Sicily: through writers' eyes

Sicily: through writers' eyes

Written and edited by
Horatio Clare

ELAND
LONDON

First published by Eland Publishing Ltd
61 Exmouth Market, London EC1R 4QL in 2006

ISBN 0 907871 94 1

Cover design and typesetting by Rose Baring & Katy Kedward
Cover image: Temple in Segesta © Hubert Stadler/CORBIS
Map © Reginald Piggott

Contents

Acknowledgements

ALL THANKS TO Barnaby Rogerson, Rose Baring and Katy Kedward at Eland Books for their commission, their expertise and their patience.

For his friendship and boundless kindness I would like to thank Daniele Trupia.

For their generous welcome and great good humour, many thanks to Paola Collura, Beppe and Tiziana Collura.

For a highly unusal and unforgettable tour of Palermo, many thanks to Lawrence Pollard.

For their expertise and advice, many thanks to Rob Ketteridge, Richard Coles and Celine Condorelli.

Without Daniella, Gina, Giovanni and the great Gianni Palermo, many of Sicily's doors would have remained closed to me – and the quiet wonders of Piana degli Albanesi unknown. Gianni also introduced me to Paolo and Francesca, to whom I am ever indebted. Thank you.

For her huge enthusiasm and tireless help with the entire project, I would especially like to thank Cindy Clare.

For their support, love and visits, many thanks to Robin Jenkins, Fliss Morgan, Mike White, Emily Simonis and John Clare.

With love and special thanks to Sally Spurring.

The publishers would like to thank the following, and gratefully acknowledge permission to reprint copyright material as follows:

From Gaia Servadio, for permission to reprint an extract from her book *Motya: Unearthing a Lost Civilisation;* from John Hopkins University

Press for permission to reprint Frank J Nisetch's translation of *Pindar's Victory Song*; from The Random House Group Ltd for permission to reprint two extracts from *The Golden Honeycomb* by Vincent Cronin, published by Harvill Press; from Cambridge University Press for permission to reprint an extract from *The Sicilian Vespers* by Steven Runicman; from Anvil Press Poetry, for permission to reprint *And Suddenly It's Evening, No Night So Clear Ever Vanquished You* and *Cool Seashore* from *Salvatore Quasimodo: Complete Poems* translated by Jack Bevan; from The Random House Group Ltd for permission to reprint an extract from *The Leopard* by Giuseppe di Lampedusa, published by Harvill Press; from Penguin Books Ltd for permission to reprint *The She-Wolf*, by Giovanni Verga, from *Cavalleria Rusticana and Other Stories*, translated by G H McWilliam; from Penguin USA for the extract from *Henry IV* by Luigi Pirandello, in *Six Characters in Search of an Author and Other Plays*; from E P Duton & Co Inc for *Adriana Takes a Trip* by Luigi Pirandello, from *Horse in the Moon: Twelve Short Stories*, translated by Samuel Putnam; from Canongate for permission to reprint an extract from *Conversations in Sicily* by Elio Vittorini; from Allen & Unwin for permission to reprint an extract from *Milocca: A Sicilian Village* by Charlotte Gower Chapman; from The Random House Group for permission to reprint an extract from *The Plague-Spreader's Tale* by Gesualdo Buffalino, published by Harvill Press; from Hesperus Press for permission to reprint an extract from *Words are Stone* by Carlo Levi, translated by Anthony Shuggar; from Gavin Maxwell Enterprises Ltd for permission to reprint an extract from *The Ten Pains of Death* (1959); from The Random House Group Ltd for permission to reprint an extract from *Midnight in Sicily* by Peter Robb, published by Harvill Press; from Hodder Headline for permission to reprint an extract from *Cosa Nostra: A History of the Sicilian Mafia* by John Dickie; from Granta for permissions to reprint an extract from *The Day of the Owl* by Leonardo Sciascia, translated by Archibald Colquhon and Arthur Oliver; from Macmillan Publishers Ltd for permission to reprint an extract from *The Snack Thief* by Andrea Camilleri, translated by Stephen Sartelli; from Mary Taylor Simeti for permission to reprint an extract from her book *On Persephone's Island: A Sicilian Journal*; from Hodder Headline for permission to reprint two extracts from *The Stone Boudoir: In Search of the Hidden Villages of Sicily*, published by Headline Review; from Serpent's Tail for permission to reprint an extract from *One Hundred Strokes of the Brush before Bed* by Melissa P and from Faber & Faber for permission to reprint *Good-bye to the Mezzogiorno* by W H Auden.

Every effort has been made to trace or contact copyright holders. The publishers would be pleased to rectify any omissions brought to their notice at the earliest opportunity.

All the extracts have been reprinted as they originally appeared in English, which accounts for any apparent discrepancies in spelling.

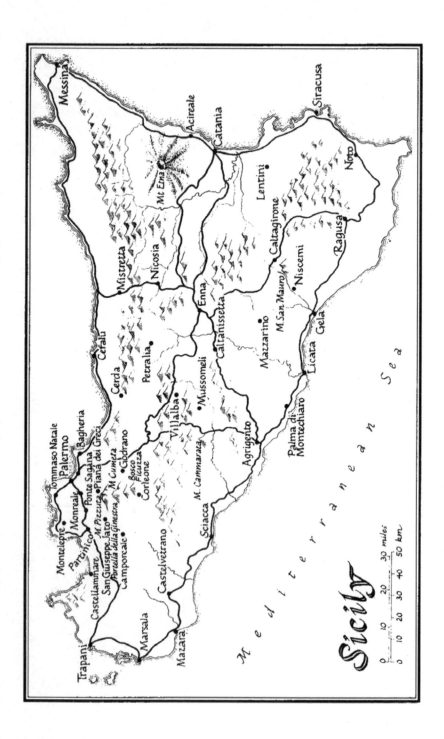

I: Arrivals

THE FIRST TIME I saw Sicily was at daybreak, from the deck of the overnight boat from Naples. The sky was fretted with grey and gold and there was Palermo, ahead of us. I had not expected the city's rearing ring of mountains, with their mists and clouds, their rocky spines, teeth and crests. To the right the leonine lump of Monte Pellegrino jutted up, to the left the mountains ranged down to the sea, and in the middle was the city. Small, open fishing boats were trailing out of it – single occupants looking up, out of their little shells, impassive, at what must have seemed the vast bulk of the ship. Palermo has seen many ships, many landfalls. Beyond the cranes of the port there were domes, baroque spires, blocks of flats and campaniles. It looked as though it was all still asleep. A man came out onto the deck in front of me. He was of young middle age, broad and not tall, in a smart dark coat. He faced the city. His head tilted back a little as he squared his shoulders and raised his chin to the prospect. He looked at the boats, the sea and the splendid Monte in its scarves of cloud, he took in the dimpled yellow crust of the city, enclosed like a coral in a reef. He gathered his breath and let it out, 'Ai...' he said, his tone somewhere between a wish, a tribute and a reproach, '...Palermo!'

He rolled the sound slightly between the syllables. 'Ai, Pa-lermo!'

I felt I could immediately appreciate, though it has taken me all my time here to understand, something of what he meant.

My flat is on the very top of a block in the new city, the grid which lies to the north of the knotted ancient heart. When I come up in the lift at supper time, it is like rising through the aromas of a gigantic feast: through all the layers of a lasagne, with a macaroni on top of it, mackerel above that, and sausages with fennel at the top. The succulence makes my head swim. But my tiny bedroom (the flat was a 'mistake', according to my landlord – the architect's grandson) has a view south across all of Palermo. When a new ship comes into port I can see its funnels. I can see the cranes of the

1

docks, and count my way inland from dome to dome until I reach the cathedral, the Duomo, then the tower of the Porta Nuova, then the countless spatter of concrete apartment blocks thrown up in the 'sack of Palermo', the mafia-backed building frenzy of the 1950s. My kitchen has a balcony which looks north, affording a spectacular and ever-changing close-up of Monte Pellegrino. All around, the humped and sharpened semi-circle of mountains joins the city to the sky.

'What is civilisation?' asked the great Russian poet, Joseph Brodsky, 'Civilisation is a city by the sea.' In Palermo, and throughout Sicily, one can see and read every twist and turn of the history of the various visions, variations and nightmares which have attended man's pursuit of this concept, civilisation. Sicily is a fascinating anthology, in stone, blood and letters, to which this book can only serve as brief introduction, a series of sample tastes. Sicilian flavours are often strong and lingering, and the reader will find many such in these pages.

It takes no imagination to see Palermo from up here, as it has been seen from afar, as a magical capital, one of the fairest cities in the world. And as a rogue, bandit town, lethally insular. It was once the most civilised, advanced, learned and cultured place in Europe. Its Norman-Arab masters created here a harmony of east and west, north and south; something European, African and Oriental that has perhaps never been surpassed: a vision before which my own time is humbled, a political and cultural symphony towards which we can only aspire. And the best part of a millennium later, in our time, Palermo has spawned, harboured and been ruled by monsters. It is an intensely evocative and eerie place.

The rhythms are peculiar. They collect the rubbish, loudly, at midnight. Six and a half hours of silence follow, interrupted occasionally by barking dogs. Then at daybreak, around six thirty, everything wakes up. By eight thirty everyone seems to have had their first coffee and a *cornetto crema*: croissants stuffed with pale custard, dusted with icing sugar, presented with a flourish, in a girdle of tissue, the way a boy might give a girl a flower. Hammers tap, drills whistle, lifts clunk, little three-wheeled pick-ups appear on street corners, lugging great carapaces of bright vegetables. The streets are flooded with schoolchildren, and again at twelve thirty, when they beseige their favourite cafés. Lunch is a serious business. No food, not even a ham, cheese and tomato panino, is prepared with anything less than loving concentration. By one everything has stopped for the meal. By two only the cafés and restaurants are still open. The city slumbers, digesting, until four, then the shutters crash open, fishmongers smash ice all over their trays again and lay out the catch; stall holders fill their racks, women descend on clothes shops, Palermitans of both sexes and all ages press their noses against the windows of shoe shops, and the butchers, bakers, supermarkets, *tabbachis,* delicatessens and bars fill with eager purchasers. The streets roar with traffic – cars chase buses and are in turn harried by scooters. The noise is astonishing, but in the old quarter, where the pale paving stones gleam like smooth old teeth, the passage of a horse and trap – hooves and steel-shod wheels combining in a racket like a building falling down – you are reminded that it was ever thus. Ohmy-God, Ohmy-God, Ohmy-God blare the sirens of ambulances. In the horse-drawn era one would have been spared the cacophony of beeping horns, but to judge by the aggrieved shouts with which motorists berate each other, it would not have been much quieter then. Girls stroll, arm in arm, eyeing up boys; couples buzz by on Vespas, the lazy turning and staring of men alerts the street to the passage of a particular beauty. By five the *granite* and *gelati* have thawed sufficiently to be scraped into cones and everyone licks ice-cream. A deep siren-blast rolls in from the port as an incoming ferry welcomes the harbour pilot. By eight it is all over: shutters down, doors shut, the flickering light of televisions play over the ceilings of living rooms. The smell of cooking is everywhere. Between nine and ten most of the town dies, except for the stop-start stroll of women taking dogs around the block, and when they have gone the city is still, abandoned to the noiseless dart of bat-eared cats. The velvet blue silence of the southern night descends, interrupted briefly at midnight by the passage of a rubbish truck.

On my first morning I went for a walk in the park. The Favorita is a kilometre-long area of dense shrubbery, citrus groves and pine wood at the base of Monte Pellegrino. It contains the Palermitans' beloved football stadium, and the hippodrome, which bustles, in the morning, with horses, training and exercising with their buggies. They spin around the track at an impressive, almost perilous speed: the drivers, their feet up higher than their hips, look as though they are in some danger, so close to their own and each other's whirling wheels, until you notice that one is smoking a cigar, and another is talking and laughing into his mobile phone, clamped between chin and shoulder. A stroll through the Favorita is not the proverbial walk in the park. First there was the huge black snake, thick as a horsewhip and twice as quick, which slashed away through the undergrowth after I had almost trodden on it. It may have been harmless but it looked like a mamba. Then there was the army: platoons of rather unthreatening soldiers, shambling along the long shady paths, for all the world as if they have been ordered to take a proper constitutional. A few wary joggers passed, then I encountered a gaggle of dissolute and disreputable looking men, hanging apparently pointlessly around a car park, up to no good. It was only eleven in the morning but they looked at me uneasily as I attempted to pass nonchalantly by, as though I was the oddball. Two buzzards floated overhead and a redstart flicked his tail, and I was just about to relax when there emerged from a bush a beautiful, milky-brown woman with matching scars on her cheeks, wearing tiny pink shorts, who looked me in the eye and pointed baldly at her crotch. In Palermo, it seems, people don't go for innocent walks in the park.

Although this book is intended to be a broadly chronological selection of writings from and about Sicily, I make no apology for opening it, as it will end, with a poem by an Englishman of the twentieth century. After all, in the dawn of discernable human time, before the Sikels and the Sikans, the first identified tribes of the island, there were the Palaeolithic people, who left their paintings, around 8000BC, in caves on Monte Pellegrino. Dwelling beside them were beings, depicted in their designs, which are still here: beasts, birds, and snakes, and no one has caught the relationship between a man and a Sicilian serpent with more feeling and acuity than D H Lawrence, who lived for a while, in 1920-21, at Taormina.

D H Lawrence
Snake

A snake came to my water-trough
On a hot, hot day, and I in pyjamas for the heat,
To drink there.

In the deep, strange-scented shade of the great dark carob-tree
I came down the steps with my pitcher
And must wait, must stand and wait, for there he was at the trough before
    me.

He reached down from a fissure in the earth-wall in the gloom
And trailed his yellow-brown slackness soft-bellied, down, over the edge
    of the stone trough
And rested his throat upon the stone bottom,
And where the water had dripped from the tap, in a small clearness,

He sipped with his straight mouth,
Softly drank through his straight gums, into his slack long body,
Silently.

Someone was before me at my water-trough,
And I, like a second comer, waiting.

He lifted his head from his drinking, as cattle do,
And looked at me vaguely, as drinking cattle do,
And flickered his two-forked tongue from his lips, and mused a moment,
And stooped and drank a little more,
Being earth-brown, earth-golden from the burning bowels of the earth
On the day of Sicilian July, with Etna smoking.

The voice of my education said to me
He must be killed,
For in Sicily the black, black snakes are innocent, the gold are venomous.

And voices in me said, If you were a man
You would take a stick and break him now, and finish him off.

But must I confess how I liked him,
How glad I was he had come like a guest in quiet, to drink at my
    water-trough
And depart peaceful, pacified, and thankless,
Into the burning bowels of this earth ?

Was it cowardice, that I dared not kill him ?
Was it perversity, that I longed to talk to him ?
Was it humility, to feel so honoured?
I felt so honoured,

And yet those voices:
If you were not afraid, you would kill him!

And truly I was afraid, I was most afraid,
But even so, honoured still more
That he should seek my hospitality
From out the dark door of the secret earth.
He drank enough
And lifted his head, dreamily, as one who has drunken,
And flickered his tongue like a forked night on the air, so black,
Seeming to lick his lips,
And lookcd around like a god, unseeing, into the air,

5

And slowly turned his head,
And slowly, very slowly, as if thrice adream,
Proceeded to draw his slow length curving round
And climb again the broken bank of my wall-face.

And as he put his head into that dreadful hole,
And as he slowly drew up, snake-easing his shoulders, and entered
    farther,
A sort of horror, a sort of protest against his withdrawing into that horrid
    black hole,
Deliberately going into the blackness, and slowly drawing himself after,
Overcame me now his back was turned.

I looked round, I put down my pitcher,
I picked up a clumsy log
And threw it at the water-trough with a clatter.

I think it did not hit him,
But suddenly that part of him that was left behind convulsed in
    undignified haste,
Writhed like lightning, and was gone
Into the black hole, the earth-lipped fissure in the wall-front,
At which, in the intense still noon, I stared with fascination.
And immediately I regretted it.
I thought how paltry, how vulgar, what a mean act!
I despised myself and the voices of my accursed human education.

And I thought of the albatross,
And I wished he would come back, my snake.

For he seemed to me again like a king,
Like a king in exile, uncrowned in the underworld,
Now due to be crowned again.

And so, I missed my chance with one of the lords
Of life.
And I have something to expiate;
A pettiness.

Taormina

The withdrawal of the life-force into an 'earth-lipped fissure' is one of the great tropes of Sicilian myth, and the return of life, spirit and sustenance from its peerlessly bountiful soil has been worshipped on the island since the Sikels, who believed in Gods below the ground, in the earth, the water and the corn. This is a land of hot springs, boiling mud, subterranean rivers which rise even from the seabed, and the great volcano, Etna. It was the goddesses of Sicily, the ancients insisted, who gave us wheat. It is supposed to have grown wild on the plain near Catania. There is, as far as I can establish, no proof of this, but any reading of the literature and history of Sicily teaches this above all things: here, what is and what is said to be, being and belief, are as two black holes in a wall, either of which might contain the serpent. Some say it is in one, some in the other, some deny its existence entirely. For example, historians believe the Sikels came from Italy in the eleventh century BC, and the Greeks, who settled three hundred years later, agreed, and thought the Sikans might have come from Spain. The Sikans themselves claimed to be autochthones, to come from the island's earth. We know that Sicily in these times was thickly forested: not until the coming of the Romans were the trees cut down and the land given to agriculture. Though the Sikels left pottery, and the Sikans stories, and perhaps syllables, surviving in the names of places, we are reliant on Greek historians, like Diodorous, for our impressions of these times. The same Diodorus who tells of Herakles swimming the straights of Messina, with the Oxen of the Sun, belonging to Geryones, ('he had the cattle taken over into Sicily, but as for himself, he took hold of the horn of a bull and swam across the passage', says Diodorus) and wrestling Eryx, the Lord of the moutain and the place which bears his name, Erice. The same Greeks held the forested island to be the home of the Cyclops, Polyphemus, and the rest of his one-eyed tribe. It is there in Diodorus and a thousand years later in Pirandello; it is there in Sciascia, in Quasimodo, in Guissepe di Lampedusa: one of the essential features of the Sicilian mind, and a tussle for all the minds that have contemplated Sicily, is the question of what is, what is told and what is imagined, and the relationship, the struggle between them. Perhaps the point is not to judge the confrontation but rather to appreciate its contortions. The island's most famous, infamous and influential product in recent history is unquestionably the poisonous fog of Cosa Nostra, 'our thing', the mafia. It began to form in the early nineteenth century, but it was not recognised, officially, in Italian law and judicial procedure, until 1982. Where the mafia are concerned, the two holes in the wall are linked at the back, and the snake is simultaneously in neither, and both.

Between the time of the Sikels, Sikans and Elymians, the three earliest known tribes, and the coming of the Greeks, Sicily's western approaches, islands and coves were taken by the Phoenecians. Perhaps the greatest race of seafarers the world has known, the Phoenicians were fearless explorers and supreme traders, and were known as navigators of genius. They did not come at first as invaders or raiders so much as businessmen. They settled islands, the mouths of rivers, and natural harbours: useful, defensible positions. They cultivated good relationships with the Sicilian tribes, who became their customers and trading partners. We know relatively little about the Phoenicians, but we have them to thank for at least two enduring marvels: their alphabet, which through the Greeks became our own, and Palermo, which the Phoenicians founded in the eighth century BC, probably marvelling that no one had already built there. The Greek name, Panormos, 'All harbour', speaks for itself.

One of the key sources of our knowledge of Phoenician life is the archaeological excavation of their town Motya, on the island of San Panteleo, a speck in a bay in the far west, just north of Marsala. By this time the Phonecians had developed something of an empire in the Western Mediterranean, known to historians as the Punic empire, away from their homeland in what is now Lebanon. Most famous was their great city of Carthage in present-day Tunisia. The writer Gaia Servadio developed a passion for the island of Motya and its story; her book, *Motya*, speaks vividly of its people.

Gaia Servadio
From *Motya: Unearthing a Lost Civilisation*

'In Motya, the Phoenicians enjoyed a twofold geopolitical advantage: their alliance and good relations with the Elymians of western Sicily and the proximity to Carthage, on the other side of the Sicilian straits,' writes Aubet. 'The fact that it was occupied without interruption from the end of the eighth to the fourth century BC makes Motya one of the best known Phoenician nuclei and one of the few in which it has been possible to analyse the whole Phoenicio-Punic cultural sequence.' On Mount Eryx, which was not strictly part of their territory, the Punics built a temple to Melqart/Heracles; another, dedicated to Astarte/Aphrodite/Venus, stood on a small plateau on the mountain's summit, just above the town. This temple became one of the best known in the ancient world not only because of its superb position but because it practised sacred prostitution. The Phoenicians deities were adopted by the Elymians, the people from Eryx, and sacred prostitution continued to be practised even in Roman times. Young women from the nobility offered themselves to the goddess; they lived in a precinct which was visited by foreigners. These would pick the women of their choice, lie with her and pay a fee to the priests of Astarte. Only then could the young woman, probably aged twelve or thirteen, go back home and start a proper family. The Phoenician Astarte, also identified as Baalat or Pene Hammon, was a powerful deity. The faithful believed that the goddess visited Africa every year and, after nine days' absence, returned home to her mountain temple. Her departure was indicated by the disappearance of the doves which were sacred to her, and her return by their reappearance. At the same time each year the image of Astarte was itself carried to Africa and brought back again.

The wanderings of Aeneas (who, according to Dionysius of Halicarnassus, is a Phoenician and not a Trojan hero, and who founded the temple of Aphrodite at Cythera in Greece), followed the same pattern as those of Cadmus. Before arriving at Carthage, Aeneas went to eastern Sicily and then on to Motya – as, in Virgil's words, he tells Dido:

> At the entrance of the bay of Syracuse, opposite the wave-beaten headland of Plemyrium, there stands an island which men of old called Ortygia. The story goes that the river-god Alpheus of Elis forced his way here by hidden passages at the mouth of Arethusa's fountain. Obeying the instructions we had received, we worshipped the great gods of the place and then I sailed, leaving behind the rich lands around the marshy river Helorus. From here we rounded Cape Pachynus, keeping close to its jutting cliffs of rock, and Camerina came into view in the distance, the place the Fates forbade to move, and then the Geloan planes and Gela itself, called after its turbulent river. Then in the far distance appeared the great walls of Acragas on its crag, once famous for the breeding of high-mettled horses. Next the wind carried me past Selinus, named after the parsley it gave to crown the victors in Greek games, and I steered past the dangerous shoals and hidden rocks of Lilybaeum.
>
> I then put into port at Drepanum, but had little joy of that shore. This was the place where, weary as I was with all these batterings of sea and storm, and to my great grief I lost my father Anchises ...

Aeneas' mother was Venus, Astarte: the earth mother, the goddess of life, youth and beauty. She had flown from Carthage in the shape of a dove, and became less pugnacious than in her Phoenician incarnation. Besides giving life, she caused death, and hence she was also the goddess of the underworld. In this guise she was later identified as the Bitter Goddess, the Greek Persephone. There were several stelae in Motya and Lilybaeum not so much dedicated to her as the goddess of darkness, entrusting the dead to her. Through these poetic words we can come to understand more of Punic life; they allow us to approach the people of Motya, even to imagine what they were like and how they might have lived – and died.

A husband lost his beautiful young wife; his regret and loss are made poetically plain in the stone he sculpted which proclaims his sorrow. In the Punic belief in death as eternal fog, he cannot but recommend his wife Allia Prima to the goddess (Astarte/Persephone); this apart, there is no afterlife, no eternal bliss for Allia Prima. But he pleads with Hermes, who is to accompany her (some Greek names of deities had already been adopted) and with the 'dark goddess', to appreciate his wife's youth and beauty. There are two inscribed sides to this stela. On the first is written:

> I beg you Hermes who keep underground, you and many of your group who cannot see images: the gift I send you, the girl, before she arrives. I question you: I give you the girl before she arrives: a beautiful gift. I give you a beautiful girl, fine gift, ears that hear, a lovely bosom, Allia Prima who has beautiful hair, a fine face, lovely eyelashes, beautiful eyes, two smooth cheeks, two nostrils, mouth, teeth, smooth ears, neck, shoulders, extremeties, I put her under the earth, that the sepulchre might be agreeable to you. I write this letter for Allia Prima.

And on the other side:

> A heart. Cerberus of Allia Prima. Beautiful neck, beautiful body, lovely knees, beautiful all and her extremities. Allia Prima I give to thee as a gift so that you pass her on to the Bitter lady. I ask you Hermes that keep them underground, you of the underworld because it is you who take away Allia Prima, a gift to Lady Persephone, I bury.

The Punics were highly superstitious, and believed that they could put a curse on their enemies by engraving threats on thin strips of lead which were fixed in places where the gods of the underworld could see them. In Latin these strips were called *defixiones* from the verb 'to nail', as the horrible words were nailed inside wells or near grottoes. This fixation with written curses has been inherited by the Spanish world (which was partly Punic) and certainly by the Punic side of Sicily ...

The most sombre aspect of the Punics' religion was that human sacrifice was carried out from the dawn of Carthage to its sunset. Although apologists for the Punics have been quick to protest that this practice has been exaggerated by the hostility of the anti-Phoenician 'press', archaeology speaks clearly, and it speaks against the apologists.

When the community was under threat, a child had to be sacrificed in order to please and placate the god. The rite was inherited from Canaanite times, when Moloch or Mot, god of the beginning and of consuming fire and the divinity who dried up springs, was a lord (Baal) who could only be satiated by human flesh. The biblical book of Jeremiah describes in chapter 35 how 'they built altars to Baal to lead their sons and daughters through the fire to Moloch' and 'to burn their children by fire as a burnt-offering to Baal'. Although this god would accept bulls and horses. children, being the most beloved possessions of their parents, were the offerings most likely to pacify him. The custom was passed on from Canaan to succeeding waves of immigrants or invaders, and continued after 1200BC, although it probably ceased earlier in the neighbouring Judaea. The Greeks and Latins abhorred the practice but the Punics, long after the Phoenicians, continued it in spite of pressure and censure from their neighbours.

Underneath the Palazzo Normani in Palermo are the remains of Punic walls. A modern walkway runs over and between them; the walls, and one small arched gate, are gently but clearly illuminated. The blocks of sandy-orange stone fit perfectly together; their designers and masons needed no cement. They date from the fifth century, the time of the rise of the great Punic metropolis in north Africa. The Punics were skilled builders: in Motya they raised six storey houses. The city of Dido has vanished, but here in the artificial twilight, three floors below the Capella Palatina, as you stare at the sweetly interlocked blocks of stone, and their desert hues, you could be gazing on the fabled walls of Carthage.

After the Phoenicians came the Greeks. They settled in eastern Sicily, founding Naxos around 735BC and Syracuse in 734. Over the next hundred years they spread along the east and southern coasts, establishing the towns of Lentini, Catania, Megara, Zancle (Messina) and Gela. This was not long after the time of Homer, when Sicily makes its first appearance on the front page of world literature.

Homer
From *The Odyssey*

... Now then saw we near
The Cyclops' late-praised island, and might hear
The murmur of their sheep and goats, and see
Their smokes ascend. The sun then set, and we,
When night succeeded, took our rest ashore.
And when the world the morning's favour wore,
I call'd my friends to council, charging them
To make stay there, while I took ship and stream,
With some associates, and explored what men
The neighbour isle held; if of rude disdain,
Churlish and tyrannous, or minds bewray'd
Pious and hospitable. Thus much said,
I boarded, and commanded to ascend
My friends and soldiers, to put off, and lend
Way to our ship. They boarded, sat, and beat
The old sea forth, till we might see the seat
The greatest Cyclop held for his abode,
Which was a deep cave, near the common road
Of ships that touch'd there, thick with laurels spread,
Where many sheep and goats lay shadowed;
And, near to this, a hail of torn-up stone,
High built with pines, that heaven and earth attone,
And lofty-fronted oaks; in which kept house
A man in shape immane, and monsterous,
Fed all his flocks alone, nor would afford
Commerce with men, but had a wit abhorr'd,
His mind his body answering. Nor was he
Like any man that food could possibly
Enhance so hugely, but, beheld alone,
Show'd like a steep hill's top, all overgrown
With trees and brambles; little thought had I
Of such vast objects. When, arrived so nigh,
Some of my loved friends I made stay aboard,
To guard my ship, and twelve with me I shored,
The choice of all. I took besides along
A goat-skin flagon of wine, black and strong ...

Of this a huge great flagon full I bore,
And, in a good large knapsack, victuals store;
And long'd to see this heap of fortitude,
That so illiterate was and upland rude
That laws divine nor human he had learn'd.
With speed we reach'd the cavern; nor discern'd
His presence there, his flocks he fed at field.

Ent'ring his den, each thing beheld did yield
Our admiration; shelves with cheeses heap'd;
Sheds stuff'd with lambs and goats, distinctly kept,
Distinct the biggest, the more mean distinct,
Distinct the youngest. And in their precinct,
Proper and placeful, stood the troughs and pails,
In which he milk'd; and what was given at meals,
Set up a creaming; in the evening still
All scouring bright as dew upon the hill.

Then were my fellows instant to convey
Kids, cheeses, lambs, aship-board, and away
Sail the salt billow. I thought best not so,
But better otherwise; and first would know,
What guest-gifts he would spare me. Little knew
My friends on whom they would have prey'd. His view
Prov'd after, that his inwards were too rough
For such bold usage. We were bold enough
In what I suffer'd; which was there to stay,
Make fire and feed there, though bear none away.
There sat we, till we saw him feeding come,
And on his neck a burthen lugging home,
Most highly huge, of sere-wood, which the pile
That fed his fire supplied all supper-while.
Down by his den he threw it, and up rose
A tumult with the fall. Afraid, we close
Withdrew ourselves, while he into a cave
Of huge receipt his high-fed cattle drave,
All that he milk'd; the males he left without
His lofty roofs, that all bestrow'd about
With rams and buck-goats were. And then a rock
He lift aloft, that damm'd up to his flock
The door they enter'd; 'twas so hard to wield,
That two and twenty waggons, all four-wheel'd,

(Could they be loaded, and have teams that were
Proportion'd to them) could not stir it there.
Thus making sure, be kneel'd and milk'd his ewes.
And braying goats, with all a milker's dues;
Then let in all their young. Then quick did dress
His half milk up for cheese, and in a press
Of wicker press'd it; put in bowls the rest,
To drink and eat, and serve his supping feast.
    All works dispatch'd thus, he began his fire;
Which blown, he saw us, and did thus inquire:
      'Ho! guests! What are ye? Whence sail ye these seas?
Traffic, or rove ye, and like thieves oppress
Poor strange adventurers, exposing so
Your souls to danger, and your lives to woe?'
    This utter'd he, when fear from our hearts took
The very life, to be so thunder-strook
With such a voice, and such a monster see;
But thus I answer'd: 'Erring Grecians, we
From Troy were turning homewards; but by force
Of adverse winds, in far diverted course,
Such unknown ways took, and on rude seas toss'd,
As Jove decreed, are cast upon this coast.
Of Agamemnon, famous Atreus' son,
We boast ourselves the soldiers; who hath won
Renown that reacheth heaven, to overthrow
So great a city, and to ruin so
So many nations. Yet at thy knees lie
Our prostrate bosoms, forced with prayers to try
If any hospitable right, or boon
Of other nature, such as have been won
By laws of other houses, thou wilt give.
Reverence the Gods, thou great'st of all that live.
We suppliants are; and hospitable Jove
Pours wreak on all whom prayers want power to move,
And with their plagues together will provide
That humble guests shall have their wants supplied.'
    He cruelly answer'd: 'O thou fool,' said he,
'To come so far, and to importune me
With any God's fear, or observed love!
We Cyclops care not for your goat-fed Jove,

Nor other Bless'd ones; we are better far.
To Jove himself dare I bid open war,
To thee, and all thy fellows, if I please.
But tell me, where's the ship, that by the seas
Hath brought thee hither? If far off, or near,
Inform me quickly.' These his temptings were;
But I too much knew not to know his mind,
And craft with craft paid, telling him the wind
(Thrust up from sea by Him that shakes the shore)
Had dash'd our ships against his rocks, and tore
Her ribs in pieces close upon his coast,
And we from high wrack saved, the rest were lost.

  He answer'd nothing, but rush'd in, and took
Two of my fellows up from earth, and strook
Their brains against it. Like two whelps they flew
About his shoulders, and did all embrue
The blushing earth. No mountain lion tore
Two lambs so sternly, lapp'd up all their gore
Gush'd from their torn-up bodies, limb by limb
(Trembling with life yet) ravish'd into him.
Both flesh and marrow-stuffed bones he eat,
And even th' uncleansed entrails made his meat.
We, weeping, cast our hands to heaven, to view
A sight so horrid. Desperation flew,
With all our after lives, to instant death,
In our believed destruction. But when breath
The fury of his appetite had got,
Because the gulf his belly reach'd his throat,
Man's flesh, and goat's milk, laying layer on layer,
Till choked up was all the pass for air,
Along his den, amongst his cattle, down
He rush'd, and streak'd him. When my mind was grown
Desperate to step in, draw my sword, and part
His bosom where the strings about his heart
Circle the liver, and add strength of hand
But that rash thought, more stay'd, did countermand,
For there we all had perish'd, since it past
Our powers to lift aside a log so vast,
As barr'd all outscape; and so sigh'd away
The thought all night, expecting active day.

15

Which come, he first of all his fires enflames,
Then milks his goats and ewes, then to their dams
Lets in their young, and, wondrous orderly,
With manly haste dispatch'd his housewifery.
Then to his breakfast, to which other two
Of my poor friends went; which eat, out then go
His herds and fat flocks, lightly putting by
The churlish bar, and closed it instantly;
For both those works with ease as much he did,
As you would ope and shut your quiver lid.
    With storms of whistlings then his flock he drave
Up to the mountains; and occasion gave
For me to use my wits, which to their height
I strived to screw up, that a vengeance might
By some means fall from thence, and Pallas now
Afford a full ear to my neediest vow.
This then my thoughts preferr'd: A huge club lay
Close by his milk-house, which was now in way
To dry and season, being on olive-tree
Which late he fell'd, and, being green, must be
Made lighter for his manage. 'Twas so vast
That we resembled it to some fit mast,
To serve a ship of burthen that was driven
With twenty oars, and had a bigness given
To bear a huge sea. Fall so thick, so tall,
We judg'd this club; which I, in part, hew'd small,
And cut a fathom off. The piece I gave
Amongst my soldiers, to take down, and shave;
Which done, I sharpen'd it at top, and then,
Harden'd in fire, I hid it in the den
Within a nasty dunghill reeking there,
Thick, and so moist it issued everywhere.
Then made I lots cast by my friends to try
Whose fortune served to dare the bored out eye
Of that man-eater; and the lot did fall
On four I wish'd to make my aid of all,
And I the fifth made, chosen like the rest.
    Then came the even, and he came from the feast
Of his fat cattle, drave in all, nor kept
One male abroad; if, or his memory slept

By God's direct will, or of purpose was
His driving in of all then, doth surpass
My comprehension. But so closed again
The mighty bar, milk'd. and did still maintain
All other observation as before.
His work all done, two of my soldiers more
At once he snatch'd up, and to supper went.
Then dared I words to him, and did present
A bowl of wine, with these words: 'Cyclop! take
A bowl of wine, from my hand, that may make
Way for the man's flesh thou hast eat, and show
What drink our ship held; which in sacred vow
I offer to thee to take ruth on me
In my dismission home. Thy rages be
Now no more sufferable. How shall men,
Mad and inhuman that thou art, again
Greet thy abode, and get thy actions grace,
If thus thou ragest, and eat'st up their race.'
    He took, and drunk, and vehemently joy'd
To taste the sweet cup; and again employ'd
My flagon's powers, entreating more, and said:
'Good guest, again afford my taste thy aid,
And let me know thy name, and quickly now,
That in thy recompense I may bestow
A hospitable gift on thy desert,
And such a one as shall rejoice thy heart.
For to the Cyclops too the gentle earth
Bears generous wine, and Jove augments her birth,
In store of such, with showers; but this rich wine
Fell from the river, that is mere divine,
Of nectar and ambrosia.' This again
I gave him, and again; nor could the fool abstain,
But drunk as often. When the noble juice
Had wrought upon his spirit, I then gave use
To fairer language, saying: 'Cyclop! now,
As thou demand'st, I'll tell thee my name, do thou
Make good thy hospitable gift to me.
My name is No-Man; No-Man each degree
Of friends, as well as parents, call my name.'
He answer'd, as his cruel soul became:

'No-Man! I'll eat thee last of all thy friends;
And this is that in which so much amends
I vow'd to thy deservings, thus shall be
My hospitable gift made good to thee.'
This said, he upwards fell, but then bent round
His fleshy neck; and Sleep, with all crowns crown'd
Subdued the savage. From his throat brake out
My wine, with man's flesh gobbets, like a spout,
When, loaded with his cups, he lay and snored;
And then took I the club's end up, and gored
The burning coal-heap, that the point might heat;
Confirm'd my fellow's minds, lest Fear should let
Their vow'd assay, and make them fly my aid.
Straight was the olive-lever, I had laid
Amidst the huge fire to get hardening, hot,
And glow'd extremely, though 'twas green; which got
From forth the cinders, close about me stood
My hardy friends; but that which did the good
Was God's good inspiration, that gave
A spirit beyond the spirit they used to have;
Who took the olive spar, made keen before,
And plunged it in his eye, and up I bore,
Bent to the top close, and help'd pour it in,
With all my forces. And as you have seen
A ship-wright bore a naval beam, he oft
Thrusts at the auger's froofe, works still aloft,
And at the shank help others, with a cord
Wound round about to make it sooner bored,
All plying the round still; so into his eye
The fiery stake we labour'd to imply.
Out gush'd the blood that scalded, his eye-ball
Thrust out a flaming vapour, that scorch'd all
His brows and eye-lids, his eye-strings did crack,
As in the sharp and burning rafter brake.
And as a smith to harden any tool,
Broad axe, or mattock, in his trough doth cool
The red-hot substance, that so fervent is
It makes the cold wave straight to seethe and hiss;
So sod and hiss'd his eye about the stake.
He roar'd withal, and all his cavern brake

In claps like thunder. We did frighted fly,
Dipers'd in corners. He from forth his eye
The fixed stake pluck'd; after which the blood
Flow'd freshly forth; and, mad, he hurl'd the wood
About his hovel. Out he then did cry
For other Cyclops, that in caverns by
Upon a windy promontory dwell'd;
Who, hearing how impetuously he yell'd,
Rush'd every way about him, and inquired,
What ill afflicted him, that he exspired
Such horrid clamours, and in sacred Night
To break their sleeps so? Ask'd him, if his fright
Came from some mortal that his flocks had driven?
Or if by craft, or might, his death were given?
He answer'd from his den: 'By craft, nor might,
No-Man hath given me death.' They then said right,
If no man hurt thee, and thyself alone,
That which is done to thee by Jove is done;
And what great Jove inflicts no man can fly.
Pray to thy Father yet, a Deity,
And prove, from him if thou canst help acquire.
　　Thus spake they, leaving him; when all on fire
My heart with joy was, that so well my wit
And name deceived him; whom now pain did split,
And groaning up and down he groping tried
To find the stone, which found, he put aside;
But in the door sat, feeling if he could
(As his sheep issued) on some man lay hold;
Esteeming me a fool, that could devise
No stratagem to 'scape his gross surprise.
But I, contending what I could invent
My friends and me from death so eminent
To get deliver'd, all my wiles I wove
(Life being the subject) and did this approve:
Fat fleecy rams, most fair, and great, lay there,
That did a burden like a violet bear.
These, while this learn'd-in-villany did sleep,
I yoked with osiers cut there, sheep to sheep,
Three in a rank, and still the mid sheep bore
A man about his belly, the two more

March'd on his each side for defence. I then,
Choosing myself the fairest of the den,
His fleecy belly under-crept, embrac'd
His back, and in his rich wool wrapt me fast
With both my hands, arm'd with as fast a mind.
And thus each man hung, till the morning shin'd;
Which come, he knew the hour, and let abroad
His male-flocks first, the females unmilk'd stood
Bleating and braying, their full bags so sore
With being unempted, but their shepherd more
With being unsighted; which was cause his mind
Went not a milking. He, to wreak inclin'd,
The backs felt, as they pass'd, of those male dams,
Gross fool! believing, we would ride his rams!
Nor ever knew that any of them bore
Upon his belly any man before.
The last ram came to pass him, with his wool
And me together loaded to the full,
For there did I hang; and that ram he stay'd,
And me withal had in his hands, my head
Troubled the while, not causelessly, nor least.
This ram he groped, and talk'd to: 'Lazy beast!
Why last art thou now? Thou hast never used
To lag thus hindmost, but still first hast bruised
The tender blossom of a flower, and held
State in thy steps, both to the flood and field,
First still at fold at even, now last remain?
Dost thou not wish I had mine eye again,
Which that abhorr'd man No-Man did put out,
Assisted by his execrable rout,
When he had wrought me down with wine? But he
Must not escape my wreak so cunningly.
I would to heaven thou knew'st, and could but speak,
To tell me where he lurks now! I would break
His brain about my cave, strew'd here and there,
To ease my heart of those foul ills, that were
Th' inflictions of a man I prized at nought.'
        Thus let he him abroad; when I, once brought
A little from his hold, myself first losed,
And next my friends. Then drave we, and disposed,

His straight-legg'd fat fleece-bearers over land,
Even till they all were in my ship's command;
And to our loved friends show'd our pray'd-for sight,
Escaped from death. But, for our loss, outright
They brake in tears; which with a look I stay'd,
And bade them take our boot in. They obey'd,
And up we all went, sat, and used our oars.
But having left as far the savage shores
As one might hear a voice, we then might see
The Cyclop at the haven; when instantly
I stay'd our oars, and this insultance used:
'Cyclop! thou shouldst not have so much abused
Thy monstrous forces, to oppose their least
Against a man immartial, and a guest,
And eat his fellows. Thou mightst know there were
Some ills behind, rude swain, for thee to bear,
That fear'd not to devour thy guests, and break
All laws of humans. Jove sends therefore wreak,
And all the Gods, by me.' This blew the more
His burning fury; when the top he tore
From off a huge rock, and so right a throw
Made at our ship, that just before the prow
It overflew and fell, miss'd mast and all
Exceeding little; but about the fall
So fierce a wave it raised, that back it bore
Our ship so far, it almost touch'd the shore.
A bead-hook then, a far-extended one,
I snatch'd up, thrust hard, and so set us gone
Some little way; and straight commanded all
To help me with their oars, on pain to fall
Again on our confusion. But a sign
I with my head made, and their oars were mine
In all performance. When we off were set,
(Then first, twice further) my heart was so great,
It would again provoke him, but my men
On all sides rush'd about me, to contain
And said: 'Unhappy! Why will you provoke
A man so rude, that with so dead a stroke,
Given with his rock-dart, made the sea thrust back
Our ship so far, and near hand forced our wrack?

Should he again but hear your voice resound,
And any word reach, thereby would be found
His dart's direction, which would, in his fall,
Crush piece-meal us, quite split our ship and all;
So much dart wields the monster.' Thus urged they
Impossible things, in fear; but I gave way
To that wrath which so long I held depress'd,
By great necessity conquer'd, in my breast:
    'Cyclop! If any ask thee, who imposed
Th' unsightly blemish that thine eye enclosed,
Say that Ulysses, old Laertes' son,
Whose seat is Ithaca, and who hath won
Surname of city-racer, bored it out.'
    At this, he bray'd so loud, that round about
He drave affrighted echos through the air,
And said: 'O beast! I was premonish'd fair,
By aged prophecy, in one that was
A great and good man, this should come to pass;
And how 'tis proved now! Augur Telemus,
Surnamed Eurymides (that spent with us
His age in augury, and did exceed
In all presage of truth) said all this deed
Should this event take, author'd by the hand
Of one Ulysses, who I thought was mann'd
With great and goodly personage, and bore
A virtue answerable; and this shore
Should shake with weight of such a conqueror;
When now a weakling came, a dwarfy thing,
A thing of nothing; who yet wit did bring,
That brought supply to all, and with his wine
Put out the flame where all my light did shine.
Come, land again, Ulysses! that my hand
May guest-rites give thee, and the great command,
That Neptune hath at sea, I may convert
To the deduction where abides thy heart,
With my solicitings, whose son I am,
And whose fame boasts to bear my father's name.
Nor think my hurt offends me, for my sire
Can soon repose in it the visual fire,
At his free pleasure; which no power beside
Can boast, of men, or of the Deified.'

I answer'd: 'Would to God I could compel
Both life and soul from thee, and send to hell
Those spoils of nature! Hardly Neptune then
Could cure thy hurt, and give thee all again.'
    Then flew fierce vows to Neptune, both his hands
To star-born heaven cast: 'O thou that all lands
Gird'st in thy ambient circle, and in air
Shak'st the curl'd tresses of thy sapphire hair,
If I be thine, or thou mayst justly vaunt
Thou art my father, hear me now, and grant
That this Ulysses, old Laertes' son,
That dwells in Ithaca, and name hath won
Of city-ruiner, may never reach
His natural region. Or if to fetch
That, and the sight of his fair roofs and friends,
Be fatal to him, let him that amends
For all his miseries, long time and ill,
Smart for, and fail of; nor that fate fulfill,
Till all his soldiers quite are cast away
In others' ships. And when, at last, the day
Of his sole-landing shall his dwelling show,
Let Detriment prepare him wrongs enow.'
    Thus pray'd he Neptune; who, his sire, appear'd,
And all his prayer to every syllable heard.
But then a rock, in size more amplified
Than first, he ravish'd to him, and implied
A dismal strength in it, when, wheel'd about,
He sent it after us; nor flew it out
From any blind aim, for a little pass
Beyond our fore-deck from the fall there was,
With which the sea our ship gave back upon,
And shrunk up into billows from the stone,
Our ship again repelling near as near
The shore as first. But then our rowers were,
Being warn'd, more arm'd, and stronglier stemm'd the flood
That bore back on us, till nor ship made good
The other island, where our whole fleet lay,
In which our friends lay mourning for our stay,
And every minute look'd when we should land.
Where, now arrived, we drew up to the sand,

23

The Cyclops' sheep dividing, that none there
Of all our privates might be wrung, and bear
Too much on power. The ram yet was alone
By all my friends made all my portion
Above all others; and I made him then
A sacrifice for me and all my men
To cloud-compelling Jove that all commands,
To whom I burn'd the thighs; but my sad hands
Received no grace from him, who studied how
To offer men and fleet to overthrow,
    All day, till sun-set, yet, we sat and eat,
And liberal store took in of wine and meat.
The sun then down, and place resign'd to shade,
We slept. Morn came, my men I raised, and made
All go aboard, weigh anchor, and away.
They boarded, sat, and beat the aged sea;
And forth we made sail, sad for loss before,
And yet had comfort since we lost no more.

Behind the fabulous myth is a credible story of adventurers in peril on a foreign shore, encountering strange and hostile natives and withdrawing under fire. Compared to what was to come the period of Greek settlement was easy; they advanced by increment, not general conquest: the Sikans and Sikels had nothing to match their arms and organisation. The Greek settlers seem to have founded towns more or less at will; over one hundred and forty years they occupied the greater part of the Sicilian coast. But the various competing towns and tribes, and the rival civilisations, Hellenic and Carthaginian, cannot have viewed one another without suspicion. Myth and story were put to work in the service of conquest. Eryx, today's Erice, a hilltop settlement and temple on what the writer Vincent Cronin calls 'the watchtower of Sicily, almost of the entire Mediterranean' was a Sikan, then an Elmyian town which came under Punic dominance, and it was famed throughout the Mediterranean world for its temple to the goddess of fertility. The Carthaginians called the goddess Ashtarte and worshipped her there. The Greeks said Herakles had been to Eryx to honour the same deity, whom they called Aphrodite. Daedalus, they said, had been there, and honoured her.

From *Diodorus Book IV*

Daedlus was an Athenian by birth and was known as one of the clan named Erechthids, since he was the son of Meion, the son of Eupalamus, the son of Erechtheus. In natural ability he towered far above all other men and cultivated the building art, the making of statues, and the working of stone. He was also the inventor of many devices which contributed to the advancement of his art and built works in many regions of the inhabited world which arouse the wonder of men. In the carving of his statues he so far excelled all other men that later generations invented the story about him that the statues of his making were quite like their living models; they could see, they said, and walk and, in a word, preserved so well the characteristics of the entire body that the beholder thought that the image made by him was a being endowed with life. And since he was the first to represent the open eye and to fashion the legs separated in a stride and the arms and hands as extended, it was a natural thing that he should have received the admiration of mankind; for the artists before his time had carved their statues with the eyes closed and the arms and hands hanging and attached to the sides.

But though Daedlalus was an object of admiration because of his technical skill, yet he had to flee from his native land, since he had been condemned for murder for the following reason. Talos, a son of the sister of Daedalus, was receiving his education in the home of Daedalus, while he was still a lad in years. But being more gifted than his teacher he invented the potter's wheel, and then, when once he had come by chance upon a jawbone of a snake and with it had sawn through a small piece of wood, he tried to imitate the jaggedness of the serpent's teeth. Consequently he fashioned a saw out of iron, by means of which he would saw the lumber which he used in his work, and for this accomplishment he gained the reputation of having discovered a device which would be of great service to the art of building. He likewise discovered also the tool for describing a circle and certain other cunningly contrived devices whereby he gained for himself great fame. But Daedalus, becoming jealous of the youth and feeling that his fame was going to rise far above that of his teacher, treacherously slew the youth. And being detected in the act of burying him, he was asked what he was burying, whereupon he replied, 'I am inhuming a snake.' Here a man may well wonder at the strange happening, that the same animal that led to the thought of devising the saw should also have been the means through which the murder came to be discovered. And Daedalus, having been accused and adjudged guilty of murder by the court of the Areopagites, at first fled to one of the demes of Attica, the inhabitants of which, we are told, were named after him Daedalidae,

Afterwards Daedalus made his escape out of Attica to Crete, where, being admired because of the fame of his art, he became a friend of Minos who was king there. Now according to the myth which has been handed down to us Pasiphae, the wife of Minos, became enamoured of the bull, and Daedalus, by fashioning a contrivance in the shape of a cow, assisted Pasiphae to gratify her passion. In explanation of this the myths offer the following account: Before this time it had been the custom of Minos annually to dedicate to Poseidon the fairest bull born in his herds and to sacrifice it to the god; but at the time in question there was born a bull of extraordinary beauty and he sacrificed another from among those which were inferior, whereupon Poseidon, becoming angry at Minos, caused his wife Pasiphae to become enamoured of the bull. And by means of the ingenuity of Daedalus Pasiphae had intercourse with the bull and gave birth to the Minotaur, famed in the myth. This creature, they say, was of double form, the upper parts of the body as far as the shoulders being those of a bull and the remaining parts those of a man. As a place in which to keep this monstrous thing Daedalus, the story goes, built a labyrinth, the passage-ways of which were so winding that those unfamiliar with them had difficulty in making their way out; in this labyrinth the Minotaur was maintained and here it devoured the seven youths and seven maidens which were sent to it from Athens.

But Daedalus, they say, on learning that Minos had made threats against him because he had fashioned the cow, became fearful of the anger of the king and departed from Crete, Pasiphae helping him and providing a vessel for his escape. With him fled also his son Icarus and they put in at a certain island which lay in the open sea. But when Icarus was disembarking onto the island in a reckless manner, he fell into the sea and perished, and in memory of him the sea was named the Icarian and the island was called Icaria.

Daedalus, however, sailing away from this island, landed in Sicily near the territory over which Cocalus reigned as king, who courteously received Daedalus and because of his genius and his renown made him his close friend.

But certain writers of myths have the following account: Daedalus remained a while longer in Crete, being kept hidden by Pasiphae, and king Minos, desiring to wreak vengeance upon him and yet being unable to find him, caused all the boats which were on the island to be searched and announced that he would give a great sum of money to the man who should discover Daedalus. Thereupon Daedalus, despairing of making his escape by any boat, fashioned with amazing ingenuity wings which were cleverly designed and marvellously fitted together with wax; and fastening these on his son's body and his own he spread them out for flight, to the astonishment of all, and made his escape over the open sea which lies near the island of Crete. As for Icarus, because of the ignorance of youth he made his flight too far aloft and fell into the sea when the wax which held the wings together was melted by the sun, whereas Dardalus, by flying close to the sea and repeatedly wetting the wings, made his way in safety, marvellous to relate, to Sicily. Now as for these matters, even though the myth is a tale of marvel, we none the less have thought it best not to leave it unmentioned.

Daedalus spent a considerable time with Cocalus and the Sicani, being greatly admired for his very great skill in his art. And on this island he constructed certain works which stand even to this day. For instance, near Megaris he ingeniously built a *kolumbrethra*, as men have named it, from which a great river, called the Alabon, empties into the sea which is not far distant from it. Also in the present territory of Acragas on the Camicus river, as it is called, he built a city which lay upon a rock and was the strongest of any in Sicily and altogether impregnable to any attack by force; for the ascent to it he made narrow and winding, building it in so ingenious a manner that it could be defended by three or four men. Consequently Cocalus built in this city the royal residence, and storing his treasures there he had them in a city which the inventiveness of its designer had made impregnable. A third construction of his, in the territory of Selinus, was a grotto where he so successfully expelled the steam caused by the fire which burned in it that those who frequented the grotto got into a perspiration imperceptibly because of the gentle action of the heat, and gradually, and actually with pleasure to themselves, they cured the infirmities of their bodies without experiencing any annoyance from the heat. Also at Eryx, where a rock rose sheer to an extraordinary height and the narrow space, where the temple of Aphrodite lay, made it necessary to build it on the precipitous tip of the rock, he constructed a wall upon the very crag, by this means extending in an astonishing manner the overhanging ledge of the crag. Moreover, for the Aphrodite of Mt. Eryx, they say, he ingeniously constructed a golden ram, working it with exceeding care and making it the perfect image of an actual ram. Many other works as well, men say, he ingeniously constructed throughout Sicily, but they have perished because of the long time which has elapsed.

Minos, the king of the Cretans, who was at that time the master of the seas, when he learned that Daedalus had fled to Sicily, decided to make a campaign against that island. After preparing a notable naval force he sailed forth from Crete and landed at a place in the territory of Acragas which was called after him Minoa. Here he disembarked his troops and sending messengers to King Cocalus he demanded Daedalus of him for punishment. But Cocalus invited Minos to a conference, and after promising to meet all his demands he brought him to his home as his guest. And when Minos was bathing Cocalus kept him too long in the hot water and thus slew him; the body he gave back to the Cretans, explaining his death on the ground that he had slipped in the bath and by falling into the hot water had met his end. Thereupon the comrades of Minos buried the body of the king with magnificent ceremonies, and constructing a tomb of two storeys, in the part of it which was hidden underground they placed the bones, and in that which lay open to gaze they made a shrine of Aphrodite. Here Minos received honours over many generations, the inhabitants of the region offering sacrifices there in the belief that the shrine was Aphrodite's, but in more recent times, after the city of the Acragantini had been founded and it became known that the bones had been placed there, it came to pass that the tomb was dismantled and the bones were given back to the Cretans, this being done when Theron was lord over the people of Acragas.

However, the Cretans of Sicily, after the death of Minos, fell into factious strife, since they had no ruler, and, since their ships had been burned by the Sicani serving under Cocalus, they gave up any hope they had had of returning to their native land; and deciding to make their home in Sicily, a part of them established on that island a city to which they gave the name Minoa after their king, and others, after wandering about through the interior of the island, seized a place which was naturally strong and founded a city to which they gave the name Engyum after the spring which flowed forth within the city.

And at a later time, after the capture of Troy, when Meriones the Cretan came to shore in Sicily, they welcomed, because of their kinship to them, the Cretans who landed with him and shared with them their citizenship; and using as their base a well-fortified city and having subdued certain of the neighbouring peoples, they secured for themselves a fairly large territory. And growing steadily stronger all the while they built a temple to the Mothers and accorded these goddesses unusual honours, adorning their temple with many votive offerings. The cult of these goddesses, so men say, they moved from their home in Crete, since the Cretans also hold these goddesses in special honour.

At first the road to Erice is very direct, rising steadily through the suburbs of Trapani, sleepy in the afternoon sun. Because it is so broad at the base, the mountain does not look as tall as it is: only a huge white cloud, pouring minutely over it like a breaker, is a clue to its great height. The climb is two thousand feet, jumping straight from the sea on its north side. Known to the Arabs as Gebel Hemed, and the Normans as Monte San Giuliano after Count Roger saw St Julian in a dream while besieging it, the base of the limestone spur is now spotted with thick grasses, prickly pears and small houses with hibiscus in their gardens. On up the road goes, until the Mediterranean is a sapphire sheet behind you, and then the road turns hard left, and you begin to really climb. Up, up through thicker grasses, the slope above so steep that you can see nothing but pines and sky, and soon the Tyrrenhian sea is far below, a huge waxing moon is rising, and it seems you are above it. Up and on up, and now the hairpin bends make you dread the journey down. It becomes cooler in the bus and soon, as if you are in an aeroplane halfway up its first steep climb, the land is a patchwork of miniatures, and the curves of the coast are visible for thirty miles, and then you are into the first skirts of the cloud and there is nothing to see but ranks of close-packed trees, sinister and still as a child's nightmare, and swirls and wraiths of cloud. At last the bus stops, between the forest and the expressionless grey walls of the town. People waiting for it puff their cheeks and hunch their shoulders; they are wearing thick jackets. It is like November outside: all the heat and the blue-bronze summer has gone, but the air is beautiful, cold and fresh.

Erice is another world. The streets are cobbled and there are no vehicles. In the eddying cloud it became a series of fog-framed glimpses; figures, footsteps, now indistinct, now suddenly clear as the cloud shifts. The town is low, narrow and quiet; one walks softly, as a visitor, marvelling, but one has the sensation that even the oldest residents and the most ancient buildings of this little place sit softly too: there is something here, much older, more powerful and enduring than any structure.

The time to meet it is just after sunrise. The streets are silent; off the main trails the cobbles are stitched with grass. The gardens at the end of the town are deserted, every pine needle is still, light lances through the trees and shafts beam between the battlements of the castle. There is a sacred feeling in the air. It makes me think of Mary in the gardens on the morning after His burial, mistaking Christ for a gardener. But we are in a time long, long before Jesus now. The clouds below part for a moment, affording a sudden image of tiny buildings, tiny roads and cars far below, like a glimpse of a distant and tentative future. Ahead, great waves of vapour are breaking on the stacked rock pinnacle atop which men worshipped their first Goddess, love, nature and all the miracles that the earth can offer, high up here, above the birds, the morning and the world. Our word venerate must come from Venere, Venus. The light changes every moment and you have never seen clouds so close: their ghostly forms and tendrils, forming and constantly reforming, cast spells, make figures, wishes and portents in the air. There is wonder here and the Gods have always attended it. It is as moving, humbling and uplifting as ever it was.

Diodorus lived in the time of Christ, in the first century BC. The flight of Daedalus takes place in the fourteenth century BC, before the Trojan war: we have skipped both back and forward in time. Returning to the state of Sicily after the first wave of Greek settlement, we find the two dominant civilisations teetering on the brink of conflict, though general conflagration does not ignite for a hundred years: that comes in the fifth century BC. In the sixth it merely smoulders. The pressures of continuing immigration from Greece adds kindling: soon after the foundation of Akragas (Agrigento) in 580BC, a band of Greeks from Knidos and Rhodes, led by a Knidian king named Pentathlus, tried to settle in Phoenician territory, in the west, near Lilybaion. The newcomers allied themselves with the Grecian populace of Selinous (Selinunte) who were fighting the Elmyians of Segesta, and their Phoenician allies. The Greeks lost and Pentathlus was killed. His followers took to the seas again, and landed on Lipari, one of the Aeolian islands, named after Liparus, father-in-law of Aeolus, the Keeper of the Winds. Here, where the African plate, the northernmost root of the Atlas mountains, meets the European plate and the geology of the Apennines, the bereft followers of Pentathlus settled, and developed a quite extraordinary social system, simple and equitable, appropriate to a community which had lost its king. There were two pressures on the settlers: to defend themselves from pirates, particularly the Etruscans, and to grow food. So they first agreed that the land would be distributed by lot, and redistributed at twenty-year intervals, then they divided themselves into two groups: half would fight off pirates while the rest would be responsible for food. Despite attacks by Etruscans, Athenians and Carthiginians, the system worked for two hundred and fifty years, until the arrival of the all-conquering Romans in 252BC. No Napoleon or Lenin could have come up with such a beautifully effective system for the management of an imperilled population: indeed, it may have been the absence of an overwhelmingly charismatic and able leader which allowed the system to flourish. The history of Sicily, and particularly in this period, is a treasure-house for students of leadership and governance.

The Greek cities rise under the domination of their first members and most powerful families, and become oligarchies. But oligarchy tends to minority, as the ruling class intermarries and resists expansion of the decision-making franchise to the growing ranks of incomers and the less well off. At some point, either by increment or by violence, the excluded majority claim their rights. Something like democracy begins. Then, in Sicily, certain individuals – magistrates, generals or men who could afford to hire mercenaries or bodyguards – place themselves above the law and award themselves the power of law-making: these are the Tyrants. In Lentini there was Panaitos, a general. In Akragas there was Phalaris, the most infamous. In the first recorded instance of a trick that the Mafia was to perfect over a thousand years later, he used public funds meant for construction to hire thugs, and seized power. He roasted his enemies in a bronze bull. He was overthrown by Telemachus, who, one story goes, gave Phalaris the awful death he had invented. He was succeeded by Theron. In Katane (Catania) the citizens gave power to a particularly wise man, Charondas, whose code of laws was later adopted by many of the Ionian communities in Sicily and Magna Graecia. From Gela came Hippokrates, who took the cities of Naxos and Lentini, and almost conquered Syracuse. After him came Gelon, who became the Tyrant of Syracuse, and the mightiest ruler in all Sicily, in all Hellas, and one of the most powerful men in the Mediterranean world.

There is much talk now of a clash of civilisations, but the year 480BC saw the real thing. In the east the Persian Xerxes was on the march. To the south, a huge fleet was assembling in the great harbours of Carthage, under the command of Hamilcar. In the autumn of that year, on the very same day, according to the popular tale, the Persians and the Carthiginians met Greek civilisation in battle: in the east at Salamis, and in Sicily, at Himera.

Herodotus
From *Polymnia*

With regard to Amilcar [Hamilcar], who was by his father a Carthaginian, and by his mother a Syracusan, and had obtained by his valour the kingly power among the Carthaginians, I understand, that when the battle was fought, and he had been routed, he disappeared, and never afterwards was found, dead or alive, any where in the world; for Gelon caused careful search to be made in all parts. The following account, however, is given by the Carthaginians themselves, and with some probability; that the barbarians fought with the Sicilian Hellenes, beginning from dawn of day to evening: for so long, it is related, the engagement lasted: meanwhile, Amilcar, abiding in the camp, was offering sacrifices, observing the tokens of success, and burning whole bodies on a huge pyre: when he beheld the rout of his army, just as he was making libations on the victims, he cast himself into the fire; and thus, accordingly, being consumed, disappeared. Whether Amilcar disappeared in this latter manner, as the Phœnicians assert, or vanished in some other manner, as the Syracusans relate, the Carthiginians not only sacrifice to him, but have likewise erected monuments to him in all their colonial towns: the largest is erected in the city of Carthage itself. So much for what took place in Sicily.

That is the Carthiginian version: according to Diodorus and the Syracusans, Gelon sent cavalry along the seashore towards the Carthiginian camp, who fooled the sentries into thinking they were friendly reinforcements from Selinunte, which was then under Punic dominance, and charged, caught Hamilcar in the act sacrificing to the god Posiedon, and killed him.

With this, and the defeat of the Persians at Salamis, Hellenic civilisation won a great victory. In Sicily, Gelon was succeeded by Hieron. Hieron was as able a warrior as his predecessor, winning a famous victory against the Etruscans off the coast of Kuma, and he was a man of culture. As the great Norman King Roger was to do in a later century, Hieron surrounded himself with the pre-eminent philosophers and poets of his time, among them Aeschylus and Pindar, the poet of victory, wisdom and magnanimous rule. The following ode was written for Hieron ten years after the great reckoning of 480BC and eloquently demonstrates Pindar's mastery of the victory song. It celebrates Hieron's championship in a chariot race at the Pythian games. Hieron has recently taken Catania, renamed it Aetna, and now celebrates himself as an Aitnaian, founder of a new city. Pindar includes a popular explanation for Aetna's eruptions in his ode: under the volcano is a giant, Typhon, imprisoned there in punishment for attempting to depose Zeus. It seems Hieron did not take the reigns at the beginning of the race in the pink of health: Pindar likens him to Philoktetes, abandoned by the Greeks on their way to Troy because he had a sore on his leg. A decade later, they learned that Troy would never fall without Philoktetes and his bow: they went back for him and the city fell. The Carthaginians and the Etruscans both feature in the ode, as, respectively, 'the Phonikian' and 'the Tyrsanoi.'

From *Pindar's Victory Songs*

    ... But let it be our lot
      to please you, Zeus, who haunt this mountain,
     brow of a fruitful land, and the city
    named for it,
              whose famed founder glorified her
    in the Pythian Games
      when the herald proclaimed her,
        together with him, Hieron,
    victor in the chariot race.
                 For men who embark on ships,
    the first blessing is a breeze to fill their sails
    and waft them on their way, for with it comes
    omen of a safe return.
             And so it is with Aitna:
    with such grace as this at her inception,
    she must retain high fame for her crowns and horses
    and the music of her triumphs.
            Lykian Phoibos, lord
    of Delos and lover of Kastalia's spring upon Parnassos,
    may you lay all this to heart willingly,
    and make this city flourish.

For all resourcefulness descends to mortals
  Only from the gods –
    if men are skilled or mighty
      or gifted in speech,
        it is from them.
        And I, yearning to praise this man,
      hope not to whirl
    my bronze-tipped javelin
off the field, but to fling it
                far beyond my rivals.
May all time continue bringing Hieron
    wealth, bountiful gifts,
      and joy of his struggles.

Well may he recall battles
  where he stood steadfast
    and took with the gods' help
      honor no Hellene plucked before,
        a lordly prize to crown his riches.
      And just now he led his army forth
    like a second Philoktetes:
  a man proud of heart
felt compelled to beg his friendship.
                So legends say
the heroes came, seeking
  Poias' archer son, worn
    by his festering sore

in Lemnos: Philoktetes, who stretched
Priam's city in the dust and put an end
to the pains of the Danaans, though he walked
With broken strength –
           there was fate in it.
So may the god watch over Hieron through coming time
and give him due season for reaping his desires.
Muse, obey me now: sing also at Deinomenes' side,
reward this four-horse chariot victory,
his father's triumph, and a joy to him no less.
Come then, a loving song for Aitna's king,

for whom Hieron founded this city
  to abide in freedom
    by the rule of Hyllos.
      So the sons of Pamphylos and Herakles,
        though dwelling under Taÿgetos' crags,
      keep the ways of Aigimios,
    Dorians forever: they left Mount Pindos
  and took Amyklai, happy men!
Today they are far-famed neighbours
                      to the twin Tyndaridai,
  riders of white horses –
    and the fame of their spear
      bursts into blossom.

May fortune such as they enjoy
  fall also to the kings and citizens of Aitna
    in the true report of men – through you, Zeus,
      their prince may follow his father,
        revering the people, leading them
      in the harmonies of peace.
    But I beseech you, son of Kronos,
  keep the Phoinikian at home,
stifle the battle-shout
               of the Tyrsanoi –
let them rue
  their pride at Kuma
   that burst into wailing for their fleet.

Such was the anguish the Syracusan king
inflicted on them when he hurled their youth
from the swift ships into the waves, saving Hellas
from the iron yoke of slavery.
             I will earn
the praise of Athens by singing of Salamis,
and of Sparta by making my theme
the battles beneath Kithairon,
where the curve-bow Persians strove and were crushed.
But when I come to the rivery field of Himera
I will sing of the Deinomenidai, conquerors of the foe.

Praise spoken in due season,
  theme after theme set down
    in quick succession, reaps
      less blame from men, for tedium
        dulls their keen attentiveness,
      and hearing others extolled
     rouses secret hatred.
  Yet do not give up your noble ways:
better men's resentment
                than their pity.
Govern the people with justice.
  Forge your speech
    on the anvil of truth.

Even a trivial spark will start a blaze
  if it fall from you
    who are steward of many, and many
      will be your witnesses, for good or ill.
      But if indeed you yearn to hear
    your name forever sounded
  in the tones of praise,
 abide in these high spirits,
go on being lavish.
             Unfurl your sails.
Don't be deceived
  by cunning thrift:
    glory follows a man,

glory alone, when he is dead, reveals
his manner of life to the lords
of song and story.
         Kroisos' mild-mannered ways
perish not, but in all lands hateful speech
oppresses Phalaris, pitiless burner of men
in the brazen bull.
        No lyres in hall
welcome him to the soft embrace of boys' voices.
Success is the first of prizes.
        To be well spoken of is second.
But he who finds them both and keeps them
wins the highest crown.

Translated by Frank J Nisetich

But victory did not bring peace to Hellas. In 431BC the Peloponnesian wars began. Athens was initially successful. In 414 in Sicily, the cities of Segesta and Selinunte were at war: Athens was allied with Segesta, Syracuse with Selinunte. Athens sent ambassadors to Segesta. It is said the Segestans dazzled them with a wealth of silver; a glimpse of the treasure of the temple of Erice. The ambassadors returned to Athens, urging the citizens to send a force to assist the Segestans, which would mean attacking and defeating Syracuse. A fierce debate broke out: the pro-war party, hungry for treasure and confident in the martial prowess of Athenians, argued that a victory in Sicily would spread fear and respect among the republic's enemies in the Peloponnese. Foremost among them was the figure of Alcibiades; young, vociferous and charismatic, eager for fame, wealth and victory. The anti-war party was led by Nicias: in a terrible irony, the man the Athenians wished to lead the expedition. The debate was chronicled by Thucydides, who would have seen it. The speeches of Nicias make compelling, and, in view of what was to come, tragic reading. Their sentiments will be familiar to anyone who has ever argued against military adventure in distant lands on what Nicias believed to be specious grounds.

> 'I say then that you wish, though leaving many enemies behind you here, to bring hither fresh ones besides, by sailing there ... Even if we conquered them, we should hardly be able to govern, so far off and so numerous as they are. But it is folly to go against men whom we could not keep under, if we conquered them ... And the Greeks in those parts would be most in awe of us, if we did not go there at all; and next to that, if after making a demonstration of our power we retired in a short time: but if we should meet with any reverse, they would very quickly despise us, and attack us in concert with our enemies here. For we all know that what is farthest off is most admired, and what gives the least room for having its fame tested.
>
> 'I bid the older men ... not to be put down through shame, in order to avoid being thought a coward if he should not vote for going to war; nor, as their opponents themselves might feel, to be madly enamoured of what they do not possess; being convinced that in very few things do men succeed through desire, but in very many through forethought.
>
> 'Good government,' Nicias concludes, 'consists in this – for a man to do his country as much good as possible, or, at least, to do it voluntarily no harm.'

Alcibiades answers him, arguing that the Sicilian cities are populated 'by a mixed rabble', 'torn by faction', and that the Peloponnesians 'were never more hopeless with regard to us' concluding: 'The state, if it remain quiet, will be worn out on itself, like anything else, and its skill in everything grow dull; while by entering into contest it will continually gain fresh experience, and will find self-defence habitual to it, not in word, but rather in deed. My decided opinion then is, that I think a state of no inactive character would most quickly be ruined by a change to inactivity; and that those men live most securely, who regulate their affairs in accordance with existing habits and institutions, even though they may be of an inferior character, with the least variation.'

It is not an argument one can easily imagine being made in public today – though one might well imagine it being held in private, in certain quarters – but the Athenians, already disposed to adventure and conquest, saw some truth in it, and voted for war.

The Athenians assembled a mighty force: one hundred and thirty warships, five thousand heavily-armed infantry and one thousand three hundred lighter troops. They were deficient in one crucial respect: Syracuse was famous for its cavalry but the Athenians took only thirty horsemen with them. At first the Syracusans disbelieved reports of the approaching threat, then rushed to prepare their defences. No sooner had the Athenians reached Sicily than Alcibiades was recalled to Athens to face charges of defacing the city's statues of Hermes, on the eve of the expedition's departure. Alcibiades set off, but rather than face his accusers he defected to Sparta, to become a valued advisor to the Spartans and Corinthians in their war with Athens. Nicias delayed, palpably reluctant to face Syracuse: he went west, to try to settle the dispute between Selinunte and Segesta, wintered at Catania, and sent ambassadors around the region in search of allies. Skirmishes were fought, including one in the great harbour of Syracuse, but the Syracusans, led and organised by Hermokrates, held their own. When the armies met on land the Athenians prevailed, though the Syracusan cavalry prevented them from pressing home any advantage.

In the spring of 414BC battle was joined in earnest. At first the Athenians had the better of it, and the Syracusans despaired. But in Sparta Alcibiades was at work, plotting the destruction of the expedition he had advocated. At his urging, a Corinthian fleet of twenty ships made for Syracuse, carrying with them one Gylippus, a Spartan general, who was to be decisive. Gylippus collected troops from other Sicilian cities, he constructed forts around Syracuse, and his men won a wall-building contest with the Athenians, in which each side tried to hem the other in. He offered the expedition a five-day truce, to withdraw from the island. He cannot have expected them to accept but it was a successful psychological tactic, rallying the spirits of the defenders. Taking advantage of the hilly land around the city, Gylippus contrived to isolate the Athenians, effectively trapping them near the city, near their ships in the Great Harbour, cut off from the north. He next attacked the invaders where they were believed to be strongest: at sea. The Great Harbour is barely two square miles of water, with a narrow mouth. The Athenians were bolstered by a fleet of reinforcements from their own city, led by Demosthenes, the best solider Athens could send, but their relief did not last long. They lost the first sea fight in the Great Harbour: there was no room for skilful sailing, the Syracusans closed with their ships and fought the crews as if on land. Worse, the Syracusans began to close up the mouth of the Great Harbour, anchoring merchant ships, triremes and smaller boats across it. The Athenians were trapped, and their hopelessness horribly apparent. Nicias, who had been sick and wounded, now assembled his disheartened soldiers, and addressed them.

Thucydides
From *The History of the Peloponnesian War*

'Soldiers of the Athenians, and of the other allies, the coming struggle will be common alike to all – for the safety and country of each of us, no less than of the enemy; since if we now gain a victory with our fleet, each one may see his native city again, wherever it may he. Nor should you be disheartened, or feel like the most inexperienced of men, who, after failing in their first attempts, ever after have the anticipation of their fear taking the colour of their disasters. But as many of you here as are Athenians, having already had experience in many wars, and all the allies who have ever joined us in our expeditions, remember the unexpected results that occur in warfare; and make your preparations with a hope that fortune may at length side with *us*, and with a determination to renew the conflict in a manner worthy of your numbers, which you see yourselves to be so great.

'Now whatever we saw likely to be serviceable against the confined space of the harbour, with reference to the crowd of ships that there will be, and the enemy's troops upon their decks, from which we suffered before, every thing has now been looked to and prepared by us also, as far as present circumstances would allow, with the co-operation of the masters of our vessels. For great numbers of bow-men and dart-men will go on board, and a multitude such as we should not have used, had we been fighting in the open sea, as it would have interfered with the display of our skill through the weight of our ships; but in the present *land-fight* which we are compelled to make on board our ships, these things will be of service. We have also ascertained the different ways in which we must adapt the structure of our vessels for opposing theirs, and especially, against the stoutness of their cheeks, from which we received most damage, we have provided grappling irons, which will prevent the ship's retiring again after it has once charged, if the soldiers on board then do their duty. For to this necessity are we reduced, that we must maintain a land-fight on board our fleet; and it seems to be our interest neither to retire ourselves, nor to suffer them to do it; especially as the shore, except so far as our troops occupy it, is in possession of the enemy.

'Remembering this, then, you must fight on as long as you can, and not be driven to land, but determine, when one ship has closed with another, not to separate before you have swept off the soldiers from your enemy's deck. And this exhortation I offer to the soldiers not less than to the sailors, inasmuch as this work belongs more to those upon deck. And we have still even now a general superiority with our troops. On the other hand, I advise the seamen, and entreat them too at the same time, not to be too much dismayed by their misfortunes, as we have now superior resources on our decks, and a larger number of ships ...

Nicias delivered this exhortation to them, and immediately commanded them to man the ships. Gylippus and the Syracusans, on the other hand, were able to perceive, from the sight of their very preparations, that the Athenians were about to engage them at sea, and the device of throwing the grappling irons had also been previously reported to them. They prepared themselves therefore on all other points severally and on this also; for they covered over with hides their prows and a considerable space of the upper part of the vessel, that the grapple, when thrown, might slip off, and not obtain any hold on them. And now, when every thing was ready, their generals, together with Gylippus, exhorted them by speaking as follows:

'That our former achievements have been glorious ones, Syracusans and allies, and that this struggle will be for glorious results in future, most of you seem to us to be aware, (for you would not else have devoted yourselves so eagerly to it,) and if any one is not as sensible of it as he ought to be, we will prove it to him. For when the Athenians had come to this country, for the subjugation of Sicily in the first place, and then, if they succeeded, for that of the Peloponnese also, and the rest of Greece; and when they possessed the largest empire enjoyed hitherto, either by Greeks of former times or of the present, you were the first men in the world who withstood their navy, with which they had borne down every thing, and have already conquered them in some sea-fights, and will now, in all probability, conquer them in this. For when men have been put down in that in which they claim to excel, their opinion of themselves in future is far lower than if they had never entertained such an idea at first; and failing through the disappointment of their boasting, they give way even beyond the degree of their power. And such, probably, is now the feeling of the Athenians.

'But in our case, both the opinion we entertained before, and with which, even while we were yet unskilful, we were full of daring, has now been confirmed; and from the addition to it of the thought that we must be the best seamen in the world, since we have conquered the best, each man's hope is doubled. And, generally speaking, it is the greatest hope that supplies also the greatest spirit for undertakings.

'... let us close with them in wrath, and consider that the feeling of those men is most lawful, with regard to their enemies, who determine, when taking vengeance on their aggressor, to glut the animosity of their heart: and that we too shall have an opportunity of avenging ourselves on our foes – the very thing which is every where said to be most sweet. For that they are our foes, and our bitterest foes, you all know; inasmuch as they came against our country to enslave it, and if they succeeded, would have imposed on our men all that was most painful; on our children and wives, all that is most dishonourable; and on our whole country, the title which is most degrading. Wherefore no one ought to relent, or deem it gain that they should merely go away without danger to us. For that they will do just the same, even if they gain the victory. But that, through our succeeding (as we probably shall do) in our wishes, these men should be punished, and should leave a more secure liberty for the whole of Sicily, which even before enjoyed that blessing; this is a glorious object to contend for. And of all hazards those are most rare, which, while they cause least harm by failure, confer most advantage by success.'

The Syracusan commanders and Gylippus having in their turn thus exhorted their men, immediately manned the ships on their side also, since they saw that the Athenians were doing it. Nicias ... led the troops down to the beach, and ranged them over as large a space as he could, that the greatest possible assistance might be given to those on board towards keeping up their spirits. Demosthenes, Menander, and Euthydemus, who went on board the Athenian fleet to take the command, put out from their own station, and immediately sailed to the bar at the mouth of the harbour, and the passage through it which had been closed up, wishing to force their way to the outside.

The Syracusans and their allies, having previously put out with pretty nearly the same number of ships as before, proceeded to keep guard with part of them at the passage out, and also round the circumference of the whole harbour, that they might fall upon the Athenians on all sides at once, while their troops also at the same time came to their aid at whatever part their vessels might put in to shore. The commanders of the Syracusan fleet were Sicanus and Agatharchus, each occupying a wing of the whole force, with Pythen and the Corinthians in the centre. When the Athenians came up to the bar, in the first rush with which they charged they got the better of the ships posted at it, and endeavoured to break the fastenings. Afterwards, when the Syracusans and their allies bore down upon them from all quarters, the engagement was going on no longer at the bar alone, but over the harbour also; and an obstinate one it was, such as none of the previous ones had been. For great eagerness for the attack was exhibited by the seamen on both sides, when the command was given; and there was much counter-manœuvring on the part of the masters, and rivalry with each other; while the soldiers on board exerted themselves, when vessel came in collision with vessel, that the operations on deck might not fall short of the skill shown by others. Indeed every one, whatever the duty assigned him, made every effort that he might himself in each case appear the best man ... So long as a vessel was coming up to the charge, those on her decks plied their javelins, arrows, and stones in abundance against her; but when they came to close quarters, the heavy-armed marines, fighting hand to hand, endeavoured to board each other's ships. In many cases too it happened, through want of room, that on one side they were charging an enemy, and on the other were being charged themselves, and that two ships, and sometimes even more, were by compulsion entangled round one. And thus the masters had to guard against some, and to concert measures against others – not one thing at a time, but many things on every side – while the great din from such a number of ships coming into collision both spread dismay and prevented their hearing what the boatswains said. For many were the orders given and the shouts raised by those officers on each side, both in the discharge of their duty, and from their present eagerness for the battle: while they cried out to the Athenians, 'to force the passage, and now, if ever they meant to do it hereafter, to exert themselves heartily for a safe return to their country;' and to the Syracusans and their allies, 'that it would be a glorious achievement for them to prevent the enemy's escape, and by gaining the victory to confer honour on their respective countries' ...

The troops on shore too, on both sides, when the sea-fight was so equally balanced, suffered a great agony and conflict of feelings; those of the country being ambitious now of still greater honour, while their invaders were afraid of faring even worse than at present. For, since the Athenians' all was staked on their fleet, their fear for the future was like none they had ever felt before; and from the unequal nature of the engagement they were also compelled to have an unequal view of it from the beach. For as the spectacle was near at hand, and as they did not all look at the same part at once, if any saw their own men victorious in any quarter, they would be encouraged, and turn to calling on the gods not to deprive them of safety; while those who looked on the part that was being beaten, uttered lamentations at the same time as cries, and from the sight they had of what was going on, expressed their feelings more than those engaged in the action. Others, again, looking on a doubtful point of the engagement, inconsequence of the indecisive continuance of the conflict, in their excessive fear made gestures with their very bodies, corresponding with their thoughts, and continued in the most distressing state, for they were constantly within a little of escaping, or of being destroyed. And thus amongst the troops of the Athenians, as long as they were fighting at sea on equal terms, every sound might be heard at once, wailing, shouting, 'they conquer,' 'they are conquered,' and all the other various exclamations which a great armament in great peril would be constrained to utter – very much in the same way as their men on board their ships were affected – until at length, after the battle had continued for a long time, the Syracusans and their allies routed the Athenians, and pressing on them in a decisive manner, with much shouting and cheering of each other on, pursued them to the shore. Then the sea forces, as many as were not taken afloat, put in to the land at different parts, and rushed from on board to the camp while the army, no longer with any different feelings, but all on one impulse, lamenting and groaning, deplored the event and proceeded, some to succour the ships, others to guard what remained of their wall; while others, and those the greatest part, began now to think of themselves, and how they should best provide for their own preservation. Indeed their dismay at the moment had been exceeded by none of all they had ever felt ... and at this time for the Athenians to escape by land was hopeless, unless something beyond all expectation should occur ...

When Nicias and Demosthenes thought they were sufficiently prepared, the removal of the army took place, on the third day after the sea-fight ... this was the greatest reverse that ever befell a Grecian army; since, in contrast to their having come to enslave others, they had to depart in fear of undergoing that themselves; and instead of prayers and hymns, with which they sailed from home, they had to start on their return with omens the very contrary of these; going by land, instead of by sea, and relying on a military rather than a naval force. But nevertheless, in consequence of the greatness of the danger still impending, all these things seemed endurable to them.

Nicias, seeing the army dejected, and greatly changed, passed along the ranks, and encouraged and cheered them, as well as existing circumstances allowed; speaking still louder than before, as he severally came opposite to them, in the earnestness of his feeling, and from wishing to be of service to them by making himself audible to as many as possible.

'Still, even in our present circumstances, Athenians and allies, must we cherish hope; for some men have, ere now, been preserved even from more dreadful circumstances than these. Nor should you think too meanly of yourselves, or yield too much to your misfortunes and present sufferings, which are beyond your desert. For my own part, though I am not superior to any of you in strength, (for you see what a state I am in through disease,) and though I consider myself to be second to none, whether in my private life or in other respects, yet now I am exposed to every danger, like the very meanest. And yet I have lived with much devotion, as regards the gods, and much justice and freedom from reproach, as regards men. And therefore my hope is still strong for the future; and my calamities do not terrify me, so much as they might. Nay, they may perhaps be alleviated; for our enemies have enjoyed good enough fortune; and if we displeased any of the gods by making this expedition, we have already been sufficiently punished for it. Others also, we know, have ere now marched against their neighbours; and after acting as men do, have suffered what they could endure. And so in our case it is reasonable now to hope that we shall find the wrath of the gods mitigated; for we are now deserving the pity at their hands, rather than of envy. Looking, too, on your own ranks, what experienced and numerous men of arms there are with you, advancing in battle-array together, do not be too dismayed, but consider that you are yourselves at once a city, wherever you may settle; and that there is no other in Sicily that would either easily resist your attack, or expel you when settled any where. With regard to the march, that it may be safe and orderly, look to that yourselves; with no other consideration, each of you, than that whatever the spot on which he may be compelled to fight, on that he will have, if victorious, both a country and a fortress. And we shall hurry on our way both by day and night alike, as we have but scanty provisions; and if we can only reach some friendly town of the Sicels, (for they, through their fear of the Syracusans, are still true to us,) then consider yourselves to be in security. And a message has been sent forward to them, and directions have been given them to meet us, and bring a fresh supply of provisions. In short, you must be convinced, soldiers, both that it is necessary for you to be brave men – since there is no place near which you can reach in safety, if you act like cowards – and, at the same time, that if you escape from your enemies now, the rest of you will gain a sight of all you may anywhere wish to see; and the Athenians will raise up again, though fallen at present, the great power of their country. For it is men that make a city, and not walls, or ships, without any to man them.'

Nicias, then, delivered this exhortation, and at the same time went up to the troops, and if he saw them any where straggling, and not marching in order, he collected and brought them to their post; while Demosthenes also did no less to those who were near him, addressing them in a similar manner. They marched in the form of a hollow square, the division under Nicias taking the lead, and that of Demosthenes following; while the baggage bearers and the main crowd of camp followers were enclosed within the heavy-armed. When they had come to the ford of the river Anapus, they found drawn up at it a body of the Syracusans and allies; but having routed these, and secured the passage, they proceeded onwards; while the Syracusans pressed them with charges of horse, as their light-armed did with their missiles. On that day the Athenians advanced about forty stades, and then halted for the night on a hill. The day following, they commenced their march at an early hour, and having advanced about twenty stades, descended into a level district, and there encamped, wishing to procure some eatables from the houses, (for the place was inhabited,) and to carry with them water from it, since for many stades before them, in the direction they were to go, it was not plentiful. The Syracusans, in the mean time, had gone on before, and were blocking up the pass in advance of them. For there was there a steep hill, with a precipitous ravine on either side of it, called the Acræum Lepas. The next day the Athenians advanced, and the horse and dart-men of the Syracusans and allies, each in great numbers, impeded their progress, hurling their missiles upon them, and annoying them with cavalry charges. The Athenians fought for a long time and the division of Nicias, taking the lead as it did, kept together and got a long way in advance; while that of Demosthenes ... was separated from the others, and proceeded in great disorder ...

Afterwards, terms were made with all the troops under Demosthenes, that they should surrender their arms, and that no one should be put to death, either by violence, or imprisonment, or want of such nourishment as was most absolutely requisite. Thus there surrendered, in all, to the number of six thousand; and the whole of the money in their possession they laid down, throwing it into the hollow of shields, four of which they filled with it. These they immediately led back to the city, while Nicias and his division arrived that day on the banks of the river Erineus; having crossed which, he posted his army on some high ground.

The Syracusans, having overtaken him the next day, told him that Demosthenes and his division had surrendered themselves, and called on *him* also to do the same. Being incredulous of the fact, he obtained a truce to enable him to send a horseman to sea. When he had gone, and brought word back again that they had surrendered, Nicias sent a herald to Gylippus and the Syracusans, saying that he was ready to agree with the Syracusans, on behalf of the Athenians, to repay whatever money the Syracusans had spent on the war, on condition of their letting his army go; and that until the money was paid, he would give the Athenians as hostages, one for every talent. The Syracusans and Gylippus did not accede to these proposals, but fell upon this division also, and surrounded them on all sides, and annoyed them with their missiles until late in the day. And they too, like the others, were in a wretched plight for want of food and necessaries. Nevertheless, they watched for the quiet of the night, and then intended to pursue their march. And they were now just taking up their arms, when the Syracusans perceived it and raised the pæan. The Athenians therefore, finding that they had not eluded their observation, laid their arms down again; excepting about three hundred men, who forced their way through the sentinels, and proceeded, during the night, how and where they could.

As soon as it was day, Nicias led his troops forward; while the Syracusans and allies pressed on them in the same manner, discharging their missiles at them, and striking them down with their javelins on every side. The Athenians were hurrying on to reach the river Assinarus, being urged to this at once by the attack made on every side of them by the numerous cavalry and the rest of the light-armed multitude, (for they thought they should be more at ease if they were once across the river,) and also by their weariness and craving for drink. When they reached its banks, they rushed into it without any more regard for order, every man anxious to be himself the first to cross it; while the attack of the enemy rendered the passage more difficult. For being compelled to advance in a dense body, they fell upon and trode down one another; and some of them died immediately on the javelins and articles of baggage, while others were entangled together, and floated down the stream. On the other side of the river, too, the Syracusans lined the bank, which was precipitous, and from the higher ground discharged their missiles on the Athenians, while most of them were eagerly drinking, and in confusion amongst themselves in the hollow bed of the stream. The Peloponnesians, moreover, came down to them and butchered them, especially those in the river. And thus the water was immediately spoiled; but nevertheless it was drunk by them, mud and all, bloody as it was, and was even fought for by most of them.

At length, when many dead were now heaped one upon another in the river, and the army was destroyed, either at the river, or, even if any part had escaped, by the cavalry, Nicias surrendered himself to Gylippus, placing more confidence in him than in the Syracusans; and desired him and the Lacedæmonians to do what they pleased with himself, but to stop butchering the rest of the soldiers. After this, Gylippus commanded to make prisoners; and they collected all that were alive, excepting such as they concealed for their own benefit (of whom there was a large number). They also sent a party in pursuit of the three hundred, who had forced their way through the sentinels during the night, and took them. The part of the army, then, that was collected as general property, was not large, but that which was secreted was considerable; and the whole of Sicily was filled with them, inasmuch as they had not been taken on definite terms of surrender, like those with Demosthenes. Indeed no small part was actually put to death; for this was the most extensive slaughter, and surpassed by none of all that occurred in this Sicilian war. In the other encounters also, which were frequent on their march, no few had fallen. But many also escaped, nevertheless; some at the moment, others after serving as slaves, and running away subsequently. These found a place of refuge at Catana.

When the Syracusans and allies were assembled together, they took with them as many prisoners as they could, with the spoils, and returned to the city. All the rest of the Athenians and the allies that they had taken, they sent down into the quarries, thinking this the safest way of keeping them: but Nicias and Demosthenes they executed, against the wish of Gylippus. For he thought it would be a glorious distinction for him, in addition to all his other achievements, to take to the Lacedæmonians even the generals who had commanded against them. And it so happened, that one of these, namely Demosthenes, was regarded by them as their most inveterate enemy, in consequence of what had occurred on the island and at Pylus; the other, for the same reasons, as most in their interest; for Nicias had exerted himself for the release of the Lacedæmonians taken from the island, by persuading the Athenians to make a treaty. On this account the Lacedæmonians had friendly feelings towards him; and indeed it was mainly for the same reasons that he reposed confidence in Gylippus, and surrendered himself to him. But certain of the Syracusans (as it was said) were afraid, some of them, since they had held communication with him, that if put to the torture, he might cause them trouble on that account in the midst of their success; others, and especially the Corinthians, lest he might bribe some, as he was rich, and effect his escape, and so they should again incur mischief through his agency; and therefore they persuaded the allies, and put him to death. For this cause then, or something very like this, he was executed; having least of all the Greeks in my time deserved to meet with such a misfortune, on account of his devoted attention to the practice of every virtue.

As for those in the quarries, the Syracusans treated them with cruelty during the first period of their captivity. For as they were in a hollow place, and many in a small compass, the sun, as well as the suffocating closeness of their not being under cover; and then, on the contrary, the nights coming on autumnal and cold, soon worked in them an alteration from health to disease, by means of the change. Since, too, in consequence of their want of room, they did every thing in the same place; and the dead, moreover, were piled up one on another – such as died from their wounds, and from the change they had experienced, and such like – there were, besides, intolerable stenches: while at the same time they were tormented with hunger and thirst; for during eight months they gave each of them daily only a cotyle of water, and two of corn. And of all the other miseries which it was likely that men thrown into such a place would suffer, there was none that did not fall to their lot. For some seventy days they thus lived all together; but then they sold the rest of them, except the Athenians, and whatever Siceliots or Italiots had joined them in the expedition. The total number of those who were taken, though it were difficult to speak with exactness, was still not less than seven thousand. And this was the greatest Grecian exploit of all that were performed in this war; nay, in my opinion, of all Grecian achievements that we have heard of also; and was at once most splendid for the conquerors, and most disastrous for the conquered. For being altogether vanquished at all points, and having suffered in no slight degree in any respect, they were destroyed (as the saying is) with utter destruction, both army and navy, and every thing; and only a few out of many returned home. Such were the events which occurred in Sicily.

The Sicilian Greeks had triumphed again but this was barely the beginning of an age of conflict on and around the island, which ended with their defeat. The Carthiginians came again, led by one Hannibal – not *the* Hannibal, but a man of the same warrior ilk. He landed at Motya, where he made his base, and attacked Selinunte, taking the city by surprise: in the quarries outside the remains of the town you can still see carved columns emerging from the rock, abandoned by their sculptors in the face of Hannibal's troops. The invader came to avenge the defeat of his grandfather, Hamilcar, and the Greeks had much to fear from him. Selinunute held out for nine days, until the walls were breached.

Selinunte, once a power to rival Syracuse, was a city conceived and built as a work of art in which its citizens would live. (One cannot help comparing this to our own time, in which settlements are built with the twin considerations of the income level of the people who will inhabit them, and the profit developers might wring from them.) It occupies a low hill between two shallow river valleys, the mouths of which formed its two harbours. It seems now almost as remote in geography as it is distant in time, a ground plan of ruins, home to a thousand lizards, on a low bluff on the far southern shore of Europe, staring across the bare seas towards Africa and a lost time. But when it thrived this was the cauldron of civilisation and conflict; Selinunte was rich and fair and its temples were quite marvellous. In 1958 they resurrected one, known as Temple E, possibly dedicated to Hera. It is a stunning structure, at once majestic and endearing, monumental and compact, the golden stone of its Doric columns and entablature testament to the city and the people it once surveyed. Four of its meotopes are now in the Palermo Museum of Archaeology. They show Herakles fighting an Amazon (one of his feet traps one of hers, preventing her escape, he has blocked her blow and is about to deliver the killing stroke); the marriage Zeus and Hera (he is reclining, tugging her down towards him, all sybaritic lust); Athena overcoming a Titan and, best of all, Artemis, Acteon and his dogs attacking him. They are all living, fluid works, but the last is quite arresting. You can almost hear the ferocious snarling of the suddenly maddened dogs. One has his teeth in Acteon's flank, another has leapt almost to head height (the hunter has him by the throat) and a third is snaking in, low to the ground, intent on the attack. Acteon is silent, perhaps panting with the effort of his desperate defence, and Artemis, with a horribly gentle, imperious gesture, is urging the dogs on, her face calm, almost smiling. Because nothing of our time is visible from the archaeological park in which Selinunte now stands, it is easy to imagine what it must have been like to live in Greek Sicily in a time of peace, under vast clear skies, surrounded by the same birdsong, warmed by the same sun and nourished by the same rich soil. The citizens of Selinunte had much to thank their Gods for, and everything to lose, when Hannibal came. As the decorations on their vases and bowls make clear, theirs was a society beset by the image and experience of war. 'Since the Selinuntines do not know how to defend their liberty, they deserve to become slaves,' Hannibal is reported to have said.

Many men were slaughtered, many women and children were taken into slavery. But Hannibal was not satisfied. He marched on Himera, where his grandfather had died. He threw siege-engines at the walls and had mines dug under them. When it seemed the city might be relieved by a force from Akragas, Hannibal spread word that he was returning to his ships at Motya, intending to sail for Syracuse. The Greek force returned to defend Syracuse, but Hannibal pressed his attack. Himera fell. Hannibal enslaved the women and children again, and assembled all the men: some three thousand. He marched them to the place where Hamilkar died, where he had them abused, tortured and finally massacred. Returning to the city, he had the walls razed, the temples destroyed and the buildings burned. Nothing was left of it. A new colony was founded, later, near the site, at the Baths of Himera, Therma Himeraia, which exists today as Termini.

The following decades saw a protracted war between Greek Sicily and Carthage. Another Carthaginian attack, led by Himilkon and a now elderly Hannibal, succeeded in taking Akragas, the city Pindar says was the fairest of all. In the course of the siege Hannibal died of plague: to assuage the Gods and reassure his men, Himilkon had his own son burned on a sacrificial fire to Moloch, the terrible Carthaginian deity.

In 405BC a man named Dionysus began a climb to power that took him to tyranny over Syracuse. He made peace with Carthage and began to build up his forces. He took the Greek cities of Naxos and Catania in 403. He strengthened the defences of Syracuse: by 402 it was the largest, and thought to be the strongest city in the world. Dionysus hired mercenaries and built quinqueremes, the biggest ships men had ever seen, with five banks of oars. He is said to have invented the catapult. When he was ready, in 397, he tore up the treaty with Carthage and made war on Motya. The battle was fought in the lagoon – Dionysus had several of his trapped ships dragged across an isthmus – and at sea, and high in the air, between siege towers and the great walls of Motya. Dionysus took the city, but the next year, in 396, Himilkon returned, and his forces retook the island for Carthage. Himilkon attacked Syracuse, but could not storm it. Fatally, it was thought, he desecrated the temple to the Sicilian Goddesses, Demeter and Persephone. Encamped in marshes near Syracuse his army caught plague; every fight went against them. Dionysus negotiated with Himilkon in secret, and for a payment of three hundred talents, Himilkon agreed to sail away at night, with his Carthaginian soldiers, leaving his allies and mercenaries to their fate. In Carthage the worried populace built an apologetic temple, alongside those of their own Gods, to Demeter and Persephone. Sicilian Goddesses, it was clear, were not to be crossed.

Today the daughters of Persephone can be seen haring through the Palermo traffic on mopeds, and perched on the back of Motoguzzis and Ducattis, multi-horsepower chariots, and smoking cigarettes behind the wheels of small Smart cars, which have been enthusiastically adopted here, perfectly suited to the city's narrow streets and mosaic parking. On the weekends they sun themselves on the beach at Mondello, distinguished from their tanned French and German sisters by a lack of mosquito bites. I am not suggesting that the little winged bloodsuckers, the accursed *zanzare*, do not bite Sicilians: merely that their bites do not erupt into pink lumps, as they do on the rest of us. The brutes come into my room at night, one at a time, whining their tiny, piercing battle cries, and feast on me until I climb out of bed, turn on the light, and murder them with my bulky copy of John Dickie's *Cosa Nostra: a history of the Sicilian Mafia*, which is now, appropriately, spattered in blood. D H Lawrence had a similar relationship with a *zanzare*.

D H Lawrence
The Mosquito

When did you start your tricks
Monsieur?

What do you stand on such high legs for?
Why this length of shredded shank
You exaltation?

Is it so that you shall lift your centre of gravity upwards
And weigh no more than air as you alight upon me,
Stand upon me weightless, you phantom?

I heard a woman call you the Winged Victory
In sluggish Venice.
You turn your head towards your tail, and smile.

49

How can you put so much devilry
Into that translucent phantom shred
Of a frail corpus?

Queer, with your thin wings and your streaming legs
How you sail like a heron, or a dull clot of air,
A nothingness.

Yet what an aura surrounds you;
Your evil little aura, prowling, and casting a numbness on my mind.

That is your trick, your bit of filthy magic:
Invisibility, and the anæsthetic power
To deaden my attention in your direction.

But I know your game now, streaky sorcerer.

Queer, how you stalk and prowl the air
In circles and evasions, enveloping me,
Ghoul on wings
Winged Victory.

Settle, and stand on long thin shanks
Eyeing me sideways, and cunningly conscious that I am aware,
You speck.

I hate the way you lurch off sideways into air
Having read my thoughts against you.

Come then, let us play at unawares,
And see who wins in this sly game of bluff.
Man or mosquito.

You don't know that I exist, and I don't know that you exist.
Now then!

It is your trump
It is your hateful little trump
You pointed fiend,
Which shakes my sudden blood to hatred of you:
It is your small, high, hateful bugle in my ear.

Why do you do it?
Surely it is bad policy.
They say you can't help it.

If that is so, then I believe a little in Providence protecting the innocent.
But it sounds so amazingly like a slogan
A yell of triumph as you snatch my scalp.

Blood, red blood
Super-magical
Forbidden liquor.

I behold you stand
For a second enspasmed in oblivion,
Obscenely ecstasied
Sucking live blood
My blood.

Such silence, such suspended transport,
Such gorging,
Such obscenity of trespass.

You stagger
As well as you may.
Only your accursed hairy frailty
Your own imponderable weightlessness
Saves you, wafts you away on the very draught my anger makes in its
     snatching.

Away with a pæan of derision
You winged blood-drop.

Can I not overtake you?
Are you one too many for me
Winged Victory?
Am I not mosquito enough to out-mosquito you?

Queer, what a big stain my sucked blood makes
Beside the infinitesimal faint smear of you!
Queer, what a dim dark smudge you have disappeared into!

Meanwhile, on the beaches of Mondello, the almost unbitten descendants of Persephone are attended by numerous Aidoneouses, now masters of persuasion rather than kidnap, but still clearly nursing the ancient desire to sweep a Sicilian girl back to the netherworld for the winter. I watched one arrive at a wedding on the back of a motorbike. She wore a black jacket and long black skirt, which rode around her thighs as she sat astride. A policeman carefully removed his whistle from his mouth and smiled. She dismounted, freeing long dark hair from her helmet. An elderly man with a tube in his nose and carrying a portable oxygen machine swayed slightly. 'Madonna santa!' he muttered – not in disapproval, as would have been the case until quite recently, but in admiration. Attitudes have changed completely, albeit slowly. In the sixteenth century the explicitly nude statues of the sumptuous Tuscan fountain in Piazza Pretoria outraged Palermitans: they still call it Piazza della Vergogna, the square of shame. Only a decade ago, in the middle of the day, the English girlfriend of a young teacher who lived opposite the Cathedral was pelted with bottles and stones as she waited for him on Corso Vittorio Emmanuele: her summer clothes made her fair game, in the eyes of her juvenile tormentors. Today, as part of the Kalsa festival, the streets of Palermo's ancient Arab quarter are hung with enormous photographs by David LaChapelle of pop-starlets and models wearing sneers and tiny scraps of lurid plastic. No one takes any notice.

The many parts Sicilian women have played through the ages – as citizens, heroines, mothers and wives; as victims, as Goddesses, domestic and otherwise, as supporters and opponents of the mafia, as champions and reformers – are worthy of a shelf of dedicated books. We come to some of the most interesting writing by and about them later in this collection, but we begin, in the time of relative peace after the first Punic war between Greek Sicily and Carthage, with a piece which places them in one of their most enduring roles: as muses, objects of men's veneration and their desire.

Very little is known about the life of Theocritus beyond his poems. He was born around 310BC and lived in Syracuse. But Theocritus was a wise, funny and tender man, and a great poet. His Idyll XI, *The Cyclops,* casts an entirely different light on the monster of the Odyssey, who seems to have led a miserable life: back-breaking farm work, maiming at the hands of Odysseus, and before that, most painful of all, unrequited love for the sea-nymph Galateia.

Theocritus
The Cylops

There is no other medicine, Nikias, against Love,
Neither by way of ointment nor of plaster, take my word,
Save the Pieran Muses. A gentle remedy
And sweet is that for men to use, yet very hard to find.
Well indeed must you know this, physician as you are,
And dearly loved beyond all others by the Muses nine.
'Twas thus at least our countryman the Cyclops eased his pain,
That Polyphemus of old time, when he loved Galateia,
And upon cheek and lips as yet his beard was scarce grown.

Not with apples nor roses did he woo, nor locks of hair,
But with sheer frenzies; all things else he reckoned as mere trifling.
Often from the green pastures would his sheep unshepherded
Wander back to the fold, while he, singing his Galateia,
There on the weed-strewn sea-beach all day from early dawn
Would sit and pine, nursing within his breast a cruel wound,
Dealt him by mighty Cypris, whose shaft had pierced his heart.
Nevertheless that cure he found; and seated on the crest
Of a tall rock, and gazing towards the sea, thus would he sing:
    'O white Galateia, wherefore thus cast off the man who loves you?
Whiter to look upon than curds, more delicate than a lamb,
Than a young calf more skittish, plumper than ripening grape!
Wherefore do you keep coming thus, whene'er sweet slumber takes me,
Only to vanish straight, whene'er sweet slumber lets me go,
Fleeing me swifter than a ewe, when the grey wolf she spies?
    I fell in love with you, dear maid, that very day when first
You came here with my mother, to gather iris flowers
Upon the mountain, and 'twas I went with you as your guide.
Thenceforth, once having seen you, I could not cease to love,
Nor can I yet. But naught you care, no by Zeus, naught at all.
    I know, beautiful maiden, why it is you shun me thus.
It is because from one ear to the other, right across
The whole width of my forehead, one long shaggy eyebrow runs,
With but one eye beneath; and broad is the nose above my lip.
Nevertheless, though I be such, a thousand sheep I feed,
And from these do I draw and drink milk of the very best.
And cheese neither in summer not in autumn do I lack,
Nor in winter's depth, but always overladen are my crates.
Then I am skilled in piping as no other Cyclops here,
And of thee, my dear sweet apple, and of myself I sing
Many a time at dead of night. Moreover eleven fawns
I am rearing for you, all with brows crescent-marked, and four bear-cubs.
    Nay, come to me, and nothing, that is yours now, shall you lack.
Leave the blue breakers of the sea to gasp against the land.
More sweetly will you pass the night beside me in my cave.
There do laurels grow, and there the slender cypress trees,
There the dark ivy, there the vine with its sweet clustering grapes;
There are cool streams of water, that from her white snows drawn
Forest-girt Etna sends me hither, an ambrosial drink.
To such delights who would prefer the sea-waves for a home?

But if my body seem too rough and shaggy for your taste,
Well, neath the ashes on my hearth oak-logs are ever smouldering,
And gladly would I suffer you to singe my very soul,
And this one eye of mine, the dearest treasure I possess.
Ah me, would that my mother at my birth had given me gills,
That so I might have dived down to your side and kissed your hand,
If your lips you would not let me: and I had brought you then
Either white snowdrops, or the soft, scarlet-petalled poppy.
Nay, but these blow in summer, those in the winter months.
So I could never bring you both these kinds at the same time.
But now my darling maiden, now I'll learn at least to swim
(If hither sailing on a ship some stranger chance to come),
And so discover why you love to dwell thus in the deep.
   Oh come forth, Galateia, and coming straight forget,
Even as I now sitting here, to go back to your home.
Be content to go shepherding and milk the flocks with me,
And learn to set the cheeses, pouring tart rennet in.
It is my mother alone who wrongs me; yes, 'tis her I blame.
Never once has she spoken to you one kind word for me,
And that although day after day she saw me wasting thinner.
I'll tell her that my head and both my feet with pain are throbbing.
Thus will I make her suffer, since I am suffering too.
   O Cyclops, Cyclops, whither are your wits gone wandering?
Nay go and weave your baskets, and gather tender shoots
To feed your lambs. If you did that, far wiser would you be.
Milk the ewe that's beneath your hand. Why pursue one who shuns you?
You'll find perchance another and fairer Galateia.
Many are the girls that call to me to play with them by night,
And each of them laughs softly, if I deign to give ear.
It's plain enough, I too on land seem to be somebody.'
   Well, thus it was that Polyphemus shepherded his love
With song, and found ease better so than if he had spent gold.

The mournful end of the Cyclops' song, as he tells himself to forget the only fish in the sea that he wants, and mulls the possibility of compensation with a more accessible girl, seems full of pathos and short on conviction. The poor rustic beast – with his beautiful agricultural metaphors! – is terminally smitten. No wonder he had a violent reaction to the intrusion of Homer's adventurers.

54

After Dionysus, who bought Plato to Syracuse but seems not to have listened to the philosopher's urgings on the virtues of non-tyrannous rule, power over the island was won by a Corinthian, Timoleon, described by the nineteenth-century historian Edward A Freeman as 'the purest hero in the whole tale of Sicily'. Timoleon, who men said had all the Gods on his side, deposed Dionysus, drove away a Carthaginian force, and marched around the island deposing tyrants. He destroyed another Punic force at the battle of the river Krimisos (the Gods sent rain and hail against the barbarians, and lightning to dazzle and terrify them) and brought down the last tyrants of Centuripa and Agyrium. It was his practice to allow his defeated enemies to live quietly as private men, and when Timoleon had freed all of Greek Sicily from tyranny, he sent for his wife and children and settled near Syracuse, on an estate, where he died.

Twenty years later, in the year 317BC, an island without tyrants came under the dominion of just one, Agathokles, who was perhaps the most remarkable of all. Agathokles, having defeated another Punic Hamilcar, promised the people of Syracuse that he would not be a tyrant. They voted him full powers. Agathokles proceeded to take city after city, resorting whenever it suited him to fearful slaughter and cruelty. He was in turn defeated by Hamilcar but escaped, regrouped at Syracuse, and decided to take the war to Carthage. For the first time in history, in the spring of 310BC, a European army landed in North Africa. Agathokles burned his boats and seized Tunis. He took all the land around Carthage and defeated its soldiers in the field, but he could not take the city. Had he not suffered rebellions in his own camp – his army was heavily composed of mercenaries – he might have succeeded. The Carthaginians were so terrified of Agathokles they burned dozens of their own children in the hope of enlisting their Gods against him. At one point their sacrificial fires ran out of control and destroyed one of their own camps; they might have been routed then, but the army of Agathokles was now in confusion and rebellion: the tyrant abandoned them and fled back to Sicily, where he vented his frustrations with massacres at Segesta and Syracuse. He ruled until 289BC, when, after twenty eight years of violent dominion, at the age of seventy two, he died. Some stories say the Syracusans gave him his funeral pyre before he had quite expired.

Sicily was once more vulnerable to the Punics, and now to the Mamertines (a mercenary band who took Messina and founded there a piratical state named after Mamers, Mars, the Latin God of war), and also to diverse tyrannies which sprang up in Tyndarion and Akragas. Relief came from old Greece in the form of Pyrrhos, said to be second only to

Alexander in military skill, but a man who gave his name to victories so hard-won that they were practically defeats. Pyrrhos had been fighting the Romans on the Italian mainland; he arrived in Sicily with elephants, the first time these extraordinary things had been seen in the west. With Greek Sicily united behind him he scaled and defeated Erice, and invaded Panormos, the first time this Punic stronghold had fallen. Recalled to face the Romans in Italy in 276BC he is said to have remarked, on his departure, 'What a wrestling ground I leave here for the Romans and Carthiginians'.

As Pyrrhos prophesied, the story of Sicily for the rest of the second century BC is the history of that struggle. They fought at sea, on the beaches, in the river valleys, and outside the towns. Cities like Akragas became Punic strongholds against the Romans, but despite various reverses, not least those masterminded by the great Hannibal, which were prosecuted by his lieutenants while Hannibal himself attacked the Italian mainland, the Romans gradually prevailed in Sicily. On several occasions indigenous populations rose against one empire's garrison and delivered themselves into the hands of the other. A new terror became known in Sicily: the horrors of a Roman victory when a besieged town fell to them. It seems that not even the worst tyrant had perpetrated anything to match the bloody excesses of Legionnaires running amok amidst a defeated population.

In 214BC the Romans turned their attention to the mightiest of all the Greek cities: Syracuse. As well as the city's long history of withstanding sieges, and all the fortifications it had acquired, the Syracusans now had a particular weapon in which to place their hopes, a peculiar and extraordinary advantage: he was a single inhabitant but he was unquestionably a genius – his name was Archimedes. Archimedes, who could move the world with a lever if he could find the right place to stand. Over two thousand years after he invented it, the Archimedes screw can still be seen at work in the salt pans near Trapani, as turning windmills draw water from one level and pour it into another. It is a sweetly simple device, like a corkscrew for water: Archimedes also invented a simple-sounding claw for lifting ships.

The man besieging Syracuse was Marcellus, 'the sword of Rome', ('by natural inclinations addicted to war', says Plutarch,) who was a masterful general, an adversary worthy of Hannibal (who accorded Marcellus great respect in battle) and seems also to have been a decent man, who followed what rules of war there were, showed mercy to defeated populations and restricted the vengeance of his soldiers. The following account of the contest between Marcellus and Archimedes was written by Plutarch, working a century after the events he describes.

Plutarch
From *Plutarch's Lives*

The land forces were conducted by Appius: Marcellus, with sixty galleys, each with five rows of oars, furnished with all sorts of arms and missiles, and a huge bridge of planks laid upon eight ships chained together, upon which was carried the engine to cast stones and darts, assaulted the walls, relying on the abundance and magnificence of his preparations, and on his own previous glory; all which, however, were, it would seem, but trifles for Archimedes and his machines.

These machines he had designed and contrived, not as matters of any importance, but as mere amusements in geometry; in compliance with King Hiero's desire and request, some little time before, that he should reduce to practice some part of his admirable speculation in science, and by accommodating the theoretic truth to sensation and ordinary use, bring it more within the appreciation of the people in general. Eudoxus and Archytas had been the first originators of this far-famed and highly-prized art of mechanics, which they employed as an elegant illustration of geometrical truths, and as means of sustaining experimentally, to the satisfaction of the senses, conclusions too intricate for proof by words and diagrams. As, for example, so solve the problem, so often required in constructing geometrical figures, given the two extremes, to find the two mean lines of a proportion, both these mathematicians had recourse to the aid of instruments, adapting to their purpose certain curves and sections of lines. But what with Plato's indignation at it, and his invectives against it as the mere corruption and annihilation of the one good of geometry, which was thus shamefully turning its back upon the unembodied objects of pure intelligence to recur to sensation, and to ask help (not to be obtained without base supervisions and depravation) from matter; so it was that mechanics came to be separated from geometry, and, repudiated and neglected by philosophers, took its place as a military art ... Archimedes, however, in writing to King Hiero, whose friend and near relation he was, had stated that given the force, any given weight might be moved, and even boasted, we are told, relying on the strength of demonstration, that if there were another earth, by going into it he could remove this. Hiero being struck with amazement at this, and entreating him to make good this problem by actual experiment, and show some great weight moved by a small engine, he fixed accordingly upon a ship of burden out of the king's arsenal, which could not be drawn out of the dock without great labour and many men; and, loading her with many passengers and a full freight, sitting himself the while far off, with no great endeavour, but only holding the head of the pulley in his hand and drawing the cords by degrees, he drew the ship in a straight line, as smoothly and evenly as if she had been in the sea. The king, astonished at this, and convinced of the power of the art, prevailed upon Archimedes to make him engines accommodating to all the purposes, offensive and defensive, of a siege. These the king himself never quite made use of, because he spent almost all his life in a profound quiet and the highest affluence. But the apparatus was, in most opportune time, ready at hand for the Syracusans, and with it also the engineer himself.

When, therefore, the Romans assaulted the walls in two places at once, fear and consternation stupefied the Syracusans, believing that nothing was able to resist that violence and those forces. But when Archimedes began to ply his engines, he at once shot against the land forces all sorts of missile weapons, and immense masses of stone that came down with incredible noise and violence; against which no man could stand; for they knocked down those upon whom they fell in heaps, breaking all their ranks and files. In the meantime huge poles thrust out from the walls over the ships sunk by the great weights which they let down from on high upon them; others they lifted up into the air by an iron hand or beak like a crane's beak, and, when they had drawn them up by the prow, and set them on end upon the poop, they plunged them to the bottom of the sea; or else the ships, drawn by engines within, and whirled about, were dashed against steep rocks that stood jutting out under the walls, with great destruction of the soldiers that were aboard them. A ship was frequently lifted up to a great height in the air (a dreadful thing to behold), and was rolled to and fro, and kept swinging, until the mariners were all thrown out, when at length it was dashed against the rocks, or let fall. At the engine that Marcellus brought upon the bridge of ships, which was called *Sambuca*, from some resemblance it had to an instrument of music, while it was as yet approaching the wall, there was discharged a piece of rock of ten talents weight, then a second and third, which, striking upon it with immense force and a noise like thunder, broke all its foundation to pieces, shook out all its fastenings, and completely dislodged it from the bridge. So Marcellus, doubtful what counsel to pursue, drew off his ships to a safer distance, and sounded a retreat to his forces on land. They then took a resolution of coming up under the walls, if it were possible, in the night; thinking that as Archimedes used ropes stretched at length in playing his engines, the soldiers would now be under the shot, and the darts would, for want of sufficient distance to throw them, fly over their heads without effect. But he, it appeared, had long before framed for such occasions engines accommodated to any distance, and shorter weapons; and had made numerous small openings in the walls, through which, with engines of a shorter range, unexpected blows were inflicted on the assailants. Thus, when they who thought to deceive the defenders came close up to the walls, instantly a shower of darts and other missile weapons was again cast upon them. And when stones came tumbling down perpendicularly upon their heads, and, as it were, the whole wall shot out arrows at them, they retired. And now, again, as they were going off, arrows and darts of a longer range, inflicted a great slaughter among them, and their ships were driven one against another; while they themselves were not able to retaliate in any way. For Archimedes had provided and fixed most of his engines immediately under the wall; whence the Romans, seeing that indefinite mischief overwhelmed them from no visible means, began to think they were fighting with the gods.

Yet Marcellus escaped unhurt, and derided his own artificers and engineers, 'What,' said he, 'must we give up fighting with this geometrical Briareus, who plays pitch-and-toss with our ships, and, with the multitudes of darts that he showers, at a single moment upon us, really out-does the hundred-handed giants of mythology?' And, doubtless, the rest of the Syracusans were but the body of Archimedes's designs, one soul moving and governing all; for, laying aside all other arms, with this alone they infested the Romans and protected themselves. In fine, when such terror had seized upon the Romans, that, if they did but see a little rope or a piece of wood from the wall, instantly crying out, that there it was again, Archimedes was about to let fly some engine at them, they turned their backs and fled, Marcellus desisted from conflicts and assaults, putting all his hope in a long siege. Yet Archimedes possessed so high a spirit, so profound a soul, and such treasures of scientific knowledge, that though these inventions had now obtained him the renown of more than human sagacity, he yet would not deign to leave behind him any commentary or writing on such subjects; but; repudiating as sordid and ignoble the whole trade of engineering, and every sort of art that lends itself to mere use and profit, he placed his whole affection and ambition in those purer speculations where there can be no reference to the vulgar needs of life; studies, the superiority of which to all others is unquestioned, and in which the only doubt can be whether the beauty and grandeur of the subjects examined, of the precision and cogency of the methods and means of proof, most deserve our admiration ... And thus it ceases to be incredible that (as is commonly told of him) the charm of his familiar and domestic Siren made him forget his food and neglect his person, to that degree that when he was occasionally carried by absolute violence to bathe or have his body anointed, he used to trace geometrical figures in the ashes of the fire, and diagrams in the oil on his body, being in a state of entire preoccupation, and, in the truest sense, divine possession with his love and delight in science. His discoveries were numerous and admirable; but he is said to have requested his friends and relations that, when he was dead, they would place over his tomb a sphere containing a cylinder, inscribing it with the ratio which the containing solid bears to the contained.

Such was Archimedes, who now showed himself, and so far as lay in him the city also, invincible. While the siege continued, Marcellus took Megara, one of the earliest founded of the Greek cities in Sicily, and capturing also the camp of Hippocrates at Acilæ, killed above eight thousand men, having attacked them whilst they were engaged in forming their fortifications. He overran a great part of Sicily; gained over many towns from the Carthaginians, and overcame all that dared to encounter him. As the siege went on, one Damippus, a Lacedæmonian, putting to sea in a ship from Syracuse, was taken. When the Syracusans much desired to redeem this man, and there were many meetings and treaties about the matter betwixt them and Marcellus, he had opportunity to notice a tower into which a body of men might be secretly introduced, as the wall near to it was not difficult to surmount, and it was itself carelessly guarded. Coming often thither, and entertaining conferences about the release of Damippus, he had pretty well calculated the height of the tower, and got ladders prepared. The Syracusans celebrated a feast to Diana; this juncture of time, when they were given up entirely to wine and sport, Marcellus laid hold of, and before the citizens perceived it, not only possessed himself of the tower, but, before the break of day, filled the wall around with soldiers, and made his way into the Hexapylum. The Syracusans now beginning to stir, and to be alarmed at the tumult, he ordered the trumpets everywhere to sound, and this frightened them all into flight, as if all parts of the city were already won, though the most fortified, and the fairest, and most ample quarter was still ungained. It is called Acradina, and was divided by a wall from the outer city, one part of which they called Neapolis, the other Tycha. Possessing himself of these, Marcellus, about break of day, entered through the Hexapylum, all his officers congratulating him. But looking down from higher places upon the beautiful and spacious city below, he is said to have wept much, commiserating the calamity that hung over it, when his thoughts represented to him how dismal and foul the face of the city would be in a few hours, when plundered and sacked by the soldiers. For among the officers of his army there was not one man who durst deny the plunder of the city to the soldiers' demands; nay, many were instant that it should be set on fire and laid level to the ground: but this Marcellus would not listen to. Yet he granted with great unwillingness and reluctance, that the money and slaves should be made prey; giving orders, at the same time, that none should violate any free person, nor kill, misuse, or make a slave of any of the Syracusans. Though he had used this moderation, he still esteemed the condition of that city to be pitiable, and, even amidst the congratulation and joy, showed his strong feelings of sympathy and commiseration at seeing all the riches accumulated during the long felicity now dissipated in an hour. For it is related that no less prey and plunder was taken here than at Carthage. For not long after they obtained also the of other parts of the city, which were taken by treachery; leaving nothing untouched but the king's money, which was brought into the treasury. But nothing afflicted Marcellus so much as the death of Archimedes, who was then, as fate would have it, intent upon working out some problem by a diagram, having fixed his mind alike and his eyes upon the subject of his speculation, he never noticed the incursion of the Romans, nor that the city was taken. In this transport of study and contemplation, a soldier, unexpectedly coming up to him, commanded him to follow to Marcellus; which he declining to do before he had worked out his problem to a demonstration, the soldier, enraged, drew his sword and ran him through. Others write that a Roman soldier, running upon him with a drawn sword, offered to kill him; that Archimedes, looking back, earnestly besought him to hold his hand a little while, that he might not leave what he was then at work upon inconclusive and imperfect; but the soldier, nothing moved by his entreaty, instantly killed him. Others again relate that, as Archimedes was carrying to Marcellus mathematical instruments, dials, spheres, and angles, by which the magnitude of the sun might be measured to the sight, some soldiers seeing him, and thinking that he carried gold in the vessel, slew him. Certain it is that his death was very afflicting to Marcellus; and that Marcellus ever after regarded him that killed him as a murderer; and that he sought for his kindred and honoured them with signal favours.

Indeed, foreign nations had held the Romans to be excellent soldiers and formidable in battle; but they had hitherto given no memorable example of gentleness, or humanity, or civil virtue; and Marcellus seems first to have shown to the Greeks that his countrymen were most illustrious for their justice. For such was his moderation to all with whom he had anything to do, and such his benignity also to many cities and private men, that, if anything hard or severe was decreed concerning the people of Enna, Megara, or Syracuse, the blame was thought to belong rather to those upon whom the storm fell, than to those who brought it upon them.

Some time after this the armies of Marcellus and Hannibal met in Italy. Plutarch records that Hannibal sent a small force stealthily forward to a wooded hill between the two camps. When Marcellus came to reconnoitre it they ambushed him, and killed Marcellus. Hannibal rode forward to view the body. Plutarch says that he was overcome with solemnity, saddened by the death of his enemy.

By 205BC all Sicily was under the rule of Rome. In that year the general Scipio set out from Sicily to meet Hannibal in battle in North Africa: Scipio won and Carthage was finished. The Punic civilisation was swallowed by the Roman. Sicily became the first great granary of Rome, the first Province, with swathes of the interior given over to corn and huge sections of the population set to work it, slaves and near-slaves, under the dominion of Roman governors, a breed of men distinguished in Sicily by their corruption, greed and brutality. It is an extraordinary fact that in these years, a century before the birth of Christ, conditions were established which were to prevail for almost the next two millennia in rural Sicily: great estates, owned by men so rich and holding such power over the lives of their tenants that the two classes, landowner and peasant, might have been inhabiting different planets, though they drew their livelihoods from the same ground and the same crops. The peasants were kept in their place by extreme poverty and a total dependence on the whims, laws and percentages of the landowners. In these times laws and rights attached themselves naturally to the wealthy at the expense of the powerless. What is surprising is that this state of affairs should have endured, effectively, into the twentieth century. The peasants' choice was thus between subservience and banditry: with their great wealth, the landowners held a monopoly on effective force. There was a third option, a general rising throughout the island, and this occurred twice in the great slave revolts in Roman Sicily; once in 134BC and again in 102BC. In each case the uprising lasted three years before it was put down. On the second occasion the Romans were forced to treat the rebellion as a major foreign war: they despatched an entire army to the island. Many of the defeated slaves were taken to Rome to die in the Circus Maximus.

In 73BC the nadir of governance in Sicily was reached with the appointment of Gaius Verres to the position of praetor of the island. We know a great deal about this repellent individual, thanks to the man to whom the Sicilians appealed, in the desperate hope that he would be able to persuade the Roman senate to rid them of Verres: Cicero. As Cicero informs the Senate, Verres was a sort of bandit kleptomaniac, who must have been ecstatic to find himself placed in authority over a place as rich in beauty, art and agriculture as Sicily.

Marcus Tillius Cicero
From *The Verrine Orations I*

The Second Speech Against Gaius Verres: Book II

But before I speak of Sicily's distresses, I feel that I should say a little of the high position of that province, of its antiquity, and of its practical importance. Your attentive consideration, due to the interests of all our allies and all our provinces, is especially due, gentlemen, to those of Sicily, for many strong reasons, the first of which is this, that Sicily was the first of all foreign nations to become the loyal friend of Rome. She was the first of all to receive the title of province, the first such jewel in our imperial crown. She was the first who made our forefathers perceive how splendid a thing foreign empire is. No other nation has equalled her in loyal goodwill towards us: once the various states in the island had embraced our friendship, they never thereafter seceded from it; and most of them, and those the most notable, remained, without a break, our firm friends. From this province therefore it was that our forefathers took that great step in their imperial career, the invasion of Africa: for the great power of Carthage would never have been crushed so readily had not Sicily been at our disposal, supplying us with corn and affording safe harbourage to our fleets. This is why Scipio Africanus, after the destruction of Carthage, richly adorned the cities of Sicily with the finest statues and memorials, intentionally setting up the most abundant memorials of the triumph of Rome among those to whom, he reckoned, that triumph gave the most delight. Yes, and Marcus Marcellus himself, known in Sicily as terrible to his enemies, as merciful to the beaten, as a faithful friend to all the rest – Marcellus not only defended those who then fought for us, but in the hour of victory spared those who fought against us. When the noble city of Syracuse, strongly fortified by art, and defended by nature against assault by land or sea, nevertheless fell before his strong arm and military skill, he left it not merely unharmed, but so richly adorned that it was a memorial alike of his victory, of his clemency, and of his self-control, since men beheld the fortress he had captured, the people he had spared, and the treasures he had left unplundered. So much respect he reckoned due to Sicily that the island of our friends was, he judged, not to be deprived even of the city of our enemies.

And accordingly our relations with the province for all purposes were always such that we looked upon her various products not as growing on their own soil, but as already added to our stores at home. When has she failed to pay us punctually her tribute of grain? When has she not spontaneously offered us what she believed that we wanted? When has she refused to supply what was ordered of her? Cato Sapiens called her in consequence 'the nation's storehouse, the nurse at whose breast the Roman people is fed.' Nay, we in our time have found, in the critical days of the great Italian war, how Sicily has been to us no mere storehouse, but like the ancient and well-filled State Treasury of our fathers' days, supplying us with hides and shirts and grain, free of cost to ourselves, to clothe, feed and equip our great armies. Yes, she does us services, great services, of which we, gentlemen, I daresay, are not even aware. Many of our citizens are the richer for having a profitable field of enterprise in this loyal province close at hand, which they can visit so easily, and where they can carry on their business so freely. To some of these Sicily supplies merchandise, and sends them away enriched with profits: others she keeps with her, to become, according to their preference, corn farmers or business men, and in short, to settle and make a home there. It is a national advantage of no trifling kind that so large a number of Roman citizens should be kept so near their own country, engaged in occupations so honest and profitable. Our tributes and our provinces constitute, in a sense our nation's landed estates; and thus, just as you, gentlemen, gain most pleasure from such of your estates as are close to Rome, so to the nation there is something pleasant in the nearness of this province to the capital.

And then again, the character of the inhabitants is such, so hardy and upright and honest, that it really reminds us of the stern old Roman manners, rather than of those which have come to prevail among us today. They have none of the failings found elsewhere among the Greeks; they are neither slothful nor self-indulgent; on the contrary, they are highly industrious, for their own and for the public good; plain-living and conscientious folk. Such, moreover, is their attachment to our own people that among them, and nowhere else, neither tax-collector nor capitalist is an object of dislike. Acts of oppression, again, on the part of the Roman officials, they have borne so patiently, time after time, that never before this day have they, as a community, sought a refuge in the sanctuary of the law and the stronghold of your protection: and yet they had to live through that awful year which brought them so low that they would certainly have been ruined but for the coming of Gaius Marcellus, sent them, it would seem, by destiny as the second Marcellus to be the saviour of Sicily; and after that they suffered under the autocratic powers conferred on Marcus Antonius. It was an inherited tradition of theirs to regard Rome as so great a benefactor of the Sicilians that they must even endure oppression, if the oppressors were Romans. Verres is the first man against whom their cities have officially sent witnesses to testify. They would, in fact, have endured even Verres in silence, if only his offences had been those of an ordinary man, offences of a recognised and organised type, or, indeed, of only a single sort, no matter what. But finding his luxury and his cruelty, his greed and his insolence, beyond their power of endurance; finding all the privileges and rights and benefits ever granted them by the Roman senate and nation reft from them by this one unscrupulous scoundrel: they made up their minds to one of two things; either to prosecute their oppressor, and secure revenge, if you would help them; or else, if you should count them unworthy of receiving your aid and succour, to abandon their cities and their homes – their countryside they already abandoned, driven from it like game by their oppressor. This was the purpose of the entreaty made by all their deputations to Lucius Metellus, that he would take over the government from Verres at the earliest possible moment; this was the state of mind that led them to pour out their tale of woe so often into their Romans supporters' ears; this was the distress that moved them to present to the consuls those petitions of theirs, which, it was plain, were not really petitions, but charges against that man yonder. And further, their distress and their lamentations succeeded in inducing myself, known to them as a man of honour and integrity, almost to abandon the fixed principle of my life in becoming the prosecutor of Verres, a step intensely repugnant to my ideas and my feelings: even though, in this particular case, I look upon myself as having undertaken the part of defender far more than that of prosecutor. And lastly, men of the highest birth and the highest rank have come to Rome, officially or as private persons, from every part of the province; every great and important city of Sicily has flung itself eagerly into the task of avenging its wrongs.

But in what circumstances, gentlemen, have they thus come to us? I feel that I must, at this point, speak to you on behalf of these Sicilians with less reserve than, it may be, they would themselves wish; I will aim at forwarding their deliverance rather than their desires. Was ever an accused person, think you, in any of our provinces, protected in his own absence against a prosecutor's investigations by such an expenditure of money and passionate effort? The quaestors of both divisions who had served under him were on the spot to oppose me, supported by lectors: and their successors, being his enthusiastic supporters, and having been liberally dealt with by him out of his fund for travelling expenses, opposed me with equal bitterness. Think of the power in the hands of a man who had, in the one province, four quaestors doing their utmost to shield and defend him; and the praetor, with all the praetor's staff, doing so much for him that it was easy to see that their field of operations had not been Sicily, which they had found empty, but the governor of Sicily, who had gone away full. They threatened the inhabitants with vengeance if they appointed deputations to give evidence against Verres, or if any of them left for Rome: they made the most liberal promises to others if only they would speak in his favour: they took important witnesses, witnesses to private charges, men summoned in person by myself, and set guards to prevent them by force from leaving the country.

Now in spite of all this, let me inform you that only one single city, that of the Mamertines, has sent an official deputation to speak in Verres' support: and the chief man of that very deputation, Gaius Heius, the most distinguished person in that city, has stated on oath in your hearing that a large cargo ship was built for Verres at Messana by workmen officially impressed; and this same representative of the Mamertines and eulogist of Verres has charged Verres with not merely carrying off his

65

personal property but plundering his home of the sacred vessels and household gods that were his family heirlooms. An impressive eulogy indeed, when the energies of those sent to deliver it are divided between praising the thief and denouncing his thefts!

Though Verres had powerful friends in Rome, Cicero eventually won the case. Before sentence could be passed on him Verres went into voluntary exile, and thus begins a pattern of ineffective Roman justice which has blighted the story of Sicily until our own time. Again and again, from Verres to the murderously corrupt Giulio Andreotti, villains disguised as politicians have found the Italian courts riddled with escape routes from their Sicilian crimes.

The turns and changes of the Roman Empire were reflected in Sicily. The Emperor Hadrian visited in 126AD, as part of his tour of his demesne. He was much taken with Aetna, as all visitors must be. When the Empire expanded to Egypt, Sicily lost its position as the great breadbasket of Rome. When the empire was shaken by division, invasion and reversal, the tremors were felt in Sicily. Two great new forces were spreading through the Mediterranean, and both came ashore in Sicily. From the north, raiding parties of Vandals and Franks sacked Syracuse in the late second century, but before them came another power, which was to prove far more mighty than force or any warrior king. It gripped even those like Alaric, the Visigoth who took Rome in 410AD, and the Vandal king Gaiseric, who raided Sicily many times in the fifth century: Christianity had come from the east.

Saint Paul, according to the Acts of the Apostles, spent three days in Syracuse, but the legends say that Saint Peter was there before him, and consecrated a church in Catania. The volcanic cavern beneath the eighteenth-century church of San Gaetano alle Grotte had an older church built into it in 1262, but the cave itself is believed to be the oldest place of Christian worship in the city, and may have heard St Peter preach. Certainly, the Sicilian calendar is rich with saints' days dedicated to early Christian martyrs. One of the first and still the most powerful, to judge by the crowds, hundreds of thousands strong, which attend her procession in February, was St Agatha of Catania, who was tortured by the Roman governor, Quinziano, and condemned, on February 4th 251, to be fried on a griddle. But the whole town witnessed that the flames would not touch her, and then felt the earthquake which put her Roman torturers to flight. Under Constantine, Christian Sicily enjoyed religious peace, but then came the Goths, Franks and Vandals, and Rome was soon unable to defend itself, much less Sicily, against them.

In the fifth century Sicily was ruled by various martial powers from the north. Gaiseric, then Odowakar the mercenary prince, then the Ostrogoth Theodoric. Then, in 533, a general from Constantinople conquered Sicily in the name of the New Rome on the Bosphorus: he was Belisarius, who would win back all of Italy in the name of his emperor, Justinian. For the next three hundred years the island was an important part of the eastern Roman Empire, Byzantium. It was governed by a series of patricians and Patriarchs, perhaps the greatest of whom was Pope Gregory the Great (590-604). Monasteries and churches were built in many places.

For a brief period, under the Emperor Constans II, who was loathed and despised in Constantinople and Rome, it looked as though Syracuse might be proclaimed capital of the Empire, but he failed to endear himself to the Sicilians either, and in 668 some of them murdered him in his bath. This was the century of the first Saracen raids on the island. Here was a people with a religion, Islam, to match Christianity; with seamanship to compare with the Phoenecians; with scholarship, learning and invention to measure up to the Greeks, and, as they soon proved, with force and organisation to surpass the Byzantines and the Romans. In 827 they came ashore at Mazara del Vallo; in 831 they took Palermo, in 878 Syracuse. The Arab conquest was a ferocious struggle: it was not until 965 that all Sicily was a Muslim-governed land. Arab rule, in terms of the scales we have been dealing in, was short: they held Palermo for barely two hundred and thirty years, less time than elapsed under Byzantine jurisdiction, but its influence was enormous, and its consequences in many ways extraordinary: it led to wonders unsurpassed in the history of the world.

II: Miracles

PARADISE IS AN ARAB word, and therefore an Arab concept. It means 'garden', which for people from north Africa and the near east implied walls girdling an area in which plants, paving, decoration and running water combine to make a heavenly space, the skilful hand of man in homage and harmony with the gifts of Allah. When they came ashore in Mazara the Arabs found in its hinterland, and then throughout the island, the raw materials for an entire paradise. Here was a heavenly climate, thick soils covered in flowers and trees, an air full of birds, an island of mountains, rivers and natural riches. Sicily had found its gardeners. The Arabs terraced and irrigated; agricultural technologies hitherto unknown on the island. They planted cotton, sugar cane, rice and citrus fruits: the oranges, lemons and limes for which Sicily would later be famous. They brought the silk worm. They taught new and better fishing methods; they sunk mines. They built drains (some of which still work, beneath Palermo) and dug canals; they banked and bridged rivers. They constructed harbours, mills, dykes and orchards. They also invented spaghetti, a form of *pasta asciutta*, dry pasta, made from durum wheat, which they grew in Sicily: the perfect food for travellers, easily carried and cooked, and which does not readily go off. They erected over three hundred mosques in the capital alone, but although they placed restrictions on Christianity (it was forbidden to read the gospel aloud or preach within earshot of a Muslim) they did not suppress it, nor Judaism. Today in the old quarters of the capital the street names are written in Italian, Arabic and Hebrew in memory of this tolerance. There were tax advantages in a conversion to Islam, but there was no ethnic or religious cleansing: quite the reverse. Under Arab rule, Palermo, Al Madinah to the Arabs, became an *agora* of the world's cultures, beliefs and languages. In the streets you could hear Latin, Greek, Germanic languages, Spanish and Arabic. The city was famous for its music, scholarship, debate and poetry. Some of the latter has

68

survived. The verses of Ibn Hamdis, for example, have been translated by Professor William Granara, of Harvard. Writers like Hamdis have a distinguished place in literary history: their work feeds the art of the Sicilian school, which flourishes in the next phase of Sicily's history, under King Roger, a Norman, which in turn was a source for Dante and Petrarch. The melting pot of the Emirate of Palermo thus contains some of the original ingredients of European literature. It must have been an inspirational place in which to live and write. Theodisius, a monk captured at the fall of Syracuse, records his impressions, on coming to Palermo, of a city 'most famous and most populous ... at our entry into the city we found an immense population of citizens and foreigners. Palermo was not inferior to its fame or to our expectations.' A merchant from Baghdad, Ibn Hawqal, thought it wealthier, larger and more splendid even than Cordoba, which was then the most famous Islamic city in the continent.

Some of the traces of the period of Arab rule can still be found in the city, but the thread of their time is almost unbroken in the place they came ashore, at Mazara del Vallo. Mazara is a little universe of its own. It seems to want for nothing, stretched out along its seafront like a dog asleep in the unblinking sun. Thanks to the fishing fleet, which is crewed by Sicilians and Tunisians, there is a quarter of the town, near the river, where Arabic is still spoken in the cafés. At night the little streets are like a stage set for a sub-tropical *Romeo and Juliet*, a Muslim-Christian love story. They are still building boats in Mazara, serious trawlers for the biggest fishing fleet in Sicily. Late at night they slip their moorings and head out to the calm dark sea. At midday the smell of fish guts and diesel baking in the sun are reminiscent of a north African port, identical to the stink of the docks in Casablanca. There is a little Norman-Arab chapel overlooking the quays and not far from it is the museum devoted to the fleet's most wonderful catch. In 1998, trawling at a depth of almost five hundred meters in the Sicilian channel, a Mazara boat caught an extraordinary thing. He has broad green muscles, streaming hair, pointed ears and alabaster eyes. He is a satyr made of bronze, a wildly beautiful, frightening thing. His sculptor has him dancing, almost flying, and to see him is to understand instantly all the throb of sex, power and fear with which the ancients associated his kind. He is live, lithe and untamed, yet he is almost two thousand four hundred years old, from an antique time, as far from the Arab conquest as the conquest is from ours: he makes the age of the Emirs seem quite recent. Our Gods and cosmologies have changed little since the Prophet Mohammed, compared to how much they changed between the time of the satyrs and the coming of Christ.

69

In Palermo there is little left, archaeologically, of the pagan time, but a column near the great south door of the cathedral bears a verse of the Koran, as do columns in the Martonara. The Kalsa quarter maintains an Arabic atmosphere. Near the Palazzo dei Normani is the Norman church of San Giovanni degli Eremiti, which adjoins an old mosque, the two buildings surrounded by gardens as paradisiacal as any Muslim could wish for.

There are disappointingly few writings from the period of Muslim rule, which was challenged in 1060 by the invasion of Count Roger, one of the Hauteville brothers, a family of Norman warrior-adventurers. He came from the mainland with the blessing of the Vatican: if he could conquer the Moors, the deal ran, he could keep the island. Roger accepted the challenge with alacrity; with a tiny force, complete self-confidence and the kind of martial excellence his countryman William was about to unleash on Harold and the British, Roger set about destroying the Arab armies. The Normans had stirrups, which allowed them to wear heavy, almost impenetrable armour, and they were expert in the use of long lances and battle axes. Their confrontation with lightly armoured Saracen soldiers might be thought of in terms of infantry against tanks. By 1091 the entire prize was taken.

The Arab conquest had undoubtedly been bloody and terrifying for the population, for all that their rule was just and peaceful – in Sicily 'Saracen' is still used like 'bogeyman', while 'a Christian' is a slang term for a good person, a known quantity – but their tolerance and magnanimity had set a precedent to which Roger now adhered. Again, Muslim and Christian lived in peace. The best of both civilisations, their beliefs, learning and cultures, grew side by side. Now law, taxation and power were tilted in favour of the Christians, but King Roger and his successors, Roger II and the two Williams (the Bad and the Good), took great interest and pleasure in the ways and skills of their Muslim subjects: their philosophy, engineering, literacy, cosmology, mathematics and writing were cherished at court. (William the Good fell headlong for the sensuality of the east, and sunk himself in a harem which the Sultans of Morocco would have recognised.) Sheiks and Emirs were not summarily overturned or dispossessed. Arab craftsmen worked alongside Greeks, Latins and locals on Norman projects, among which were many churches and chapels: and here we come to the wonders.

Many writers have attempted to describe the Palatine Chapel. It takes a rare combination of passion, scholarship and aesthetic sensitivity to do it any sort of justice. In 1953 a young American chucked in his London job in publishing and brought his wife and child to Sicily to seek his literary fortune: his name was Vincent Cronin, and his book about Sicilian art and architecture, *The Golden Honeycomb*, is the product of just such a combination.

Vincent Cronin
From *The Golden Honeycomb*

The Palazzo Reale is a vast collection of buildings of many periods and divers styles erected on an eminence at the western side of the city. Here in the ninth century the Arabs constructed a military post which was later enlarged by the Normans and decorated in the Arab and Byzantine styles. This was the most productive period of the palace, when the Cappella Palatina was built and art flourished under the patronage of Norman kings. Under their successors, the Germans, the palace became a centre of learning famous throughout Europe, and here, especially during the reign of the enlightened Frederick II, himself the best of early Sicilian poets, flourished the first school of poetry in the Italian language. The cloistered courtyards have not yet relinquished the spirit of that golden age, when a second Athens rose on a more western stretch of the Mediterranean, and the conversation of artists still echoes through the arcades. During the vicissitudes of later history the building was subject to destruction and reconstruction so that, apart from the Chapel, of the original Norman epic there remains only a single stanza, the Sala di Re Ruggero. It is a small room in perfect condition, encrusted with mosaics of hunting scenes, of birds and trees and convoluted foliage, against a golden background, an image of the great hall of the Zisa before its destruction. The room was built fifty years before the Cappella Palatina, and the Arab influence, with its tendency to abstraction and aversion from realism, for example in the treatment of the peacocks, is much more evident. This room leads abruptly to civilisations which it is not yet time to regard, to eighteenth-century apartments hung in purple damask, and these in turn to a still later ballroom, in green and yellow, built by the Bourbons. Indeed, the great variety of styles so overlap that neither within nor without is it possible to be certain into which century one has strayed. In Sicily this simultaneity of time constantly bewilders, suggesting that all beauty exists in an eternal present.

The buildings composing the Palazzo Reale, which are fused to form a single frontage without unity, have a pleasing exterior which, however, lacks grandeur. To the south stands the oldest part, a courtyard built by the Spaniards in the sixteenth century, surrounded on four sides by arcades in three storeys. As framework and support stand Norman foundations, for the staircase of these arcades gives entrance to the Cappella Palatina, founded by King Roger and dedicated to St Peter. Of all the glories of Sicily, this chapel is among the most beautiful, a myriad-coloured miniature of Christian civilisation. If the treasure-house of the Martorana was pillaged, this casket is overflowing with all the jewels of the East; if Palermo is loud with suggestions of Norman architecture in the Sicilian manner, phrases as it were of a fragmentary poem, here is the text written out in full, the manuscript illuminated in gold; if the vicissitudes of history have tangled the skeins of Sicilian art, here is a masterpiece they dared not touch. It is royal, it is golden, it is Christian, it is a home, one is blasphemously tempted to think, almost worthy of God.

The building is not large – no more than a hundred feet in length – for, intended as a court chapel, it has been incorporated in the structure of the palace, so that of the exterior only the south wall is visible, facing the courtyard and the sunshine. From dazzling light, reflected in the cream-coloured walls of this arcade, one enters to darkness, which in turn gives way to a deeper, dimmer, more mysterious light. At first only the main outlines can be distinguished: the form, which is that of a Greek cross; figures looking down from all sides; and the golden eastern arch illuminated from the cupola. Only after many minutes, when the eye has grown accustomed to the dark, gilded light, does the chapel rise from its own shadows to stand revealed in full splendour.

What is to be chosen first, for everything within these walls puts forward its own particular mode of beauty to be admired? The more immediately evident takes precedence. The nave is divided from the aisles by ten pillars, some of granite, some of cipolin marble, exquisitely moulded and with gilded capitals. The sanctuary, reached by five stairs, is surmounted by a cupola. At the right stands the pulpit, an integral part of the chapel, raised on columns, in front of which soars a marble candelabrum, thirteen feet in height, designed for the Paschal candle. This ornament, undamaged, is a fine example of twelfth-century Norman carving, and depicts symbolic animals in convoluted shapes, intertwined with saints and a figure of God the Father. It is grey in colour and its tall, tapering form leads the eye upwards to the roof of the nave, to which it provides the ideal harmonic introduction. This roof is made of wooden stalactites in the Arab style, and its added dimension contrasts admirably with the necessarily flat walls. Moreover, while its dark brown colour sets off the golden mosaics, it is itself sufficiently elaborate to withstand their brilliance. The floor, also, is in Arab style, being of white marble, patterned with rose, green and golden tesserae in oriental abstract shapes. These are matched in the lower half of the walls. The lowest space is decorated by a frieze of mosaics and this is surmounted by white marble divided into alternating panels, one showing a Maltese Cross, the other slabs of porphyry.

This, the main section of the lower walls, is in turn surmounted by an even more elaborate frieze of tesserae. Thus the whole of the lower walls, including the pulpit and its pillars, is a progressive elaboration of the motif of the floor, culminating in the tesserae which cover the entire upper half of the walls, the pointed arches and their soffits, the cupola and apses. The thickness of the outside walls is shown at the windows, five in each aisle, five on each side of the clerestory, and eight small apertures in the cupola. At the back of the nave, raised on steps, is a dais for the royal thrones.

All this is magnificent, but set beside the figured mosaics it is nothing, for the chapel is its mosaics, as the dancer is her dance. Largest of all are the three great figures of Christ. In the cupola looking down directly on the sanctuary is Christus Pantocrator, with large eyes, thick hair and beard, holding a closed book. The light falls directly on his face, revealing an expression of great power mingled with compassion. Before even one is aware of a reaction, it has compelled homage and abasement. In the central apse above the high altar is a figure of Christ blessing, with book open, and fingers of the right hand separated in benediction. This mosaic, by its half-vertical, half-horizontal position in the conch, admirably suggests the dual nature of its subject. Finally, at the back of the nave, between St Peter and St Paul, is a mosaic of the enthroned figure of Christ, the only one of the three representations to portray the whole body.

The oldest mosaics are those in the sanctuary, the scenes on the south wall being distinguished by the Greek lettering beside them. They are in five main panels. In the centre is the Transfiguration, on the left the Baptism of Our Lord, on the right the Raising of Lazarus. Above is the Flight into Egypt, and beneath, balancing it, the Entry into Jerusalem. All these Gospel scenes are intrinsically dramatic and lend themselves well to simple yet graphic representation. Because the modern world is so accustomed to Scripture as a written text, it forgets that to many people of the Middle Ages the Gospel was preached by picture and mystery play, forms more effective to some than the spoken or written word. Indeed, the image can be taken farther still, and in the gold background to this Scripture in pictures can be seen the equivalent of the great gold initial letters in decorated manuscripts of the same period.

This dramatic instinct is evident in such a scene as the Entry into Jerusalem. At the extreme left walk eight of the Apostles, not all fully visible, their faces tense with ill-concealed fear. In front of them Christ, his eyes shadowed with sadness, his hand raised in benediction, sits on a white donkey led by an eager St Peter. The road, silver in colour, shows up well the green palm branches which have been scattered on it. A palm tree divides the groups, and on the right stand six men and a woman at the entrance to Jerusalem, their faces betraying every sign of dissimulation. In the foreground four children, with all the enthusiasm and animation of youth shown in their rapid movements, are tearing off their clothes to spread before the donkey, and it is these figures which Christ is blessing. The colours are green, rose, and mauve on silver and white, the background as always being of gold. The road which at the extreme left is very wide in order to contain the large interlaced group of figures simply narrows to a point at the city gate: the road is not important. This concentration on essentials at the expense of logical realism is again evident in a scene above, where the angel is shown appearing to St Joseph in a dream. St Joseph is shown wrapped in something white, which, though it looks like neither, is both the bedcover and sleep: no distinction is made in Byzantine iconography between the symbol and the thing symbolised. Thus, everything in creation can be used as a figure: bird, beast, flower, or fish.

The other main scenes in the building depict stories from the Old Testament and incidents in the lives of St Peter and St Paul. On the panels below the cupola is a particularly dramatic scene, similar to one in the same position in the Martorana. On the left is the angel Gabriel, on the right Our Lady, and in the centre out of a blue, round heaven is stretched simply a hand, the hand of God the Father, from which speeds a dove in a line of light to Our Lady. The impact is instantaneous, because so simple and dramatic, yet there is nothing superficial about the work, and the details are finely executed. In these mosaics, as in mime and ballet, the position and gesture of the hands are all-important. Thus the angel Gabriel's outstretched hand at once delivers a message and commands; that of Our Lady, held close to the side, palm lifted vertically, protests her unworthiness. This feature reveals one of the great secrets of the mosaics: they appeal immediately and overwhelmingly yet possess such spirit, such subtlety both of form and colour, that they are never fully fathomed. The faces overawe, yet remain inscrutable: the scenes appear simple, yet their delicacy of colour and imagination of detail are highly complex and original qualities which would outlast a lifetime of marvelling.

The interior of the Cathedral of Monreale is not merely an extraordinary synthesis of the Norman, Byzantine, Sicilian and Arab art: it is also a meeting of narrative and architecture; art and literature intertwined. Its mosaics tell stories, from the biblical to the contemporary (William the Second is shown offering his new cathedral to the Virgin Mary) which unfold both sequentially and at once. The viewer is subject to a downpour of beauty, life, drama and action so intense as to entirely wash time away. You do not stand at an angle to the events depicted, just a little below them, almost among them. The experience is analogous to that of a believer swept up in the events of Holy Week: there is no temporal skin between the present and the eternal. These things, one feels, happened, are happening and will happen, once, now and forever. The details of the mosaics are entrancing, and there are some distinctively Sicilian touches. The feeding of the five thousand has become the feeding of about fifty, they have already polished off the fish, leaving only heads, tails and bones, and there is much more bread in large barrels than they will ever get through (a meal in a Sicilian house often consists of no less than what an Englishman would consider three main courses, plus at least two starters, sweets and fruit). In the scene of the Ark floating on the flood, drowned corpses bob in the water, and Noah's raven has alighted on one, for a grisly and acutely-observed feast. The blood spurting from Abel's head looks as though it was done by someone who had seen the kind of wound Cain's club would have inflicted.

A delightfully skewed portrait of the Norman Kingdom of Sicily was written in 1185 by Abu'l-Husayn Muhammad ibn Ahmad ibn Jubayr, a scholar, born in Valenica, who had been living and working peacefully as a secretary in the great court of Granada until the day the Moorish Governor of that city summoned him on some business matter, and offered him a cup of wine. Ibn Jubayr, a devout Muslim, refused. His master, infuriated, ordered him to drink 'seven cups, by Allah!' Trembling, Ibn Jubayr obeyed. It must have been a miserable sight, for the Governor was struck with remorse, and ordered the cup filled, seven times over, with golden dinars, which he poured into his secretary's lap. At which point some of us might have withdrawn, offered a prayer of penitence and thanks, and lived happily, and wealthily, ever after. Not Ibn Jubayr. A man who had never journeyed outside Spain, he saw at once that one of his most repeated prayers had been answered: Allah had granted him the opportunity to risk death by accident, illness, war (this was the time of Saladin's conflict with the crusaders), brigands, pirates and drowning, and to discharge his duty of pilgrimage. He set out for Mecca. He took a ship to Egypt, travelled by caravan to the Red Sea, crossed it, braved the reefs of the Arabian shore and its scalding deserts, and arrived at Mecca. After visiting the tomb of the Prophet in Medina he travelled again by caravan to Baghdad, Aleppo and Damascus. In the crusader city of Acre he found a Genoese ship bound for the west, laden with hundreds of Christian pilgrims returning from Jerusalem, and went with them. This voyage, terrifying and sincerely perilous (and all the worse for Ibn Jubayr, who was not a happy sailor) ended with a shipwreck on the coast of Sicily, where our hero would have met his death, had it not been for the miraculous appearance of the then King of Sicily himself, William the Good. Even for a mediaeval manuscript, the origin and survival of this one is remarkable, and doubly cheering, as its writer is so charming, devout, and sometimes – perhaps not entirely unintentionally – hilarious.

From *The Travels of Ibn Jubayr*

The Month of Ramadan the Venerated (580)
December 6th – January 4th, 1185
May God in His grace and favour let us share His blessings and during it accept our prayers. There is no Lord but He

On the morning of the 1st day of this month we observed before us the Mountain of Fire, the famous volcano of Sicily, and rejoiced thereat. May God Most High reward us for what we have endured, and end (our days) with the best and most magnificent of His favours. May He animate us in all circumstances to gratitude for what He has bestowed on us. A favourable wind then moved us from that place, but on the evening of Saturday the 2nd of the month its force increased and drove the ship with such speed that in but an instant it had brought us to the mouth of the strait. Night had fallen. In this strait the sea is confined to a width of six miles and in the narrowest place to three. The sea in this strait, which runs between the mainland and the island of Sicily, pours through like the 'bursting of the dam' and, from the intensity of the contraction and the pressure, boils like a cauldron. Difficult indeed is its passage for ships. Our ship continued on its course, driven by a strong wind from the south, the mainland on our right and the coast of Sicily on our left.

When it came to midnight on Sunday the 3rd of the blessed month (of Ramadan), and we were overlooking the city of Messina, the sudden cries of the sailors gave us the grievous knowledge that the ship had been driven by the force of the wind towards one of the shore lines and had struck it. At once the captain ordered that the sails be lowered, but the sail on the mast called the 'ardimun' [artimone] would not come down. All their efforts they exerted on it, but they could do naught with it, because of the strain of the wind. When they had laboured in vain, the captain cut it with a knife piece by piece, hoping to arrest the ship. During this attempt the ship stuck by its keel to the ground, touching it with its two rudders, the two shafts by which it steers. Dreadful cries were raised on the ship, and the Last Judgement had come; the break that has no mending and the great calamity which allows us no fortitude. The Christians gave themselves over to grief, and the Muslims submitted themselves to the decree of their Lord, finding only and clinging and holding fast to the rope of hopefulness in the life to come. In turn the wind and the waves buffeted the ship until one of its rudders broke. The captain then threw out one of the anchors, hoping to take hold with it, but to no purpose. He cut its rope and left it in the sea. When we sure that (our time) had come, we braced ourselves to meet death, and, summoning our resolution to show goodly patience, awaited the morn or the time of destiny. Cries and shrieks arose from the women and the infants of the Rum. All with humbleness submitted themselves (to the will of God), and 'men were despoiled of their manhood'.

We, meanwhile, were gazing at the nearby shore in hesitance between throwing ourselves in to swim and awaiting, it might be, relief with the dawn from God. We formed the resolve to remain. The sailors lowered the long-boat into the sea to remove the most important of their men, women, and effects. They took it one journey to the shore, but were unable to return, and the waves threw it in pieces on the beach. Despair then seized our spirits; but while we were suffering these vicissitudes, dawn shone and aid and succour came from God. We made certain of our eyes, and there before us was the city of Messina less than half a mile away.

We marvelled at the power of Great and Glorious God in the management of His designs, and said:

'Many are taken off in death upon the threshold of their house.'

The sun then rose and small boats came out to us. Our cries had fallen on the city, and the King of Sicily, William himself, came out with some of his retinue to survey the affair. We made speed to go down to the boats, but the violence of the waves would not allow them to reach the ship. We at last descended into them at the end of the terrible storm ... The strangest thing that we were told was that this Rumi King, when he perceived some needy Muslims staring from the ship, having not the means to pay for their landing because the owners of the boats were asking so high a price for their rescue, enquired, this King, concerning them and, learning their story, ordered that they be given one hundred ruba'i of his coinage in order that they might alight. All the Muslims thus were saved and cried, 'Praise be to God, Lord of the Universe.'

The Christians took from the ship all that they had had therein. The next day the waves had shattered it and thrown it in pieces on the shore: a lesson to those who saw, and 'a sign to those who pondered' [Koran XV, 75]. Wonder fell upon us for our deliverance; and to Great and Glorious God we renewed our thanks for His beneficent offices and gracious decrees, and for preserving us from the falling of this fate upon us on the mainland, or on one of the islands inhabited by the Rum where, even had we been saved, we should have been for ever slaves. Help us, Great and Glorious God, to render thanks for these gifts and favours, and for this merciful solicitude and compassion. All this is in His power, and it is His faculty to be kind and beneficent. There is no God but He. Another sign of the loving-kindness and benevolence of Great and Glorious God towards us in this disaster was the presence of this Rumi king. But for that, all within the ship would have been robbed of everything, or all the Muslims might have been placed in servitude, for such was their custom. The arrival of the King at this city was on account of his fleet, which was being built and which proved a saving mercy to us. Praise be to God for His avouched and beneficent care. There is no God but He.

Recollections of the city of Messina
May God restore it (to the Muslims)

This city is the mart of the merchant infidels, the focus of ships from the world over, and thronging always with companies of travellers by reason of the lowness of prices. But it is cheerless because of the unbelief, no Muslim being settled there. Teeming with worshippers of the Cross, it chokes its inhabitants, and constricts them almost to strangling. It is full of smells and filth; and churlish too, for the stranger will find there no courtesy. Its markets are animated and teeming, and it has ample commodities to ensure a luxurious life. Your days and nights in this town you will pass in full security, even though your countenance, your manners [lit. 'hand'] and your tongue are strange.

Messina leans against the mountains, the lower slopes of which adjoin the intrenchments of the town. To its south is the sea, and its harbour is the most remarkable of maritime ports, since large ships can come into it from the seas until they almost touch it. Between them and the shore is thrown a plank over which men come and go and porters take up the baggage; thus no boats are needed for loading and unloading save for ships anchored far out ...

The prosperity of the island surpasses description. It is enough to say that it is a daughter of Spain in the extent of its cultivation, in the luxuriance of its harvests, and in its well-being, having an abundance of varied produce, and fruits of every kind and species.

But it is filled with the worshippers of the Cross, who promenade in its upper districts and live at ease in its sheltered parts. The Muslims live beside them with their property and farms. The Christians treat these Muslims well and 'have taken them to themselves as friends' [Koran XX, 41], but impose on them a tax to be paid twice yearly, thus taking from them the amplitude of living they had been wont to earn from that land. May Almighty and Glorious God mend their lot, and in His goodness, make a happy recompense their heritage.

The mountains are covered with plantations bearing apples, chestnuts and hazelnuts, pears, and other kinds of fruits. There are, in Messina, no Muslims save a small number of craftsmen, so the Muslim stranger there will feel lonely.

The finest town in Sicily and the seat of its sovereign, is known to the Muslims as al-Madinah, and to the Christians as Palermo. It has Muslim citizens who possess mosques, and their own markets, in the many suburbs. The rest of the Muslims live in the farms (of the island) and in all its villages and towns, such as Syracuse and others. Al-Madinah al-Kabirah ['the great City' – Palermo], the residence of their King, William, is however the biggest and most populous, and Messina is next ...

Their King, William, is admirable for his just conduct, and the use he makes of the industry of the Muslims, and for choosing eunuch pages who all, or nearly all, concealing their faith, yet hold firm to the Muslim divine law. He has much confidence in Muslims, relying on them for his affairs, and the most important matters, even the supervisor of his kitchen being a Muslim; and he keeps a band of black Muslim slaves commanded by a leader chosen from amongst them. His ministers and chamberlains he appoints from his pages, of whom he has a great number and who are his public officials and are described as his courtiers. In them shines the splendour of his realm for the magnificent clothing and fiery horses they display; and there is none of them but has his retinue, his servants, and his followers.

This King possesses splendid palaces and elegant gardens, particularly in the capital of his kingdom, al-Madinah. In Messina he has a palace, white like a dove, which overlooks the shore. He has about him a great number of youths and handmaidens, and no Christian King is more given up to the delights of the realm, or more comfort and luxury-loving. William is engrossed in the pleasures of his land, the arrangement of its laws, the laying down of procedure, the allocation of the functions of its chief officials, the enlargement of the splendour of the realm, and the display of his pomp, in a manner that resembles the Muslim Kings. His kingdom is very large. He pays much attention to his (Muslim) physicians and astrologers, and also takes great care of them. He will even, when told that a physician or astrologer is passing through his land, order his detainment, and then provide him with means of living so that he will forget his native land. May God in His favour preserve the Muslims from this seduction. The King's age is about thirty years. May God protect the Muslims from his hostility and the extension of his power.

One of the remarkable things told of him is that he reads and writes Arabic. We also learnt from one of his personal servants that his *'alamah* is: 'Praise be to God. It is proper to praise Him.' His father's *'alamah* was: 'Praise be to God in thanks for His beneficence.' The handmaidens and concubines in his palace are all Muslims. One of the strangest things told us by this servant, Yahya ibn Fityan, the Embroiderer, who embroidered in gold the King's clothes, was that the Frankish Christian women who came to his palace became Muslims, converted by these handmaidens. All this they kept secret from their King. Of the good works of these handmaidens there are astonishing stories.

It was told to us that when a terrifying earthquake shook the island this polytheist [a Muslim would deem William to be so, since he accepted the dogma of the Trinity] in alarm ranged round his palace, and heard nothing but cries to God and His Prophet from his women and pages. At sight of him, they were overcome with confusion, but he said to them: 'Let each invoke the God he worships, and those that have faith shall be comforted.'

The pages, who are the leaders of his state and the managers of his affairs, are Muslims, there being none who do not, voluntarily and for a heavenly reward, fast in the holy month [of Ramadan], and give alms that they might be nearer to God. They redeem prisoners and bring up their young ones, arranging for their marriage and giving them assistance, and doing all the good they can. All this is done by Great and Almighty God for the Muslims of this island and is one of the mysteries of His care for them.

In Messina we met one of their leading and most distinguished pages called 'Abd al-Massih, whose wish (to see us) had been conveyed to us. He entertained us with regard and generosity, and then spoke openly to us, revealing his close-guarded secrets. He had first looked about his audience-room, and then, in self-protection, dismissed those servants about him whom he suspected. He then questioned us about Mecca – may God hallow it – and about its venerable shrines, and those of Holy Medina and of Syria. As we told him he melted with longing and fervour, and asked if we would give him some blessed token we had brought from Mecca and Medina – may God hallow them – and begged us not to be sparing of what we could give him. 'You can boldly display your faith in Islam,' he said, 'and are successful in your enterprises and thrive, by God's will, in your commerce. But we must conceal our faith, and, fearful of our lives, must adhere to the worship of God and the discharge of our religious duties in secret. We are bound in the possession of an infidel who has placed on our necks the noose of bondage. Our whole purpose therefore is to be blessed by meeting pilgrims such as you, to ask for their prayers and be happy in what precious objects from the holy shrines they can give us to serve us as instruments of faith, and as treasures on our bier (in token of the life to come).' Our hearts melted in compassion for him, and we prayed that his end might be happy, and gave him some of our treasures as he wished. Profusely he expressed his thanks and gratitude, and told us in confidence of his colleagues the other pages, who have a notable repute for good works. In the release of prisoners they most acquire merit in God's eyes, and all their servants are of a like temper.

Another singular circumstance concerning these pages is that when in the presence of their Lord and the hour for prayer is at hand they will leave the chamber one by one that they might make their prayers. They sometimes do so in a place where the eye of their King might follow them, but Almighty and Glorious God conceals them. They thus continue to labour in their purpose, covertly advising the Muslims in their unending struggle for the faith. May God, in His grace, advantage them and bring them to a happy end.

In Messina, the King has a shipyard containing fleets of uncountable numbers of ships. He has a similar yard at al-Madinah [Palermo].

We lodged (in Messina) at an inn, and stayed there nine days. Then, on the night of Tuesday the 12th of the holy month (Ramadan) and the 18th of December, we embarked on a small ship sailing to al-Madinah. We steered close to the shore, so that we might keep it within sight. God sent us a light breeze from the east that most pleasantly urged us on our way. So we sailed along, bending our gaze on the continuous cultivations and villages, and on the fortresses and strongholds at the tops of the lofty mountains. To our right we saw nine islands [Aeolian or Lipari], rising up like lofty mountains in the sea, close to the shores of Sicily. From two of them [Vulcano and Stromboli] fire issues unendingly, and we could see the smoke ascending from them. At the close of night a red flame appeared, throwing up tongues into the air. It was the celebrated volcano. We were told that a fiery blast of great violence bursts out from air-holes in the two mountains and makes the fire. Often a great stone is cast up and thrown into the air by the force of the blast and prevented thereby from falling and settling at the bottom. This is one of the most remarkable of stories, and it is true.

As for the great mountain in the island, known as the Jabal al-Nar [Mountain of Fire = Etna], it also presents a singular feature in that some years a fire pours from it in the manner of the 'bursting of the dam'. It passes nothing it does not burn until, coming to the sea, it rides out on its surface and then subsides beneath it. Let us praise the Author of all things for His marvellous creations. There is no God but He.

Recollections of the town of Shafludi [Cefalu]
May God restore it (to the Muslims)

Cefalu is a coastal town, with an ample produce from its soil and with many commodities, beset with vine and other trees, and having well-ordered markets. A community of Muslims lives there. Set over the town is a mountain, on whose large circular summit is a fortress, than which I have never seen any more formidable. They hold it in readiness for any sea attack that a fleet from the lands of the Muslims – may God render them victorious – might make upon them unawares.

Recollections of the town of Thirmah [Termini]
May God deliver it (to the Muslims)

Better situated than the place we have just described, this town is strongly fortified, and surmounts and towers above the sea. The Muslims have a large suburb, in which are their mosques. The town has a high and impregnable fort, and in its lower part is a thermal spring which serves the citizens as baths. It enjoys an extreme fertility and abundance of victuals; indeed, the whole island in this regard is one of the most remarkable in God's creation. We passed Thursday the 14th anchored in a river below the town into which the tide from the sea flowed and ebbed, and there we stayed the night of Friday. The wind then changed to the west, and we had no way to sail.

Between us and our destination, al-Madinah, the town known to the Christians as Palermo, lay five and twenty miles, and we feared that we would be held long at Termini. But we thanked God Most High for His gracious favour in having (already) brought us in two days across a passage that stayed other ships, as we were told, twenty or thirty days and more; and on the morning of Friday in the middle of the holy month, we rose determined to journey overland by foot. We discharged our design, and, carrying some of our effects, and having left some of our companions to guard the chattels remaining in the ship, we set forth.

We travelled along a road like a market so populous it was, with men coming and going. Groups of Christians that met us themselves uttered the first greetings, and treated us with courtesy. We observed in their attitude and insinuating address towards the Muslims that which would offer temptation to ignorant souls. May God, in His power and bounty, preserve from seducement the people of Muhammad – God's blessings upon him.

We came at last to Qasr Sa'd [Solanto Castle], which lies a parasang from Palermo, and being seized with fatigue, turned aside and passed the night in it. The castle is on the seashore, and is lofty and ancient, for it was built in the time of the Muslim occupation of the island. It always was, and still is, by the grace of God, inhabited by pious (Muslims). Around it are numerous tombs of ascetic and pious Muslims, and it is known for its grace and blessedness, being visited by men from all countries. Opposite it is a spring known as 'Ayn al-Majnunah [the Spring of the Mad Woman]. The castle has a strong iron door. Inside are the living quarters, and commanding belvederes, and well-planned suites; the place indeed has all the conveniences of living. At its summit, is one of the finest mosques in the world. It is an oblong building with long arcades spread with spotless mats of a workmanship such as I have never seen better; and within it are hung forty lamps of brass and crystal. In front of the mosque is the broad road which girdles the upper part of the castle. In the lower part is a well containing sweet water.

We passed the most pleasing and agreeable night in that mosque, and listened to the call to prayer, which long we had not heard. We were shown high regard by the residents of the mosque, amongst whom was an imam who led them in the obligatory prayers and, in this holy month, the *tarawih* [special and additional prayers of twenty prostrations, performed in the month of Ramadan].

Near this castle, about a mile away in the direction of Palermo, is a similar castle known as Qasr Ja'far, which contains a spring of sweet water.

We noticed on this road churches prepared for the Christian sick. In their cities they have them after the model of the Muslim hospitals, and we have seen their like at Acre and Tyre. We marvelled at such solicitude.

After the morning prayers, we bent our way to al-Madinah. On arrival we made to enter, but were stopped and directed to a gate near the palace of the Frankish King – may God relieve the Muslims of his dominance. We were then conducted to his Commissioner that he might question us as to our intentions, as they do in the case of all strangers. Over esplanades, through doors, and across royal courts they led us, gazing at the towering palaces, well-set piazzas and gardens, and the ante-chambers given to the officials. All this amazed our eyes and dazzled our minds, and we remembered the words of Almighty and Glorious God: 'But that all mankind would become one people (i.e. infidels), we would have given those who denied merciful God silver roofs for their houses, and stairways to mount to them' [Koran XLIII, 33, gold and silver having no value in the sight of God].

Amongst the things we observed was a hall set in a large court enclosed by a garden and flanked by colonnades. The hall occupied the whole length of that court, and we marvelled at its length and the height of its belvederes. We understood that it was the dining-hall of the King and his companions, and that the colonnades and the ante-chambers are where his magistrates, his officials, and his stewards sit in presence.

The Commissioner came out to us, walking majestically between the servants who surrounded him and carried the train of his robes. We looked upon a stately old man with long white moustaches, who questioned us in supple Arabic as to our design and our country. We told him, and he showed pity for us, and, with repeated salutations and invocations, ordered that we be allowed to depart. He gave us much cause to wonder. His first question to us had been for news of Constantinople and what we knew of it, but alas we had nothing we could tell him. We shall give news of it later.

One of the strangest examples of seducement into waywardness that we witnessed happened as we left the castle, when one of the Christians seated at the gate said to us: 'Look to what you have with you, pilgrims, lest the officials of the Customs descend on you.' He thought, of course, that we carried merchandise liable to customs duty. But another Christian replied to him saying, 'How strange you are. Can they enter into the King's protection and yet fear? I should hope for them (to receive) nothing but thousands of *rubayyat*. Go in peace, you have nothing to fear.' Overwhelmed with surprise at what we had seen and heard, we departed to an inn where we took lodgings on Saturday the 16th of the holy month and the 22nd of December. On leaving the castle, we had gone through a long and covered portico down which we walked a long way until we came to a great church. We learnt that this portico was the King's way to the church.

Recollections of al-Madinah [Palermo], the capital of Sicily
May God restore it (to the Muslims)

It is the metropolis of these islands, combining the benefits of wealth and splendour, and having all that you could wish of beauty, real or apparent, and all the needs of subsistence, mature and fresh. It is an ancient and elegant city, magnificent and gracious, and seductive to look upon. Proudly set between its open spaces and plains filled with gardens, with broad roads and avenues, it dazzles the eyes with its perfection. It is a wonderful place, built in the Cordova style, entirely from cut stone known as kadhan [a soft limestone]. A river splits the town, and four springs gush in its suburbs. The King, to whom it is his world, has embellished it to perfection and taken it as the capital of his Frankish Kingdom – may God destroy it.

The King's palaces are disposed around the higher parts, like pearls encircling a woman's full throat. The King roams through the gardens and courts for amusement and pleasure. How many – may they not long be his – palaces, constructions, watch-towers, and belvederes he has, how many fine monasteries whose monks he has put in comfort by grants of large fiefs, and how many churches with crosses of gold and silver! May it be that God will soon repair the times for this island, making it again a home of the faith, and by His power delivering it from fear to security. For He can perform what He desires.

The Muslims of this city preserve the remaining evidence of the faith. They keep in repair the greater number of their mosques, and come to prayers at the call of the muezzin. In their own suburbs they live apart from the Christians. The markets are full of them, and they are the merchants of the place. They do not congregate for the Friday service, since the khutbah is forbidden. On feast-days (only may) they recite it with intercessions for the 'Abbasid Caliphs. They have a qadi to whom they refer their law-suits, and a cathedral mosque where, in this holy month, they assemble under its lamps. The ordinary mosques are countless, and most of them are used as schools for Koran teachers. But in general these Muslims do not mix with their brethren under infidel patronage, and enjoy no security for their goods, their women, or their children. May God, by His favour, amend their lot with His beneficence.

One point of resemblance between this town and Cordova – for one thing always resembles another in some direction – is its having in the middle of the new city an old one known as the Qasr al-Qadim [the old Castle], just as there is in Cordova – God protect it. In this old castle are mansions like lofty castles with towers hidden in the skies, bewildering the sight with their splendour.

One of the most remarkable works of the infidels that we saw was the church known as the Church of the Antiochian. We examined it on the Day of the Nativity

[Christmas Day], which with them is a great festival; and a multitude of men and women had come to it. Of the buildings we saw, the spectacle of one must fail of description, for it is beyond dispute the most wonderful edifice in the world. The inner walls are all embellished with gold. There are slabs of coloured marble, the like of which we had never seen, inlaid throughout with gold mosaic and surrounded by branches (formed from) green mosaic. In its upper parts are well-placed windows of gilded glass which steal all looks by the brilliance of their rays, and bewitch the soul. God protect us (from their allurement). We learnt that its founder, after whom it was named, spent hundred-weights of gold on it. He had been vizier to the grandfather of this polytheist King. This church has a belfry supported by columns of coloured marble. It was raised cupola over cupola, each with its separate columns, and is therefore known as the Columned Belfry, and is one of the most wonderful constructions to be seen. May God, in His kindness and benevolence, soon exalt it with the adhan ['call to prayers', i.e. make it a Muslim mosque].

The Christian women of this city follow the fashion of Muslim women, are fluent of speech, wrap their cloaks about them, and are veiled. They go forth on this Feast Day dressed in robes of gold-embroidered silk, wrapped in elegant cloaks, concealed by coloured veils, and shod with gilt slippers. Thus they parade to their churches, or (rather) their dens [a play on the words *kana'is*, 'churches', and *kunus*, 'dens'], bearing all the adornments of Muslim women, including jewellery, henna on the fingers, and perfumes. We called to mind – in the way of a literary witticism – the words of the poet: 'Going into the church one day, he came upon antelope and gazelle.'

We invoke God's protection for this description which enters the gates of absurdity and leads to the vanities of indulgence, and seek protection also from the bewitchment that leads to dotage. In truth He is the Lord of power and forgiveness.

Seven days we spent in this city, living in a hostel used by Muslims. We left it on the morning of Friday the 22nd of this holy month and the 28th of December, bound for Trapani, where there are two ships, one waiting to sail to Andalusia and the other to Ceuta. We had sailed to Alexandria in this, and both were carrying pilgrims and Muslim merchants.

Through a line of continuous villages and farms we trended, observing land, both tilled and sown, such as we had never seen before for goodness, fertility, and amplitude. We compared it to the *qanbaniyah* [Latin, *campania*, 'countryside', a relic of the Roman occupation] of Cordova, but this soil is choicer and more fertile.

We passed one night only on the road at a place called 'Alqamah [Alcamo], a large and spacious town with markets and mosques. Its inhabitants, and those of the farms we had passed on our way, were Muslims all. Leaving 'Alqamah at daybreak on Saturday the 23rd of the holy month and the 29th of December, we passed, not far from it, a castle called Hisn al-Hammah [the Castle of the Baths]. It is a large place with many thermal springs which God throws up from the ground charged with special elements, and so hot that the body can hardly bear them. We passed one on our road and, dismounting from our animals, refreshed our bodies by bathing in it. We arrived at last at Trapani in the late afternoon of that day and lodged in a house that we hired for the purpose.

Recollections of the town of Atrabanish [Trapani]
May God restore it (to the Muslims)

Trapani is a small city enclosed by walls, and white as a dove. It possesses an excellent harbour, most suited for shipping, and is therefore much used by the Rum, particularly those who sail to the Barr al-'Adwah [the coast of Africa]. Between it and Tunis is only a day and a night's journey, and the voyage is never stayed, winter or summer, save when the wind is unfavourable. Otherwise, the crossing by that course is very short.

Trapani is furnished with markets and baths and all the commodities needed in a town. But it lies in the throat of the sea, which encompasses it on three sides. It is joined to the land by only a narrow strip, and the yawning sea waits to engulf the rest. Its people indeed say that the sea will assuredly swallow it. May the end of its days be remitted. But the future is veiled from all save God Most High.

The low prices, resulting from the wide cultivation, make life easy and comfortable in this town, where the Muslims and the Christians have each their mosques and their churches. Near to its eastern corner and inclining to the north, is a great mountain of immense height. At its summit is an isolated crag, on which is a Rumi stronghold connected to the mountain by a bridge. Near to it on the mountain the Rum have a large town, the women of which are said to be the fairest of all the island. God grant that they be made captives of the Muslims. On the mountain are vineyards and cornfields, and we learnt that it has some four hundred springs. It is called Jabal Hamid [Mount St. Julian], and its ascent is quite easy on one side, its people saying that through it Sicily may be conquered. God grant that it be. But in no case will they allow a Muslim to ascend to it, and for this reason they have prepared this strong fortress. Should they apprehend aught, they would collect their women inside it and cut the bridge, leaving a great ditch between them and those on the heights of the adjacent mountain.

It is a strange fact that this town should have all these springs, as described, while Trapani, lying in the plain, should have no water save in a well at some distance from it, and in the not deeply sunk wells of its houses where it is brackish and cannot be swallowed.

At Trapani we found the two ships waiting to sail to the west. We hope, if God wills, to embark on the one bound for Spain. May God with His favour vouch unto us His accustomed beneficent offices.

To the west of Trapani, and about two parasangs from it, are three small close-lying islands called Malitimah [Maritimo], Yabisah [Levanzo], and al-Rahib [Favignana], which was named after a monk who lived on its summit in a fortress-like building that serves as a place of ambush for the enemy. The other two islands are uninhabited, and in this lives no one but the monk we have mentioned.

The Month of Shawwal (580)
January 5th – February 2nd, 1185
May God grant us His grace and favour

The new moon commenced on the night of Saturday the 5th of January, according to testimony given to the Hakim of Trapani to the effect that the new moon of the month of Ramadan had been seen on the night of Thursday and that the people of the capital of Sicily, already described, had begun the fast on that Thursday. The people therefore began their festival of the ending (of the month of fasting) after taking count from that Thursday. We prayed, on this holy feast-day, in a mosque in Trapani with a group of its inhabitants who had refrained, for a proper reason, from going to the *musalla* [place of prayer, where the *khutbah* was recited]. We offered up the traveller's prayer. May God restore every stranger to his homeland. The remainder of the people, with timbal and horn, went to the *musalla* with their magistrate. We marvelled at this, and at the Christian's tolerance of it.

Having agreed on the price of our passage in the ship going, within the will of God, to Spain, we turned our minds to provisions for the journey. But God alone can assure our help and easement, for there arrived an order from the King of Sicily stopping all ships from sailing from the shores of his island. It seems that he is preparing a fleet, and no ships may sail until the fleet has left. May God frustrate his designs, and may he not achieve his ends. The Genoese owners of the two ships hurried aboard to protect themselves from the Wali, but he relaxed as the result of a bribe the Genoese gave him, so that they remained in their ship and awaited a wind on which to sail ...

The people of Trapani are making conjectures as to the destination of the fleet this tyrant is preparing. As to its numbers, some say there are three hundred sail, between galleys and dromonds, while others say there are more, and that a hundred ships carrying victuals are to accompany it. May God frustrate it, and turn fortune against it. Some men say its destination is Alexandria – may God guard and defend it – and others Majorca – God defend it – while yet others say Africa – God defend it ...

There are others who see the levy as intended solely for Constantinople the Great, because of the momentous news which has come concerning it; news which inspires the soul with bodings of strange events, proving incontestably the truth of the traditions transmitted from the Chosen One [Muhammad] – God's blessings upon him. The report had it that the sovereign of Constantinople [Manuel Comnenos] had died and left the kingdom to his wife, who had a young son. But his cousin had usurped the throne, killed the widow, and seized the boy. A son of the rebel had been enjoined to kill the boy, but, his heart being moved to compassion, he had released the youth, who after many hazards, had been brought by destiny to this island. He arrived in wretched state as a menial, being servant to a monk, and concealing his royal figure in a lackey's cloak. But the secret came out and the affair was disclosed, for the cloak was of no avail. When by order of William King of Sicily the youth was brought before him and questioned, he declared that he was the serf and servant of the monk. But a party of Genoese on their way to Constantinople confirmed his identity and proved that it was he. There were besides, the signs and indications of royalty that shone from him, amongst which, as it was related to us, was the following:

It happening that King William went forth on one of his feast-days, the people had disposed themselves to greet him, and the youth in question was placed amongst the personal suite. All bowed deeply in humility and deference to the King that his looks might fall upon them: all save the youth, who did not incline deeply in salutation. Then was it known that his royal dignity had held him from giving the reverence of a subject. King William took great care of him, bestowing on him a dwelling-place and keeping him under most careful protection for fear that his cousin the rebel might do him mischief unawares.

He had a sister famed for her beauty with whom the usurping cousin had become enamoured. Yet he could not marry her, for the Rum do not take their kinswomen in marriage. But impetuous love, blind and deafening desire, and the transports that lead their possessor to bliss and then desert him, impelled him to take her and go with her to the Emir Mas'ud, Prince of Darub [Cilician Gates] and of Quniyah [Iconium, or modern Konia] and the lands of the foreigners adjoining Constantinople. Of the zeal of this Emir for Islam we have already spoken in these writings. It is enough to tell you that the Prince of Constantinople still pays tribute to him, and propitiates him by ceding some neighbouring territories.

In the presence of the Emir, he embraced, together with his (beloved) cousin, the creed of Islam; and a golden crucifix which had been heated by fire, he trampled beneath his feet. This, according to their fashion, is the surest way of renouncing the Christian religion and giving allegiance to the faith of Islam. He then married his cousin and achieved the object of his desire. Finally, he took the Muslim armies to Constantinople and entered it with them, slaying of its inhabitants some fifty thousand of the Rum. He was aided in his enterprise by the Aghr.....n, who are a sect of the people of the Book. They speak Arabic, and for all other sects of their race they bear a concealed enmity. They do not allow the eating of pork. The citizens weakened themselves by their dissensions, and God struck the spring of strife between them so that the Muslims seized Constantinople.

Its countless riches were taken to the Emir Mas'ud, who placed over forty thousand Muslim horsemen in the city, which now adjoined the Muslim lands. This conquest if it be true, is one of the greatest portents of the Day of Judgement. God best knows of hidden things.

We found this story to be spread about the island on the tongues of the Muslims and Christians alike, who believe it, and have no doubts about it. News of it had been brought by some Rum ships which had arrived from Constantinople, and the first question of the King's Commissioner when we were brought before him on our entry into Palermo had been whether we had news of Constantinople. We knew nothing, and did not understand the meaning of the question until later.

They then enquired concerning the question of the King of Constantinople, this youth, and the rebel's pursuit of him, for he has spies who seek to kill him; indeed, because of this the youth is kept near to the Prince of Sicily, so closely guarded that an eye-glance can hardly fall on him. We were told that he is a tender shoot of youth with the rosy hue of a stripling, slender and with a royal splendour about him. He studies with diligence the Arabic and other tongues, is distinguished for his kingly bearing, and is sagacious, despite his youthful age and inexperience.

Now, as it is reported, the Sicilian King intends to despatch the fleet to Constantinople, in shame for this youth and what befell him. But however these designs may fare, Almighty and Glorious God will drive him back with losses, showing him the unblessed nature of his way, and raising tempests to confound him. For as He desires so can He accomplish. This news from Constantinople – God grant that it be true – is one of the greatest miracles and awaited manifestations of the world. God indeed is all-powerful in His decrees and in what He pre-determines.

The Month of Dhu 'l-Qa'dah (A.H. 580)
February 3rd – March 4th, 1185
May God accord us His grace and favour

The new moon rose on the night of Monday the 4th of February, while we awaited in Trapani the end of winter and the sailing of the Genoese ship in which we hoped to travel to Andalusia. Pray God – Mighty and Glorious is He, and to be praised – may bless our aim, and help us with His grace and favour in our designs.

During the time of our stay in this town, we learnt painful things about the grievous state of the Muslims in this island concerning their relations with the worshippers of the Cross – may God destroy them – their humiliation and abasement, their state of vassalage under the Christians, and the duress of the king, bringing the calamities and misfortunes of apostasy on those of their women and children for whom God had ordained such suffering.

The King sometimes used force as a means of making some of their *sheiks* renounce their faith. There is the story of recent years concerning one of the learned doctors in Muslim law in the capital of their tyrant king. He is known as Ibn Zur'ah, and was so pressed by the demands of the officials that he declared his renunciation of Islam and plunged into the Christian religion. He diligently memorised the New Testament, studied the usages of the Rum, and learnt their canon law, until he was accepted into the body of priests who give judgement on law-suits between Christians. When a Muslim case arose, he would give judgement on that too, based on his previous knowledge of the Muslim religious law; and thus recourse was made to his decisions under both codes. He owned a mosque opposite his house which he converted into a church. God protect us from the results of apostasy and false ways. With all this, we heard that he but concealed what was really his true faith; and it may be that he took advantage of the exception allowed for in God's words, 'Save he who, being under compulsion, yet in his heart believes' [Koran XVI, 106].

During the last few days there has come to this town the leader and Lord of the Muslim community in this island, the Qa'id Abu 'l-Qasim ibn Hammud, commonly known as Ibn al-Hajar. This man belongs to that noble house on the island of which the eldest son successively assumes the Lordship (of the Muslims). We were further told that he is an upright man, liking good, loving his kind, full of acts of charity such as ransoming prisoners, and distributing alms to travellers and stranded pilgrims, together with many noble deeds and generous acts.

The town became greatly disturbed on his arrival. He had recently been out of favour with this tyrant, who had confined him to his house, on charges preferred against him by his enemies, who traduced him with untrue stories, including that of corresponding with the Almohades – whom God support. He would have been destroyed, but for the Guardian Angel, and even then suffered a series of divestments which exacted from him more than thirty thousand dinars. He was parted from all the houses and properties which he had inherited from his forebears, and at last was without wealth. More recently the tyrant had taken him back in his favour, and had granted him a post in his government. But he discharged his duties like a slave, his person and his property impounded.

When he arrived at Trapani, he expressed a wish to meet us. We met and he revealed to us such matters concerning his and his people's relations with their enemies as to draw tears of blood from the eyes and melt the heart in suffering.

For instance, he said to me, 'I have wished to be sold (as a slave), I and my family, that perhaps the sale would free us from the state we are in and lead to our dwelling in Muslim lands.' Reflect on a state of affairs which could lead this man, notwithstanding his great authority and exalted rank, his large household, his sons and his daughters, to make such a choice. For him and for all the Muslims of this island, we begged of Almighty and Glorious God a happy deliverance; and upon every Muslim standing in worship before Great and Glorious God lies the duty of offering prayers on their behalf. In tears ourselves, we left him crying. But our spirits had been enriched by the nobleness of his actions, his rare qualities, the soundness of his judgement, his limitless beneficence and generosity, and the goodness of his character and nature.

When in Palermo we had seen houses belonging to him, his brothers, and members of his house, which were like lofty and superb castles. The condition of these men, in a word, was exalted, and his was so in particular. During his time here he has performed many good deeds towards those pilgrims who are poor or distressed, mending their affairs, and giving them the money for the cost of their journey, as well as provisions. May God prosper him for it, and give him by His grace, his just reward.

The (Muslim) people of this island suffer, amongst other tribulations, one that is very sore. Should a man show anger to his son or his wife, or a woman to her daughter, the one who is the object of displeasure may perversely throw himself into a church, and there be baptised and turn Christian. Then there will be for the father no way of approaching his son, or the mother her daughter. Conceive now the state of one so afflicted in his family or even in his son. The dread of their falling to this temptation would alone shorten his life. The Muslims of Sicily therefore are most watchful of the management of their family, and their children, in case this should happen. The most clear-sighted of them fear that it shall chance to them all as it did in earlier times to the Muslim inhabitants of Crete. There a Christian despotism so long visited them with one (painful) circumstance after the other that they were all constrained to turn Christian, only those escaping whom God so decreed. But the word of chastisement shall fall upon these infidels. God's will shall prevail: there is indeed no God but He.

So great is the standing of this al-Hamudi [Abu Kassim] amongst the Christians – may God destroy them – that they declare that if he turned Christian, not a Muslim in the island but would follow him and imitate his act. May God protect them all, and deliver them, in His grace and favour, from their plight.

We came upon another striking example of their state, such as breaks the spirit in pity and melts the heart in compassion. One of the notables of this town of Trapani sent his son to one of our pilgrim companions, desiring of him that he would accept from him a daughter, a young virgin who was nearing the age of puberty. Should he be pleased with her, he could marry her; if not, he could marry her to any one of his countrymen who liked her. She would go with them, content to leave her father and her brothers, desiring only to escape from the temptation (of apostasy), and to live in the lands of the Muslims. Her father and brothers were disposed to this proposal, since they themselves might find escape to Muslim lands when the embargo that impeded them should be suspended. The man sought after, in order to earn a heavenly reward, accepted the offer, and we helped him to seize an opportunity which would lead him to the felicities both of this world and the next.

We ourselves were filled with wonder at a situation which would lead a man to give up so readily this trust tied to his heart, and to surrender her to one strange to her, to bear in patience the want of her, and to suffer longings for her and loneliness without her. We were likewise amazed at the girl – may God protect her – and at her willingness to leave her kin for her love of Islam, and her wish 'to seize a solid handle' [Koran II, 256; XXXI, 22]. May Almighty and Glorious God protect and guard her and console her by uniting her to her own and, by His grace, confer on her His favours. When her father had consulted her as to the project she had said, 'If you hold me back, the responsibility (before God) will be yours.' The girl was motherless, but had two brothers and a little sister from the same father.

The Month of Dhu 'l-Hijjah (A.H. 580)
March 5th – April 3rd, 1185
May God accord us His favour and blessings

... We passed the night ready for travelling – God grant that our journey be expeditious – and on the morning of the Feast of Sacrifice we were on the deck of the ship. May God help us to endure tribulation in it. We are more than fifty Muslims. May God protect all, and in His grace and favour, unite them to their native lands. Praise be to Him who can ensure this. We were eager to sail, but the wind was not propitious, and for twelve days we came and went between the ship and the shore, being each night disposed to sail. At last God allowed us to put to sea on the morning of Tuesday the 21st of Dhu 'l-Hijjah, the 25th of March.

As far as the population of Sicily was concerned the period of Norman rule was not without burden: the feudal system they established ensured that all powers of taxation and justice remained in the hands of the court and the King's officials. It was an advance on the Roman system of slavery, but not a great leap forward. The point of it was to place the population in a pyramid of beholden layers, designed to yield the maximum number of knights and retainers to the King, should he need them for war. The pyramid had three levels: the King and his generals, the Barons, and the vassals, as the peasants were called. As the historian of Southern Italy, Tommaso Astarita puts it, 'Even after its military function declined, feudalism continued to dominate southern society until well into the nineteenth century, and its effects have yet to disappear entirely from southern life.' However, the Sicilians appreciated being governed by a power based in the island, and one which built beautifully and reverently, and accrued Europe-wide respect and esteem for its learning and culture, and one which created a high society in which all the many races and previous civilisations of the island had a place. A fragment of a tombstone from the period, now displayed in Zisa Palace, is inscribed with Latin, Greek, Hebrew and Arabic. The Zisa, from Al-Azis, the Magnificent, is a superb thing, high, strong and elegant, standing between the western edge of old Palermo and the mountains, aligned so that one peak, Cozzo San Isidorio, is perfectly framed by its tall windows. It is three double storeys high, arched and crenulated, entirely Moorish in design. Fountains and a water channel glittered through mosaic floors on the ground level, feeding a pool in front of the palace. On the walls, designs of men and birds echoed the work at Monreale and the Palatine Chapel. A thoroughly secular place, built for pleasure on the edge of a hunting estate, it gives a strong sense of the ease, power and ambition of its Norman lords, and their great affinity for the art and way of life of the Arabs they had displaced.

The seeds of the poetry of the Sicilian school were planted in the enlightened court of Roger II, and they flowered under Frederick II, son of Henry VI of Swabia, to whom the last Norman king, William the Good, yielded the throne. Troubadors from Provence, at that time the foremost poets in Europe, were welcomed to Frederick's Palermo. The Sicilian poets adapted Troubador songs, and produced the first movement of Italian literature. Among their inventions was one of the signature forms of Western literature: the sonnet. The character of the poetry of the Sicilian School will be recognised by students of English as a kind of courtly love, in which a longing lover writes with hopeless devotion to an idealised and inaccessible woman. Frederick II was himself an accomplished writer of such pieces, but had he lived in freedom, his son Enzo, who was taken prisoner by the Bolognese, and died in a Bologna prison after twenty-three years of confinement, would surely have surpassed him.

Enzo, King of Sardinia
On the Fitness of Seasons

There is a time to mount; to humble thee
    A time; a time to talk, and hold thy peace;
    A time to labour, and a time to cease;
A time to take thy measures patiently;
A time to watch what Time's next step may be;
    A time to make light count of menaces,
    And to think over them a time there is;
There is a time when to seem not to see.
Wherefore I hold him well-advised and sage
    Who evermore keeps prudence facing him,
        And lets his life slide with occasion;
And so comports himself, through youth to age,
    That never any man at any time
        Can say, Not thus, but thus thou shouldst have
          done.

The work of Jacopo Da Lentini provides a more conventional model of the work of the Sicilian school. The imagery of this sonnet – one of the earliest examples of the form – might not seem strange to a Sicilian, or anyone familiar with the snows of the great volcano, the sweet and bitter Sicilian fruits, and the vexed history of the island's familial power struggles.

Jacopo da Lentino

I have seen the clear sky produce rain,
And darkness give off light,
And burning fire turn into ice,
And cold snow give off heat;

And sweet things become very bitter,
And bitterness produce sweetness,
And two enemies remain at peace,
And between two friends hatred arise.

But I have seen an even stranger thing with love:
For I was stricken, and it cured me by striking;
With fire it extinguished the fire that burned in me.

The life it gave me was death;
The fire that soothed me now will not cease
For so fierce is love that I can find no peace.

Jacopo is an able writer, but not a master. Dante called him 'the Notary of Lentini', damning indeed, given the way writers look at lawyers. But Jacopo succeeds in expressing gentle and genuine feeling, which seems entirely natural and unaffected, through the rhyming and rhythmic strictures of the mighty new form of the sonnet. Even without a fluency in Italian, any reader can appreciate his interweaving of sound and sense in this piece, thanks to the straight forward pronunciation of the language.

Jacopo Da Lentino
Of His Lady in Heaven

I have it in my heart to serve God so
    That into Paradise I shall repair, –
    The holy place through the which everywhere
I have heard say that joy and solace flow.
Without my lady I were loth to go, –
    She who has the bright face and the bright hair,
    Because if she were absent, I being there,
My pleasure would be less than nought, I know.
Look you, I say not this to such intent
    As that I there would deal in any sin:
    I only would behold her gracious mien,
    And beautiful soft eyes, and lovely face,
That so it should be my complete content
    To see my lady joyful in her place.

The Emperor Frederick, *Stupor Mundi*, 'the Wonder of the World' held power in Germany, as well as Sicily and the Italian south, and took a comparatively bloodless part in the successful fifth Crusade, which saw him negotiate his coronation as King of Jerusalem. He was a collector of gems, coins, exotic animals, manuscripts, languages (he spoke German, Latin, Italian and some Arabic), antiques and people: Leonardo Fibonacci, thought to have been principally responsible for the introduction of Arabic numerals to Europe, lived at Frederick's travelling court. Frederick was often on the move, but his heart was in the land of his birth: on visiting the Holy Land he remarked that God could not have seen the south of Italy, or He would not have so praised the promised land He offered to the Jews.

Frederick died in 1250, leaving a vacuum at which some despaired and others celebrated. The Papacy was particularly cheered: between Gregory IX and Innocent IV, Frederick had been excommunicated a record three times, declared the anti-Christ and officially deposed from his position of Holy Roman Emperor. The Popes were jealous and fearful of him, covetous of the Kingdom of Sicily and resentful of his tolerance towards Muslims and his interest in Islamic culture.

Frederick's legitimate heir, Conrad, died after only four years. Manfred, Frederick's son by his favourite mistress, was crowned King of Sicily in 1258, having been excommunicated in 1255 – an insult, one feels, which must have been greeted with ironic cheers in Palermo: he had a long way to go if he was going to surpass his father in Pope-baiting. Unfortunately for Manfred and for Sicily, new powers were on the rise in Europe. The reconquest of Spain saw the ascendancy there of the kings of Aragon, while in France Charles of Anjou took control of Provence and accrued influence in northern Italy. In return for promises to respect the Pope's lordship over Sicily and to lead a Crusade, Pope Clement IV crowned Charles King of Sicily in Rome. The rival kings, Charles and Manfred, met in battle at Benevento in February 1226. Manfred was killed and Sicily became the possession of Charles of Anjou, ruled, garrisoned and administered by the French. The Sicilians were once again subjects of a distant potentate; bad enough, and exacerbated by the character of French rule in the island, which became notorious for its corruption and disrespect. A Mediterranean-wide plot began to simmer, involving Emperor Michael of Constantinople, who was greatly afraid of Charles (the King planned an expedition against him, which would make him master of the entire Christian world); King Peter of Aragon, the strongest rival to Charles in Europe; and the Sicilians, represented in the writings of Petrarch and Boccaio by the mysterious figure of John of Procida, a doctor who had won the favour of Frederick II while he lived. He now served Manfred and travelled the various courts, an intriguing sort of diplomatic James Bond figure in popular history, who even won the support of Pope Nicholas III, whom John had cured from illness as a young man, and whom he now wooed with Byzantine gold.

The writer and distinguished historian Steven Runciman takes up the tale in 1282 with the Angevin fleet of Charles moored in Messina, a favourite crusader stop-over, preparing to sail for Constantinople, while an Aragonese fleet assembles in Barcelona, bound, supposedly, for conquest in north Africa.

Steven Runciman
From *The Sicilian Vespers*

Easter fell early in the year 1282, on March 29th. Throughout Holy Week the island of Sicily was outwardly calm. A great Angevin armada lay at anchor in Messina harbour. Royal agents toured the island commandeering all the stores of grain that they could find and rounding up herds of cattle and of pigs, to provide food for the expedition, and horses for the knights to ride, regardless of the peasants' sullen resentment. The Royal Vicar, Herbert of Orléans, governor of the island, was in residence at Messina, in the castle of Mategriffon, the 'terror of the Greeks', which Richard Cœur de Lion had built a century before. In Palermo the justiciar, John of Saint-Rémy, kept the feast in the palace of the Norman kings. None of the French officials and none of the soldiers who commanded the forty-two castles from which the countryside was policed noticed more than the habitual unfriendliness shown them by the subject race. But amongst the Sicilians themselves as they celebrated the resurrection of Christ with their traditional songs and dancing in the streets, the atmosphere was tense and explosive.

The Church of the Holy Spirit lies about half a mile to the south-east beyond the old city wall of Palermo, on the edge of the little gorge of the river Oreto. It is an austere building, without and within. Its foundation-stone was laid in 1177 by Walter Ophamil, or 'of the Mill', the English-born Archbishop of Palermo, on a day made sinister by an eclipse of the sun. It was the custom of the church to hold a festival on Easter Monday, and on Easter Monday of that year people came crowding as usual from the city and the villages around, to attend the Vesper service.

There was gossiping and singing in the square as everyone waited for the service to begin. Suddenly a group of French officials appeared to join in the festivities. They were greeted with cold, unfriendly looks, but they insisted on mingling with the crowd. They had drunk well and were carefree; and soon they treated the younger women with a familiarity that outraged the Sicilians. Among them was a sergeant called Drouet, who dragged a young married woman from the crowd and pestered her with his attentions. It was more than her husband could bear. He drew his knife and fell on Drouet, and stabbed him to death. The Frenchmen rushed up to avenge their comrade and suddenly found themselves surrounded by a host of furious Sicilians, all armed with daggers and swords. Not one of the Frenchmen survived. At that moment the bell of the Church of the Holy Spirit and of all the churches of the city began to ring for Vespers.

To the sound of the bells messengers ran through the city calling on the men of Palermo to rise against the oppressor. At once the streets were full of angry armed men, crying 'Death to the French' – 'moranu li Franchiski' in their Sicilian dialect. Every Frenchman that they met was struck down. They poured into the inns frequented by the French and the houses where they dwelt, sparing neither man, woman nor child. Sicilian girls who had married Frenchmen perished with their husbands. The rioters broke into the Dominican and Franciscan convents; and all the foreign friars were dragged out and told to pronounce the word 'ciciri', whose sound the French tongue could never accurately reproduce. Anyone who failed in the test was slain. The Justiciar, John of Saint-Rémy, shut himself in the old royal palace; but most of the men of his garrison had been away holiday-making in the town. The few that remained could not hold it for him. He was wounded in the face during a skirmish at the entrance before fleeing with two attendants out of a window through the stables. They found horses and rode at full speed to the castle of Vicari, on the road into the interior. There they were joined by other refugees who had escaped the massacre.

By the next morning some two thousand French men and women lay dead; and the rebels were in complete control of Palermo. Their fury had calmed down sufficiently for them to think of the future. Representatives of each district and each trade met together and proclaimed themselves a Commune, electing as their Captain an eminent knight called Roger Mastrangelo. Three vice-captains were appointed, Henry Baverio, Nicholas of Ortoleva and Nicholas of Ebdemonia, with five counsellors to assist them. The Angevin flag was torn down, and everywhere replaced by the Imperial eagle which Frederick II had allotted as a badge to the city of his childhood. A letter was sent with ambassadors to the Pope asking him to take the new Commune under his protection.

Already news of the rising was spreading throughout the island. Runners hurried out during the fierce Monday night from Palermo to tell all the towns and villages to strike at once, before the oppressor could strike back. On the Tuesday the men of Palermo themselves marched out to destroy the castle of Vicari, where the Justiciar and his friends were taking refuge. The garrison was too small to resist for long; and the Justiciar offered to surrender if he were allowed to go down to the coast and embark for his native Provence. As the negotiations were beginning one of the besiegers fired an arrow at him and shot him dead. It was the signal for a general massacre of everyone inside the castle.

Throughout the week news came of further uprisings and slaughtering of the French. The first town to follow the example of Palermo was Corleone, twenty miles to the south. After killing the French it too proclaimed itself a Commune. On April 3rd its captain, Boniface, sent three envoys to Palermo to give the news and to suggest common action. The two Communes decided to send troops in three directions, westwards towards Trapani, southward towards Caltanissetta and eastward towards Messina, to rouse the rest of the island and co-ordinate its efforts. As the rebels approached each district, the French fled or were massacred. In two towns only they were spared. The Vice-Justiciar of Western Sicily, William Porcelet, who lived at Calatafimi, had won the love of the Sicilians by his benevolence and his justice. He and his family were escorted with honour to Palermo and were allowed to embark for Provence. The town of Sperlinga, in the centre of the island, prided itself on its independence of view. The French garrison there was unharmed and was able to retire safely to Messina.

In Messina there was no rising. The Vicar, Herbert of Orléans, had a strong garrison. The great Angevin fleet was in the harbour. Messina had been the only city in the island to which Charles's government had shown any favour; and its leading family, the Riso, supported his régime. On April 13th, a fortnight after the Vespers, when all the west and centre of the island was in rebel hands, the Commune of Palermo sent a letter to the people of Messina, asking them to join the rebellion. But the Messinese were cautious. With Herbert and his garrison dominating them from the castle of Mategriffon and with the king's ships lying off the quay, they preferred not to commit themselves. Instead, on April 15th a Messinese army troop, under a local knight, William Chiriolo, moved south to the neighbouring city of Taormina, to protect it against the fury of the rebels. At the same time Herbert sent the Messinese noble, Richard Riso, in command of seven local galleys to blockade Palermo harbour and if possible to attack its fortifications. The Palermitans hastened to display the banner of Messina with its cross alongside their banner on the walls, to show that they regarded the Messinese as their brothers; and Richard's sailors refused to fight them. The galleys remained off the harbour maintaining an unenthusiastic and inefficient blockade.

In Messina opinion was swaying round in favour of the revolt. Many of its citizens were also citizens of Palermo who had moved to Messina when it became the administrative centre. Their sympathies were with their native city. Herbert began to lose confidence. He determined to make sure of Taormina and sent a troop of Frenchmen there under a Neapolitan, Micheletto Gatta, to replace the Messinese garrison. William Chiriolo and his men were offended by this lack of trust in them. They came to blows with the French and took them all prisoner. Two or three days later, on April 28th, Messina broke out into revolt. Most of the French had already retired to the castle of Mategriffon; and the massacres were on a smaller scale than at Palermo. Herbert blockaded himself in the castle, but he was obliged to abandon the fleet, which was set on fire and utterly destroyed. The Messinese declared themselves to be a Commune, under the protection of the Holy Church. They elected as their captain Bartholomew Maniscalco, who had played the chief part in organizing the revolt.

That same day three distinguished citizens of Messina arrived back from King Charles's court at Naples. They were Baldwin Mussone, a former judge, and Baldo and Matthew Riso. Mussone at once threw in his lot with the Commune, and Maniscalco resigned the captaincy to him next morning. One of the younger Risos, the doctor Parmenio, tried to persuade his uncles Baldo and Matthew to join the rebellion; but they and the rest of the family remained faithful to Charles and took refuge with Herbert in the castle. They found that Herbert was already giving up the struggle. After a preliminary attack had been made on the castle, he negotiated with Mussone and obtained a safe-conduct for himself and his staff. Two galleys were put at their disposal on condition that they sailed directly to Aigues-Mortes in France and promised never to return to Sicily. Herbert gave his word; but as soon as he was clear of the harbour he ordered the galleys to sail to Catona, just across the Strait. There he found Peter Ruffo, Count of Catanzaro, who was the richest noble in Calabria and loyal to Charles. They assembled troops to prepare for a counter-attack on Messina.

The Chatelain of the castle of Mategriffon, Theobald of Messy, with seventy French sergeants and their wives and children, was allowed similar terms. The whole company was placed in another ship, with orders to sail to Aigues-Mortes. The loyal members of the Riso family were kept as prisoners by the Commune in the castle of Mategriffon, where they were joined by Micheletto Gatta and his Frenchmen, who had been brought up under escort from Taormina. Messengers had already been sent to Palermo to tell of the events at Messina and of the foundation of the sister-Commune; and the Messinese ships still hovering off the port were ordered home. Their commander, Richard Riso, managed to slip away to Calabria. When the vice-commander Nicholas Pancia sailed round into Messina harbour he met the ship carrying the Chatelain Messy and his party. Pancia had already heard that Herbert of Orléans had broken his promise to retire to France and suspected that Messy was about to follow his example. The ship was detained and all its company cast into the sea and drowned.

When order was restored in Messina the Commune elected four counsellors to assist the captain. They were all of them local judges, Raynald of Limogia, Nicholas Saporito, Peter Ansalano and Bartholomew of Neocastro, who later wrote a history of the great events. Next it was decided, significantly, to send news to Constantinople, that the Emperor Michael should know that his chief enemy had been crippled. No doubt he might then in gratitude send more of his gold to the islanders. It was difficult to find a messenger to go on the perilous journey; but a Genoese merchant, Alafranco Cassano, volunteered his services. His nationality would protect him if he were detained by one of Charles's ships. He reached Constantinople a few weeks later and was given an immediate audience with the Emperor. Michael, when he heard the news, gave thanks to God and hastened to add to the autobiographical memoir that he was preparing for his son the significant words: 'Should I dare to claim that I was God's instrument in bringing freedom to the Sicilians, I should only be stating the truth.' His agents and his gold had indeed played their part in planning the uprising; and the uprising had not only freed Sicily; it had also saved his Empire. Charles's great expedition against Constantinople had now to be postponed for ever.

Charles was at Naples when in the first days of April a messenger sent by the Archbishop of Monreale told him of the massacre at Palermo. He was angry; for it meant the postponement of his eastern expedition for a while. But he did not at first take the revolt seriously. It was a local affair, he thought, with which his Vicar, Herbert of Orléans, could deal. He merely ordered the vice-admiral Matthew of Salerno to take four galleys to attack Palermo. The order was given on April 8th; but when Matthew arrived off Palermo he found the Messinese squadron already cruising ineffectually outside the harbour and did not venture to press any attack. When Messina joined in the revolt, the Messinese ships attacked him and captured two of his galleys. He retired with the others to Naples.

It was the rising in Messina and the destruction of his fleet there that brought Charles to realize the seriousness of the rebellion. 'Lord God,' he cried, 'since it has pleased You to ruin my fortune, let me only go down by small steps.' He set about seeing that the steps should be small. The eastern expedition was countermanded. Instead, the ships and men assembled in his Italian ports were summoned to the straits of Messina, and he himself set out to command the force which should reduce the rebel island.

He had the full support of the Pope. When in April an envoy from Palermo arrived at Orvieto to ask the Holy See to take the new Commune under its protection, Pope Martin refused to grant him an audience. The island still hoped that Martin would relent. In the first days of May Messina joined Palermo and the other cities in sending three ambassadors to his court. They came solemnly into his presence before the whole Consistory chanting three times the words: 'Lamb of

101

God, Who bearest the sins of the world, have mercy upon us.' But the Pope replied bitterly repeating three times the words in the Passion, 'Hail, King of the Jews – and they smote Him.' The embassy had no other answer from him. Instead, on May 7th, Ascension Day, he issued a Bull of excommunication against the rebel Sicilians and against anyone who should give them aid. A second Bull excommunicated Michael Palaeologus 'who calls himself Emperor of the Greeks', and a third Guy of Montefeltro and the Ghibellines of northern Italy.

Charles had another sympathetic friend in his nephew King Philip of France. He wrote in April to the French court to inform Philip that active steps might be needed to prevent the revolt from having serious consequences. When Messina rebelled, he wrote again to ask for help against the rebels. In response two of his nephews, Philip's brother Peter, Count of Alençon, and Robert of Artois, prepared to send a party of French nobles to Italy. Charles's son, Charles of Salerno, who was in Provence at the time, was told to go to Paris to arrange for further co-operation with the French court. To King Philip the main danger seemed to come from Aragon. He had already warned Charles to beware of the Aragonese king; and Charles had not heeded him. He was convinced that the great Aragonese fleet assembled in the harbour of Fangos was destined for an attack against Sicily, in spite of all King Peter's protests that he was going crusading in Africa. Before he had heard that Messina was lost to Charles he had sent an embassy to King Peter, who was already with his fleet. It reached Port Fangos on May 20th and gave Peter a letter in which Philip demanded assurances that the fleet would not be used against Charles. If it were, he warned, he would regard it as an hostile act and would send an army against Aragon.

His warning was ineffectual. Peter merely answered that he was, as he had always maintained, preparing for an expedition to Africa. In fact, the Sicilian revolt had taken Peter by surprise. His agents had planned it; but he had counted on Charles's expedition against Constantinople taking place. Then, when the Sicilian kingdom was bared of its best soldiers, Sicily was to revolt and he would intervene. The Sicilians, abetted by the Byzantine Emperor, had forestalled him. When the news of the massacre at Palermo reached him, he did nothing. It was only after the revolt at Messina and the destruction of Charles's ships there that he decided to act. Even so, he moved cautiously. He would genuinely sail to Africa and fight the Moors there while waiting to see what would happen in Sicily. On June 3rd he sailed out of Port Fangos at the head of a great flotilla of men-of-war and transports, heading for the Algerian coast.

To maintain his pretence, he sent a special envoy to the Pope to ask for his blessing for his crusade and for the usual indulgences. Martin was not deceived. He gave a curt reply to the ambassador. The Swiss knight, Otto of Grandson, who was acting as Edward of England's agent at Orvieto, reported on June 11th to his employer that everyone at the papal court expected the King of Aragon to intervene in Sicily. But Peter was in no hurry. His fleet put in at Port Mahon in Minorca, which was still a Muslim emirate, though tributary to the Aragonese crown. The emir hastened to supply the fleet with generous provisions, but sent a secret messenger to Tunis to warn its king of the expedition. When the fleet arrived at Collo, on the Algerian coast, Peter learnt that his ally, the governor of Constantine, whose detachment from the Tunisian kingdom and whose conversion the expedition was supposed to achieve, had been suddenly attacked by the Tunisians, as a result of the Minorcan message, and had been put to death. His elimination deprived the crusade of its object. But Peter remained on with his soldiers at Collo, conveniently close for watching events in Sicily.

The Sicilians were meanwhile preparing themselves to meet King Charles's counter-attack. Charles did not hurry his preparations. He meant, when he struck, to strike hard and decisively. The ships and men destined for the eastern campaign were gathered together at Catona on the Calabrian shore of the Straits. Peter of Alençon and Robert of Artois were summoned with their French knights to join the Angevin army. Contingents were diverted from Provence, from the expedition that had been going to sail up the Rhône and refound the Kingdom of Arles. The Guelfs of Florence sent a troop under Count Guy of Battifolle, with the banner of the city and fifty young squires to whom King Charles promised knighthood. Ships were hired from Venice, Pisa and Genoa, to take the place of those that the Messinese had destroyed. It was a formidable army which King Charles himself joined as commander-in-chief on July 6th. Nineteen days later he led it across the Straits and encamped in the vineyards just to the north of Messina.

Pope Martin hoped that the Sicilians would be alarmed into submission without fighting. They still maintained that their Communes were under his protection. On June 5th he had appointed one of his ablest ministers, Cardinal Gerard of Parma, to be his legate in the island with orders to obtain its unconditional surrender. Five days later, to supplement his efforts, King Charles issued a long ordinance reforming the administration of the island. Royal officials were in future forbidden to indulge in any form of extortion; they were not to sequester goods or beasts or commandeer boats without payment, not to force towns and villages to give them gifts nor to imprison citizens on inadequate grounds, nor to annex their lands, crimes which the ordinance admitted to have been committed in the days before the rising. But the promise of these reforms left the Sicilians unmoved. They had suffered too much at the hands of the Angevins, and their pride had been roused. They were ready to fight against odds. Already on June 2nd the Messinese had foiled an attempt of the Angevins to land forces at Milazzo, on the north-east coast of the island. Nor was their spirit broken when three weeks later an Angevin detachment effected a landing there and defeated with heavy losses the Messinese militia which tried to drive them back. The only results of their defeat were that the Messinese broke into the Castle of Mategriffon where the members of the Riso family were imprisoned and dragged them out to death, and that they removed the judge Baldwin Mussone from the office of Captain, judging him to be inefficient and lukewarm. In his place they elected Alaimo of Lentini, one of the three Sicilian nobles who had taken the lead in John of Procida's intrigue. He proved a more vigorous commander, whose only fault was his subservience to his wife, Machalda of Scaletta, an heiress of humble origin and vast ambition. At the moment she was not by his side; she had gone with some of her vassals to Catania, where she had tricked the frightened French garrison into surrendering to her and then had put them to death, taking control of the city herself.

Alaimo worked hard to put the defences of Messina into good order. Foreign volunteers came to swell his forces; there were several Genoese galleys and their crews, regardless that some of their compatriots had been hired by King Charles; there were twelve galleys from Ancona, and, unexpectedly, twelve from Venice, manned by men who disliked King Charles and his policy. The Sicilians had been promised help from Pisa; but the Pisans had just begun a war against Genoa and withdrew the galleys that they were sending. The only Pisans to take part in the Sicilian war were the crews of four galleys hired out to King Charles. They were in the forefront of his forces and made themselves particularly objectionable to the men of Messina. Towards the beginning of August the defenders were joined by fifty Aragonese nobles and their followers, who had left their King's army in Africa as volunteers to help the Sicilian cause.

Charles launched his first serious attack against Messina on August 6th, with an attempt to storm the quarter at the end of the peninsula which protected the harbour. He was driven back with very little loss to the defenders. Two days later his men tried to storm the fortified heights of Capperrina, at the north-west edge of the city, furthest from the sea. After the failure of an attack by daylight, his men returned to the assault after dark, but were discovered and discomfited by the prompt action of two local women, whose names, Dina and Clarentia, are recorded with honour in the chronicles. These successes encouraged the Sicilians. It was an unusually rainy month; and the mud hindered the attack more than the defence. The citizens, women as well as men, took their turns in manning the defences. They sent spies to the enemy camp, notably a Franciscan friar, Bartholomew of Piazza, who had made a thorough inspection of the Angevin army before it crossed the Straits. The city was further encouraged by a report that the Holy Virgin herself had been seen blessing the defence. But Charles was taking his time. His army was large and strong and his fleet greatly outnumbered the Sicilians', and both awaited reinforcements. He tightened his blockade of Messina till the moment should come for the final assault.

During the lull after his first attacks, he sent the papal legate, Cardinal Gerard, into the city. The Messinese gave an honourable welcome to the representative of the Pontiff whom they declared to be their overlord. The Captain, Alaimo, formally offered to place Messina in his hands if the Pope would declare himself Protector of the Commune. The cardinal replied that the Church would give back the city to its faithful son, Charles, to whom the whole island lawfully belonged. Alaimo snatched back the keys of the city which he had handed to Gerard and declared in a loud voice that it was better to die in battle than to submit knowingly to a hated enemy. The cardinal was sent back to the royal camp.

After the failure of the legate's mission Charles pressed on with the attack. On August 15th another attempt was made to storm the wall at Capperrina, but it too failed. The blockade was tightened. The citizens were ready to suffer for their cause, but they were saved from starvation by exceptionally good crops of fruit and vegetables from the allotments within the walls and exceptionally large hauls of fish from the harbour. An attack on the north wall on September 2nd equally failed. On September 14th Charles ordered a general assault. The fighting that day was fiercer than ever before. But once again the assailants made no progress; and after two of the nobles standing by Charles had been killed by a stone hurled from the walls, he called off the attack and retired to his camp. From there he wrote to Alaimo to promise him that if he would surrender and would proclaim Charles in the city, he would be rewarded with hereditary estates wherever he wished and money to pay for the expenses of the war. All that Charles asked was that six citizens of Messina, whom he would choose, should be handed over for punishment. Every other citizen of Messina would be pardoned.

Alaimo contemptuously rejected the offer. He and his government realized their danger; but they had hopes now of a saviour. When the Pope through his legate rejected their scheme to turn Sicily into a group of Communes under the authority of the Holy See, they understood that they must find another solution for the island's future. One was at hand.

When King Peter of Aragon sent an embassy to Pope Martin to ask for papal blessing for his crusade, he had little hope of a friendly answer. His chief ambassador, the Catalan William of Castelnou, had instructions to pause on his return journey at Palermo and to make contact with the rebel leaders there. The Palermitans knew by now that nothing would make the Pope desert King Charles's cause. The Sicilians had been unwilling at first to substitute the rule of one foreign potentate for that of another. But they could not stand alone. Queen Constance of Aragon was after all the representative of the House of Hohenstaufen and the ultimate heiress of the great dynasty of kings. Her husband was near at hand with a splendid armament. Prudence and legitimacy alike counselled them to accept Peter and Constance as their king and queen. When William of Castelnou sailed on to join his master at Collo, he brought with him three envoys from Sicily. One was a Messinese noble called William, who had been living at Palermo, the other two were judges from Palermo, whose names were unknown.

The Sicilian delegation came before King Peter at the camp at Collo and made obeisance to him, telling him of the plight of their orphan island. The Lady Constance, they said, was their lawful queen to whom the crown should be given, and after her to her sons, the Infants of Aragon. They implored him to come and rescue them and to see that his queen enjoyed her rights. Peter received them honourably but hesitated to commit himself. Four days later a ship arrived bearing two knights and two burghers from Messina, who had slipped through the Angevin blockade. At the same time three other citizens from Messina made their way to Palermo to announce that they were joining in the appeal to King Peter. Peter still affected to be diffident. But he had consulted his army leaders and found them willing to follow him to Sicily. After a due show of modesty he graciously announced that he would accede to the Sicilians' request. He would sail to Sicily and would place his wife upon the throne of her ancestors. He promised the islanders that their liberties should be respected and that all should be as it had been in the days of Good King William. He then sent William of Castelnou once again to the papal court with a careful and pious explanation of his motives.

Towards the end of August the Aragonese camp at Collo was dismantled. For three days the army authorities piled men, horses, arms and provisions into the waiting galleys and transports. The Sicilian ship hurried home to announce to the islanders that its crew had seen King Peter embarking. Some two days later, on August 30th 1282, the great host of Aragon, with the King at its head, disembarked at Trapani. The rebellion in Sicily was now a European war.

For the next four hundred years Sicily was under Aragonese and then Bourbon rule. The story of this period is not written in books but in stones. Sicilian literature went quiet, even if Sicily did not. Society stratified – under Spanish viceroys, Spanish, Italian and Sicilian nobility built churches and lived in palaces, baronial figures owned the great estates, and the peasants lived and died the way they had for centuries. This is not the place to survey the vast Sicilian hoard of European architectural treasure: the Italian Gothic achievements of the thirteenth century, the Sienese sculpture of the fourteenth century, the Catalan architecture of the fifteenth or the renaissance architecture and town planning.

But we will pause briefly to consider the miracles of the Sicilian Baroque which followed the earthquake of 1693, when architects like Rosario Gagliardi, G B Vaccarini, Francesco Battaglia and Andrea Palma created masterpieces like the cathedral façade in Syracuse (Palma), the Rococo marvel of the Palazzo Biscaria in Catania (Battaglia) and the entire town of Noto (Gagliardi and Vincenzo Sinatra), the last being a realised vision of Grecian brilliance; an entire new town conceived and built as a work of art (though you would not know it, on arrival at the railway station).

Noto is a very peculiar place today, peaceful, stunningly beautiful, with its baroque churches, public buildings and squares laid out evenly, the stones glowing peachy-gold, pinkish-yellow, orange and lemon, under the sun. It is a stunning, dignified and musical response to a horrific event: 'In the year 1693, on January 11th, came an earthquake of such horrible violence that the ground seemed to billow like the sea, the hillsides swayed and tumbled, and in one dreadful instant the town collapsed, killing one thousand persons,' recorded Friar Filippo Tortora, quoted by Nino Azzaro, a photographer and historian of Noto, who says in the introduction to his book of pictures of the city 'the aim of this book is that of showing the world that folly of human wits which is Noto.' The translation by Paola Ruggieri seems apt: Noto is a kind of folly, a little miracle at the end of Europe. In the mornings and evenings the centre resembles an extraordinary museum, tended by droves of little old men in jackets and hats, who line the benches of the corso; they seem slightly bemused at their dominance: many of the young have left, and the centre is presently covered in scaffolding, as frantic efforts are finally made to rescue its World Heritage-designated splendour from collapse.

Vincent Cronin describes his favourite relic of the Baroque period, and teases from it a digression on that favourite Sicilian subject: sweets.

Vincent Cronin
From *The Golden Honeycomb*

Diodorus has put on record that the first artist to work in Sicily also dedicated his genius to the service of a cult, fashioning a votive offering for the mountain goddess of Erice. The original Sicilian work of art took a religious form, and since to originate in any field is also to start a tradition, the sacred element has remained dominant until the present day ...

The masterpiece of Sicilian baroque is the church of St Caterina, consecrated in 1664, facing the Martorana in the Piazza Bellini [in Palermo]. As soon as one enters, one experiences that absolute satisfaction together with a penumbra of bewilderment which only a perfect work of art can give. Every visible square inch of this vast building (it is almost two hundred feet in length) has been cultivated to add its yield to the total harvest of beauty. A garden in full bloom, a granary heaped to the rafters with corn, an orchard teeming with fruit – none of these gives quite the same effect of abundance, for none has been harmonised and concentrated with deliberate and inspired art. The combination of colours – rose-brown, white and black – and the added dimension given by the relief work are the immediately striking features, conveying a sense of *chiaroscuro* and pale light which draws one into the nave. The interior takes the form of a cross, with a dome but without aisles. Pilasters run the length of the walls, separating the six side chapels, each of which is as richly decorated as the nave, and each having its distinctive pattern of inlaid marble. On a single pilaster there are carved as many as twelve cherubim in relief, each one perfectly executed, whether conspicuous or hardly visible high above the nave. At the base of each pilaster is carved a biblical scene – almost the only doctrinal evidence in a world of pure nature: one of them represents Jonah and the whale, with a magnificent Spanish galleon in relief, its rigging of metal wire. The richness of the meanest chapel here would dignify the high altar of many another church. That of St Caterina in the south transept shows the *tour de force* at its highest pitch. Here the detail of decoration is carried to a point beyond which all form would disappear under the weight of ornament and the whole would be lost in the profusion of the parts. It is as though the flowers in a large garden had attained such luxuriance that it is uncertain whether the garden has not reverted to its primeval state; as though a snowstorm had been depicted in the medium of marble; as though a frenzied mind, the mind of a Rimbaud, were throwing out powerful and extravagant images before tumbling over the verge of madness. The first principle is that nothing shall remain simple: the straight line of a column must be twisted, or the flutings painted: the bases must be inlaid with bulging pieces of marble: the recesses must be filled with flowers: at all costs nothing must remain bare, lest it prove that other worlds exist, simpler and quieter than this extravangance of flowers and frozen fountains, abandoned to a perpetual state of tension.

St Caterina used to be famous for its preserved pumpkin and blancmange, and the Martorana opposite for its *frutti* of sweet almond paste. If the taste for sweet cakes was introduced by the Saracens, it was the growth of the religious houses during the Counter-Reformation which developed cake-making into an art, and curiously enough the decoration on present-day cakes recalls nothing so much as the polychrome interior of St Caterina – a significant sidelight on this form of baroque architecture.

Each religious house specialised in one particular form of confectionery or pastry, and since this was one of the principal means of livelihood competition became sufficiently intense to produce a wealth of designs and recipes. The fact that many daughters of noble parents chose the religious life perhaps accounts for the fastidious and elaborate decoration of the cakes. All are typically Sicilian in their extravagant colour and cloying sweetness. The simplest sort is the imitation of fruit or vegetable, smaller than life size, made in almond paste. As though in some fabulous greenhouse, strawberries and cherries, figs and oranges, apples and pears all ripen together in the confectioner's window, as they once did at the church doors. The small orange-coloured *nespole* which appear in May and taste half-apricot, half-orange, are shown cut in half, revealing the large seeds which resemble chestnuts. Wild strawberries and raspberries are fashioned with such cunning that it is almost impossible, before they are tasted, to distinguish them from the real. Heaped together in a wide bowl, their opulence of colour is as cloying as their tropically sweet taste.

If these almond-paste imitations out-colour nature, the actual fruits are candied to preserve what in the natural order of things would perish. As though embalmed in sweet spices, the rind of the fruit persists, its true essence lost in the taste of sugar. In this candied confectionery the colour becomes darker and autumnal, like the rich brown shade of heather honey. Both the imitated and preserved fruits, however, possess only a surface excellence, for they have that heavy, overpowering taste which Sicilians find pleasing in food.

The larger cakes are minor works of sculpture. Like severe Roman baroque architecture, the inside is of little interest: as in most Sicilian cakes it consists of a cassata layered with curds, enclosed in pistachio-marzipan. All the confectioner's skill and invention are lavished on the external decoration, which is as varied as three dimensions and a round shape will allow. Candied oranges halved with cherries on a chocolate base; a chequered carpet of cherry jam, in which are set waterlilies made of pistachio cream with petals of half almonds; a garden built up like a bas-relief with a succession of quartered preserved fruits; a coat-of-arms composed entirely of star-mouldings in coffee and chocolate cream; a Catherine wheel spun with spirals of rainbow-coloured icing: as varied as the pattern of snowflakes ... They are new, exotic, perfumeless flowers, coloured stuccoes, triumphs of architecture, their mouldings as finely worked and fretted as any Saracen portal or window. They are marble inlays more gorgeous than those of the church of S. Caterina, vivid and intricate as the wheels of a Sicilian cart. But, by contrast, they are as perishable as the butterflies and flowers they resemble: no other artist unless it be the maker of fireworks fashions such ephemeral materials as the confectioner. In the shop window his cakes attract the passer-by as jewellery or silverware would, but to sell them is to destroy his handiwork with his own hands: annihilation is the price of success. As in an oriental slave market, in the confectioner's shop beauty is bought only to be consumed.

When we next encounter Sicily we find it no longer a subject for conquest, nor a Kingdom to wonder at, nor a prize to prospect. It has become a destination, an accretion of all its histories, a subject for study and description for the new breed of European man: the curious tourist.

For a fair account of the kind of place the island had become by the eighteenth century we need a classicist, an architectural historian, a botanist, naturalist, geologist, scholar, rigorous social observer, trained in public administration, and a supremely gifted writer. Johann Wolfgang von Goethe was all of these. He arrived in Palermo in April 1787. He had fled Germany the year before, internationally famous for his novel *The Sorrows of Young Werther*, and practically enslaved in Weimar by duties, obligations, adulation and work: his prodigious administrative efficiency made him indispensable to the city authorities there, and he was in constant social demand. He was exhausted, so one night he set out for Italy, slipping away like a thief. Goethe makes a wonderful travelling companion. He is interested in everything and has an entire library of references in his head. He is a master of the art of looking; really looking. Anyone who has ever tried to draw a building or a scene will know how much we miss in our first, second and third glances at a thing. Goethe misses nothing. The best descriptions of how he does it, how he sees, occur early in his diaries and letters. The passages describing Venice and his journey there are spectacular. By the time he gets to Sicily the writer's fervour and fascination have relaxed somewhat: the south has done its gentle work on him.

Johann Wolfgang von Goethe
From *Letters from Italy*

Sunday April 1st, 1787
About three in the morning a violent storm. Half asleep and dreaming, I went on with the plan of my drama; in the mean time there was great commotion on deck; the sails were all taken in, and the vessel pitched on the top of the waves. As day broke the storm abated, and the sky cleared up. Now Ustica lay right on our left. They pointed out to me a large turtle swimming a great distance off; by my telescope I could easily discern it, as a living point. Towards noon we were clearly able to distinguish the coast of Sicily with its headlands and bays, but we had got very far to the leeward, and tacked on and off. Towards midday we came nearer to the shore. The weather being clear, and the sun shining bright, we saw quite distinctly the western coast from the promontory of Lilybæum to Cape Gallo.

110

A shoal of dolphins attended our ship on both bows, and continually shot ahead. It was amusing to watch them as they swam along, covered by the clear transparent waves at one time, and at another springing above the water, showing their fins and spine-ridged back, with their sides playing in the light from gold to green, and from green to gold.

As the land was direct on our lee, the captain lay to in a bay behind Cape Gallo. Kniep failed not to seize the opportunity to sketch the many beautiful scenes somewhat in detail. Towards sunset the captain made again for the open sea, steering north-east, in order to make the heights of Palermo. I ventured several times on deck, but never intermitted for a moment my poetical labours; and thus I became pretty well master of the whole piece. With a cloudy sky, a bright but broken moonlight, the reflection on the sea was infinitely beautiful. Paintings, in order to heighten the effect, generally lead us to believe, that the reflection from the heavenly luminaries on the water has its greatest breadth nearest to the spectator, where it also possesses its greatest brilliancy. On this occasion, however, the reflection was broadest at the horizon, and, like a sharp pyramid, ended with sparkling waves close to the ship. During the night our captain again frequently changed the tack.

Monday April 2nd, 1787
This morning, about eight o'clock, we found ourselves over against Palermo. The morning seemed to me highly delightful. During the days that I had been shut up in my cabin, I had got on pretty well with the plan of my drama. I felt quite well now, and was able to stay on deck, and observe attentively the Sicilian coast. Kniep went on sketching away, and by his accurate, but rapid pencil, many a sheet of paper was converted into highly valuable mementoes of our landing, which, however, we still had to wait for.

Palermo, Monday April 2nd, 1787
By three o'clock pm, we at last, after much trouble and difficulty, got into harbour, where a most glorious view lay before us. Perfectly recovered from my sea-sickness, I enjoyed it highly. The town facing north, lay at the foot of a high hill, with the sun (at this time of day) shining above it. The sides of the buildings which looked towards us, lay in a deep shade, which, however, was clear, and lit up by the reflection from the water. On our right Monte Pellegrino, with its many elegant outlines, in full light; on the left the coast, with its bays, isthmuses, and headlands, stretching far away into the distance; and the most agreeable effect was produced by the fresh green of some fine trees, whose crowns, lit up from behind, swayed backwards and forwards before the dark buildings, like great masses of glow-worms. A brilliant haze gave a blueish tint to all the shades.

Instead of hurrying impatiently on shore, we remained on deck till we were actually forced to land; for where could we hope soon to find a position equal to this, or so favourable a point of view?

Through the singular gateway, which consists of two vast pillars, which are left unconnected above, in order that the tower-high car of St Rosalia may be able to pass through, on her famous festival, we were driven into the city, and alighted, almost immediately, at a large hotel on our left. The host, an old, decent person, long accustomed to see strangers of every nation and tongue, conducted us into a large room, the balcony of which commanded a view of the sea, with the roadstead, where we recognised our ship, Monte Rosalia, and the beach, and were enabled to form an idea of our whereabouts. Highly satisfied with the position of our room, we did not for some time observe that, at the farther end of it, was an alcove, slightly raised, and concealed by curtains, in which was a most spacious bed, with a magnificent canopy and curtains of silk, in perfect keeping with the other stately, but old fashioned, furniture of our apartment. This display of splendour made me uneasy; so, as my custom was, I wished to make an agreement with my host. To this the old man replied that conditions were unnecessary, and he trusted I should have nothing to complain of in him. We were also at liberty to make use of the ante-room, which was next to our apartment, and cool, airy, and agreeable from its many balconies.

We amused ourselves with the endless variety of views and endeavoured to sketch them one by one in pencil, or in colours, for here the eye fell upon a plentiful harvest for the artist.

In the evening the lovely moonlight attracted us once more to the roadstead, and even after our return riveted us for some time on the balcony. The light was peculiar – the repose and loveliness of the scene were extreme.

Palermo, Tuesday April 3rd, 1787

Our first business was to examine the city, which is easy enough to survey, but difficult to know; easy, because a street a mile long, from the lower to the upper gate, from the sea to the mountain, intersects it, and is itself again crossed, nearly in its middle, by another. Whatever lies on these two great lines is easily found; but in the inner streets a stranger soon loses himself, and without a guide will never extricate himself from their labyrinths.

Towards evening our attention was directed to the long line of carriages ... in which the principal persons of the neighbourhood were taking their evening drive from the city to the beach, for the sake of the fresh air, amusement, and perhaps also for intrigue.

It was full moon about two hours before midnight, and the evening was in consequence indescribably glorious. The northerly position of Palermo produces a very strange effect; as the city and shore come between the sun and the harbour, its reflection is never observed on the waves. On this account, though it was one of the very brightest of days yesterday, I found the sea of a deep blue colour, solemn, and oppressive; whereas, at Naples, after noon-day, it gets brighter and brighter, and glitters with more airy lightness, and to a greater distance.

Kniep has today left me to make my pilgimages and observations by myself, in order that he might accurately sketch the outline of Monte Pellegrino, the most beautiful headland in the whole world.

Palermo, Wednesday April 4th, 1787
In the afternoon we paid a visit to the fertile and delightful valley at the foot of the Southern Mountains, running by Palermo, and through which the Oreto meanders. Here, too, is a call for the painter's eye, and a practised hand to convey an idea of it. Kniep, however, hastily seized an excellent point of view at a spot where the pent-up water was dashing down from a half-broken weir, and was shaded by a lovely group of trees, behind which an uninterrupted prospect opened up the valley, affording a view of several farm buildings.

Beautiful spring weather, and a budding luxuriance, diffused over the whole valley a refreshing feeling of peace, which our stupid guide marred by his ill-timed erudition, telling us that in former days, Hannibal had fought a battle here, and circumstantially detailing all the dreadful feats of war which had been perpetrated on the spot. In no friendly mood I reproved him for thus fatally calling up again such departed spectres. It was bad enough, I said, that from time to time the crops should be trodden down, if not by elephants, yet by men and horses. At any rate, it was not right to scare away the peaceful dreams of imagination by reviving such tumults and horrors.

The guide was greatly surprised that I could, on such a spot, despise classical reminiscences; and I, too, could not make him understand how greatly such a mingling of the past with the present displeased me.

Still more singular did our guide deem me, when at all the shallow places, of which many were left quite dry by the stream, I searched for pebbles, and carried off with me specimens of each sort. I again found it difficult to make him understand that there was no readier way of forming an idea of a mountainous district like that before us, than by examining the nature of the stones which are washed down by the streams, and that in so doing, the purpose was to acquire a right notion of those eternally classic heights of the ancient world.

And, indeed, my gains from this stream were large enough: I carried away nearly forty specimens, which, however, may be comprised under a few classes. Most of these were of a species of rock, which, in one respect, might be regarded as a sort of jasper or hornblende; in another, looked like clay-slate. I found some pebbles rounded,

113

others of a rhomboidal shape, others of irregular forms, and of various colours. Moreover, many varieties of the primeval limestone, not a few specimens of breccia, of which the substratum was lime, and holding jasper, or modifications of limestone. Rubbles of muschelkalk also were not wanting.

The horses here are fed on barley, chaff (*hackerling*) and clover. In spring they give them the green barley, in order to refresh them – *per rinfrescar* is the phrase. As there are no meadows here, they have no hay. On the hillsides there are some pasturelands, and also in the cornfields, as a third is always left fallow. They keep but few sheep, and these are of a breed from Barbary. On the whole they have more mules than horses, because the hot food suits the former better than the latter.

The plain on which Palermo lies, as well as the districts of Ai Colli, which lie without the city, and a part also of Baggaria, have for their basis the muschelkalk, of which the city is built. There are, for this purpose, extensive quarries of it in the neighbourhood. In one place, near Monte Pellegrino, they are more than fifty feet deep. The lower layers are of a whiter hue. In it are found many petrified corals and other shell-fish, but principally great scallops. The upper stratum is mixed with red marl, and contains but few, if any, fossils. Right above it lies the red marl, of which, however, the layer is not very stiff.

Monte Pellegrino, however, rises out of all this; it is a primary limestone, has many hollows and fissures, which, although very irregular, when closely observed are found to follow the order of the strata. The stone is close, and rings when struck.

Palermo, Thursday April 5th, 1787
We have gone carefully through the city. The style of architecture resembles for the most part that of Naples; but the public buildings, for instance the fountains, are still further removed from good taste. Here there is no artistic mind to regulate the public works; the edifices owe both their shape and existence to chance accidents. A fountain, which is the admiration of the whole island, would, perhaps, never have existed, had not Sicily furnished a beautiful variegated marble, and had not a sculptor, well practised in animal shapes, happened to be in favour precisely at the time. It would be a difficult matter to describe this fountain. In a moderately-sized site stands a round piece of masonry, not quite a staff high. The socle, the wall, and the cornice are of variegated marble. In the wall are several niches in a row, from which animals of all kinds in white marble, are looking with stretched-out necks. Horses, lions, camels, and elephants are interchanged one with another; and one scarcely expects to find, within the circle of this menagerie, a fountain, to which, through four openings, marble steps lead you down to draw from the water, which flows in rich abundance.

The same nearly may be said of the churches, in which even the Jesuits' love of show and finery is surpassed – but not from design or plan, but by accident – just as artist after artist, whether sculptor or carver, gilder, lackerer, or worker in marble chose, without taste or rule, to display on each vacant spot his own abilities.

Amidst all this, however, one cannot fail to recognize a certain talent in imitating natural objects; for instance, the heads of the animals around the fountains are very well executed. By this means it is, in truth, that the admiration of the multitude is excited, whose artistic gratification consists chiefly in comparing the imitation with its living prototype.

Towards evening I made a merry acquaintance, as I entered the house of a small dealer in the Long Street, in order to purchase some trifles. As I stood before the window to look at the wares, a slight breeze arose, which eddying along the whole street, at last distributed through all the windows and doors the immense cloud of dust which it had raised. 'By all the saints,' I cried, 'whence comes all the dust of your town – is there no helping it? In its length and beauty, this street vies with any in the Corso in Rome. On both sides a fine pavement, which each stall and shop-holder keeps clean by interminable sweeping, but brushes everything into the middle of the street, which is, in consequence, so much the dirtier, and with every breath of wind sends back to you the filth which has just before been swept into the roadway. In Naples busy donkeys carry off day by day the rubbish to the gardens and farms. Why should you not here contrive and establish some similar regulation?'

'Things with us are as they are,' he replied; 'we throw everything out of the house, and it rots before the door; you see here horse-dung and filth of all kinds – it lies there and dries, and returns to us again in the shape of dust. Against it we are taking precautions all day long. But look, our pretty little and ever-busy brooms, worn out at last, only go to increase the heap of filth before our doors.'

And oddly enough it was actually so. They had nothing but very little besoms of palm-branches, which, slightly altered, might have been really useful; but as it was, they broke off easily, and the stumps were lying by thousands in the streets. To my repeated questioning, whether there was no board or regulations to prevent all this; he replied, 'A story is current among the people that those whose duty it was to provide for the cleansing of our streets, being men of great power and influence, could not be compelled to disburse the money on its lawful objects; and besides that there was also the strange fact that certain parties feared that if the dirty straw and dung were swept away, everyone would see how badly the pavement beneath was laid down. And so the dishonesty of a second body would be thereby exposed. 'All this, however,' he remarked, with a most humorous expression, 'is merely the interpretation which the ill-disposed put upon it.' For his part, he was of the opinion of those who maintained that the nobles preserved this soft litter for their carriages, in order that, when they take their drive for amusement in the evening, they might ride at ease over the elastic ground. And as the man was now in the humour, he joked away at many of the abuses of the police – a consolatory proof to me that man has always humour enough to make merry with what he cannot help.

Palermo, April 14th, 1787

Towards evening I paid a visit to my friend the shopkeeper, to ask him how he thought the festival was likely to pass off; for tomorrow there is to be a solemn procession through the city, and the Viceroy is to accompany the host on foot. The least wind will envelop both man and the sacred symbols in a thick cloud of dust.

With much humour he replied: In Palermo, the people look for nothing more confidently than for a miracle. Often before now on such occasions, a violent passing shower had fallen and cleansed the streets partially at least, so as to make a clean road for the procession. On this occasion a similar hope was entertained, and not without cause, for the sky was overcast, and promised rain during the night.

Palermo, Sunday April 15th, 1787

And so it has actually turned out! During the night the most violent of showers have fallen. In the morning I set out very early in order to be an eyewitness of the marvel. The stream of rain-water pent up between the two raised pavements had carried the lightest of the rubbish down the inclined street, either into the sea or into such of the sewers as were not stopped up, while the grosser and heavier dung was driven from spot to spot. In this a singular meandering line of cleanliness was marked out along the streets. On the morning hundreds and hundreds of men were to be seen with brooms and shovels, busily enlarging this clear space, and in order to connect it where it was interrupted by the mire; and throwing the still remaining impurities now to this side, now to that. By this means when the procession started, it found a clear serpentine walk prepared for it through the mud, and so both the long robed priests and the neat-booted nobles, with the Viceroy at their head, were able to proceed on their way unhindered and unsplashed.

I thought of the children of Israel passing through the waters by the dry path prepared for them by the hand of the Angel, and this remembrance served to ennoble what otherwise would have been a revolting sight – to see these devout and noble peers parading their devotions along an alley, flanked on each side by heaps of mud.

On the pavement there was now, as always, clean walking; but in the more retired parts of the city whither we were this day carried in pursuance of our intention of visiting the quarters which we had hitherto neglected, it was almost impossible to get along, although even here the sweeping and piling of the filth was by no means neglected.

The festival gave occasion to our visiting the principal church of the city and observing its curiosities. Being once on the move, we took a round of all the other public edifices. We were much pleased with a Moorish building, which is in excellent preservation – not very large, but the rooms beautiful, broad, and well proportioned, and in excellent keeping with the whole pile. It is not perhaps suited for a northern climate, but in a southern land a most agreeable residence. Architects may perhaps some day furnish us with a plan and elevation of it.

We also saw in most unsuitable situations various remains of ancient marble statues, which, however, we had not patience to try to make out.

Alcamo, Wedesday April 18th, 1787
At an early hour, we rode out of Palermo. Kniep and the Vetturino showed their skill in packing the carriage inside and out. We drove slowly along the excellent road, with which we had previously become acquainted during our visit to San Martino, and wondered a second time at the false taste displayed in the fountains on the way. At one of these our driver stopped to supply himself with water according to the temperate habits of this country. He had, at starting, hung to the traces a small wine-cask, such as our market-women use, and it seemed to us to hold wine enough for several days. We were, therefore, not a little surprised when he made for one of the many conduit pipes, took out the plug of his cask, and let the water run into it. With true German amazement, we asked him what ever he was about? Was not the cask full of wine? To all which, he replied with great nonchalance: he had left a third of it empty, and as no one in this country drank unmixed wine, it was better to mix it at once in a large quantity, as then the liquids combined better together, and besides you were not sure of finding water everywhere. During this conversation the cask was filled, and we had some talk together of this ancient and oriental wedding custom.

And now as we reached the heights beyond Mon Reale, we saw wonderfully beautiful districts, but tilled in traditional rather than in a true economical style. On the right, the eye reached the sea, where, between singular shaped headlands, and beyond a shore here covered with, and there destitute of, trees, it caught a smooth and level horizon, perfectly calm, and forming a glorious contrast with the wild and rugged limestone rocks. Kniep did not fail to take miniature outlines of several of them.

We are at present in Alcamo, a quiet and clean little town, whose well-conducted inn is highly to be commended as an excellent establishment, especially as it is most conveniently situated for visitors to the temple of Segeste, which lies out of the direct road in a very lonely situation.

Alcamo, Thursday April 19th, 1787

Our agreeable dwelling in this quiet town, among the mountains, has so charmed us that we have determined to pass a whole day here. We may then, before anything else, speak of our adventures yesterday. In one of my earlier letters, I questioned the originality of Prince Pallagonia's bad taste. He has had forerunners and can adduce many a precedent. On the road towards Mon Reale stand two monstrosities, beside a fountain with some vases on a balustrade, so utterly repugnant to good taste that one would suppose they must have been placed there by the Prince himself.

After passing Mon Reale, we left behind us the beautiful road, and got into the rugged mountain country. Here some rocks appeared on the crown of the road, which, judging from their gravity and metallic incrustations, I took to be ironstone. Every level spot is cultivated, and is more or less prolific. The limestone in these parts had a reddish hue, and all the pulverized earth is of the same colour. This red argillaceous and calcareous earth extends over a great space; the subsoil is hard; no sand underneath; but it produces excellent wheat. We noticed old very strong, but stumpy, olive trees.

Under the shelter of an airy room, which has been built as an addition to the wretched inn, we refreshed ourselves with a temperate luncheon. Dogs eagerly gobbled up the skins of the sausages we threw away, but a beggar-boy drove them off. He was feasting with a wonderful appetite on the parings of the apples we were devouring, when he in his turn was driven away by an old beggar. Want of work is here felt everywhere. In a ragged toga the old beggar was glad to get a job as house-servant, or waiter. Thus I had formerly observed that whenever a landlord was asked for anything which he had not at the moment in the house, he would send a beggar to the shop for it.

However, we are pretty well provided against all such sorry attendance; for our Vetturino is an excellent fellow – he is ready as ostler, cicerone, guard, courier, cook, and everything.

On the higher hills you find every where the olive, the caruba, and the ash. Their system of farming is also spread over three years. Beans, corn, fallow; in which mode of culture the people say the dung does more marvels than all the Saints. The grape stock is kept down very low.

Alcamo is gloriously situated on a height, at a tolerable distance from a bay of the sea. The magnificence of the country quite enchanted us. Lofty rocks, with deep valleys at their feet, but withal wide open spaces, and great variety. Beyond Mon Reale you look upon a beautiful double valley, in the centre of which a hilly ridge again raises itself. The fruitful fields lie green and quiet, but on the broad roadway the wild bushes and shrubs are brilliant with flowers – the broom one mass of yellow, covered with its pupilionaceous blossoms, and not a single green leaf to be seen; the white thorn cluster on cluster; the aloes are rising high and promising to flower; a rich tapestry of an amaranthine-red clover, orchids and the little Alpine roses, hyacinths, with unopened bells, asphodels, and other wild flowers.

The streams which descend from Mt Segeste leave deposits, not only of limestone, but also of pebbles of hornstone. They are very compact, dark blue, yellow, red, and brown, of various shades. I also found complete lodes of horn, or fire-stone, in the limestone rocks, edged with lime. Of such gravel one finds whole hills just before one gets to Alcamo.

Segeste, April 20th, 1787
The temple of Segeste was never finished; the ground around it was never even levelled; the space only being smoothed on which the peristyle was to stand. For, in several places, the steps are from nine to ten feet in the ground, and there is no hill near, from which the stone or mould could have fallen. Besides, the stones lie in their natural position, and no ruins are found near them.

The columns are all standing; two which had fallen, have very recently been raised again. How far the columns rested on a socle is hard to say; and without an engraving it is difficult to give an idea of their present state. At some points it would seem as if the pillars rested on the fourth step. In that case to enter the temple you would have to go down a step. In other places, however, the uppermost step is cut through, and then it looks as if the columns had rested on bases; and then again these spaces have been filled up, and so we have once more the first case. An architect is necessary to determine this point.

The sides have twelve columns, not reckoning the corner ones; the back and front six, including them. The rollers on which the stones were moved along, still lie around you on the steps. They have been left in o rder to indicate that the temple was unfinished. But the strongest evidence of this fact is the floor. In some spots (along the sides) the pavement is laid down, in the middle, however, the red limestone rock still projects higher than the level of the floor as partially laid; the flooring, therefore, cannot ever have been finished. There is also no trace of an inner temple. Still less can the temple have ever been overlaid with stucco; but that it was intended to do so, we may infer from the fact that the *abaci* of the capitals have projecting points probably for the purpose of holding the plaster. The whole is built of a limestone, very similar to the travertine; only it is now much fretted. The restoration which was carried on in 1781, has done much good to the building. The cutting of the stone, with which the parts have been reconnected, is simple, but beautiful. The large blocks standing by themselves, which are mentioned by Riedesel, I could not find; probably they were used for the restoration of the columns.

The site of the temple is singular; at the highest end of a broad and long valley, it stands on an isolated hill. Surrounded, however, on all sides by cliffs, it commands a very distant and extensive view of the land, but takes in only just a corner of the sea. The district reposes in a sort of melancholy fertility – every where well cultivated, but scarce a dwelling to be seen. Flowering thistles were swarming with countless butterflies, wild fennel stood here from eight to nine feet high, dry and withered of the last year's growth, but so rich and in such seeming order that one might almost take it to be an old nursery-ground. A shrill wind whistled through the columns as if through a wood, and screaming birds of prey hovered around the pediments.

Castel Vetrano, Saturday April 21st, 1787
From Alcamo to Castel Vetrano you come on the limestone, after crossing some hills of gravel. Between precipitous and barren limestone mountains, lie wide undulating valleys, everywhere tilled, with scarcely a tree to be seen. The gravelly hills are full of large bolders, giving signs of ancient inundations of the sea. The soil is better mixed and lighter than any we have hitherto seen, in consequence of its containing some sand. Leaving Salemi about fifteen miles to our right, we came upon hills of gypsum, lying on the limestone. The soil appears, as we proceed, to be better and more richly compounded. In the distance you catch a peep of the Western sea. In the foreground the country is everywhere hilly. We found the fig-trees just budding, but what most excited our delight and wonder was endless masses of flowers, which had encroached on the broad road, and flourish in large variegated patches. Closely bordering on each other, the several sorts, nevertheless, keep themselves apart and recur at regular intervals. The most beautiful convolvoluses, hibiscuses, and mallows, various kinds of trefoil, here and there the garlic, and the galega-gestrauche. On horseback you may ride through this varied tapestry, by following the numberless and ever-crossing narrow paths which run through it. Here and there you see feeding fine red-brown cattle, very clean-limbed and with short horns of an extremely elegant form.

The mountains to the north-east stand all in a line. A single peak, Cuniglione, rises boldly from the midst of them. The gravelly hills have but few streams; very little rain seems to fall here; we did not find a single gully giving evidence of having ever overflowed.

In the night I met with a singular incident. Quite worn out, we had thrown ourselves on our beds in anything but a very elegant room. In the middle of the night I saw above me a most agreeable phenomenon – a star brighter, I think, than I ever saw one before. Just, however, as I began to take courage at a sight which was of good omen, my patron star suddenly disappeared, and left me in darkness again. At daybreak, I at last discovered the cause of the marvel: there was a hole in the roof, and at the moment of my vision one of the brightest stars must have been crossing my meridian. This purely natural phenomenon was, however, interpreted by us travellers as highly favourable.

The interior of the island strikes the traveller as a poet's territory more than a prose writer's; at the very least it takes a poet's sensibility. The stars are very bright in Sicily; this autumn I have been beguiled almost every night by Venus and the planet Mars, hanging like a lantern in the southern sky. The mountains swing and swell in rearing symphonies of rock and green; the sunburned lands have a silent, indifferent ferocity. In spring – the Italian *primavera* seems a better word for it – the valleys and pastures run with flowers. For a sense of the country it is worth abandoning chronology for some of the poems of one of Sicily's Nobel Laureates, the poet Salvatore Quasimodo, who was born in Syracuse in 1901, the son of a station master. His first collection, *Waters and Lands* came out in 1930. Quasimodo did various jobs before he became a Professor of Italian Literature at the University of Milan: he built roads and held administrative posts in the Ministry of Public Works. Though he spent large chunks of his life in northern Italy, his homeland is everywhere in his work, and his first collection is entirely devoted to her.

Salvatore Quasimodo
And Suddenly It's Evening

Each of us is alone on the heart of the earth
pierced by a ray of sun:
and suddenly it's evening.

No Night So Clear Ever Vanquished You

No night so clear ever vanquished you
if you open yourself up to laughter and all seems to touch
a stairway of stars
that once in dream came spiralling down,
putting me back in time.

Then God was fear of a closed room
where a dead one lies,
centre of all things,
clear sky and wind, ocean and cloud.

And my throwing myself on the ground,
my crying the name out loud in the silence
was sweetness of feeling myself alive.

Cool Seashore

I compare my man's life to you,
cool seashore, drawing pebbles and light
and forgetting with the new wave
the one that once the air's moving gave voice to.

If you rouse me I listen,
and every pause is sky I lose myself in,
calm of trees and the night's transparency.

Just before Goethe, another highly literate tourist arrived on the island. Patrick
Brydone recorded his impressions of Sicily in a series of letters written in the
summer of 1770 to his friend William Beckford. They make a fine companion
to Goethe's more cerebral pieces: Brydone, also an acute observer, is less of a
social scientist than Goethe, and more interested in people and stories.

> *Palermo June 19th 1770*
> The approach to Palermo is fine. The alleys are planted with fruit trees,
> and large American Aloes in full blow. Near to the city we passed a place
> of execution, where the quarters of a number of robbers were hung up
> upon hooks, like so many hams; some of them appeared newly executed,
> and made a very unsightly figure. On our arrival, we learned that a priest
> and three others had been taken a few days ago, after an obstinate defence,
> in which several were killed on both sides; the priest, rather than submit
> to his conquerors, plunged his hanger into his breast, and died on the
> spot: the rest were executed.

July 1770

The Sicilians are very animated in conversation, and their action for the most part is so just and so expressive of their sentiments, that without hearing what is said one may comprehend the subject of their discourse. We used to think the French and Neapolitans great adepts of this art; but they are much outdone by the Sicilians, both in variety and justness of gesticulation.

The origin of this custom [goes] so far back as the time of the earliest Tyrants of Syracuse, who, to prevent conspiracies, had forbid their subjects, under the most severe penalties, to be seen in parties talking together. This obliged them to invent a method of communicating their sentiments by dumb show, which they pretend has been transmitted from generation to generation ever since.

Regardless of the source of the story, Brydone was absolutely right about the eloquence of Sicilian gestures. As well as countless improvisations there are certain formulae: the edge of one hand smacked up into the underside of the other means 'let's go!' A finger screwed into the corner of the mouth says 'sweet', or toothsome. Shoulders and chest thrust forward, arms slightly back, is a loud protest of ignorance. My particular favourite, a cupped hand brushing the underside of the raised chin with the fingertips, is a denial and contradiction, much deployed by my friend Paolo, a retired professor of Greek and Latin from Agrigento. Paolo had a visceral loathing for the airs, antics and pronouncements of the Prime Minister at the time of my stay, Silvio Berlusconi. When Paolo is describing some rightist scheme he makes this gesture, his hooded eyes glittering, and looks as though he is miming a man up to his neck in shit – where most left-leaning Italians, and large sections of the judiciary and the press, believe Berlusconi to be.

The Sicilian ladies marry very young, and frequently live to see the fifth or sixth generation. You will expect, no doubt, that I should say something of their beauty: In general they are sprightly and agreeable, and in most parts of Italy they would be deemed handsome. The ladies here have memorable fine hair, and they understand how to dress and adorn it to the greatest advantage. It is now only used as an embellishment, but in former times we are told, that like that of Sampson it was found to be the strength and protection of their country. Their historians relate (in whose reign I believe is rather dubious) that their city had suffered a long siege from the Saracens, and was greatly reduced to famine, but, what distressed them still more, there were no materials to be found for the making of bowstrings, and they were on the point of surrendering. In this dilemma, a patriotic dame stepped forth, and proposed to the women, that the whole of them should cut off their hair, and twist it into bowstrings. This was immediately complied with. The heroism of the women, you know, must ever excite that of their men. The besieged, animated by this gallant sacrifice of the fair, renewed their defence with such vigour, that assailants were beat off; and a reinforcement soon arriving, the city was saved. The ladies still value themselves on this story, which you may believe has not been forgotten by their bards. The hair of our ladies (says one of their quaint poets) is still employed in the same office; but now it discharges no other shafts than those of cupid; and the only cords it forms are the cords of love.

One of the highlights of Brydone's visit, and certainly one of the phenomena which excites the most comment from him, was his encounter with the Sirocco. It seems he had heard much about it, and like all British and Irishmen he was much enthused by the prospect of some remarkable weather: he was not all disappointed. August is the traditional time to flee Palermo's heat, but the July of 1770 evidently brought some scorching days too.

On Sunday we had the long expected Sirocco wind, which, although our expectations had been raised pretty high, yet I own it greatly exceeded them. Friday and Saturday were uncommonly cool, the mercury never being higher than seventy two and a half; and although the Sirocco is said to have set in early on Sunday morning, the air in our apartments, which are very large, with high ceilings, was not in the least affected by it at eight o'clock, when I rose. I opened the door without having any suspicion of such a change; and indeed I was never more astonished in my life. The first blast of it on my face felt like the burning steam from the mouth of an oven. I drew back hard and shut the door, calling out to Fullarton, that the whole atmosphere was in a flame. It felt somewhat like the subterranean sweating stoves at Naples; but still much hotter. In a few minutes we found every fibre greatly relaxed, and the pores opened to such a degree, that we expected soon to be thrown into a profuse sweat. I took the thermometer out to the open air, where it immediately rose to one hundred and ten, and soon after to one hundred and twelve. The sun did not appear the whole day, otherwise I am persuaded that the heat must have been insupportable; on that side of the platform which is exposed to the wind it was with difficulty that we could bear it for a few minutes. I attempted to take a walk in the street to see if any creature was stirring, but I found it too much for me, and was glad to get upstairs again.

This extraordinary heat continued till three o'clock in the afternoon, when the wind changed at once, almost to the opposite point of the compass, and all the rest of the day it blew strong from the sea. It is impossible to conceive the different feeling of the air. The wind no sooner changed to the North, than it felt extremely cold, and we were soon obliged to put on our clothes, for till then we had been almost naked.

I own to you my curiosity with regard to the Sirocco is now thoroughly satisfied: nor do I at all wish for another visit of it during our stay in Sicily. Many of our acquaintance laughed at us for exposing ourselves so long to it; and they were surprised that our curiosity should lead us to make experiments at the expense of our persons. They assure us, that during the time it lasts, there is not a mortal to be seen without doors, but those whom necessity obliges. All their doors and windows are shut close, to prevent the external air from entering; and where there are no window-shutters, they hang up wet blankets on the inside of the windows.

I have seen an old fellow here, who has written upon it. He says it is the same wind that is so dreadful in the sandy deserts of Africa, where it sometimes proves mortal in the space of half an hour.

I met the *sirocco* once or twice, but never at murderous pitch. In Agrigento in October it was welcomed by one restaurant-owner like the reappearance of an old friend whom he thought had gone with the summer. The Sicilians start dressing in jackets and even scarves with the first abating of the heat, in late Autumn, when the tourists are still in shorts, and while I was still marvelling at an apparently endless summer. The beach at Mondello was still busy until November. Salvatore Quasimodo took the memory of the wind north with him, and looked for it when he returned.

Salvatore Quasimodo
Street in Agrigentum

The wind is still there that I remember
kindling the manes of horses coursing
oblique across the plains; a wind
that stains and gnaws the sandstone and the heart
of the doleful telamons lying
felled on the grass.
Ancient soul grey with bitterness
you return with the wind, sniff
the delicate moss that clothes
the giants thrust down from the sky.
How lonely you are in the space that remains to you;
and greater your grief, if you hear again the sound
as it moves far off and opens out to the sea
where morning Hesperus now creeps.
The marranzano twangs
sad in the carter's throat as he climbs
slow the moon-sharpened hill
in the murmur of saracen olive trees.

Agrigento would have been a beautiful town, with its Arab streets climbing the hill to the cathedral, with its promenades, soft sea views and the famous ridge of Greek temples, but it has been throttled, garrotted by a knotted grey noose of motorways and junctions. Modern man's contribution to the incomparable beauty of the Sicilian landscape is almost everywhere appalling. Where our predecessors raised temples to everything that is best in man, God and nature, in our time we chose to worship the automobile. An observer cannot help but feel that the stupefying piles of money which must have gone into the construction of the roads – halfway between runways and railway lines, which fly imperiously over the valleys rather than following their contours – would have been better off burned, which would at least have prevented huge chunks of it falling into the hands of the mafia, which despite the claims of some writers, traditions and no doubt the killers themselves, was still at least half a century from formation at the time of Brydone's visit.

Sicily in the later eighteenth century was still under Bourbon rule, in the form of Ferdinand IV, regent of the south of Italy and Sicily (in 1816 this would be formalised as the Kingdom of the Two Sicilies with Palermo and Naples as its capitals). The king was a Neapolitan in everything but blood and name: he had not been crowned in Palermo, where he was still Ferdinand III; he did not even visit his island until 1798, when a post-revolutionary French army invaded Italy from the north. Ferdinand sent an army to Rome in the hope of restoring papal rule and bringing down the republic the French established there, but the manoeuvre failed. The King then raided his city's banks, took as much of Naples' art and as many of its artefacts as he could cram into his ships, and fled to Palermo, escorted by the Royal Navy – then commanded in the Mediterranean by Horatio Nelson, who had recently returned from fighting the French off the Egyptian coast at the battle of the Nile. In 1799 the Neapolitans established a republic in the king's absence, but a French withdrawal, a British blockade of the Bay of Naples and a counterrevolutionary army led by one Cardinal Ruffo, all combined to strangle it.

British policy was principally concerned with the fight with France and French-backed republicanism. In the service of that aim, Nelson's ships and British troops restored Bourbon rule in Naples with much shameful bloodletting. One of the admiral's aides wrote 'We commit the most horrible infamies to put the stupidest of kings back on his throne.'

In December 1799, before his return to Naples, Ferdinand threw a great party for Nelson in the Royal Palace in Palermo: he presented the one-eyed warrior with a laurel crown, a diamond-studded sword, and the Dukedom of Bronte, a small town, tipped in a jumble down the west side of Etna, between tortured old lava flows. No doubt the admiral was touched, but his mind was surely on other things. His personal life was exciting, since he had fallen in love with the beautiful Lady Emma Hamilton, who had thrown herself at him in Naples (her husband, Sir William, did nothing to prevent the affair, and the three now travelled as a unit) and he could see busy professional times ahead, thanks to Napoleon Bonaparte, who was now in power in France.

Six years later Nelson was dead, having won the battle of Trafalgar; Emma was spending the money he and William had left her, on her way to penury; the French were back in Naples (Napoleon declared the existence of the Naples Bourbons 'incompatible with the peace of Europe and the honour of my crown') and Ferdinand back in Sicily, protected once again by the Royal Navy. He crowned himself Ferdinand IV, and then, with the eventual fall of Napoleon in 1815, he started again, renumbering himself Ferdinand I of the Kingdom of the Two Sicilies. As the popular Sicilian rhyme put it: 'You were the fourth, you were the third, now you call yourself the first. If you continue with this joke ('scherzo') you'll end up a zero.'

British influence in Sicily had a number of effects, which may have seemed minor at the time, but which were to have significant consequences. Nelson had ordered a great deal of wine for his fleet, which vitalised the industry of Marsala, and, to prevent scurvy, had been prepared to pay good money for lemons and limes. The seeds of Sicily's next great export crop were planted, and with them, as we shall see, the seeds of its great curse.

The British had pushed Ferdinand into issuing a limited constitution for the island in 1812, but with their retreat, Ferdinand rolled back his reforms. As Ferdinand's successors, Francis I and Ferdinand II ignored the island, concentrating on defending Naples from the Austrians, discontent grew in Sicily. In 1839 in Naples gas lights appeared in the main streets, and the San Carlo theatre, while in Sicily one observer saw the peasants 'feed upon herbs, clothe themselves in rags, and sleep huddled up together in smoky huts amidst the stench of a dunghill.'

When the great year of revolutions came, 1848, Sicily was more than ready. Indeed, the rising in Sicily began a good month before that in Paris: the wind that was to overturn so many power-structures in Europe that year first blew in Palermo, on January 12th, when rioting broke out and revolutionary committees formed, demanding the reissue of the 1812 constitution. On January 15th Bourbon troops shelled the city from the safety of the Royal Palace, earning Ferdinand II his Sicilian title 'Re Bomba', King Bomb. Three weeks later the whole island was in revolt. The rebellion lasted until May 1849 when Bourbon troops entered Palermo and began reprisals: many hundreds were jailed, executed or exiled. The repressive, corrupt and despotic rule of the south fell further and further out of step with the rest of Europe. William Gladstone visited the kingdom in 1850 and pronounced it 'the negation of God erected into a system of government.'

The kingdom tottered on, an international pariah, whose populace seethed with a sullen desire for vengeance and freedom, until 1859 and the death of Ferdinand. His son, Francis II, was twenty-three, and not a forceful youth. In April 1860 rioting broke out again in Palermo, and in May, Guiseppe Garibaldi sailed to Sicily from Genoa with his thousand, and landed in Marsala. In less than a year the Francis was in exile and the southern Kingdom gone.

The birth of modern Italy, and Sicily, was thus attended by violent revolution, upheaval and death. Garibaldi bought Sicily freedom from the Bourbons, but in his wake were left violence, lawlessness, poverty and corruption. The elites protected their holdings by force, and the new Italian state failed to impose any significant control on the island. While the peasants remained overwhelmingly illiterate and desperately poor, there were vast profits to be made from lemons, limes, land and the sulphur mines. The term 'mafia' was banded about whenever there was trouble, and there was often trouble. The government blamed this mysterious Sicilian force for the widespread resistance of the population to taxation, conscription and state authority, as if there was something malign in the very character of the island and its people. Not for the last time, a lazy and inaccurate government insult greatly enhanced the prestige and notoriety of what was then a loose association of criminal gangs which were forming like blood clots in the arteries of the island's wealth.

An encompassing portrait of Sicily in the 1860s was written in the 1950s by an aged Sicilian aristocrat, Giuseppe Tomasi di Lampedusa. If his novel, *The Leopard*, (*Il Gattopardo*) is not in your luggage or your head when you visit Sicily then you have a great treat, some would say a life-changing experience, awaiting you when you return home (though you might purchase a copy in English in the Feltrinelli shop on the Via Maqueda, Palermo).

For those of us with literary ambitions, Lampedusa provides a simultaneously daunting and delightful model. To write a book which will ensure your fame and good name centuries after your death, which will bring pleasure and enlightenment to all who read it, which will endure in freshness and beauty as only great art endures, is, if you follow Lampedusa, not such a complicated achievement.

You will need to travel: Lampedusa made a small tour to London in his youth. You will need to learn languages and read massively, and with great art and attention: Lampedusa was an authority on the novel; his commentaries on Stendhal, Dickens and Shakespeare are supremely simple and penetrating tutorials. You will need to think, learn, listen and observe above all else: Lampedusa never did a stitch of work, beyond his reading, writing and some teaching. His familial wealth allowed him to dedicate his time to the life of his mind. You will need to understand, quietly and completely, the history and character of your subject and your place; you will need to feel it and comprehend it in your very blood. Then, when you are ready, and it may take a long time before you are, you simply sit down with a pen somewhere comfortable, paying no attention to things like publishers, agents, the appetites of the reading public, the literary marketplace or anything else, and write out your masterpiece. Then you can die, assured that you have done something worthwhile with your time on earth. Lampedusa lived to have his manuscript rejected by publishers, but not long enough to see it rediscovered, published, translated, and become a world-wide sensation. Ah, well. One imagines him shrugging in heaven, lighting a phlegmatic cigarette, and lifting an eyebrow at the way it all turned out.

The Leopard is the story of the last year in the life of Don Fabrizio, Prince of Salina, a Sicilian noble and the last of his line. It recounts the courtship and marriage of his nephew, Tancredi, to the beautiful Angelica Sedara, daughter of a prototype rural Mafioso. (He is not named as such explicitly, but Sedara's character and doings leave the issue in no doubt.) The action takes place at the beginning of the 1860s, as Garibaldi's red-capped thousand sweep away the remains of the Bourbon regime. The novel's great political insight is simple, and truly Sicilian: everything must appear to change, so that everything – the corruption, brutality and unfairness of power and wealth – might remain the same. Its understandings of the human character and conditions are more complex.

This excerpt, which comes near the end of the book, might serve as a sample of some of its many flavours. It is hoped that it will whet the appetite, and it will certainly not exhaust it. It may be enjoyed without fear of spoiling the plot.

Giuseppe Tomasi di Lampedusa
From *The Leopard*

A Ball

November, 1862

The Princess Maria Stella climbed into the carriage, sat down on the blue satin cushions and gathered around her as many rustling folds of her dress as she could. Meanwhile Concetta and Carolina were also getting in; they sat down in front of her, their identical pink dresses exhaling a faint scent of violets. Then a heavy foot on the running board made the barouche heel over on its high springs; Don Fabrizio was getting in too. The carriage was crammed, waves of silk, hoops of three crinolines, billowed, clashed, mingled almost to the height of their heads; beneath was a tight press of foot-gear, the girls' silken slippers, the Princess's russet ones, the Prince's patent leather pumps: each suffered from the other's feet and could find nowhere to put his own.

The mounting steps were folded, the footman given his orders. 'To Palazzo Ponteleone.' He got back on to the box, the groom holding the horses' bridles moved aside, the coachman gave an imperceptible click of his tongue, and the barouche slid into motion.

They were going to a ball.

Palermo at the moment was passing through one of its intermittent periods of social gaiety; there were balls everywhere. After the coming of the Piedmontese, after the Aspromonte affair, now that spectres of violence and spoliation had fled, the few hundred people who made up 'the world' never tired of meeting each other, always the same ones, to exchange congratulations on still existing.

So frequent were the various and yet identical parties that the Prince and Princess of Salina had moved to their town palace for three weeks so as not to have to make the long drive from San Lorenzo almost every night. The ladies' dresses would arrive from Naples in long black cases like coffins, and there would be an hysterical coming and going of milliners, hairdressers and shoemakers; of exasperated servants carrying excited notes to fitters. The Ponteleone ball was to be one of the most important of that short season; important for all concerned because of the standing of the family, the splendour of the palace and the number of guests; particularly important for the Salina who would be presenting to 'society' Angelica, their nephew's lovely bride-to-be. It was still only half-past ten, rather early to appear at a ball if one is Prince of Salina, whose arrival should be timed for when a fête is at its height. But this time they had to be early if they wanted to be there for the entry of the Sedàras, who were the sort of people ('they don't *know* yet, poor things') to take literally the times on the gleaming invitation card. It had taken a good deal of trouble to get one of those cards sent to them; no one knew them, and the Princess Maria Stella had been obliged to make a visit to Margherita Ponteleone ten days before; all had gone smoothly, of course, but even so it had been one of those little thorns that Tancredi's engagement had inserted into the Leopard's delicate paws...

The girls, incomprehensible beings for whom a ball is fun and not a tedious worldly duty, were chatting away gaily in low voices; the Princess Maria Stella felt her bag to assure herself she'd brought her little bottle of sal volatile; Don Fabrizio was enjoying in anticipation the effect of Angelica's beauty on all those who did not know her and of Tancredi's luck on all those who knew him too well. But a shadow lay across his contentment; what about Don Calogero's tail-coat? Certainly not like the one worn at Donnafugata; he had been put into the hands of Tancredi, who had dragged him off to the best tailor and even been present at fittings. Officially the result had seemed to satisfy him the other day; but in confidence he had said, 'The coat is the best we can do; Angelica's father lacks *chic*.' That was undeniable; but Tancredi had guaranteed a perfect shave and decently polished shoes. That was something.

Where the Bambinai slope comes out by the apse of San Domenico the carriage stopped; there was a faint tinkle and round the corner appeared a priest bearing a ciborium with the Blessed Sacrament; behind, a young acolyte held over him a white canopy embroidered in gold; in front another bore a big lighted candle in his left hand and in his right a little silver bell which he was shaking with obvious enjoyment. These were the Last Sacraments; in one of those barred houses someone was in a death agony. Don Fabrizio got out and knelt on the pavement, the ladies made the sign of the Cross, the tinkling faded into the alleys tumbling down towards San Giacomo, and the barouche, with its occupants given a salutary warning, set off again towards its destination, now close by.

They arrived, they alighted in the portico; the coach vanished into the immensity of the courtyard, whence came the sound of pawing horses and the gleams of equipages arrived before.

The great stairs were of rough material but superb proportions; from every step country plants spread rustic scents; on the landing between flights the amaranthine liveries of two footmen, motionless under their powder, set a note of bright colour in the pearly grey surroundings. From two high little grated windows came a gurgle of laughter and childish murmurs; the small Ponteleone grandchildren, excluded from the party, were looking on, making fun of the guests. The ladies smoothed down silken folds; Don Fabrizio, *gibus* under an arm, was head and shoulders above them, although a step behind. At the door of the first drawing-room they met their host and hostess; he, Don Diego, white-haired and paunchy, saved from looking plebeian only by his caustic eyes, she, Donna Margherita, with, between coruscating tiara and triple row of emeralds, the hooked features of an old priest.

'You've come early! All the better! But don't worry, *your* guests haven't appeared yet.' A new thorn pierced the sensitive fingertips of the Leopard. 'Tancredi's here already too.' There in the opposite corner of the drawing-room was standing their nephew, black and slim as an adder, surrounded by three or four young men whom he was making roar with laughter at little tales that were quite certainly indecent; but his eyes, restless as ever, were fixed on the entrance door. Dancing had already begun and through three, four, five ante-chambers came notes of an orchestra from the ballroom.

'We're also expecting Colonel Pallavicino, who did so well at Aspromonte.' This phrase from the Prince of Ponteleone was not as simple as it sounded.

On the surface it was a remark without political meaning, mere praise for the tact, the delicacy, the respect, the tenderness almost with which the Colonel had got a bullet fired into General Garibaldi's foot; and for the accompaniment too, the bowing, kneeling and hand-kissing of the wounded Hero lying under a chestnut tree on a Calabrian hillside, smiling from emotion and not from irony as he might well have done (for Garibaldi, alas, lacked a sense of humour).

At an intermediate stage of the princely psyche the phrase had a technical meaning and was intended to praise the Colonel for the aptness of his dispositions, the timely deployment of his battalions, and his ability to carry out successfully against the same adversary what Landi had so unaccountably failed to do at Calatafimi. At heart, though, Ponteleone thought that the Colonel 'did so well' by managing to stop, defeat, wound and capture Garibaldi, in so doing saving the compromise so laboriously achieved between the old state of things and the new.

Evoked, created almost by the approving words and still more approving thoughts, the Colonel now appeared at the top of the stairs. He was moving amid a tinkle of epaulettes, chains and spurs in his well-padded, double-breasted uniform, a plumed hat under his arm and his left wrist propped on a curved sabre. He was a man of the world with graceful manners, well-versed, as all Europe knew by now, in hand-kissings dense with meaning; every lady whose fingers were brushed by his perfumed moustaches that night was able to re-evoke from first-hand knowledge the historical incident so highly praised in the popular press.

After sustaining the shower of praise poured over him by the Ponteleone, after shaking the two fingers held out to him by Don Fabrizio, Pallavicino merged into the scented froth of a group of ladies. His consciously virile features emerged above snowy white shoulders, and an occasional phrase came over. 'I sobbed, countess, sobbed like a child'; or 'He looked fine and serene as an archangel.' The male sentimentality enchanted ladies reassured already by the musketry of his Bersaglieri.

Angelica and Don Calogero were late, and the Salina family were thinking of plunging into the other rooms when Tancredi was seen to detach himself from his little group and move like a dart towards the entrance: the expected pair had arrived. Above the ordered swirl of her pink crinoline Angelica's white shoulders merged into strong soft arms; her head looked small and proud on its smooth youthful neck adorned with intentionally modest pearls. And when from the opening of her long kid glove she drew a hand which though not small was perfectly shaped, on it was seen glittering the Neapolitan sapphire.

In her wake came Don Calogero, a rat escorting a rose: though his clothes had no elegance this time they were at least decent. His only mistake was wearing in his buttonhole the Cross of the Order of the Crown of Italy recently conferred on him; but this soon vanished into one of the secret pockets in Tancredi's tail-coat.

Her fiancé had already taught Angelica to be impassive, that fundamental of distinction ('You can be expansive and noisy only with me, my dear; with all others you must be the future Princess of Falconeri, superior to many, equal to all'), and so she greeted her hostess with a totally unspontaneous but highly successful mixture of virginal modesty, neo-aristocratic hauteur and youthful grace.

The Palermitans are Italians after all, and so particularly responsive to the appeal of beauty and the prestige of money; apart from which Tancredi, however attractive, being also notoriously penniless, was considered an undesirable match (mistakenly, as was seen afterwards when too late); and so he was appreciated more by married women than by marriageable girls. This merging of merits and demerits now had the effect of Angelica being received with unexpected warmth. One or two young men might well have regretted not having dug up for themselves so lovely an amphora brimming with coin: but Donnafugata was a fief of Don Fabrizio's, and if he had found that treasure there and then passed it to his beloved Tancredi, one could no more be jealous of that than of his finding a sulphur mine on his land; it was his property, there was nothing to be said.

But even this transient resentment melted before the rays of those eyes. At one moment there was quite a press of young men wanting to be introduced and to ask for a dance; to each one of them Angelica dispensed a smile from her strawberry lips, to each she showed her card in which every polka, mazurka and waltz was followed by the possessive signature: Falconeri. There was also a general attempt by young ladies to get on familiar terms; and after an hour Angelica found herself quite at her ease among people who had not the slightest idea of her mother's crudity or her father's rapacity.

Her bearing did not contradict itself for an instant; never was she seen wandering about alone with head in the clouds, never did her arms move from her body, never was her voice raised above the murmur (quite high anyway) of the other ladies. For Tancredi had told her the day before, 'Now darling, we (and so you too now) are more attached to our houses and furniture than we are to anything else; and nothing offends us more than carelessness about those; so look at everything and praise everything; anyway Palazzo Ponteleone is worth it; but as you're not just a girl from the provinces whom everything surprises, always put a little reserve into your praise; admire, but always compare with some arch-type seen before and known to be outstanding.' The long visits to the palace at Donnafugata had taught Angelica a great deal, so that evening she admired every tapestry, but said that the ones in Palazzo Pitti had a finer border; she praised a Madonna by Dolci but remembered that the Grand Duke's had a more expressive melancholy; even of the slice of tart brought her by an attentive young gentleman she said that it was excellent, almost as good as that of 'Monsu Gaston', the Salina chef. And as Monsu Gaston was positively the Raphael of cooks, and the tapestries of Palazzo Pitti the Monsu Gaston of hangings, no one could complain, in fact everyone was flattered by the comparison; and so from that evening she began to acquire the reputation of a polite but inflexible art expert which was to accompany her quite unwarrantably throughout her long life.

While Angelica reaped laurels, Maria Stella gossiped on a sofa with two old friends, and Concetta and Carolina froze with their shyness the politest partners. Don Fabrizio was wandering round the rooms; he kissed the hands of ladies he met, numbed the shoulders of men he wanted to greet, but could feel ill-humour creeping slowly over him. First of all he didn't like the house; the Ponteleone hadn't done it up for seventy years, it was still the same as in the time of Queen Maria Carolina, and he, who considered himself to have modern tastes, was indignant. 'Good God, with Diego's income it wouldn't take long to sweep away all these consoles, all these tarnished mirrors! Then order some decent rosewood and plush furniture, and so live in comfort himself and stop making his guests go round catacombs like these. I'll tell him so in the end.' But he never told Diego, for these opinions only stemmed from his mood and his tendency to contradiction; they were soon forgotten and he himself never changed a thing either at San Lorenzo or Donnafugata. Meanwhile, however, they served to increase his disquiet.

The women at the ball did not please him either. Two or three among the older ones had been his mistresses, and seeing them now, weighed down by years and daughters-in-law, it was an effort to imagine them as they were twenty years before, and he was annoyed at the thought of having thrown away his best years in chasing (and catching) such slatterns. The younger women weren't up to much either, except for one or two: the youthful Duchess of Palma, whose grey eyes and gentle reserve he admired, Tutú Làscari also, with whom, had he been younger, he might well have found himself in unique and exquisite harmony. But the others ... it was a good thing that Angelica had emerged from the shades of Donnafugata to show these Palermitans what a really lovely woman was like.

There was something to be said for his strictures; what with the frequent marriages between cousins in recent years due to sexual lethargy and territorial calculations, with the dearth of proteins and overabundance of starch in the food, with the total lack of fresh air and movement, the drawing-rooms were now filled with a mob of girls incredibly short, improbably dark, unbearably giggly. They were sitting around in huddles, letting out an occasional hoot at an alarmed young man, and destined, apparently, to act only as background to three or four lovely creatures such as the fair-haired Maria Palma, and the exquisite Eleonora Giardinelli, who glided by like swans over a frog-filled pool.

The more of them he saw the more put out he felt; his mind, conditioned by long periods of solitude and abstract thought, at one moment, as he was passing through a long gallery where a numerous colony of these creatures had gathered on the central *pouf*, got into a kind of hallucination; he felt like a keeper in a zoo looking after some hundred female monkeys; any moment he expected to see them clamber up the chandeliers and hang there by their tails, swinging to and fro, showing off their behinds and loosing a stream of nuts, shrieks and grins at pacific visitors below.

A religious evocation, oddly enough, drew him away from this zoologic vision. For from the group of crinolined monkeys rose a monotonous, continuous sacred cry. 'Maria! Maria!' the poor creatures were perpetually exclaiming. 'Maria, what a lovely house!' 'Maria, what a handsome man Colonel Pallavicino is!' 'Maria, how my feet are aching!' 'Maria, I'm so hungry! When does the supper-room open?' The name of the Virgin, invoked by that virginal choir, echoed throughout the gallery and changed the monkeys back into women, for the *ouistiti* of the Brazilian forests had not yet, as far as he knew, been converted to Catholicism.

Slightly nauseated, the Prince passed into the room next door, where were encamped the rival and hostile tribe of men; the younger were off dancing and those now there were only the older ones, all of them his friends. He sat down a little among them; there, instead of the name of the Queen of Heaven being taken in vain, the air was turgid with commonplaces. Among these men Don Fabrizio was considered an 'eccentric'; his interest in mathematics was taken almost as sinful perversion, and had he not been actually Prince of Salina and known as an excellent horseman, a tireless shot and a fair womaniser, his parallaxes and telescopes might have exposed him to the risk of outlawry. Even so they did not say much to him, for his cold blue eyes, glimpsed under the heavy lids, put would-be talkers off, and he often found himself isolated, not, as he thought, from respect, but from fear.

He got up; his melancholy had now changed to black gloom. He had been wrong to come to this ball; Stella, Angelica, his daughters, could easily have coped with it alone, and he at this moment would have been happily ensconced in his study next to the terrace in Villa Salina, listening to the tinkling of the fountain and trying to catch comets by their tails. 'Anyway, I'm here now; it would be rude to leave. Let's go and have a look at the dancing.'

The ballroom was all golden; smoothed on cornices, stippled on door-frames, damascened pale, almost silvery, over darker gold on door panels and on the shutters which covered and annulled the windows, conferring on the room the look of some superb jewel-case shut off from an unworthy world. It was not the flashy gilding which decorators slap on nowadays, but a faded gold, pale as the hair of certain nordic children, determinedly hiding its value under a muted use of precious material intended to let beauty be seen and cost forgotten. Here and there on the panels were knots of rococo flowers in a colour so faint as to seem just an ephemeral pink reflected from the chandeliers.

That solar hue, that variegation of gleam and shade, made Don Fabrizio's heart ache as he stood black and stiff in a doorway: this eminently patrician room reminded him of country things; the chromatic scale was the same as that of the vast wheat fields around Donnafugata, rapt, begging for pity from the tyrannous sun; in this room, too, as on his estates in mid August, the harvest had been gathered long ago and stacked elsewhere, leaving, as here now, a sole reminder in the colour of burnt up useless stubble. The notes of the waltz in the warm air seemed to him but a stylisation of the incessant winds harping their own sorrows on those parched surfaces, today, yesterday, tomorrow, forever and forever. The crowd of dancers among whom he could count so many near to him in blood if not in heart, began to seem unreal, made of the raw material of lapsed memories, more labile even than that of disturbing dreams. From the ceiling the gods, reclining on gilded couches, gazed down smiling and inexorable as a summer sky. They thought themselves eternal; but a bomb manufactured in Pittsburgh, Penn., was to prove the contrary in 1943.

'Fine, Prince, fine! They don't do things like this nowadays, with gold leaf at its present price!' Sedàra was standing beside him; his quick eyes were moving over the room, insensible to its charm, intent on its monetary value.

Quite suddenly Don Fabrizio felt a loathing for him; to the rise of this man and a hundred others like him, to their obscure intrigues and their tenacious greed and avarice, was due the sense of death looming darkly over these palaces; it was due to him and his colleagues, to their rancour and sense of inferiority, their incapacity for putting out blooms, that the black clothes of the men dancing reminded Don Fabrizio of crows veering to and from above lost valleys in search of putrid prey. He felt like giving a sharp reply and telling him to get out of his way. But he couldn't; the man was a guest, he was the father of that dear girl Angelica; and maybe, too, he was just as unhappy as others.

'Fine, Don Calogero, fine. But our young couple's the finest of all.' Tancredi and Angelica were passing in front of them at that moment, his gloved right hand on her waist, their outspread arms interlaced, their eyes gazing into each other's. The black of his tail-coat, the pink of her interweaving dress, looked like some unusual jewel. They were the most moving sight there, two young people in love dancing together, blind to each other's defects, deaf to the warnings of fate, deluding themselves that the whole course of their lives would be as smooth as the ballroom floor, unknowing actors set to play the parts of Juliet and Romeo by a director who had concealed the fact that tomb and poison were already in the script. Neither was good, each self-interested, turgid with secret aims; yet there was something sweet and touching about them both; those murky but ingenuous ambitions of theirs were obliterated by the words of jesting tenderness he was murmuring in her ear, by the scent of her hair, by the mutual clasp of those bodies destined to die.

III: People of the Earth

I N THE RICH, SOPHISTICATED, 'modern' north, when they wish to be dismissive and scornful, they call Sicilians and other southerners *terroni*, people of the earth. The Sicilians retort with *pollentoni*, pollenta-eaters; a cutting riposte, from the perspective of this island, where some of the best food in Europe is grown, eaten, caught and cooked. But *terroni* has a ring to it, too; summoning images of a small, sun-flayed race, with soil under their nails and the smell of livestock about them, barely fit for the rich, fast place the continent would like itself to be. Crossing south eastern Sicily by train and watching an old goatherd with a nut-brown face leading his flock down one of the yellow-white hills, his short, strong stride perfectly matched to the gradient of the hard, rippled hills on which he makes his living, you can see that this *is* a man of the earth, and a proud one. It is not a soft life, and within the living memory of the older islanders, surviving by what is on and under the Sicilian soil has been a grim struggle. The sulphur mines around Caltanisetta, for example, saw working conditions as dreadful as can be imagined, and many of the workers were children. No wonder the island bred men for whom any insult was mortal, and women accustomed to seeing their men die before their time.

One writer, whose life straddled the transformation of the island from the Kingdom of Two Sicilies to modern Italy, caught the condition of its working people, and made great, telling and revolutionary art of it, in the way that Dickens did for the English, and Zola for the French. Giovanni Verga was born in Catania in 1840, and died there in 1922. The son of a landowner, he published novels, plays and short stories, and came to be seen as the founder of Verismo, the Italian realist school of literature. One famous story, *Cavelleria Rusticana*, was turned into an opera by Pietro Mascagni. The one-act production was a sensational hit when it was produced in Rome in May 1890; at the age of twenty six, Mascagni reckoned the success of the first night had made him rich for life. The simple, passionate and violent depiction of Sicilian life ticked every box in the mainland mind concerning the nature and situation of the islanders. It was true, as the contemporary anthropologist, researcher and writer Leopoldo Franchetti observed during his tour of the island in 1876, that the government had failed to establish effective law, order or a monopoly of violence on the island, and that it was consequently plagued by banditry and score-settling, but this was the worst of it, not the whole of it, as the opera-goers might have thought. Verga's novel *I Malavoglia*, was published in English as *The House by the Medlar Tree*, and later filmed by Lucino Visconti as *La Terra Trema* (1948). It is the story of the struggle of the Malavoglia family, a clan of fishermen and women, living, or rather, surviving, in the village of Aci Trezza, near Catania. An attempt to better themselves, to put their fishing boat to more lucrative use, brings disaster. The author seems extremely pessimistic about the possibility of progress, or even its desirability. Lampedusa's hero, Don Fabrizio, echoes Verga in the implicit suggestion that here in Sicily nothing has changed and nothing will ever change, as though alternatives, socialist or capitalist, are even less attractive than stasis. Thus for a foreign reader there is an intriguing contradiction in Verga, whose clarity of vision seems to condemn the conditions of his subjects, but the dynamic of whose stories offers no hope or impetus for their improvement. Here is a realist writer, whose mastery of the demands of plots and stories leads him to dramatise moments of high crisis – his work has been compared to classical Greek drama. That these moments were reflections of reality is certain, but though they were not the whole story, they became it, in the eyes of the outside world. His work reinforces a stereotypical picture of a primitive, backward place, cursed with lawless killers, commonly described now as 'mafia', even as it shows the complexity and humanity of its inhabitants. The detail of Verga's stories, the way people talk, think and feel, shows a race of individuals as sophisticated as any, but one which is horribly held back, in the absence of the possibility of true social progress, transfixed and hemmed in by their conditions and traditions. One of the foremost critics of our day, James Woods, compares Verga's short stories to those of Chekov. It strikes the reader as just, but this is a Chekov with knives and axes.

Here, then, for its detailed characterisation and its blazing and incendiary heroine, comes *The She-Wolf.*

Giovanni Verga
From *Cavalleria Rusticana and Other Stories*

The She-Wolf

She was dark-haired, tall and lean, with firm, well-rounded breasts, though she was no longer young, and she had a pale complexion, like someone forever in the grip of malaria. The pallor was relieved by a pair of huge eyes and fresh red lips that looked as though they would eat you.

In the village they called her the She-Wolf because, no matter what she had, she was never satisfied. The women crossed themselves whenever they saw her coming, lone as a stray bitch, with the restless and wary appearance of a starving wolf. She would gobble up their sons and their husbands in the twinkling of an eye with those red lips of hers, and draw them to the tail of her skirt and transfix them with those devilish eyes, as though they were standing before the altar at St Agrippina's. Luckily the She-Wolf herself never set foot inside the church, either at Easter or at Christmas or to hear Mass or to go to confession. Father Angiolino of St Mary of Jesus, a true servant of God, had lost his soul on her account.

Maricchia, poor girl, a good and worthy soul, shed tears in secret because she was the She-Wolf's daughter and nobody would ever want to marry her, even though she too had a fine trousseau tucked away in a chest and a patch of decent land in the sun, like any other girl in the village.

Then it happened that the She-Wolf fell in love with a handsome young fellow back from the army, when the two of them were hay-making on the notary's farm. She'd fallen for him lock, stock and barrel, her flesh burning beneath her thick cotton bodice, and, staring into his eyes, she was overcome with the kind of thirst you would experience down in the valley on a hot midsummer day. But he just kept scything calmly away, head down over the hay, saying, 'What's the matter, Pina?' In the vast expanse of the fields, where all you could hear was the chirping of the crickets as they leapt, with the sun beating straight down, the She-Wolf tied up sheaf after sheaf, bundle after bundle, showing no sign of fatigue, never looking up for an instant, never putting her lips to the flask, just as long as she could be there behind Nanni, while he scythed away, asking her every so often, 'What is it you want, Pina?'

One evening she told him, while the men, exhausted from their long day's labours, were nodding off to sleep in the barn, and the dogs were filling the dark air of the countryside with their howling, 'It's you I want! You that are beautiful as the sun, and sweet as the honey! I want you!'

'It's that unmarried daughter of yours that I want,' Nanni replied, laughing.

The She-Wolf thrust her hands into her hair, tearing at the sides of her head without uttering a word, then strode off and stayed away from the barn. But when the olive-crushing season came round in October, she set her eyes on Nanni again because he was working next door to where she lived, and the creaking of the press kept her awake the whole night long.

'Pick up that sack of olives,' she said to her daughter, 'and come with me.'

Nanni was pushing the olives under the mill wheel with his shovel, and shouting 'Gee up there!' to the mule to keep it moving.

'Do you want my daughter Maricchia?' Pina asked.

'What are you going to give her?' Nanni replied.

'She's got the things her father left, and she can have my house into the bargain. All you need to leave me is a corner of the kitchen to spread out my palliasse.'

'In that case we can talk it over at Christmas,' said Nanni.

Nanni was covered in grease and sweat from the oil and the fermenting olives, and Maricchia wanted nothing whatever to do with him, but when they got home her mother grabbed her by the hair and said to her through clenched teeth:

'If you don't take him, I'll kill you!'

You would have thought the She-Wolf was ill, and people were saying that when the Devil grows old he goes into hiding. She never wandered about the village any more, she didn't stand on the doorstep flashing those crazy eyes of hers. Her son-in-law, whenever she fixed those eyes on him, began to laugh, and pulled out his scapular to bless himself with. Maricchia stayed at home, breastfeeding the children, while her mother went off to the fields to work alongside the men; just like a man, in fact, digging, hoeing, rounding up the cattle, and pruning the vines in all weathers, in January with an icy wind from the east, or August with a *sirocco* from the south, when at the end of the day the mules would be drooping their heads and the men would be sitting asleep, propped against the wall with their mouths hanging open. 'In hours that run from dusk till dawn goes no good woman ever born,' and Pina was the only living soul you could see out and about, picking her way over the torrid stones of the country lanes, across the parched stubble of the boundless fields that stretched into the heat haze of the far distance towards Etna, shrouded in mist, where the sky bore down on the horizon.

'Wake up!' said the She-Wolf to Nanni, who was lying asleep in the ditch under the dust-laden hedgerow, resting his head between his arms. 'Wake up, I've brought you some wine to wet your throat.'

Nanni opened his eyes wide, stupefied, still half-asleep, to find her standing over him, white-faced, thrusting her breasts towards him and fixing him with her coal-black eyes, and he stretched out his hands, groping the air.

'No! No good woman's abroad from dusk till dawn!' bewailed Nanni, pressing his face down again into the dry grass of the ditch as hard as he could, with his fingernails tearing at his hair. 'Go away! Go away! Keep away from the barn!'

She did go away, did the She-Wolf, tying up her splendid tresses as she went, staring ahead of her towards the hot fields of stubble with her coal-black eyes.

But she kept going back to the barn, and Nanni said nothing. In fact, whenever she was late arriving, in hours that run from dusk till dawn, he would go and wait for her at the top of the ashen-white, deserted lane, with beads of sweat standing out on his forehead. And afterwards he would thrust his hands through his hair and repeat every time, 'Go away! Go away! Don't come back to the barn!'

Maricchia wept day and night, and stared at her mother with tear-filled eyes aflame with jealousy, looking like a wolf-cub herself, everytime she saw her returning pale and silent from the fields.

'You wicked slut!' she cried. 'You wicked slut of a mother!'

'Shut up!'

'You thief! Thief!'

'Shut up!'

'I'll tell the police sergeant, that's what I'll do!'

'Go ahead and tell him!'

She did go ahead, with her children clinging round her neck, totally unafraid, and without shedding a tear. She was like a mad woman, because now she too loved the husband they had forced upon her, all greasy and covered in sweat from the fermenting of the olives.

The sergeant had Nanni called in, and threatened him with prison and the gallows. Nanni stood there sobbing and tearing his hair. He denied nothing, and didn't even try to make excuses.

'I was tempted!' he cried. 'I was tempted by the Devil!'

He threw himself at the sergeant's feet, pleading with him to send him to prison.

'For pity's sake, sergeant, take me out of this hell on earth! Have me killed, send me to prison, never let me set eyes on her again, ever!'

But when the sergeant spoke to the She-Wolf, she replied, 'No! I kept a corner of the kitchen to sleep in, when I gave him my house as a dowry. The house is mine. I don't intend to leave it.'

Shortly after that, Nanni was kicked in the chest by a mule, and was at death's door. But the parish priest refused to bring him the bread of Christ until the She-Wolf left the house. The She-Wolf went away, and her son-in-law could then prepare to take his leave of the world as a good Christian. He confessed and made communion with such an obvious show of repentance and contrition that all the neighbours and onlookers were in tears at the bed of the dying man. And it would

143

have been better for him if he had died then and there, before the Devil returned to tempt him and to take him over body and soul as soon as he recovered.

'Leave me alone!' he said to the She-Wolf. 'For God's sake, leave me in peace! I stared death in the face! That poor Maricchia is in despair! The whole village knows all about it now! It's better for both of us if I don't see you...'

He would have liked to tear out his eyes so as not to see the eyes of the She-Wolf, who made him surrender body and soul when she fixed them upon him. He no longer knew what to do to release himself from her spell. He paid for Masses for the souls in Purgatory, and asked the parish priest and the sergeant to help him. At Easter he went to confession, and did penance in public by crawling on his belly for six feet over the cobblestones in front of the church. After all that, when the She-Wolf returned to torment him, he said to her:

'Listen! Just you stay away from the barn, because if you come looking for me again, I swear to God I'll kill you!'

'Go ahead and kill me,' replied the She-Wolf. 'It doesn't worry me. I can't live without you.'

When he saw her coming in the distance, through the sown fields, he stopped digging at the vine with his mattock, and went and wrenched the axe from the elm. The She-Wolf saw him coming, pale with frenzy, the axe glittering in the sun, but she never stopped for a moment or lowered her gaze as she carried on walking towards him, with her hands full of bunches of red poppies, devouring him with her coal-black eyes.

'Ah!' Nanni stammered. 'May your soul roast in Hell!'

Translated by G H McWilliam

Almost a contemporary of Verga, and inspired by him, is Sicily's other Nobel laureate, one of the most significant dramatists of the twentieth century, and perhaps the greatest playwright of modern Italy, the son of a sulphur merchant, born near Agrigento in 1867, whose house you can still visit there, not far from the so-called Valley of the Temples: Luigi Pirandello.

The house is a little museum now, its large, quiet rooms are full of photographs and playbills, the former in black and white, the latter in vivid colour. The later pictures show an elegant Sicilian gentleman, apparently enjoying life, though slightly bemused by the fuss it is making of him. His face, as an older and successful man, is gaunt, the brow deeply lined. His wife Antonietta Portulano suffered a breakdown when the couple lost Pirandello's inheritance to a flood which destroyed his father's sulphur mine. Antonietta became obsessively jealous and delusional, but for years Luigi refused to have her committed. He lived with her, and wrote around her, until her insanity threatened their daughter's safety. Madness, delusion and extreme mental and emotional crises are never far from the centre of his work; in his last great play, *Henry IV*, they are the explicit subject. Beyond the terrace of his house, and visible through most of the windows is the water, 'the African sea' as he called it. Behind the face of genteel integrity the house presents, there seems another current in its atmosphere: something contemplative, sad and austere, perhaps nothing more than an echo of the mood of the sea on a grey day, and perhaps an echo of the mind of its master.

Luigi Pirandello
From *Henry IV*

Henry IV: This is how it is! When we are not resigned, out come our desires. A woman who wants to be a man... an old man who wants to be young... None of us lie or pretend! There's little doubt about it: in good faith we have fixed ourselves, all of us, in a fine concept of our own selves. Nevertheless, Monsignor, while you hold tight, clinging with both your hands to your holy cassock, there slips away, down your sleeves, like a snake shedding its skin, something you are not aware of: life, Monsignor! And it's a surprise when you see it materialize there all of a sudden in front of you, escaping from you. Spite and anger against yourself, or remorse, also remorse. Ah, if only you knew how much remorse I found before me! With a face that was my very own face, but so horrible, that I could not look at it...

Translated by Mark Musa

It would be a disservice to quote at length from Pirandello's extraordinary plays, which need a theatre more than a page: the writer, producer and later founder of the Arts Theatre in Rome did things with drama which have to be experienced to be appreciated. *Six Characters In Search of an Author* is exactly that: the characters invade a rehearsal and demand to be allowed to act out their own play, while challenging 'real' figures, like the stage manager (and by extension the audience) with the assertion that they, the 'characters', being fixed and unchanging creations, are more real, and stable, than those who watch them. At its first production in Rome the audience rioted. Fortunately, his short stories, though not as revolutionary as his theatre, are a Sicilian feast.

Luigi Pirandello
From *Horse in the Moon: Twelve Short Stories*

Adriana Takes a Trip

It was thirteen years, now, since Adriana Braggi had stopped going out; she no longer left the old house, shrouded in a cathedral-like silence, which she had entered as a youthful bride. She was no longer to be glimpsed behind the windowpanes, even by those few passers-by who, from time to time, mounted the steep and slippery, half-crumbling path, overrun with shrubbery, which was so deserted that the grass was to be seen growing between its pebbles.

At the age of twenty-two, when, after barely four years of married life, her husband had died, she also had undergone something resembling a death to the world. She was now thirty-five, and still went clad in the same funereal black which she had donned that first day; a black silk handkerchief hid her beautiful brown hair, no longer cared for but carelessly caught up in a couple of braids and knotted at the back of her neck. But with it all, a serenity that was half sorrow and half peace rested graciously upon her pale and delicate face.

No one wondered at these cloistral habits in that Sicilian mountain town; for the strict customs of the place all but required the jealously guarded wife to follow her husband to the grave, and widows were expected to shut themselves up like this, in perpetual mourning, until death.

So far as that goes, the women of the few respectable families in the place, both married and unmarried, were almost never seen in the street; they went out only on Sundays, to go to Mass, and, upon rare occasions, to exchange calls upon one another. At such times, they decked themselves in the richest and most fashionable attire, imported from the leading shops of Palermo or Catania, and made a great display of gold and jewelry. This, however, was not done out of coquettishness; for, grave and embarrassed in manner, they always walked with burning cheeks and downcast eyes, close beside husband or father or older brother. Such a show of luxury was almost obligatory; and those calls or those few steps to the church were veritable excursions, to be prepared for a day in advance. The good name of the family was at stake, and the men were sticklers in the matter; they, indeed, were the punctilious ones, inasmuch as they desired to show that they knew how to spend, and were able to spend, money upon their women folk.

Obedient and submissive always, the women dressed to suit the men's wishes, in order not to disgrace the latter. Following these brief appearances, they would docilely return to their household cares, and, if they were wives, would wait for the children to come, all that God might choose to send (for that was their cross). If they were maids, they would wait until their parents said to them, one fine day: 'There you are; marry him.' They would marry him; and the men were content to receive from their wives this lifeless and loveless fidelity.

Only a blind faith in the compensations of a life to come could have kept them from despairing, or could have rendered endurable the heavy, inert drabness in which their days went by, one after another, every day like another, in that little mountain town which was so silent, beneath the deep and ardent blue of the sky, that it seemed uninhabited, with its narrow, badly paved streets which ran between the rows of limestone cottages with their clay gutter pipes and their uncovered tin eaves-troughs.

At the end of these tiny streets, one had a view of an undulating expanse of brimstone-parched earth. Arid beneath an arid sky, the earth stretched away in a motionless silence, lulled by the hum of insects, by the chirp of stray crickets, by the distant crowing of a cock or the barking of a dog; and from it there arose like a cloud, into the dazzling midday light, the odor of withered, thickly clustered weeds, with a fainter manurey whiff of stables.

There was a scarcity of water, even in the well-to-do households; and in the huge courtyards in which the streets appeared to end were old-time open cisterns. It rained but little, even in winter; and when it did rain, it was a holiday. All the women would then set out tubs and pails, basins and casks, and would stand in the door-ways with their camlet dresses tucked between their knees, watching the rain as it poured in torrents down the steep paths and listening to it as it gurgled in the eaves and gutter-pipes and fell into the cisterns. The rain bathed the pebbled paths, it bathed the walls of the houses, and everything seemed to breathe more freely in the pleasing fragrance of the water-drenched earth.

The men contrived to find distraction of one sort or another in the business of everyday living, and went for company of an evening to the café or to the Casino; but as for their lovelessly wedded wives, they who, from childhood, had been compelled to extinguish every instinct that pointed to worldly vanity, after they had attended like the drudges that they were to their household tasks, always the same, they had nothing to look forward to but a wretched boredom, a baby on their laps or a rosary in their hands, as they waited for their lord and master to come home.

Adriana Braggi had not, as a matter of course, loved her husband.

Of a very weak constitution and in a constant state of excitement on account of his uncertain health, her husband had abused and tyrannized over her for four long years, having been so unreasonable as to be jealous of his own older brother, whom he was conscious of having grievously wronged – or rather, in reality, betrayed – in marrying Adriana. For here again, custom prevailed; and of all the sons of a well-to-do family, one only, the oldest, was supposed to take a wife, in order that the family substance might not be dissipated through a number of heirs.

Cesare Braggi, the older brother, had never shown any signs of resentment for this betrayal; possibly for the reason that the father, who died shortly before the wedding took place, had designated him as the head of the family and had commanded that the second-born, upon his marriage, should remain obedient to the older son.

Upon coming into the old Braggi mansion, Adriana had experienced a certain humiliation in the knowledge that she was thus subject to her brother-in-law. Her position had later become an annoying and an irksome one, when her husband, in a fit of jealousy, had let it slip out that Cesare had intended marrying her himself. She had found it hard to face her brother-in-law after that; but the more her embarrassment grew, the less the latter seemed inclined to exert his authority over her; he had welcomed her, from the very first day, with a frank and winning cordiality, and had treated her as if she had been a sister.

He was mild-mannered, and in conversation, in attire, and in every other respect manifested the innately fine instincts of a gentleman; neither his association with the uncouth country folk, his daily tasks, nor those habits of relaxation and idleness which a wretchedly empty provincial existence tended to induce for a number of months each year had succeeded in hardening him; they had not so much as altered him in the slightest degree.

For a number of days each year, often for so long as a month, he would leave the little town and business behind, and would go to Palermo, to Naples, to Rome, to Florence, to Milan, by way of plunging into life, of taking, as he put it, a civilization-bath. And he would come back from these trips younger in mind and body.

Adriana, who had never set foot outside her native province, upon seeing him thus return to the big old house, where time appeared to be stagnating in a death-like silence, was conscious, upon each occasion, of a secret, indefinable feeling of turmoil.

Her brother-in-law brought back with him the breath of a world which she was not able even to picture.

And this feeling of turmoil was heightened by her husband's harsh laugh, as he listened to an account of his brother's spicy adventures; she would become angry and then shudder, when her husband that evening came to join her in their

148

bedroom, aroused by his brother's tales to a state of eager over-excitation. The anger, the shudder were for him, and grew all the stronger as she perceived that, on the other hand, her brother-in-law's respect and reverence for her were all the time increasing.

When her husband died, Adriana was quite dismayed at the thought of having to remain alone in the house with her kinsman. She had, it is true, her pair of little ones who had been born to her in those four years of married life; but although a mother, she had never succeeded in overcoming, in her brother-in-law's presence, her instinctive young girl's timidity. This timidity, it must be stated, was not willful on her part; but there it was; and she blamed for it her late and jealous husband, his exceedingly suspicious and domineering ways, and the sly watch he had all the while kept on her.

Cesare Braggi, with fine sensitiveness, had thereupon invited the mother to come and stay with her windowed daughter; and little by little, Adriana, freed from her husband's hateful tyranny, and thanks to her mother's companionship, had been able to find, if not perfect peace, at least some rest for her soul. She had given herself over utterly to the care of her children, lavishing upon them all the love and all the tenderness that had been able to find no outlet in a degrading marriage.

Each year, Cesare continued to make his month's trip to the Mainland, bringing back with him gifts not only for her, but for the grandmother and for his nephews, toward whom he always exhibited the most thoughtful fatherly affection.

Without the presence of a man, the women were afraid in the house, especially of a night. During the days when he was gone, it seemed to Adriana that the silence, grown deeper and darker was holding some unimaginable disaster in suspense above them: and there, at the top of that steep and lonely path, the creaking of the old cistern pulley, stirred by a passing breeze, would produce in her an indescribable anxiety. But could she expect that he, merely for the sake of the two women and the children, who, after all, were not his – could she expect that, tired out from his year's work, he should deprive himself of the one recreation that he had? He might have taken no thought of them whatsoever, but, seeing that his brother had prevented his having a family of his own, have gone on living his own life, unhampered by any ties; and instead – how could she help realizing it? – with the exception of this brief vacation period, his only interest was in the house and in his orphan nephews.

In the course of time, all sorrow was numbed in Adriana's heart. Her sons were growing up, and she was glad that they could grow up under such a guardian as their uncle. Her own devotion had now become absolute, and it was occasion for wonderment to her if brother-in-law or sons displayed any inclination to elude the extreme good care that she bestowed upon them. It seemed to her that she could never do enough. And of whom was she to have thought, if not of them?

Her mother's death had been a blow to her; she had lost the one companion that she had. She gradually had come to the point where she was able to talk with her mother as with a sister. What was more, with her mother there, she had been able to think of herself as yet young, which she was in spirit. With her mother gone and with those two nearly grown sons, one sixteen, the other fourteen, and each as tall as his uncle, she was beginning to feel old, and to look upon herself as being old.

She was in this frame of mind, when she became conscious for the first time of a vague indisposition, a feeling of weariness, a slight bearing-down sensation in one shoulder and in the chest, and a certain dull pain which occasionally ran down her whole left arm, becoming a shooting pain that took her breath away.

She did not complain; and no one might have been any the wiser, if, one day at table, she had not had, unexpectedly, one of these convulsive attacks.

The old family physician was called in; and he, from the very start, was gravely alarmed by the symptoms that he found. His alarm increased, after he had made a long and careful examination.

The trouble was in the lungs. But what was the nature of the trouble? The old doctor, with the assistance of a colleague, attempted a puncture by way of finding out, but without any result. Then, noting a certain induration of the glandular tissue above and below the shoulder-blade, he advised Braggi to lose no time in taking his sister-in-law to Palermo, letting it be clearly understood that he feared an internal tumor, which might, possibly, prove incurable.

To go at once was out of the question. After thirteen cloistered years, Adriana was quite unprovided with the necessary clothes for appearing in public or for traveling. They must send to Palermo at once, to fit her out as speedily as could be done.

As for Adriana, she raised every objection that she could think of, assuring her brother-in-law and her sons that she no longer felt so bad... Take a trip? The mere thought of it gave her a shiver. This was just the time when Cesare was in the habit of going on his month's vacation. If she went along, she would only be in the way, would spoil all the pleasure in it for him. No, no, she would not hear of it under any conditions. And anyway, who would look after the children while she was gone? Who would look after the house? Such were the difficulties that she raised; but brother-in-law and sons demolished them with a laugh. She, however, stubbornly insisted that the trip would do her more harm than good. Why, merciful heavens, she no longer knew what a street looked like, would not know how to behave in the street! For pity's sake, for pity's sake, why wouldn't they leave her in peace!

The two lads were jubilant when the gowns and hats arrived from Palermo.

With the big boxes wrapped in wax paper, they gleefully stormed their mother's room, shouting and clamoring that she must put her new things on, at once. They wanted to see their little mother all dressed up, as they had never seen her before; and they were so insistent in every way that there was nothing for her to do but to give in, just to please them.

The gowns were black; they, too, were mourning gowns, but very expensive and marvelously made. Knowing nothing of fashions any more, she was very clumsy, and was at a loss as to how to set about putting them on. How was she ever to button all those hooks and eyes? And heavens, look at that collar; was it supposed to be as high as that? And those sleeves, with all those puffs... were they wearing them like that now?

The boys, meanwhile, kept up a clamor outside the door:

'Ready, mother? Ready yet?'

As if their mother had been dressing for a party! They did not stop to think of what those clothes were for; and she herself, the truth is, at this moment, did not give a thought to the subject.

When, in a flush of self-consciousness, she raised her eyes to the wardrobe mirror, she experienced a sudden violent feeling that was almost one of shame. This gown, which set off so daringly her bosom and her hips, made her look as young and slim as a girl. She had been feeling old of late; but now, of a sudden, she was young, beautiful – another being!

'What am I thinking of! What am I thinking of! Out of the question!' she exclaimed, twisting her neck and lifting a hand to put the mirror back in place.

Her sons, hearing this exclamation, started pounding and kicking at the door, until it seemed that they would break it in, shouting for her to open the door and let them have a look at her.

But how could she! No! She was ashamed. Why, she looked like a caricature! No, no...

The door threatened to come crashing in at any moment. There was nothing to do but open it.

The boys were dazzled at first by this unforeseen transformation. Their mother, out of self-defense, kept saying: 'No, no, go away! No, no, it's out of the question! What are you thinking of?' – when her brother-in-law suddenly appeared upon the scene. Oh, for mercy's sake! She made an effort to flee, to hide herself, as if he had come upon her nude. But her sons held her fast and showed her off to their uncle, who laughed at her embarrassment.

'But it really suits you very well!' he said at last, becoming serious. 'Look up.'

With an effort, she raised her head.

'I feel as if I were at a masquerade...'

'Nothing of the sort! Why should you? I tell you, it's very becoming. Turn a little – like that, to one side...'

She obeyed, forcing herself to appear calm; but her bosom, under her tight-fitting gown, rose and fell, betraying her inner agitation, occasioned by the calm and careful examination on the part of this most expert of connoisseurs.

'It is very nice. And what about the hats?'

'Regular baskets!' Adriana exclaimed, almost in fright.

'Ah, but they're wearing them large now.'

'But how shall I ever be able to get them on my head? I shall have to do my hair a different way.'

Cesare turned to look at her once more, with an unperturbed smile.

'That's right,' he said. 'You have so much hair...'

Her sons approved:

'Yes, yes, Mother, that's good girl! Do your hair right away!'

There was sorrow in Adriana's smile.

'Just see what you're making me do,' she said, turning to her brother-in-law.

It was decided that they were to leave the next morning.

Alone with him!

Here she was, accompanying him on one of those trips the very thought of which had once so disturbed her. She had but one fear now, that of letting her perturbation become apparent to the man who sat opposite her, wholly attentive to her, but calm as ever.

This calm of his, which was altogether natural, made her feel like blushing for her own upset condition. It was then that, by way of overcoming her shame and giving herself courage, she had recourse to a half-conscious fiction, letting him think that her perturbation was due to another cause: the novelty of the trip and the inrush of so many new impressions upon her shy and shut-in mind. And the strength that she found in her need (which, after all, was not so reprehensible when you looked at it like that) she attributed to the duty that was hers of not exhibiting too much astonishment in the presence of one who, for so many years, had been so thoroughly familiar with the ways of the world and so thoroughly the master of himself, and who might be bored or displeased by such an exhibition on her part. It must, as it was, seem ridiculous enough in a woman of her age, that childlike wonderment which danced in her eyes.

She, accordingly, forced herself to restrain the joyously feverish eagerness of her glance, forced herself not to be continually turning her head from one window to the other, as she was tempted to do, in order not to lose a single one of all these sights, upon which, for the first time in her life, her eyes like fugitives were now resting. She forced herself to conceal her astonishment, to overcome her curiosity, which might have helped her in keeping alertly awake, and which might have overcome that dull, dizzy feeling produced by the rhythmic rumble of the wheels and the illusory flight of hills and trees and hedgerows.

It was her first time on a train. At every instant, at every revolution of the wheels, she had the impression of taking a step forward into an unknown world, a world that was suddenly created in her soul, under appearances which, however close at hand they may have been, yet seemed to her distant, and which gave her, along with the pleasure she took in beholding them, a very faint and indescribable feeling of pain, occasioned by the thought that they had always existed like this, outside the realm of her own existence and imagination – the pain of being but a stranger and a transient in the midst of it all, and of knowing that all these things, without her, would have gone on living their own lives and fulfilling their own individual destinies.

Here were the low roofs of a hamlet: doors and windows, streets and steps. The people who lived there were shut in upon this little plot of earth, with their own customs and occupations, just as she for so many years had been shut up in that little mountain village. Beyond that which their eyes could see, nothing existed for these folk. The world to them was a dream. One by one, they were born, grew up and died, without ever having seen what she had just seen upon this trip, which was so little when one thought of how large the world was, and which yet seemed to her so very, very much.

As she glanced around, from time to time, she encountered her brother-in-law's smiling gaze.

'How do you feel?' he inquired.

'Very well,' she replied, with a nod of the head.

A number of times, he came over to take the seat beside her, in order to point out to her and give her the name of some remote part of the country where he had been, – that mountain there, which towered so threateningly; anything that stood out in the landscape, and which he conceived might hold a special interest for her. He did not realize that all these sights, even the least of them, were awakening in her a tumultuous swarm of new sensations, or that the information which he gave her, the things he pointed out to her, in place of kindling her interest to a higher pitch, tended rather to diminish and to cool the fervor induced by that wavering image of grandeur which she, bashfully, and still with that indefinable feeling of pain, was building up for herself out of this manifold and unknown world.

Furthermore, amid all this inner turmoil of sensations, his voice came bringing darkness rather than light, a poignant darkness that brought her up violently; and then it was, that the feeling of pain became sharper, more distinct. She blamed herself for her ignorance, and was aware of a dimly hostile resentment at all these sights which, suddenly and too late, had come to brim her eyes and make their way into her soul.

At Palermo, the next day, as they came down the flight of steps that led to the clinic, following an interminable consultation, she understood from the effort her kinsman made to hide his alarm, from the exaggerated solicitude with which he had insisted upon having the doctor's orders repeated to him, and from the doctor's manner in replying – she understood, clearly enough, that sentence of death had been passed upon her, and that this poisonous mixture, of which she was to take a few drops, with the utmost precaution, twice a day before meals, was nothing more than a merciful deception or the viaticum of a prolonged death-agony.

And yet, half-stupefied and nauseated by the smell of ether throughout the place, she had barely stepped from the shadow of the stair into the street, into the dazzling sunset light, beneath a flaming sky which, from the direction of the sea, seemed to fall precipitously like a huge and gleaming cloud upon the distant Corso; she was no sooner aware, amid this golden glow, of the throng of vehicles and the noisy, swarming crowd, of clothes and faces lighted up with purple glints and of the wavering colored light, like that of precious stones, that danced over all, from shop-windows, from signs, from mirrors along the street, when – life, life, that was all she asked – she was conscious of a riotous incursion of life into her soul, through the gateways of her excited, over-excited senses – an intoxication that was all but divine. Nor did she feel any anxiety; she did not so much as give a passing thought to death, death that was so near at hand and so inevitable, death that she already was carrying about inside her, hidden away there in that punctured spot under her left shoulder-blade, which still pained her at moments. No, it was life, life! This inner overwhelming hubbub now made its way from her mind to her throat, and something like an old, old pain that had been long buried in the depths of her being surged up. Here she was, bursting into tears; but they were tears of joy.

'It's nothing – nothing... ' she assured her brother-in-law, with the brightest of smiles shining through her tears. 'It seemed to me... I don't know... Come on, come on...'

'To the hotel?'

'No... No... '

'We'll go have dinner, then, at the 'Chalet,' down by the sea; to the Foro Italico; what do you say?'

'Yes, wherever you like.'

'That's fine. Come along! We'll see the promenade at the Foro; we'll hear the music... '

They took a cab and went to meet that gleaming, kindling cloud.

Ah, what a night that was for her, at the 'Chalet': the moon and the illuminated Foro, with its incessant clatter of twinkling carriages, amid the odor of seaweed and the scent of orange blossoms wafted in from the gardens! She was bewildered, as by a superhuman enchantment, but one to which she was unable wholly to abandon herself, by reason of a certain anguish, the hateful anguish of doubt – doubt that all was as it appeared to be, so extremely distant and impersonal did it seem; memory, consciousness, thought alike were fused in the far-away infinity of dreams.

The same impression, but intensified, laid hold of her again the following morning, as, in a carriage, they rolled down the enormous deserted lanes of the Parco della Favorita. At a certain point, she gave a sigh. It was as if she were coming to herself, as if she were coming out of that distance, and were now able to measure it, without, however, breaking the spell or impairing the intoxication of that sunlit dream, there among those plains, which likewise seemed to melt away into a dream without end, in a mystic, wonder-filled silence.

And without any volition of her own, she turned to glance at her brother-in-law, and smiled up at him out of gratitude.

But even as she smiled, she suddenly felt a keen, deep-rooted pity for herself, condemned as she was to die at the very moment when so many beauties, so many marvels were unfolding before her astonished eyes – a life such as might have been her own, such as so many of her fellow-creatures lived. And she felt that it had, perhaps, been a cruel thing for them to force her to come upon this trip.

It was not long afterward that the carriage finally drew up in a distant lane, and she descended on her brother-in-law's arm for a nearer view of the Fountain of Hercules. She stood there before the fountain, under the cobalt-blue of the sky, which was so intense that it seemed almost black against the fulgent marble whiteness of the demigod's statue, a-top a tall column that rose from the middle of the wide basin. The divinity was bending over to look down into the glassy water, upon which a few leaves and a few greenish-colored algae were floating, their shadows being reflected at the bottom of the pool. At each lightest ripple on the surface of the water, she could see a fine mist arise to bathe the impassive faces of the two sphinxes that stood guard over the basin, and at the same time, she could feel her own face being pensively flecked by a cooling zephyr from the water, and her numbed mind at once expanded in a great, a boundless silence; it was as if the light from a yet more distant heaven had come to her in this fathomless void, to lend her its vivifying flame. She felt that she was now, as it were, touching eternity and acquiring a clear-seeing, limitless knowledge of everything, of that infinity which lay concealed in the soul's mysterious depths; she felt that she had lived, and that it was enough to have lived, for the reason that, for an instant, for that one instant, she had tasted eternity.

She suggested to her brother-in-law that they go back that same day. She wished to go home in order to leave him free, after those four days which he had already lost from his vacation. He would lose yet another day in seeing her home; then, he would be at liberty to set out again, on his annual jaunt to those more distant lands, far, far away, beyond the turquoise sea. He need have no fear, since she was certain not to die so soon, during the month that he was gone.

She did not tell him all this; she only thought it, and asked him to please be so good as to take her back to their own country.

'No, why should I?' was his reply. 'We're here now. You're going with me to Naples. Just to make sure, we'll see a few other doctors down there.'

'No, no, please, Cesare! Let me go home. It's no use!'

'What do you mean? It's the only thing to do. We'll feel safe, then.'

'But don't we know already all there is to know? There's nothing the matter with me; I'm well enough; can't you see for yourself? I'll take my medicine. That's all that's necessary.'

He looked at her gravely, and said:

'Adriana, I want to – so much.'

She could make no further reply; she was like any other woman of her country, whose business it was not to question anything that the male held to be proper and fitting. The thought occurred to her that he wanted to satisfy his own conscience, by not relying upon the word of one doctor alone, so that, back home, in the days to come, when she was dead and gone, folks might be able to say: 'He did everything he could to save her; he took her to Palermo and all the way to Naples...' Or possibly, he really hoped that some better doctor down there might find that he could cure her after all, might find some remedy that would save her? Or perhaps – Ah, yes, this was what she ought to believe – knowing that she was lost and that nothing could save her, he was determined, now that he had her along with him, to give her this last, extraordinary pleasure, as a slight compensation for the cruel blow that fate had dealt her.

She, however, had a horror, a veritable horror of that stretch of water to be crossed. Merely to look at it with such a thought in mind took her breath away; it was as if she had been expected to swim across.

'You'll see,' he smilingly reassured her. 'You won't notice a thing on a little crossing like that. Just look, how calm it is. And then, you'll see what it's like on a steamboat. You won't notice it at all.'

Was she to confess to him the dark and anguished forebodings that arose in her at sight of the sea? If she were once to leave the shores of this island, which seemed so far away from her own little nook in the world and so wholly strange to her, and where she had already been so unaccountably perturbed – if she were to leave these shores and go adventuring with him, farther away still, lost with him in that enormous, mystery-laden expanse – if she were to do this, she knew that she would never again return to her own home, that she would never again cross that water alive. But could she tell him all this? No, these were forebodings that she dared not phrase even to herself; she preferred to believe that it was, simply, a terror of the sea, due to the fact that she had never before seen so large a body of water, even from a distance; and now, she was to cross it...

They embarked that very evening for Naples.

Adriana at first, as the steamer moved away from the pier and left the harbor behind, had been stunned by the confusion and uproar, by the noisy, vociferating throng surging up and down the gangplank, by the creaking of the cranes and all the tumult of embarking; and then, she beheld everything gradually receding from her, growing smaller and smaller: the people on the wharf, who still stood waving their handkerchiefs, the harbor, the houses, everything; until the city became but a vaporous streak, shot through here and there with wan-gleaming lights, as it lay in its broad cloister-like valley, walled in by reddish-gray mountains. Once more, she was lost in a dream, a marvelous dream, but one that brought her a wide-eyed dismay, heightened by the fact that the steamer, big as it undoubtedly was, nevertheless shook fragilely to the ominous, timed splash of the propellers: they were now in the grip of those two unthinkable immensities, sky and sea.

He smiled at her dismay and, inviting her to a promenade, slipped an arm through hers protectingly, with an intimacy which he had never before permitted himself. He led her down to a point where they could see the shiny, powerful steel pistons that moved the propellers; but she, upset by this unaccustomed intimacy, could not stand the sight, nor the puff of warm, fetid air that struck her in the face. She felt faint and lay back, her head practically resting upon his shoulder; but at once, she regained control of herself, as if terrified by the instinctive gesture of abandonment to which she had just yielded.

'Do you feel bad?' he again inquired, more solicitously than ever.

Unable to reply, she shook her head. They strolled arm-in-arm toward the stern and stood there gazing at the long phosphorescent ship's wake, in a sea that had turned black beneath a star-dusted sky, as the enormous smokestack incessantly belched forth its slow, dense puffs, which seemed to be glowing with the heat of the engines. Finally, to complete the spell, the moon came up out of the sea; through the smoke clouds on the horizon, as from behind a lugubrious mask, it arose threateningly, to keep a silent and a terrifying watch over these, its watery dominions. Then, by degrees, it grew more luminous, keeping strictly within its own snowy circle of light, beneath which the sea lay in an endless expanse of palpitant silver. And then it was that Adriana felt coming up within her all the anguish and all the alarm occasioned by these raptures which were now transporting her, and which led her irresistibly, exhausted as she was, to hide her face in his bosom.

It happened at Naples, as they were leaving a café-concert where they had dined and spent the evening. Accustomed as he was, on his annual trips, to leaving places of this sort of a night with a lady on his arm, he now, in offering Adriana this courtesy, darted an unexpectedly ardent glance beneath the latter's big, plumed hat, and at once, instinctively, pressed her arm to his side, quickly and forcefully. That was all. The conflagration broke.

In the darkness of the carriage that took them back to the hotel, as they clung together, mouth to mouth in an insatiable kiss, she in a few moments told him everything, everything that he, but a moment back, in an instant, in a flash, in that one darting glance, had divined: the life she had led during all those years of silent martyrdom. She told him how always, always, without wanting to, without knowing that she did, she had loved him; and he told her how, from his boyhood days, he had wanted her, had dreamed of making her his, as she now was – his, his!

They were in a frenzied delirium, which it seemed would never spend itself, the violence of which was augmented by their consciousness of the death-sentence that hovered over her, and by their passionate desire to make up, in these few days that were left them, for all those lost years, those years of stifled longing and of hidden, feverish love. They felt the need of losing themselves utterly, of blinding themselves to what they had been to each other during those years, the falsely honest appearances they had kept up, down there in that stern little town, to the citizens of which their love, their marriage on the morrow would have appeared a sacrilege and a profanation.

Their marriage? Never! Why should she force him into that act, so disgraceful for all concerned? Why should she thus bind him to her, she who had so little a while to live? No, no: love; she would take love, a frantic and overwhelming love, for the few days that this trip would last: an elopement from which she was never to come back; an elopement to death.

She could not go back now and face her sons. She had sensed all this dimly, when she left. She had known that, once having crossed the sea, all would be over for her. And now, it was away, away; she wanted to fly away, farther, farther away, arm-in-arm with him, like this, blindly, all the way to death.

And so they went on, on to Rome, and on to Florence, and on to Milan, seeing little or nothing of what lay in their path. Death, which nestled in her, and which transfixed her at times, seemed to be lashing her onward, whipping up her ardor.

'It is nothing!' she would say, at every attack, every pang. 'It is nothing!'

And she would give him her mouth, with the pallor of death on her face.

'Adriana, you are suffering...'

'No, no, it is nothing! What does it matter to me?'

On their last day at Milan, before leaving for Venice, she caught sight of her haggard face in the glass. And when, after the night trip, there burst upon her in the silence of the dawn the superbly melancholy dream-like vision of a city emerging from the water, she understood that she had met her fate at last, and that it was here her journey was to end.

But she wanted to have her day in Venice. All day until evening, all day until nightfall, down the silent canals, in a gondola. And all night long, she remained awake with a strange, haunting impression of that day: a day of velvet.

The velvet of the gondola? The velvety shadows of certain canals? Who can say! The velvet lining of a coffin.

The next morning, when he had left the hotel to mail some letters for Sicily, she came into his room and found upon his stand a torn envelope. She recognized the handwriting of her elder son. She raised the envelope to her lips and kissed it despairingly, then went back into her own room, took from her leather purse the phial with the poisonous mixture still intact, threw herself down upon the unmade bed, and drained it off at a gulp.

Translated by Samuel Putnam

It is fortunate, given the imbalance in the number of male and female Sicilian writers, that the greatest among the men wrote so well about women. The following is an extract from *Conversations in Sicily* (*Conversazione in Sicilia*) by Elio Vittorini. The son of a railway worker, like Quasimodo, Vittorini published this, his first major book, in 1930, when he was twenty two. He had attended school for only eight years, and had worked to support himself as a construction labourer while writing short stories, and building towards this little masterpiece. *Conversations in Sicily* is narrated by a young man who has come back to Sicily after fifteen years away to see his mother, whom his father has recently deserted. The novel begins with a short but affectionate note from his father, saying that he has left, and urging his son to keep an eye on his mother. The narrator takes a train south. This section comes early in the book, not long after the protagonist has reached his mother's house.

Elio Vittorini
From *Conversations in Sicily*

XV

'Where are you off to?' I called after her.

She replied in a voice sounding suffocated, as if coming from under a pall of dust: 'I'm getting a melon!' And I felt sure that she was in some unused room with a low roof – the attic.

I waited. There was no longer any herring on our plates, nor the smell of herring in the kitchen. My mother returned with a long melon in her hand. 'A fine one, isn't it?' she said. 'A winter melon!'

She smiled, and she seemed a ghost, herself and the memory of her, twice real with the melon in her hand, as in the line-keepers' cottages in my childhood.

'We used to have melons in winter, too,' said I.

'Yes,' said my mother. 'I used to bury them under the straw in the hen-coop. Now I keep them here in the attic. I've got about ten of them.'

'In the hen-coop?' I said. 'It was always a mystery where you kept them! We could never find out. You seemed to be storing them inside yourself. And every so often, like on a Sunday, you'd produce one. You'd vanish like you did now, and return with a melon... It was a mystery...'

'I expect you all used to search for them everywhere,' said my mother.

'Of course,' said I. 'If they'd been in the hen-coop, we'd have found them.'

'They were there all the same,' said my mother. 'But in a hole dug in the ground with the straw on top.'

'Ah, that's where they were!' said I. 'And we used to think you stored them somehow inside yourself...'

My mother smiled. 'Is that why you used to call me Melon Mummy?' she asked.

'Did we call you Melon Mummy?' said I.

'Or Mummy of the Melons perhaps... Don't you remember?'

'Mummy of the Melons!' I exclaimed.

The melon, laid on the table, revolved gently towards me, once, twice. The green of its hard rind had delicate veins of gold. I bent down and sniffed.

'Ah, that's it!' I said. 'That's it all right.'

Not only did I get the penetrating smell of the melon; but the old smell like that of wine in the wintry solitude of mountains, along the deserted railway line, and like that of the tiny dining-room, with its low roof, in the line-keepers' cottages.

I looked about me.

'Isn't there any piece of our furniture here?' I asked.

'Not one,' said my mother. 'Some of the crockery and the kitchen things are ours... The blankets, and the linen. We sold up the furniture when we came here...'

'But what made you decide to come here?' I asked.

'I made the decision. This is my father's house and there's no rent to pay. He built it bit by bit, on Sundays... Where did you expect us to go?'

'I don't know...' said I. 'But it's certainly very far from the railway! How can you live without even seeing the line?'

'What d'you want to see the line for?' said my mother.

'I'd have thought it mattered to you... You used to go out and stand at the barrier with a flag when it passed.'

'Yes, if I didn't send one of you,' said my mother.

'Ah, you sent one of us sometimes?' I exclaimed.

Her reply did not matter. I could remember that I was on special terms with the train, as if we had engaged in a dialogue together; for a moment I found myself trying to recall the things it had told me, as if I looked upon the world in the light of what I had learnt from it during our conversations.

I said: 'There was a certain place where we lived right near the station. Serradifalco, I think. We couldn't see the station, but we could hear the goods trucks banging against one another during the shuntings...'

I remembered the winter, the vast emptiness of the undulating landscape, not a tree to be seen, not a leaf, and the earth smelling wintry, like a melon; and that noise.

'I'd like to hear that noise!' I said.

'Cut the melon,' cried my mother.

I pressed on the hard skin, and the knife instantly sank in. Meanwhile my mother had brought wine and glasses. The wine was poor stuff, but the melon lay halved before us and we inhaled the perfume of wintry melon ...

XVIII

Then my mother began to wash up. There was no running water, and she washed the dishes in an earthenware basin filled with hot water; at the same time she began a spasmodic whistling.

'Will you give me a hand?' she said, as she picked the first plate out of the hot water. I rose and prepared to do so. She scrubbed the plate with a little ash, handed it to me and, pointing to a pail of cold water, told me to rinse the plate and wipe it. We proceeded in this way with the other plates and dishes, my mother whistling and singing, and I watching her.

She sang old tunes without the words, softly, sometimes humming, sometimes whistling, with an occasional trill. She was a strange sight, this woman of some fifty years, with her face that didn't look old; though rather withered by the years, yet not old, even youthful; with her chestnut, almost blond, hair; with her red blanket around her shoulders, and father's big shoes on her feet. I looked at her hands, large, worn and rugged, completely different from her face, for they could be the hands of a man who felled trees or tilled the soil, while her face was somehow that of an odalisque. 'These women of ours,' I thought, not meaning Sicilians, but women in general, whose hands were without softness in the night, and, perhaps, at times, unhappy on that account, jealous and savage; to have the heart and face of an odalisque, yet not her hands with which to bind their men to them. I thought of my father and myself, and of all men, with our need of soft hands to caress us, and I seemed partly to understand our restiveness with women; how we were ready to desert them, our women with their hands rough and bony, almost masculine, so hard in the night; and how the odalisque-woman by her mere touch could enslave us like a queen. It was this, I thought, that rendered alluring people reared in luxury, the entire bureaucratic-military structure of society, the hierarchies and dynasties, the princes and kings of the story-books; the notion of the woman with soft, tended hands. To know that they existed was enough to enable us to perceive what they were like, these women, and to see them remote and inaccessible with their horses, their banners and eunuchs. And that was why, I thought, fairs and seraglios were liked, with their trumpets and flags. Amidst all the fun, our gaze would wander from our own womenfolk to seek other women – I, my father, every man – to seek something else in those other women, without for a moment supposing that it was the caress of soft hands that we sought. How mean we were, I thought, as I looked at my mother's shapeless hands, her shapeless feet clad in the old pair of men's shoes – parts of her other nature that had to be ignored and remain nameless. But all this while my mother was singing, singing like a bird, humming and whistling and giving an occasional trill. Her hands and feet did not matter, even her age did not matter. All that mattered was that she sang and was a bird, the mother-bird of the air and – among her eggs – of the light, the mother-bird shedding light.

'Well,' said I, 'I expect you pass your time like this when you're alone.'

'Like this?' said my mother.

'Yes,' said I. 'Singing.'

My mother shrugged her shoulders and looked as it perhaps she wasn't aware that she was singing.

'Don't you mind being alone?' I added.

She gave me her squinting look of perplexity, wrinkled her brow, and said: 'If you think I should feel the loss of your father's company, you're mistaken... What makes you think that? Because you're lending a hand?'

'Why?' said I. 'Wasn't he a good companion? I expect he also used to help wash up.'

'That doesn't mean I should feel lonely without him...' said my mother.

'But he was a nice man!' said I.

'I don't need a nice man about the house!' said my mother. 'That was my misfortune, his being nice!'

'I wish you'd explain yourself better,' said I.

'Your grandfather, you see, wasn't nice...' said my mother. 'He didn't call the women queens, he didn't write verses to them.'

'I expect he didn't like them,' said I.

'Didn't like them?' said my mother. 'He liked them ten times more than your father did. But he didn't call them queens. When he liked one of them, he carried her down to the valley. There are many here in the village who still remember him. And many at Piazza, too.'

'And you complain of Father?' I said. 'I think that with your character you might have been worse off being Grandfather's wife...'

'Worse off?' exclaimed my mother. 'How worse off?'

'Well,' said I. 'Grandfather carried them down to the valley, and Father wrote poetry to them. I think you'd have found those escapades in the valley more painful than poems...'

'Not at all!' said she. 'I wouldn't have minded if he'd only carried them down to the valley.'

'What?' said I. 'He'd carry them down to the valley and write verses as well?'

'Of course,' cried my mother. 'And call them queens, treat them like queens. He was a nice man. And if any woman had a nice name, like Manon, for example – he seemed to go quite mad. And that was ridiculous at his age.'

'Who was called Manon?' I asked.

'That was the equestrienne in the circus,' said my mother. 'It was on her account I sent him away... Because her name was Manon. But he always treated them like queens. He was a nice man.'

There was a pause, but I didn't speak. My mother seemed to be waiting, so I said: 'He was a nice man.'

'That was the worst of it,' said she. 'I wouldn't have minded if he'd just carried them down to the valley. Instead he'd come and tell me: 'My dear, if you were a girl, you could be called Manon.''

'What's wrong with that?' said I.

'What was wrong was that he treated them like queens, not like dirty sows. And God only knows what he made them believe. That's the worst of it. I couldn't look down my nose at them.'

'Ah, you couldn't look down your nose at them?' I said, thinking to myself: Strange woman!

'He made them believe God only knows what, and they would look at me as if they were God only knows what... They'd come to my house, railwaymen's wives, peasant women. They were calm and brazen. They wouldn't lower their eyes. They'd look at me as if they were God only knows what. And I couldn't look down my nose at them.'

Strange woman, I thought.

'That was the worst of it,' my mother went on. 'He made them feel they mattered far more than me! And they looked at me as if they did matter far more than me! He called them queens. He didn't let them think they were just dirty sows. And I couldn't look down my nose at them...'

That's what she said, and I kept thinking: Strange woman! Strange woman! And I almost laughed to myself. I knew what we men were like, perhaps odious – like my father and myself – yet right, after all, in our enthusiasm for women's company, and in encouraging them to think God only knows what. And internally, I almost laughed.

XIX

Taking up the broom, my mother moved about the place sweeping. She was luxuriating in her role of mother and woman, while I, almost laughing to myself, kept thinking that she herself might well have been one of those she called dirty sows, a queen – despite her rough hands – for other men, mysterious, a queen-bee and mother of enthusiasms.

Why not, I thought to myself.

Hers was too rich a maternal sense to have let her play the role of a mere wife, an insignificant, wretched creature worn out in keeping track of her husband's enthusiasms for other women. She had too much old honey in her, moving about the kitchen as she now did, so tall, with her almost blond hair, and the red blanket about her shoulders. She was too full of old honey to have ever been a pathetic creature. And almost laughing to myself, I said: 'You're a strange woman! So you would have liked them to know they were sows?'

'I would,' said my mother. 'I would have liked to laugh at the matter...'

'You're a strange woman!' I said. 'You'd have laughed at the matter?'

'Naturally. I wouldn't have minded at all! I'd have laughed at it. But he didn't treat them like sows...'

'Why should he have done that?' said I. 'They had husbands like you and children like you.'

'That's all very well,' said my mother. 'No one was forcing them to behave like sows...'

'Was it so dirty, what they did? Didn't they do the same as you did with him? Or were they doing something else?'

'Something else?' cried my mother.

She stopped sweeping for a moment.

'What d'you mean, something else?' she said. 'They did the same thing, of course. What else could they do?'

'Well, then?' said I. 'They had husbands like you. They had children like you. They were doing nothing dirtier than you did with him... Why should he have treated them like dirty sows?'

And my mother said: 'But he wasn't their husband, he was my husband...'

'That's the difference, is it?' I said. I laughed to myself. I saw her standing bewildered in the middle of the kitchen, with the broom in her hand, having

164

stopped sweeping, and I laughed to myself. 'I don't understand your reasoning,' I said.

And, laughing to myself, I resolved to hazard the blow. 'I don't understand your reasoning,' I repeated. And I added: 'Were you a dirty sow when you did the thing with other men?'

My mother did not blush. Her eyes kindled, her mouth closed, hard, her whole body went hard, and the old honey within her was stirred. She did not blush.

And laughing inwardly, I said: 'Because I assume you also went down to the valley...' I was happy to stir the old honey within her and, laughing inwardly, I became loquacious.

'You haven't passed all your time in a kitchen,' I said. 'You've also been down in the valley with someone!'

'Oh!' said my mother. She stood like a stone image in the middle of the kitchen, the old honey stirred within her, but not blushing, not ashamed. 'Oh!' she said, looking down her nose at me.

When she said this, she was more than my mother, she was a mother-bird, a mother-bee, but the old honey in her was too old, and it calmed itself, and lay still, crafty, and I, after all, was a son of twenty-nine, almost thirty years, unknown to her during half of my life, during the past fifteen years, just a stranger from the street as to that half of me; and so, continuing to sweep, she said: 'Well, I expect he deserved my going with other men once or twice!'

Laughing to myself, I thought: Ah, the old sow!

I said: 'Of course he deserved it!'

Then I asked: 'Several times? With several men?'

'Oh!' my mother exclaimed. 'D'you think I put myself out for those men?'

'Of course not,' I said. 'I wanted to know if you'd been with one or two...'

'With one! With one!' said my mother. 'It was a mistake, the other time; it doesn't count.'

'A mistake?' said I. 'How a mistake?'

'It was with a chum of ours while we were at Messina,' said she. 'After the earthquake... It was a mix-up, really. I was very young, and it wasn't mentioned any more.'

'Oh, really!' said I. 'And with the other man?'

'Oh!' said my mother. 'With the other man, that was by accident!'

'Was he also a chum of ours?' I asked.

My mother said: 'It was someone I didn't know.'

'Someone you didn't know?' I exclaimed.

'Is that so strange?' said my mother. 'You don't know everything that went on.'

'I expect he must have raped you!' I said.

'Raped?' said my mother.

The tone in which my mother said this made me laugh to myself. Then, observing her as if from some other spot in the world, and not from there in her very own kitchen, and in her very own Sicily, I asked: 'But where was it? Were we already living in the line-keepers' cottages?'

XX

'We were at Acquaviva,' said my mother.

I was listening to her now from some other place in the world, and I imagined Acquaviva to be somewhere very remote, a lonely spot lost in the mountains. But I said: 'But we were all grown-up at Acquaviva. It was after the war.'

'What d'you mean by that?' said my mother. 'Ought I to have asked your permission because you were grown-up? You were eleven. You used to go to school and play games...'

So it was in those solitary places, Acquaviva, San Cataldo, Serradifalco; the children would be at school, packed off on the goods train, or playing in the hollows of that undulating countryside, the men busy with the hoe, the mothers with their washing or something else, everyone wrestling with his own devil, alone under that limitless sky.

It was marvellous – so far away in space. My mother said it had been a terrible summer. Not a trickle of water, this meant, in all the torrent-beds within a radius of some sixty miles, nothing but stubble everywhere, from east to west. And not a house to be seen for ten or fifteen miles in any direction, except, along the railway track, the line-keepers' cottages engulfed by the solitude. A terrible summer also meant not a single patch of shade throughout those hundreds of miles, crickets exploding in the sun, snail-shells emptied by the sun, everything aflame with the sun. 'It was a terrible summer,' repeated my mother.

She had finished sweeping and was putting things away in the kitchen. She wouldn't talk of her own accord but was willing to reply to my questions. 'Was it morning? Was it afternoon?' I asked.

She said: 'I think it was afternoon. There were no wasps, no flies, there was nothing... It must have been afternoon.'

'And what were you doing?' I asked.

'I had made the bread...' she said.

So it was like this: for miles and miles around the odour of serpents dead in the sun, and then, all of a sudden, the smell of freshly-baked bread about a solitary house.

'I had made the bread,' said my mother.

'And then?' I asked.

'I was washing,' my mother said. 'We had a tub outside by the well, and it must have been the afternoon because it was just the tub that cast a shadow... I always used to wash in the afternoon.'

So it was afternoon, and there was the smell of freshly-baked bread about the house. There was a well, with water that had come by train in a cistern-truck, and a woman washing. But my mother would not tell her tale, though she replied to my questions. I asked: 'And he?'

'He was a wayfarer,' said my mother.

'A wayfarer!' I cried.

'Yes, someone who travelled about on foot,' said my mother.

'Those miles and miles without a drop of water... without a cottage...'

My mother said: 'Yes. With a small haversack containing a change of clothes, and wearing a soldier's uniform without any stars, with an old reaper's cap on his head. He had taken off his shoes, and carried them, tied together, on his shoulder...'

'Had he come from far?' I asked.

'I think so,' said my mother. 'He told me he had passed through Pietraperzia, Mazzarino, Butera, Terranova and a hundred other places. But he seemed to have come directly from where the war had ended. He was still dressed like a soldier, but he didn't have on any stars.'

'All the way on foot?' I said. 'Through Terranova, Butera, Mazzarino, Pietraperzia?'

My mother said: 'On foot... by that day he'd been going forty-eight hours without seeing a village or a living soul.'

'And he hadn't eaten for forty-eight hours? Hadn't drunk for forty-eight hours?' said I.

My mother said: 'Longer than that... The last place he'd passed was a cattle farm. There the dogs didn't allow strangers to approach. That's what he told me, and meanwhile he'd drunk a pailful of water.'

She stopped, as if she had nothing more to say, and I asked her: 'He only wanted water?'

'He wanted anything else he could get,' said my mother. 'In fact he didn't ask, but I gave him a small loaf of bread that I had baked less than an hour before. I seasoned it for him with oil, salt and marjoram, and he sniffed the air and the smell of the bread and said: 'God be praised!''

Once again my mother stopped and wouldn't proceed with her tale, though she answered my questions. I asked her something – I no longer know what – and my mother said that she didn't want the man to hunger or thirst for anything; that she wanted to see him sated, and it seemed a Christian and charitable act to appease his hunger and thirst for other things.

'Blessed old sow,' I thought to myself.

'But, after all, he just stopped on his way!' I said.

'No,' said my mother, 'the man came back on other afternoons.'

'He was from these parts, then?' said I. 'He wasn't a wayfarer?'

'He was a wayfarer. He was on his way to Palermo and he'd crossed the whole of Sicily.'

'Was he going to Palermo? Or did he go to Palermo?'

'He was going, but didn't go. He went as far as Bivona. He found work there, in a sulphur-mine, and stayed on.'

'At Bivona?' said I. 'But Bivona is far from Acquaviva...'

'It's the other side of the mountains. About twenty miles... All the places are about twenty miles away from Acquaviva.'

'No,' said I. 'Casteltermini is less than twenty miles away. Why didn't he stop at Casteltermini?'

'Perhaps there was no work at Casteltermini. Or perhaps he wanted to go on to Palermo, but having got to Bivona, he changed his mind.'

'He did twenty miles on foot to come and see you?' said I.

'Twenty coming, and twenty going. He was a wayfarer... And he came back on the seventh day after that afternoon.'

'Did he come back several times?' said I.

'Various times. He used to bring me little gifts. Once he brought me a honey-comb. It perfumed the whole house.'

'Oh!' I exclaimed. And I said: 'How's that he didn't come back?'

'That's it,' said my mother. She was about to continue, but she looked at me and said: 'You don't ask me if it was the Great Lombard?'

'Oh!' I exclaimed. 'Why? What's he to do with it?'

'I think it was him,' said my mother. 'I think he used to think of his other duties. Isn't a Great Lombard someone who thinks of his other duties?'

'He thought of his other duties?' I exclaimed. 'He? The wayfarer?'

'Yes,' said my mother. 'Towards the winter there was a strike in the sulphur mines, and the peasants were also rioting. Trains passed by full of the Armed Police...'

Now my mother was talking freely. There was no need to prompt her.

'The railwaymen didn't come out on strike,' she went on. 'The trains passed full of the Armed Police. More than a hundred died at Bivona. Not of the Armed Police. Of them...'

'And you think he was among them?' said I.

'That's what I think,' said my mother. 'Because otherwise wouldn't he have come back?'

'Ah!' said I. I observed my mother. She had nothing more to do in the kitchen. She was quiet and placid, and with her hand she was ironing her dress against her leg. Blessed old sow, I thought to myself once again.

Translated by Wilfrid David

In the story's middle distance is a portrait of the island in the early years of the twentieth century. Unrelieved poverty in the interior drove vast numbers to flee overseas: by 1900 Sicily was one of the busiest centres of the emigration in the world. Thousands left for the United States, South America and Australia; by 1914 one and a half million Sicilians had left. Conditions for the majority of those who remained were relatively primitive. Up to forty percent of Sicilians were illiterate when *Conversations in Sicily* was published; up to sixty percent of those living inland. Vittorini himself was an emigrant, albeit only to the mainland. Under the explosive sun, amid the wild and rearing hills, the peasant struggle continued: against the landscape, and the bandits, and the weather, and the market, and each other. And now many of the bandits were organised, and living in the towns and villages, indistinguishable to outsiders from the rest of the population: the Mafia had truly arrived. Where it came from and how it grew will be detailed in the next section, but for a glimpse of how it effected the lives of the rural poor, and much, much else besides, there is a rather amazing book by an American, a woman from Chicago named Charlotte Gower Chapman, who learned Sicilian among immigrants in her native city, and set out for the island's interior in 1928. After immersing herself in the life of a small, isolated community she wrote *Milocca: A Sicilian Village* and posted it home. It got lost in the mail, and reappeared somehow in 1978, when it was published. It is a fascinating and intricately detailed account: this extract, though something of an overview of village life, affords a glimpse into the heart of the mysterious interior.

Charlotte Gower Chapman
From *Milocca: A Sicilian Village*

Milocca, the village selected as the scene of this study, lies in the south-west corner of the Province of Caltanissetta, about eighty miles south from Palermo and slightly to the east. The surrounding country is rugged and quite bare of any but cultivated trees. In the late summer the broken landscape is burned to a yellowish white, with here and there gray outcrops of gypsum. The heavily eroded valleys and hillsides look like a gigantic relief map. It is no garden land but stark and, as seen from the train, apparently uninhabited. But in May, before the grain is cut, it is easy to see that here is no deserted waste. Every inch of tillable ground is cultivated. The inhabitants live in towns situated on higher ground, away from the malarial river valley which the railroad follows. Occasionally the walls of their closely grouped houses can be seen from the train. They are yellowish gray like the rest of the landscape.

The rare travellers who wish to reach Milocca descend at the railroad station at Campofranco. Here one of the largest of the Sicilian sulphur mines and an establishment for making chemical fertilizer form the basis of a small industrial settlement. The town of Campofranco, where most of the labourers live, can just be seen at the top of a hill on the opposite side of the river. There is no bridge and no road to the village. In the summer the river Platani can be crossed dry-shod as it winds about its broad pebbly bed. In the winter one must go about by the bridge and the station of Sutera, three kilometers north.

To reach Milocca it is necessary to ford first the Platani and then the Gallo d'Oro which flows into the larger river somewhat below the station. Then an abrupt ascent, a relatively level winding road, and the first outlying sections of Milocca appear. Before the centre of the village, with its piazza and the church, is reached there is still another deep stream bed to pass. The distance is perhaps six miles in all, over a rocky trail so difficult that the journey required at least two hours.

The centre of town is a group of houses clustered about the church. In 1901 there were but thirty-nine inhabitants in this section. In a quarter century the number has increased to something like two hundred. This is the largest of the thirty-five groups of houses which constitute the political unit known as Milocca. It is the business centre. Here are most of the stores, the administrative offices, the only church, the mill, the inn, the residences of the doctors and the midwife, as well as the shops of most of the artisans. It is here that men congregate to exchange opinions concerning local happenings or what they know of national affairs. The annual fairs and such occasional attractions as a traveling circus are held on the square itself.

About this centre the other local divisions of the village are scattered. The circumference of the area that they cover is approximately five miles. They vary in their distance from the centre of the community from a few rods to two miles. Most of them are more than half a mile distant. Only five contain any shops where merchandise may be purchased. No meat is sold outside the centre of town. The pharmacy is the only outlying shop which is not duplicated in the Centro Urbano.

This scattered arrangement of the village is unusual in Sicilian towns. The more typical arrangement of a village is illustrated in the town of Campofiorito, where two thousand people live in the centre of town, in houses which for the most part are side by side with no intervening spaces, save the narrow paved streets, while only sixty-seven persons live in scattered houses in the country. Milocca's peculiarity in this respect is in part responsible for the town's reputation of backwardness. I was assured that it was a community 'forgotten by God and by man,' completely without the comforts of civilization.

Very little of the present town antedates the eighteenth century. In 1740 the monastery of San Martino was established by monks of the Benedictine order. A few peasants settled near the monastery, more or less attached to it as cultivators of its land. In 1866 the Church was dispossessed of its lands, and those of the monastery of San Martino were assigned to the commune of Sutera. Subsequently small plots of land were distributed among the enterprising poor of Sutera at very reasonable terms of purchase. The long difficult road, impassable in winter, that lies between Milocca and Sutera made it impossible for these new landholders to maintain their residences in the parent community, and small clumps of houses were built near their fields. The insecurity of the countryside, long habits of close communal dwelling, and the need to be reasonably near a supply of potable water all combined to prevent the building of isolated farm houses. Thus the groups of dwellings which comprise the existing community were formed. They are still known as *robbe*, literally farmsteads, in the common speech, although an official attempt has been made to rechristen them 'villages,' and in spite of the fact that a *robba* may contain ten or twenty families.

Besides the small farms which resulted from the distribution of the Church lands, there were, in and about Milocca, certain large estates, usually the property of absentee landlords. These latifondi, known locally as *feudi*, are no longer in existence within the communal territory. This fact alone sets Milocca off from the majority of the communes in the province, more than a third of whose area is held in one hundred and twenty-two large estates of more than 494 acres each. However, the Milocchese are entirely familiar with the *latifondo* system, with its large semi-fortified manor houses where the laborers live during the week, returning to their homes only for the weekend, unless they take their families with them, so that the establishment is a little village in itself. A number of young men still go to work on the estates in the neighbouring communes of Buompensiere, Racalmuto, and Campofranco, and in 1920, under the leadership of a local zealot, the labourers armed and took by force six of these estates. This local socialist movement was only moderately successful. For forty-five stirring days they held the *feudi*, maintaining a force of a hundred men in each to defend the place from counterattack and to keep it going. Once when the people of Sutera came out to aid in the recapture of one of the seized estates, the women of Milocca went into battle and helped their men keep what they had taken. The whole matter was finally settled, with the Milocchese allowed to rent half the land they had conquered, pending legislation. At present two of the estates are managed by the local co-operative bank and two more are rented by wealthy local men.

The 1920 uprising was part of the post-war unrest which manifested itself all over Italy, with workers seizing factories in the north and land in the south. The Milocchese phase was fathered by a small number of active socialists and was organized and led by Don Toto Angilella, an active member of a rising merchant family. Associated with him was a self-styled lawyer from Grotte, a mining town to the south. It may have been at this time, or possibly on an earlier occasion, that this visiting enthusiast set up the free and independent socialist state of Milocca, with the red flag flying over the town hall. If this was a separate venture, it was somewhat less successful than the other, for according to all accounts, the republic lasted only twelve hours, before the military police appeared and quelled the rebellion. The hero of the occasion was obliged to leave Italy, and his exploit has apparently vanished from memory, but not from the records of the police.

Although the Milocca uprising was one of many such expressions of discontent and unrest all over the country and was fomented by one who preached a doctrine popular throughout Europe, it may also have had certain local causes. The larger part of the settlement of Milocca had remained a part of the commune of Sutera, while a few *robbe* lay within the territory of Campofranco and were politically attached to that commune. As Milocca grew in size it acquired a church, telegraph and post office, and a number of resident merchants and artisans. It had its own administrative officers, a *sindaco* and a town council, and a registrar of births and deaths. However, its taxes were paid to the parent commune, and Milocca got very little in return in the way of public services. The roads within the village and leading out of it were in deplorable condition, the cemetery was not kept up, and when Sutera provided itself with water piped from the Madonie mountains the dependent commune derived no benefit. Whether the ordinary citizen was aware of these grievances or not is a question, but they were seized upon by certain leading citizens who set about working to obtain political autonomy for Milocca. One of the leaders in this movement was the same Don Toto Angilella who led the land seizures in 1920. The socialist and the autonomist movements thus had the same leader and the general post-war unrest was further complicated by local problems. The grievance of the landless peasant against the great landlords was bound up with the griefs of waterless Milocca against Sutera. Thus the people of Sutera were found fighting on the side of the dispossessed capitalists against the Milocchese, despite their common economic and class interests.

When the Fascist government established itself, it sought to abolish all other political parties. In Milocca this resolved itself into the question: Which of the local factions should control the local Fascisti? This question became particularly acute when the town was granted autonomy in December, 1923. The first Prefect's Commissar of the new commune was appointed from outside, but the position of secretary to the local Fascist Party was given to one of the local conservatives. There is a story that when the news of autonomy reached Milocca, this man and Don Toto immediately mounted and raced to the provincial capital. The conservative had the better horse and was given the appointment. However, when a local Commissar was eventually appointed (1927), it was Don Toto Angilella, the former socialist leader.

When the first Commissar arrived in town, each of the local factions strove to outdo the other in welcoming him. Each provided a band with which to greet him and great discussions arose on what should be the order of their going. An agreement was finally reached that one band should lead on the trip from town and the other on the way back. The faction which led out failed to keep its agreement and the resulting strife and confusion greatly perturbed the new official, whose inaugural address was rendered almost inaudible by the disaffected faction and its musicians, who continued to parade merrily throughout the discourse.

Of course the leading citizens all joined the Fascist party, and their wives made up the *Fascio femminile*. Active participation in these groups, however, tended to follow the old tradition. When the Angilellas were in control of local affairs, the Cipollas of the opposed faction were noticeably inactive. Their women did not march with the women Fascists in the parades that marked all political celebrations, nor did they help in soliciting memberships to the Red Cross. On one occasion two of the younger members of this group publicly refused to rise when the Fascist marching song, *Giovanezza*, was played. When the Cipolla faction had its turn in power, the Angilellas tended to be equally uncooperative.

This political division within the town is one of the most important features of the local life. No person who is at all active in public life can ignore it, and very few can avoid being affected by it in one way or another. At times the rift between the two parties is more serious than at others. In 1928-9 it was very marked, for one of the most important members of the Cipolla faction was in prison charged with being a member of the Mafia, and his friends tended to blame his arrest upon the Angilellas. Five years earlier the young people of the two factions had been very friendly, but during the period of observation, there was no contact between them. A generation earlier a Cipolla had eloped with one of the Angilella daughters, precipitating a long period of active antagonism, for the girl's father maintained that his political rival had connived at the match just to bring shame on the Angilella family. Business contacts bring the men of the two parties together in outwardly amiable relations, but the women of their families meet only on occasions of death or serious illness, when etiquette prescribes calls of condolence.

The precise position of the Mafia in relation to these political divisions is no clearer than is the exact nature of the Mafia itself. Legally the Mafia is known as an association for crime. Whether it is a single organization, or a series of local gangs comparable to those which have become familiar in the United States, is not easily ascertained. It is certain, however, that it was very powerful politically in all parts of Sicily, and that certain bands were in close co-operation. It was very strong in Milocca, which seems to have afforded by its isolation a safe retreat for bandits whose business headquarters were in other towns. The exploits of these persons seem to have caught the popular imagination much more than the incidents of political strife mentioned above. Some of the stories go back as much as twenty years, to an almost legendary figure whose various successes in outwitting the police form a cycle of stories that are told with delight.

The greatest development of Mafia activity seems to have been in the tumultuous post-war years. Those were days when a woman saw her husband go off to the fields and did not know whether he would return alive, or whether he would be killed with his own mattock by the men who stole his mules; when no one went abroad after dark, and if necessity forced him out dared not give greeting to anyone he met, however familiar the dark figure, lest his acquaintance kill him as an inconvenient witness to his wanderings. Men who had to ride long distances went in groups, or took a police guard, and even that was not secure, for one traveller was murdered despite the presence of an armed guard. Law-abiding citizens did not dare incur the disfavour of the *mafiusi*, and almost anyone who had extensive property in the country was obliged to protect himself by extending favours to them. It is this latter fact that may well explain why the Cipolla faction seems to have been in closer league with the associated criminals than were the Angilellas, for the former had flocks and fields to protect, while the latter had none.

The extirpation of the Mafia in Milocca came in January, 1928. A vigorous campaign against crime had been waged in Sicily since 1925, under the capable direction of Prefect Cesare Mori, who combined the forces of the military police and the militia in surrounding and attacking the various strongholds. By June, 1927, the greater part of the work was done, and there remained only small isolated bands to deal with. One of these had representatives in Milocca. According to popular report, many of the names of the guilty men were turned in to the authorities by the mother of a bandit who had been murdered by one of his fellows in the course of some quarrel within the band. The police descended in force, by night, and proceeded to make their arrests. Some of their victims escaped, in spite of the suddenness of the attack, but the members of their families were taken and held in their stead. If this did not produce the desired persons, all their livestock was confiscated. The little square in Milocca must have presented a strange spectacle that January morning, filled with bleating sheep, goats, horses and mules, while the police station was full of weeping women. No one felt safe. A bride who set out to make her nuptial calls was ordered back to her home, for this was no time to be abroad. Pity was mixed with fear, pity for the unhappy animals, the bereft families, the arrested men, and even for the police, who had come without adequate provisions and had to beg bread from the terrified townspeople. Finally the police and their captives set off to Mussomeli, a distance of more than ten miles over difficult country, taking with them the families and flocks belonging to the men who had not as yet given themselves up. In Mussomeli the prisoners were put in jail, to be sent later to various prisons to await trial. The men whose property was seized eventually made their appearance and their hostages returned home, somewhat travelworn. At this time between thirty and fifty men were seized. A few had been taken earlier, and arrests continued from time to time for more than a year, as bits of information implicated more persons. In the fall of 1928, there were about one hundred Milocchese men in prison awaiting trial. In the early part of 1930 a few were released for lack of evidence against them.

The incarceration of so many local men was not without important effects upon the life of the village during the period in which this study was made. On my arrival, a rumour got about that I was carrying on investigations in regard to the prisoners, and so might be influential in getting them released. As long as this rumour was current, everyone sought to please the stranger. The belief may never have died completely, for no arrested man was ever described to me as anything but entirely innocent and a true saint. At the same time, the action of the government in making the arrests and destroying crime was always praised. A very few people went so far as to suggest that the cleansing had not been so thorough as it might have been. As it was, it had put the entire community into a sort of mourning. Religious occasions were not celebrated with the usual splendour, for most of the men who had been active in such affairs were behind the bars. Prison-widows were numerous, and some were in serious financial difficulties so that for a time relief was administered to them in the form of free meals and condensed milk and flour for nursing mothers. The funds for this relief were soon exhausted. One woman had deviated from the path of virtue in the absence of her husband, and was condemned as much for her levity in a time of bereavement as for her unchastity. Crime itself had come almost to a full stop.

To the Fascist regime Milocca owes not only the suppression of the Mafia but also the attainment of the coveted political autonomy.

Milocca began first to benefit from its autonomy when a local Commissar, Don Toto Angilella, was appointed in 1927. Within a short time a number of improvements had been made: a sanitary officer was appointed, a pharmacy installed, and the old midwife replaced with one who had received training. Roads were repaired, kerosene lamps set up to light the streets in the business centre on moonless evenings, and improvements were made on the springs which provide Milocca's water.

There were other attempts to make Milocca less rural: manure piles were banished from the vicinity of houses, horsemen were obliged to dismount when

175

passing through the centre of town, houses on the village square were required to have a new coat of whitewash, and it was forbidden to throw dirty water in the streets ...

This population of Milocca is almost entirely agricultural. The sulphur mine which lies within the commune's territory is owned and operated by outsiders. The only industrial establishment in town is the mill, which employs six men constantly and two or three more in the autumn when the olive-press is in operation. About seventy other persons – teachers, professional men, officials, artisans and merchants – earn their livings in ways not directly connected with agriculture or husbandry. There are a dozen or more herdsmen, many of whom are also concerned with small-scale farming.

The principal crop of the district is wheat, which forms the staple in the local diet, and also the largest export product. Almonds, broad beans and sumac are also raised for export, and a small surplus of olive oil, wine, cheese, hay and wool is likewise sold out of town. The life of the town moves in accordance with the rhythms of the agricultural year. Debts are paid and leases terminate on the fifteenth of July, after the wheat harvest. Building is done, marriages performed, religious and popular feasts are celebrated during the lulls in agricultural activity. School attendance varies with the demands which the family farm-work makes upon the children of the household. Local prosperity varies from year to year, as the seasons are favorable or unfavorable for the crops. A bad year is spoken of as a 'year of hunger.'

The key position of agriculture in the local economy is reflected in the Milocchese conception of wealth. The man who owns land is considered to be more truly wealthy than one who can boast of nothing more than money in the bank. High social standing is dependent either on education or property in land, but is assured only in the families which possess both.

The importance of agriculture in Milocchese life is typical of many Sicilian communities. It is, however, not entirely characteristic of this region in Sicily, where sulphur and rock salt mines are abundant. Fourteen of the twenty-two communes in the Province of Caltanissetta have populations which include miners. In the past, some Milocchese worked in the local mine, but in the late 1920s, it was more profitable to work in the fields, for miners' daily wages were two lire (twenty percent) less than those of field labourers.

The people of Milocca live in houses of one or two rooms built of gypsum rock covered over with gympsum plaster. The walls are thick, but easily penetrated by the moisture of the winter rains. In two-room houses the second room is built above the other. In the older houses the floor is supported by a masonry vault. Newer buildings make use of metal cross beams. Where there is a second story, the upper room is reserved for the family, and the lower room serves for storage and to house the domestic animals, or it may be rented as a shop, schoolroom, or to a poorer family. The upper room is reached by an outside staircase which runs up the side of the building. Not infrequently an opening is let in the floor to permit the householder to keep an eye on his stock in the room below. The dwelling room is usually paved with tiles, which may be plain and reddish-gray or glazed and decorated in designs of blue, white and green. The latter are more admitted and are easier to keep clean. The roof is made of canes, lashed together, smeared with plaster, and overlaid with a double layer of red tiles. Only in the better houses is a plaster ceiling provided for the upper room. Ground-floor rooms are without windows, and receive their only light from the doorway. The upper rooms have large french windows giving on the street. If the family can afford it, there is an iron balcony upon which the doors open.

When houses are built close together, two adjoining ones may use the same staircase, which is then roofed over and provided with a front wall, with a door at the foot of the stairs. The houses of wealthy persons tend to follow the general pattern described, save that one family may occupy two or more two-storey units. There is but one staircase, of the type described, and the upper rooms have connecting doors.

The single-room houses provide shelter not only for the family, but also for the livestock. For these, mangers may be built of masonry, usually near the door. Beneath the mangers, an enclosed space may be provided for the chickens. In a corner is a small raised open hearth where cooking is done. There is no chimney, and smoke escapes through the roof or by a small hole left for the purpose high on the wall. One or more beds, a table, several wooden chests, and a few chairs share the rest of the space with piles of wheat, broad beans and straw. Clothing, utensils and harness are hung from pegs let into the plaster walls. In such an establishment, it is possible that provision be made for cooking out-of-doors in fair weather, and the bread oven is also outside. This is built of plaster, lined with tile, and shaped like a beehive. It has a protective wall of masonry, and a roof above it. In some cases the chickens are kept under the oven.

In the two-room houses, the lower story is reserved for the animals. If the family includes a grown son, he may sleep here. This room also serves for the storage of straw and fuel, as well as for the harness and field implements. Grain is stored in bins constructed in the floor of the upper room, filling the spaces in the sides of the supporting vault. The upper room is reserved for living purposes. A separate kitchen may be built at the head of the staircase. The bread oven is usually outside. Persons who own this type of house usually can boast a *chiffonier*, which replaces the less-admired chest. Otherwise, there is no material difference in the furniture.

The houses of the wealthy usually contain a *salotto*, where guests are received. This consists of a small settee and several matching chairs which are grouped about a small table. If the house is large, the *salotto* is established in a room of its own. Otherwise, it is placed in one corner of a bedroom. These houses also may have embroidered hangings at the windows and a small rug to embellish the *salotto*. Otherwise rugs are lacking in all houses. The best type of kitchen stove, erroneously known as a steam-kitchen (*cucina a vapore*) is a tile stove, with enclosed hearths, and a flue.

These houses are, on the whole, well-suited to the Milocchese climate and mode of life. Their high ceilings and thick walls keep them relatively comfortable during the heat of summer. The absence of windows is not serious in view of the amount of time which is spent out-of-doors. In winter, when the temperature falls to freezing on the coldest days, they are of course impossible to heat. Large copper pans are filled with ashes and the glowing husks of almonds, and about these the family huddles, wrapped in shawls. Small braziers in the form of copper buckets may also be provided for the use of the individual, to be held in the lap or placed under the chair as convenience dictates. On the worst days, in homes where the walls are already darkened by smoke, a bonfire may be built in the middle of the floor, more for the cheering effect of its flames than for any extra heat that it may give. The structure of the building reduces fire risks to a minimum. Fortunately the winter is short.

The lack of storage space in the home is correlated with a very simple manner of living. Guests are seldom invited in, so that there is no need of more dishes than the few required for the family. One platter may serve for the entire household, and all customarily drink from a single glass. For cooking little more is needed than a large pot for boiling spaghetti, a smaller vessel for making sauce, and a frying pan. Water is kept in the large earthen-ware jars in which it is brought from the well. All food-stuffs are purchased in small quantities. Flour is ground as it is needed for making bread, which is stored away in a basket or placed in one of the chests. There is no need for refrigeration, for milk is bought only when it is to be used at once, butter plays no part in the local diet, and in summer meat is cooked as soon as it is purchased. Fruits and vegetables which are stored for winter use are hung on the walls or buried in the wheat ...

If living conditions are bad in Milocca, it is largely because of its isolation. While many of the surrounding towns have a water supply piped in from the Madonie mountains, the Milocchese depend upon three or four natural springs of potable water, and as many more whose water is too bitter for any use but washing and watering the stock. In the summer, a drought of unusual severity may cause a serious shortage. Even in ordinary times, water is so valuable that as much as possible of it is made to serve a double purpose. Plants are always watered with soapy water which has already been used for washing hands or dishes or both, and very often dishes are washed in the water in which the spaghetti has been boiled. A woman who throws quantities of water into the street is apt to be reproved as a wanton waster.

Electricity is another utility which the Milocchese lack. In this, however, they are not much behind many other small towns in Sicily. The lack is not greatly felt, for the rhythm of daily life is largely determined by the movements of the sun. The men leave for the fields before sunrise, and return shortly after sunset. On their return, supper is served and the ordinary family goes to bed early. Kerosene lamps are used during the brief hours when any artificial illumination is required ...

Milocchese diet centres around bread and its close relative, spaghetti, which in its various forms is known as *pasta*. In most families the baking is done by the women of the household. A sufficient quantity of wheat is taken from the bin under the floor, cleaned with care, and sent to the mill for grinding. When the flour returns, it is sifted several times to remove the bran, and then mixed with warm water, salt, and a bit of the fermented dough from the previous week, to form a stiff dough. This is worked on a special wooden platform by means of a thick bar attached to one end of the board with a hinge. It is strenuous work and requires at least two people, one of whom turns the heavy mass of dough. Neighbours may drop in to help in this process or exchange gossip with the workers. Kneading by hand succeeds the heavier manipulation, and loaves are made. These may take various forms, depending on the whim and the skill of the housewife. The simplest form is a round loaf, with a long semi-circular gash on the top. More elaborate forms which almost anyone can make are the 'fish' and the 'pistol'. The top of the loaf may be left plain, glazed with white of egg or covered with poppy seeds or sesame. As soon as they are made, the loaves are put to bed, literally, and covered with all the available blankets and shawls. While they are rising, the oven is heated by a fire of straw and twigs built inside it. When both it and the bread are ready, the oven is swept out, and the loaves put in with a long wooden shovel kept for this purpose. A flat stone door closes the oven and is sealed in place with wet ashes. The sign of the cross is made over the door, and the bread is left for an hour or so to take care of itself. The finished bread is dusted and kept in a basket. It is of a yellowish colour and close texture. Butter is not eaten with it, but hot bread may be seasoned with olive oil, salt, pepper and grated cheese, as a treat for the children or for visitors. Every woman is convinced of the superiority of her bread to that of any other women in the community and of the excellence of the bread of Milocca over that of any other town. Bread is never lightly treated. Before each new loaf is cut the sign of the cross is made on it with the knife, and the knife is kissed. No loaf is ever put down bottom-side up. It is the 'providence of God' and is to be respected.

Pasta is served at only one meal a day, usually in the evening when the man of the house is back from the fields. During the day each member of the family satisfies his hunger when it makes itself felt, by taking a piece of bread and fruit, nuts, some cheese, salted sardines, or possibly an egg, with or without a swallow of wine. The untranslatable word *campanaggio* refers to any of these things which are eaten with the bread. The man in the fields may cut himself a raw artichoke or a bunch of grapes for his *campanaggio*, or his employer may provide something in the way of cheese, onions, or boiled greens.

At present most of the families in Milocca manage to afford to buy the spaghetti manufactured at the mill. In former days this was a luxury, and *pasta* was used only on festive occasions. Some women still make their own at home, in the form of a sort of noodle. A few possess small presses for making spaghetti. Almost everyone makes home-made pasta occasionally for a change, although as a general rule they prefer the mill variety. The *pasta* is served in a variety of ways: with the conventional tomato sauce, with the juices from meat which has been cooked in a casserole, or with vegetables. The last fashion is the cheapest and the most common. People are very particular as to the degree to which their *pasta* is cooked and the form of *pasta* used, and some can detect the almost imperceptible difference between the Milocchese *pasta* and that purchased in other towns. (Since the Milocchese mill is owned by the Angilellas, some of the most violent of the Cipolla partisans insist on buying *pasta* which is imported.)

For the production of these staples of the diet, Milocca is quite self-sufficient. Although the average daily consumption of wheat per person is a pound and a half, three times as much is exported as is consumed locally. Since the local wheat is not suitable for the commercial manufacture of pasta, the mill imports annually about two thousand five hundred quintals of semolina, one-third of which is re-exported to neighboring towns in the form of spaghetti. That which is utilized locally comprises approximately one-fourth of the wheat consumed.

Most of the foods that are used to accompany and dress these farinaceous staples are likewise of local production. All the milk is supplied by local goats, and the flocks of sheep furnish enough cheese for the community and a small quantity for export. The increase of these flocks provides the meat, with the occasional and rare addition of pork or beef when one of the two dozen pigs is slaughtered or a draught animal meets an accidental death. Chickens are raised in large numbers and their flesh adorns the table at high feasts. However, their most important contribution to the diet and to the local economy is their eggs. These serve as legal tender in the local stores and are also bought up by peddlers from other towns.

The roadside affords a wide selection of edible plants, and many farmers give over a corner of a field to a vegetable garden that may be sufficiently extensive to provide a surplus which is sold to neighbours. These gardens, however, do not supply all the vegetables consumed and many are brought in by the same itinerant peddlers who are the agents in the exportation of eggs. What is true of vegetables also applies to fruits, save that these are imported in smaller quantities.

Salt fish is kept in stock by local dealers and small quantities of fresh fish are occasionally brought up from Porto Empedocle, but these items play a very small part in the Milocchese diet. Local vineyards supply most of the wine drunk in Milocca and a small surplus for export. The little wine that is imported is regarded by its purchasers as superior to the local product and a luxury.

All the olive oil used is produced locally and some is exported. Olives are also salted and dried, but the difficulties in transportation make it unprofitable to export them in this form. Almonds, on the other hand, are raised primarily for exportation and their local consumption is regarded as something of an extravagance. Families in modest circumstances frequently depend on the produce of their few almond trees to provide their supply of ready cash for the year. Other uses are also made of the almond. The outer husk is burned to make a sort of ash soap used in laundering and the hard shell serves as fuel in the braziers.

The domestic animals that are kept about the house and not put out to graze are fed mainly on wheat straw, eked out with dried broad beans. Large quantities of these legumes are raised, for in the local system of crop rotation a given field is sown to broad beans and to wheat in alternate years. These beans serve also for human consumption but are considered a delicacy only when they are green. More than half the crop is exported. The part played by hay, oats and barley in the diet of Milocchese livestock is very small. A very little hay is exported.

While Milocca produces more than enough foodstuffs to keep its inhabitants and their domestic animals alive, certain of the imports may be regarded as necessities. Chief among these is salt. Sugar, coffee and pepper are really luxuries, without which people might, and in former days did, get along. Honey was used for sweetening and some of the older recipes for candies and cookies call for it instead of sugar. Wine is still the usual beverage in poorer homes.

Importations become more significant when one leaves the foodstuffs to consider household equipment and wearing apparel. Here again there has been a change with the times. It is now possible to buy in Milocca mattress ticking, sheeting, toweling, and cotton stuff for making underwear and men's shirts, but in the past all these fabrics were woven at home from flax of one's own raising. Flax is still grown and looms are set up, but it is customary to buy cotton thread for the warp and use homespun only for the weft. Cloth made in this way is admittedly inferior to that made with homespun warp, but it is much easier to weave. Wool is also spun and woven into saddle bags. Some of it is exported. All outer clothing for both sexes is made up from textiles purchased in the local stores or from wandering vendors. Caps and shoes are bought ready made, and the local cobblers subsist mainly on repair work, although a particularly skillful one is occasionally commissioned to make a pair of boots. Stockings are usually homemade, of coarse cotton thread which is used again after they are worn out for the weaving of dish towels.

Kerosene has almost entirely replaced olive oil for the illumination of homes, though a few of the poorer families still make use of oil lamps very similar to those of ancient Greece. The kerosene and the fuel oil used at the mill are brought in, as are all household utensils and farm implements. The local carpenters and smiths import all the wood and iron that they use. Tiles for roofs and floors likewise come from outside. One of the most important imports is chemical fertilizer, most of which is brought up from the Campofranco station.

All these materials had to be brought in on the backs of mules or donkeys until the automobile road to Milocca was completed in 1929. Even then the most direct connections with the railroad and with Racalmuto, Campofranco and Sutera were over narrow mule tracks, so that only a few carts made their appearance in town. In view of the difficulties of transportation, the presence in Milocca of such large objects as a piano and a Diesel engine seems little short of miraculous, and the wonder does not cease when interested parties relate how such things were brought across country on sledges drawn by bullocks winding about in their efforts to find the most level and least hazardous path.

The isolation affects more than the material comforts of the people. No one travels for pure pleasure, except for the rare honeymoon trips taken by wealthy couples. Convention dictates that a man take his new bride on some excursion during the first year of his married life, but not everyone can manage this, and many brides must content themselves with a visit to the fair at the festa of Saint Anthony and an ice under the white awning of one of the temporary booths. Or a bride may be taken to a similar festa at Racalmuto or Campofranco, if her husband wishes to buy a donkey or there are religious duties to be performed. Most women have never been on a train, nor even seen one except as their excursions into the country have taken them to the heights at the edge of the river valley from where one can see far off the thread of tracks and, with luck, white smoke and a tiny train. Men have a wider experience in these things, for most of them have served their time as soldiers, and as such have been sent even as far as the continent where homesickness, strange foods and life in barracks did little to foster in them a taste for wandering. Life and its interests centre in Milocca, and in those far away outposts of Milocca in Pennsylvania and Alabama from which come letters telling of the birth of grandchildren, the illness of a brother, or the marriage of a nephew to a fine girl, though a Turk (the term applied to all non-Catholics regardless of nationality or creed). The lure of America is strong, especially to the younger peasants who dream of riches gained by labour lighter than that which they know, riches with which they could return, buy land, and settle down as respected proprietors. Even the dangers of sea travel and the prospect of the bad bread and the stale, unhealthy air of America are not deterrents in view of the advantages to be gained. But, failing America, they feel no urge to go to other parts of their own country or to the African colonies. Occasionally someone remarks that it must be pleasant to go about and see the countries and cities of the world, but the general opinion is that a traveller's life is full of wear and tear.

Even secondhand reports on life outside the local community, such as may be gleaned from newspapers or books, excite but little interest. Only eight newspapers come to Milocca and these reach possibly thirty people. News of the Mafia trials was the chief topic of interest in 1929. As the wedding of the Prince of Piedmont approached, this event aroused some enthusiasm, possibly because there was hope that prisoners would be released in honor of the occasion. There was some excitement about the reconciliation between Mussolini and the Pope, just as there was in any action of Il Duce. The border incidents along the Riviera occupied much space in the papers, but only served to confirm the legendary hatred between the Sicilians and the French, and as far as this was concerned, the tale of the Sicilian Vespers in 1282 was a much better story than any that the news had to offer.

The general absence of interest in world affairs may be a result of the illiteracy of the people. In 1931 according to official reports, the percentage of illiterates in the total Sicilian population over six years of age was forty. Probably in Milocca this figure should be somewhat higher, for the school reports given above would indicate that only 62.2 percent of the children attend school for even a part of the year, and their elders were even more lax about their education. In Milocca there were many who could make out to draw their own names, and so might pass as literate, although incapable of writing or reading anything else. Others could manage to read or write after a fashion, but with so much difficulty that they reserved their accomplishment for occasions of strict necessity. Possibly a dozen people in town read for pleasure, mostly women, some of whom read religious pamphlets and others the few old novels which they might have or the serial story in the newspaper.

Under such conditions life is of course limited, but it is by no means monotonous. The annual cycle of seasons provides a change of occupation for both men and women, variations in the diet, and new diversions. Beyond this, there is always enough local gossip to occupy attention. An ordinary wedding provides conversation for more than a week, what with the dowry of the bride, the gifts presented her by the groom and the comments of the prospective mothers-in-law. An elopement is an even greater boon to social intercourse, for there are first the threats of the outraged parents of both parties, the eventual reconciliation with one or both households, and finally the arrangements of the marriage, all of which

183

bring to mind similar occasions in the past for comparison and contrast. An arrest, a birth, diseases or death in the family or among the livestock, family or neighbourhood quarrels or the report of a legacy from America all provide occasions for comment which no one finds dull. First fruits and the condition of crops are discussed with enthusiasm, and if there is really no news at all, one can always fall back on stories or companionable silence. At all times of the year men congregate in the square of a Sunday morning, and there is always a group about the mill. A woman's contacts are mainly limited to her immediate neighbours as they help each other in the heavier household tasks or sit in the sun before their doorways, knitting, spinning, or cleaning wheat. Most Milocchese families are reunited in the evening, except in the summer when advantage may be taken of the night's coolness to harvest grain or carry it to the threshing-floor. In the summer they may sit outside to enjoy the air and a bit of conversation with their neighbours.

The agricultural year properly begins with the planting season, which starts in the middle of September and continues through October and even into December. The local code of the Fascist Syndicate requires that sowing be completed before December 15th. This can be enforced only on rented land, when the owner chooses to cite the law against a lazy tenant. Wheat is sown when the land is first plowed, but fields which are to be planted to broad beans require more preparation and the spreading of manure. Plowing usually requires the services of two draught animals and two men. If the farmer is too poor to own the necessary animals or to hire help, he may prepare the land himself, using a mattock to break the earth. Preparation by hand is preferred for broad beans. These are planted as late as possible, and always after All Soul's Day (November 2nd). Delay minimizes the dangers of the plants becoming afflicted by a parasite known as the *lupa*.

While plowing and planting are the main concerns of men during the fall months, the women are engaged in other activities, some of which require masculine aid. In September the almonds are cracked, so that the meats may be sold and the shells kept for fuel. The green husks have already been removed and are being burned for ash soap. The flax is dried, pounded and its straw removed. The latter operation requires a skilled hand and there are men who specialize in this work in its season. With the middle of September the grape harvest begins, taking both men and women to the vineyards. The treading is done as soon as the grapes are gathered, and the wine put to ferment in barrels to be ready for Saint Martin's Day (November 11th), when any proper wine should be ready for testing. After the grapes, the olives are gathered, usually by women, and the men take them to the press to be made into oil. When the rains begin, the roadsides are full of greens which may be gathered to supplement the tomatoes, squash and eggplant in the garden. If one does not care to gather greens, passing vendors sell swiss chard,

184

escarole and celery. But a trip to the country is worth while, for snails are out and can be cooked in tomato sauce to make an excellent *campanaggio*.

October sees the first of the year's lambs butchered for meat. It also gives work to men who come from other towns to trim the olive and almond trees. Only two men in Milocca are adept at this work, which earns almost three times as much as ordinary field labour. The cuttings are used for fuel by the owner of the trees. In this month, the women who intend to weave next year plant a small patch of flax in a corner of one of the fields prepared by the men.

Christmas and the holidays usually mark some respite in the work, but vineyards must be cultivated and pruned and there may be late sowing to be done. The winter rains make it impossible to go to the fields on many days, and the men stay around home or lounge about the square or at the mill. When the weather is very cold, one may stay in bed to keep warm. Greens are gathered, but the only garden plant available is kohlrabi. Oranges are ripe.

In February the grain has begun to sprout and must have three cultivations by hand before it grows too tall. The broad beans must also be cultivated. Artichoke plants are cut as a vegetable – *carduna*. Vendors bring in the first cauliflowers. In this month, the almond trees bloom, the bitter ones deep pink, the sweet ones greyish white, like puffs of smoke in the distance. By this time most of the women have finished their spinning, and those who intend to weave are preparing to set up the looms.

By early April the grain is already so high that donkeys must be muzzled so that they will not eat the stalks which grow to the very edge of the narrow paths. From now on no work can be done in the fields, except in the vineyards where cultivation continues and the vines must be cleared of the shoots which persist in coming out from the wild-grape root into which slips of wine grapes have been grafted. Gardens are made in this month by setting out seedlings available in local stores – tomatoes, eggplant, peppers, and lettuce. Squash and melon seeds, carefully saved from fine examples of last year's crop, are planted in little hills. By this time the rains have practically ceased and greens can no longer be gathered in the country. Green almonds are eaten with husk, shell and all from the time that they are as large as lima beans.

Weaving is finished by the beginning of May, and the women who have new cloth spend their mornings bleaching it by dampening the long strips and stretching them on the grass. This is also the month for building new houses. By the end of the month it is time to harvest the broad beans, pulling up the entire plant. The sheep are sheared and the flax is pulled up. During this month men have gathered *ddisa*, a tough wild grass which is used to bind the sheaves of grain. They have also made ready for the harvest the circular threshing floors. Capers are gathered from plants which grow wild. The main dish of the month is green broad beans, which, like the almonds, are eaten at all stages.

By the beginning of June the busy season has begun. The ordinary wages of ten lira have begun to rise, and may be tripled or even quadrupled before harvesting is done. The beans may be threshed before the wheat is cut. By the eighth of June some farmers are already threshing their wheat, an activity which continues well into July. Once the wheat has been cut and carried to the treading-floor, where the mules do the treading, the men stay by it on guard, for piles of harvested wheat are a temptation to thieves and afford an opportunity to enemies for anonymous revenge. The women carry food to the men where they work, and select dishes that will be especially nourishing. A great variety of fruits and vegetables are available: mulberries, cherries, medlars, lettuce, escarole, artichokes, squashes, cucumbers, potatoes, green beans, and the first tomatoes. Women beat out at home such small crops as lentils and chickpeas, and the flax gets a preliminary beating to remove the seed.

By the middle of July the harvest is over. The grain has been threshed, divided between tenant and owner at the threshing floor, and the grain and straw have been carried home. The beans are already stored. This is the period to pay debts and do any moving that is to be done. Figs, pears, and the first tomatoes are ripe in Milocca, and the short apricot season is at an end. By the end of the month the first melons appear. This is the time to gather brush and heavy wild grasses for fuel and to quarry local rock for building purposes. These are distinctly odd jobs, and most of the men are about the square a great deal of the time.

Tomatoes are abundant by the beginning of August, and are cooked down, strained, and the extract put to dry against storage for winter use. Prickly pears, known locally as *ficudinnia*, are ripe and provide a popular *campanaggio*. The few men who raise sumac for export cut it and tread it out when it is dry. The almond harvest begins, giving employment to many young women of poor families. As soon as the almonds are gathered they are husked and dried in the sun. The flax is put to soak in the streams, now that harvest is over and there is no danger that men working in the fields will get malaria from the stench of the rotting stems. As the grapes ripen, a guard may be kept in the vineyard. The year ends with the feasts of Saint Anthony and the Addolorata, each with its fireworks and animal fair.

Nicknames in Milocca

The following nicknames are personal, and are based on characteristics of the individuals who now bear them:

La Greca/the Greek:	The woman has a speech defect
Lu Calavris/the Calabrian:	Uses modes of address indiscriminately
Lu Tortu/the crooked:	A cripple

Grattalora/cheesegrater:	A man with a pock-marked face
La Funcia/the snout:	A woman with protruding lips
Vapurettu/little steamboat:	A fat priest who moves rapidly and puffs
Passa cantannu	passes singing
La Vacca/the cow:	A woman with large breasts
Notaru/notary:	The bearer was a broker, but not a notary
Pantaluni/pantaloons:	The man had once used this word as a euphemism for trousers
Mala figura/poor figure:	It was said that the man always cut a poor figure in his dealings with others
Lu Signuruzzu/the little Lord:	From his mild, Christ-like manner
Lu Barattieri	Flustered one
Lu Presidenti/the president:	It did not seem that he had ever been president of anything
Lu Lungu/the long:	A tall man
Lu Russu/the red:	A man with red hair

Certain nicknames derive from the place of origin of the person or family:

Narisi	from Naro
Cummatinara	from Comitini
Mussumulisa	from Mussomeli

More rarely, a sort of nickname grows up as the result of some constant association with another, usually better known, individual:

d' 'u dutturi	of the doctor. The bearer had spent a number of years in attendance upon Dr Callari
d' 'a Gnura Angela	applied to the children of a well-known widow

In the Regional Gallery of Sicily in Palermo, the Palazzo Abatellis, is an extraordinary fresco, *The Triumph of Death*, by an unknown master of the fifteenth century. Death, a madly-grinning skeleton, rides a spectral, almost cubist horse, and fires a volley of arrows ahead of him, aiming at kings, bishops, noblemen and women. The arrows are shown sticking out of people's necks, out of their breasts and backs, and the victims lie in grey-faced heaps, or clutch their wounds, their faces stricken with terror, as the ghastly horse thunders towards and over them. Behind death, the poor, the old and the ordinary are gathered on the other side of the scene, praying for a release which, for now at least, death denies them. They have nothing to fear from his arrows, while the rich and powerful have everything to lose. The Sicilian relationship with death is shown here at its most sardonic and ambivalent. From the markets, strewn with lovingly displayed corpses, to the blood-soaked history of conquest, crime and violence, Sicily is a place richly conversant with mortality. Five hundred years after *The Triumph of Death* was painted, a Sicilian writer named Gesualdo Buffalino created something like the fresco's literary equivalent: *The Plague-Spreader's Tale (Diceria dell'untore)*. A young soldier, having escaped death in the second world war, returns to Palermo with tuberculosis. He believes he is going to die, but, while consigned to a sanatorium with other similarly condemned sufferers, he falls in love with Marta, a young dancer, who also has the disease. Their relationship takes place in the shadow of this looming fate, with the beat of the awful horse's hooves in their ears. But when it finally arrives, death comes with a twist. This extract describes the couple's happiest day.

Gesualdo Buffalino
From *The Plague-Spreader's Tale*

Of all the days of my life that Sunday, August the eighteenth, is one of the three or four which, whenever I set out to attain the rapture of living over again, I re-enact from start to finish. But perhaps I should explain... My relationship with my past smacks of depravity: I embalm it within myself, I forever caress it, as some caress the corpse of a loved-one. The strategies I employ to retrieve it are the usual two. First I visit myself as a tourist, at a leisurely pace, pausing before each plaster ornament, each scrap of majestic bric-à-brac: as a poacher of memories, I don't want to scare the game. But then I dispense with politeness and buttering up, piercing my past with ruthless Parthian glances, swift to seize and to flee. From the moments I there unearth (and how many I have lived just in order to remember them!) I am unable to elicit thoughts, for I don't have a strong head, and thinking either scares or wearies me. But flashes, glimpses, that's different... flashes of light and shade, and that inkling of recognition tucked away for years with millions of others in an invisible coffer behind my brow... At times I feel it would take a mere nothing, a whit more strength or a demon prompter, and I would burst the barrier – I, even I, scornful of Not-to-be, timid of To-be, would achieve the miracle of the Encore, delectable Re-being...

To re-be... that is indeed the question. For there is neither act nor magic spell but fails me, and what little struggles to rebirth beneath my eyelids, in the very instant of illumination blinds me. In the end it leaves me nothing but words. Worse still if they are the very words, warm, plump and moist, which I stuff my mouth with now as I did then, either bolting them down or spewing them up, a tyro on stage with first-night jitters. Or, elbows leant on the railings of my sequestration, craning out to gaze at the seething below, the living silver, the snarling and beguiling houndvoice of life, the merriment and magnificence, the banners, the abominations, the tears, the unhoped-for reprieves, the exorbitant punishments, and all the wars and the lawsuits of grief versus grief... Metaphors perhaps, though I knew not of what; and fortuitous at that, since no divinity had prepared or provided for them, since the old kinematograph had flickered out and died before my very eyes, like the drops of a shower that vanish as soon as fallen. Nothing for it but to put myself up for auction, offer myself for sale as an eloquent, big-hearted charlatan: madamina, this is the catalogue... (But for all that still capable of lust, of frenzy, of action. Still game enough to struggle, even with a foot or two in the grave, even at the risk of tightening, inch by inch, the noose they'd flung round my neck...)

Well then, on the morning of that memorable Sunday, stripped to my undervest, I shaved a sketchy reflection of myself in the plate-glass of the veranda, while whistling, to the general annoyance, a Verdi air, a *scherzo* or a *follia*. Nor had I failed to wake up ten times in the course of the night to consult the luminous alarm-clock on the bedside-table, and in the intervals of sleep to dream of her as I had seen her the evening of the show, in that soaring figure which dancers call *ballon*. A vision that had readily come to blend with others of mine, childhood Easters in my home town, and me on my father's shoulder watching the rocking ascent of a gaily-coloured squadron of fire-fed tissue-paper airships, camels and big fat women and pot-bellied barrels, which a light wind wafted like kites towards a cloud...

So, as I say, I shaved, not without bloodshed and heroic manly sticking-plasters, and then set forth, sparing barely an unpitying shudder for the bulky brass-handled coffin on a trolley wheeled along the corridor by soft-fingered Sister Casimira. The corpse that was to occupy it was not one of my mob, so all the more speedily did I hasten to join the off-duty party assembled at the foot of the stairs. Too speedily in fact, for I ran full tilt into the gaunt frame of the Wizard, causing him to drop the spectacles he was polishing with a handkerchief.

'In a hurry?' he enquired, while retrieving a detached earpiece; and then, after an ambiguous whinny from me, 'Yes or no?'

In the forceps of these monosyllables I opted for the more polite, though against my will, and with the mental reservation that I would allow him to detain me only a minute or two.

'Would you do me a favour while you're in town?' he went on, straightening his silk Shylockian skullcap, knocked skew-whiff by the impact. 'You only have to pop down to the docks.'

'If it doesn't take too much of my time,' I returned coldly, though really rather chuffed by that sort of olive-branch he seemed to be offering, after so many weeks of friction and standoffishness. Intrigued, too, by the request, seeing that on a previous outing his commission had been of the choicest: to play the spy after midday Mass at La Martorana, and report back to him about his wife, how she was dressed, whether she was laughing, whether she took her lover's arm...

Not this time. The voice that bent close to my ear when I asked 'What is it?' simply told me 'Go jump in the sea,' and with such grating facetiousness and acrimonious itch to pick a quarrel that I was left with no choice, since I was hastening to a love-tryst, but to fling back an unimaginative 'Same to you with knobs on' and make good my escape.

At the main gate the old porter Carabillò, ever ready with an ancient saw, said '*petra smossa nun pigghia lippu*,' and I went on my way with a smile, telling myself that all the moss that had gathered on the stone of my soul would take more than a weekly outing in town to scrape off. But on my way to the tram-stop I was touched, I couldn't help it, at the sight of a hesitant youngster just out of a cab: certainly a new recruit for our monastery, come to relieve the outward-bound corpse, such was the effort with which he carried a suitcase identical in all respects to mine, and on his shoulders the burden of his germ-infested youth, the tonnage of a mountain pitching into ruin. 'Is this the way in?' he enquired in a boyish, anxious voice. I answered with a nod and left him at the gate, in one hand his suitcase and in the other, poor innocent, his admission papers, a buff envelope stuffed with clinical notes, diagnoses, prognoses...

Waiting for a woman! There's a pleasure in the agony of waiting for someone who doesn't come, a quite heady emotion akin to that of losing at cards minute by minute, chip by chip. With this pleasure I now spiced up my fantasies, leaning against a wall covered with photographs of soldiers under the legend HAVE YOU SEEN THESE MEN?, while time passed and not a sign of Marta, there by the soft-drinks stall where she had promised to meet me.

No, not a sign of her, and I dwelt, with a sharp grim smart of yearning, on her limbs – those effluents of humours – on her spittle, her oozings, sweats, tears and exudations; and on herself, damned in her issues of blood, triumphant in her haemoptyses. How strange to fall in love with a body that eats, secretes, excretes and is dense with villi, papillae, Malpighian islands... Names from my pre-war schooldays, that I now repeated to myself, recalled through the roar of the years to help me study the geology of that dank sepulchre of flesh with all the meticulousness of a general, on the eve of invasion, poring over a map of the enemy territory...

Thus wrapped in thought, it eventually came as a surprise when I suddenly caught sight of her crossing the road; and not only because she acted so furtively, turning round twice to glance over her shoulder, but especially because she popped out from an unexpected direction, from a side-alley that made me wonder what route it could possibly be the end of.

'I've had to come a long way round – *buscar el levante por el poniente,*' she laughed. 'Who should be on the tram but Panzera, Dr Grifeo's evil genius. He had his eye on me, and I got the impression he was on my trail.'

I noticed in passing that she did not call the Skinny Wizard the Skinny Wizard, though my attention was far more for her light mauve organdy frock with white polka dots, from which emerged the pale bare sticks of her arms, and the upward jet of the neck, and the face I know not whether the more proud or somnambular, the eyes like timorous butterflies and the sickle-shaped plump lips from which, whatever words emerged, you seemed to catch the strains of an old-world pavane.

What a posh dust-jacket, I thought, for such a doomsday-book of dungheaps and unwholesome ponds! How she repels me! How I adore her! And I grabbed her hand and hurried her along the pavement almost at a run. She protested, she laughed, for a while she complied, but finally she was seized by a fit of coughing and forced me to stop, and we sat on some church steps like two teenagers.

Upon which she noticed that the heel of one shoe was coming adrift, and she blamed me and scolded me for it, still coughing and laughing and dabbing at her mouth with a lawn handkerchief bearing an embroidered monogram that was certainly not an M. 'I'm not falling for it, there are too many clues and too obvious,' I told myself, as an habitual devourer of detective stories, sensing that with some hoax or crafty scheme in mind, though maybe only to coax more attention, she wanted to cut a figure with me as the protagonist of perversions and mysteries, as perhaps until recently, in some cloud-cuckoo-land, she had really fancied herself to be. Now less than ever did I believe in the pinch of white powder from a small packet in her handbag, introduced sneakily into her nostril. No, I didn't believe it, but maybe it was all to the good: it would help to get her going...

Meanwhile the first thing was to get the shoe mended, though she promptly put on airs about continuing barefoot and in flight, levitating above the lake of asphalt like Titania or a Peri, whichever I preferred: 'I fly, I walk on water,' she proclaimed. 'I'm quite used to working miracles.'

Personally, and more prosaically, I set off on foot, leaving her sitting there for the few minutes it took to summon the local cobbler from the ramshackle hovel where he kept bed and bench. Even on a Sunday he was only too glad of the few coppers for the job, throwing in as a bonus, as he worked on the spot, the monologues of a small-time philosopher copiously insalivated with the vanity of pouring them into the ear of such a fetching foreigner as Marta. One of them amused her, a tale about Firrazzano or some such crafty fellow who chased Death away by sprinkling salt on his tail. But she frowned when I asked the cobbler if he could spare us a handful of salt. She then insisted on going to see two theatres, the Massimo and the Politeama, although they were miles away. And she caressed their doorways with her fingers as one strokes a beloved cheek.

I pointed to the pillars high in the façade. 'They're carved out of stone from my home town,' I told her. 'My grandfather owned a quarry famous all over Sicily. He it was who brought the rough blocks here to be worked. They crossed the whole island from end to end on a contraption like they used to build the pyramids, with ropes and rollers, drawn by ten horses. And all along the route the windows were flung open...'

She liked this story too, but in her changeable way, 'You can't take me in,' she said. 'I've had better guides to better theatres. And they didn't exhibit the randy, impatient look I can see in your eyes.'

She realized she had offended me, and slipped her arm through mine.

So arm in arm we strolled around for hours, and Marta, despite a touch of fever, seemed to cope with the effort. In fact at times she even found things to amuse her, at others (it was a way she had) a chance to inflate any object or event into a symbol. As when she spotted two volumes on a bookstall and bought them for me as being right up our street. One of them, unstitched, greasy, the work of a certain Mattia Naldi, discoursed upon the plague and ways of warding it off in the Year of Our Lord Sixteen Hundred and Something; the other, which I still possess, indeed 'it lies before me as I write', came from an anonymous hand of the newborn Nineteenth Century: *Guide to the Royal Madhouse in Palermo, Written by a Lunatick in his Convalescence, Printed at the Sign of the Ancient Masons...*

So midday came and we sought out a trattoria. There, pausing over her plate and eyeing the spoon in her hand. Marta started talking again, slowly, between two bouts of coughing.

'Yes, the analysis is reassuring, and they say they only let you out if you're clean. And yet I feel, I *know*, that every breath I breathe out is poison, that everything I touch or that touches me gets infected. Even that doorpost at the Politeama just now. Even this spoon. And I feel, I know, that everywhere I go I am spreading and smearing death – on walls, on napkins, on the rims of dishes... I'm sometimes struck with the idea of wilfully exploiting such a boundless power to hatch and spread. I see myself entering a house, and it's got to be a happy home; I see myself spitting scrupulously in every part of every room, here on a pillow-case, there on a baby's bottle. An idea like this, such a mixture of evil and infantility, one can't help wondering what seeds have been nursed in me to bring such a thing to the surface. What catacombs and hidden dungeons can it have escaped from? I feel more and more curious about myself.'

I interrupted her: 'Do you know what they say in my dialect, for infecting someone? *Ammiscari*, they say. It means mixing – mixing oneself with someone else. It implies that there's a transfer, a flowing of oneself into the other, just as mystical, perhaps, as that of two other solemnities as different as could be: communion with God in the Host, and the blending of two friendly bodies in a bed.'

And so saying I kissed her in front of all present, tried to turn the caprices of remorse that were troubling her thoughts to laughter and an overture: after all we were together there to answer the purposes of love...

Translated by Patrich Creagh

The end of the war and its aftermath brought as much turmoil and suffering to the island as the course of the conflict. First, in 1943, came the allied attack, when Palermo, Messina and many other towns were heavily bombed by British and American planes. Then came the invasion – which, despite ferocious fighting on the east coast, was not as bloody as it might have been, thanks to an alliance between the Americans and the Mafia, which saw many Sicilian and Italian garrisons surrendering, deserting their German 'allies' – and then the real trouble started, in the turbulent post-war period, when various factions battled for control of the island's destiny. They included, very broadly, the left and the communists, who demanded land reform and redistrubtion; the separatists, some of whom wished Sicily to be independent, while others wanted it to become part of the United States of America; the right, who wished to defeat the left at any cost; the landowners and the wealthy, who were anxious to hang on to their quasi-feudal power-structures and privileges, and the Mafia, who were determined to back the winning side, while milking all the others. Over all this, first AMGOT, the Allied military government, then the Italian state attempted to exercise control. The attempt by the former to cleanse power of fascism led to the resurrection and in many places enshrinement of the mafia: here were people who understood how Sicily worked, and were only too pleased to get things done for the new power in the land, knowing that it would soon move on. The disarray of the latter did nothing to alter this. The great writer and journalist, Carlo Levi, who had been exiled to Eboli by the fascists – and there written the magnificent *Christ Stops at Eboli* – returned to Sicily several times after the war, and recorded what he found. His writings about the island have recently been published in English by Hesperus.

Carlo Levi
From *Words are Stones: Impressions of Sicily*

The road continued to climb, running through an increasingly desolate landscape. Now we met no one: only an ice-cream vendor on a motorcycle raced by us at speed, and I don't know who he was going to sell ice cream to in those mountains. A cold wind was blowing, the sky clouded over and became grey, the sun had vanished when suddenly, at a turning in the road, we saw Lercara Friddi in the distance. With its low houses, it stretched out along the earth, and to the left lay a barren expanse, grey and yellowish, covered with little conical hills of yellow slag: these were the mines. In a few minutes we were in the main street of Lercara: as soon as we stepped out of the car, we realised that we had walked into the midst of a battle, in a town that seemed to be in a state of siege.

Hundreds of armed *carabinieri* thronged the streets, walking into stores, sitting in their trucks parked at the edge of the road, or strolling along, in patrols. The street was filled with people; gazes – direct, oblique and sidelong – were levelled at us from all directions. There was a palpable tension in the air, a diffuse passion, as if all those people, engaged in some unknown activity, were motivated by profound and important matters, and were awaiting grave and decisive events, making all the faces alert and wary.

This was no ordinary afternoon in a country village: this was a day of anticipation, typical of a city in a state of civil war. A strike was on: the first strike to be held in living memory; everyone was fully involved. I had come, out of simple curiosity, to visit an old sulphur mine in one of the thousands of villages of rural stagnation; and instead I found myself in a place in ferment, in a state of flux and change, filled with new emotions, impassioned actions and focused, violent determination, where something that had previously not existed was burgeoning in the hearts of the people.

My companions were tired and hungry. We had stopped, by chance, in front of the only tavern, a tavern without a sign and, at that hour of the afternoon, without customers. For that matter, there was nothing to eat, nothing but eggs and cheese. On the pavement, a powerfully built young man walked back and forth, twenty steps up and then twenty steps back. He wore a cap, poised provocatively on the back of his head, and a suit of heavy, good-quality salt-and-pepper tweed. The sleeves of his jacket and the cuffs of his trousers were a little too short, and the expression on his face was dull and ferocious. On his upper lip was a pencil-thin moustache, his gaze was indirect and fleeting, and his gait was at once insolent and worried. If the Mafia (which does not exist) were to exist, this was, I thought to myself, the typical and distinctive appearance of a *mafioso*. He looked at our parked

194

car, studied it, then walked off only to retrace his steps. Other men who looked like him, with the same unwelcoming appearance, violent and treacherous, were walking on the opposite pavement, or else stood leaning against the walls of the houses, hands in pockets and eyes attentive beneath half-lidded gazes, as if peering out through a venetian blind or prison bars. Other men, dressed in the clothing of the poor, walked down the middle of the street, or stood conversing.

It was quite a while before our eggs were ready: the family that owned the tavern was eating spaghetti, amidst clouds of flies, and were in no hurry. They were pretty close-mouthed about the strike: they didn't know who we were. All they would say was that the sulphur mine was occupied by the police that the strike had been going on for over a month, and that the miners, who received their pay at the end of each working week, had been surviving thus far on credit from shopkeepers but that perhaps, since this was the first of the month, they would return to work, as they could no longer pay their debts and he said it in a way that made it impossible for me to understand whether he devoutly wished or deplored this capitulation to hunger. But I was able to reconstruct, at least in part, what had happened, a bit from them, a bit from a tobacconist, a bit from a *carabiniere*, and a bit from a passer-by, and even more from an old newspaper that I found lying on a table.

From what I was able to surmise from these fleeting and fragmentary pieces of evidence, the sulphur mines of the Lercara basin, all managed and, in practical terms, owned by Signor N, the gentleman to whom I had been directed, are hopelessly antiquated, operating with prehistoric methods. There are no adequate safety measures, the work is done in pitiable conditions, women and children work there as well, and the pay is far below the minimum wages established in the general contracts. And yet everything went forward in a context of absolute stagnation: days and years went by, unchanging, because there is nothing more stable, reliable, and unchanging than a feudal regime. There was no union organisation here, at least until three months ago: it seemed as if the resigned fatalism of the poor would endure for ever. But on June 18th, a seventeen-year-old boy, Michele Felice, a *caruso*, was working in the mine when he was crushed by a boulder that dropped from the roof of a gallery, and was killed. This is a common occurrence: the dead boy's father had had his leg crushed in a sulphur mine collapse. A deduction was made to the dead boy's final pay packet because, by dying, he had failed to complete his working day; and the five hundred miners each had an hour's pay deducted too – the hour in which work had been halted to remove the boulder from the boy's body and carry it up, from the bottom of the mineshaft, into daylight. An ancient sense of justice was triggered, an age-old desperation found, in this occurrence, a visible symbol, and the strike began. It lasted twenty days, then it came to a halt, and then began again, following a series of firings in reprisal, and by this point it was a strike for specific union demands, for wages, insurance, safety and the freedom to organise; the strike was still going on, nor was it clear what the outcome would be.

With this sketchy information, we left the tavern, and enquired where we could find Signor N. He was just a short distance away, in his office, overlooking the street, on the same pavement where the men that I had noticed when I first arrived were walking up and down, restlessly keeping an eye on things.

The office was more like a warehouse, divided in two by a partition wall, separating a lobby from the office, with a work table and several chairs. The walls were bare. Sitting in the lobby was an old man, huge, heavy, massive, with a short powerful neck, an open-necked shirt and a shabby grey suit: a head covered with leathery skin, with enormous jaws, a mouth bristling with teeth, and small, evasive eyes behind the thick lenses of a pair of metal glasses. This was Signor N, the subcontractor and foreman of the mines. How can I describe him? Perhaps only a painting could adequately render the aura of that face, the atmosphere that enveloped it, the uncommon manner of his gestures. His face was impassive and inscrutable and yet at the same time it was enlivened by grimaces expressing feelings different from those we are accustomed to perceiving: a mixture of cunning, extreme mistrust, mingled confidence and fear, arrogance and violence and even, perhaps, a certain wit: and yet all these elements seemed to be fused in that face in a way that was distant and alien to us, as if the tone of the emotions, and the very appearance of the face belonged to another era, of which we have nothing more than an archaic hereditary recollection.

I had the distinct impression of being in the presence of a rare representative of a lost race, not a man of today, or yesterday or even a hundred years ago, but one of those who had lived a thousand years ago, in that period of history that has left practically no documentation at all, a time that we can only imagine. He welcomed us with extreme wariness. We could not tour the mines: they were garrisoned by the military police: not even he could enter. He was not interested in knowing who I was: if I wrote books, he had never heard of them. The visiting-card of introduction that I had given him, and that he turned over and over scornfully in his hands, meant nothing to him: he could not remember who that gentleman might be: certainly not a mine owner, he had never met him, he did not know him or his name. If, as I claimed, I had come to see the sulphur mines, I could turn around and go back home. To win him over, I could think of nothing better than to praise a large painting hung on the lobby wall (a white-leadish painting by a local painter, a certain Gattuso, which depicted, appropriately enough, the entrance of one of the mines), and finally, to compliment him on his face, which deserved a painting of its own, or at least a photograph. 'Of me, a photograph?' he exclaimed. 'No, that's prohibited, absolutely forbidden. No one has ever taken my picture, and no one ever will. My doctor forbids it,' he added, with a smile that revealed a formidable row of teeth, 'and so does my pharmacist.' As he said these words, he noticed that B had his photographic equipment on a strap around his neck, ready to use; and to make sure that no one took his picture, Signor N rose to his feet, huge and heavy as a boulder, and placed himself, back to back, against B: he thus made sure that he could not be surprised. In the meanwhile, Signor N's two sons had entered the office, two young men who stood at the door, along with others, young and old, and I had no idea who they were. I told him to be careful, that photographers were dangerous individuals, capable of anything, and in the meanwhile B, who might have been small but who was also strong and powerfully built, was squirming and turning. Signor N matched his movements, pirouetting, and remaining clamped to him, so that the two were soon rotating in the middle of the room, in a sort of cautious and very slow dance, as if they were acting out a ballet of mistrust. B was very sharp: at a certain point he fired off a flash, at nothing in particular: Signor N took a step in surprise, and B took advantage of the moment to launch, like the Jupiter of photography, a second flash of light, and succeeded in photographing him, saying the whole time that it was only a joke, and that there was no film in the camera. 'I've taken pictures of Churchill too, in the bath,' he said; and Signor N seemed to be amused by the game and the comparison, and, becoming apparently more agreeable, he invited us into his office and asked us to sit across from his desk. Here he repeated that he could not show us the mine, and anyway it was empty and not in operation, but if we really wanted to, we could try to obtain permission from the police inspector. The strike? It would be over very soon: the workers had no money to pay their debts. It was a political matter, a political strike. Now he was beginning to remember the gentleman who had given me the visiting-card, sure, it was Don Nicola, a part-owner of one of the mines in the Lercara basin. If I was a writer, then I should read a pamphlet that had been written against him, and tell him what I thought. It was full of lies and incredible gross exaggerations. He summoned one of his sons, and told him to give me a copy of the pamphlet, buy me an espresso, and show me how to get to the sulphur mines.

The son accompanied us to the café, and our progress was followed by a hundred eyes; there he told the barista to find a copy of the pamphlet for me. But both B and I had the distinct impression, rightly or wrongly, that while he was asking him to look for it, he winked one eye and waved a hidden 'no' with one hand. In the end, he made us promise that we would come back to the office for the pamphlet; and then we got in the car and left together. We drove down streets lined with low houses, we passed by the church, in the miners' quarter, we drove out of town, and we were immediately in front of the sulphur mines. Once we came to a stop, the young man said that he had to go home, and ran off.

197

B and I stood there, looking out over the empty landscape. Beneath us, along the path, in the last light of day, peasants were returning from the fields, with a donkey and a she-goat, looking straight ahead of them. But in front of us, silence and solitude enshrouded the cones of slag, the earth stained yellow with sulphur, the cracked and ramshackle smokestacks, like ruins of towers. A departing veil of pink, purple and violet hung in the chilly grey sky of sunset, over the hellish yellow of the earth. From one of those malevolent hillocks leapt a man in black, holding a rifle at the ready. Running as if he were attacking a position, he came rolling towards us at high speed. Behind him, five *carabinieri* appeared, in their country uniforms, carrying submachine guns and following the man at a run; they immediately surrounded us and shouted orders not to move. The man in black was a private guard working for Signor N: he could not let us through, he said, unless we showed an authorised document from Signor N or unless he was present himself; we could enter only if N ordered it – our word was not sufficient. The five *carabinieri* with their improbable black moustaches were even less accommodating, and seemed to be determined to investigate the matter of our presence in some depth, and with ill intentions; a display of eloquence, though it failed to move us a single step forward, did secure permission to leave, without further delay or harm.

And so we returned to town, in the spreading darkness. Before we reached the houses, a man sprang out of the shadows and, through the open car window, hastily thrust two copies of the pamphlet into my hands. 'Take them, read them,' he said, running along beside the car as we continued driving. It was a booklet entitled, '*Accusation from the Sulphur Mine* – A Letter from Lercara Friddi', by Mario Farinella: the pamphlet that Signor N had promised; and yet it did not seem to me that the man who had brought the pamphlet, and his impassioned voice, had come from N's camp.

At the entrance to town, a large crowd awaited us: men, women and children blocked the road, their arms locked, and surrounded the car as soon as it came to a halt. They were miners. 'Who are you people?' they cried. 'You have been to the mine. Who sent you?' The women, with children in their arms, seemed especially infuriated, and also especially threatening. I stepped out of the car and explained who I was, and said that I was a friend. Someone there knew who I was, and the faces and voices softened immediately. 'But why did you go to see N? Why didn't you come to us?' they asked. They begged my pardon for having mistaken me for an emissary or agent of the subcontractor; one of the miners had followed me all afternoon, with no idea who I was; he had watched me drink a coffee with N's son, and then go to the sulphur mines, which they too were blocking off. And so they had assembled their forces, they had gathered to stop me, they had assumed I was up to no good, and now they were glad to discover their mistake. It was a miner who had thrust the pamphlets into my hands, someone who had been at the café, and had also seen the discouraging hand signals of the young N, and had run to get copies for me. In an instant, there was a change in those sullen and hostile faces, and in the half-light, I saw them shine with trust and cheerful friendliness! They asked me to come with them, they would tell me everything about the mine, they wanted me to hear those things and write about them. I promised I would come to see them: first I wanted to go back to see Signor N, as I had promised.

Signor N welcomed me, this time, with a broad contented smile: a smile that became even broader when I told him that first the *carabinieri* had been about to arrest me, and then the miners had been on the verge of giving me a beating. He was sitting down, surrounded by a retinue of friends and trusted collaborators, who stood along the walls. I suspected, perhaps wrongly, that the fact that I had encountered difficulties had been his wish, or his desired source of amusement, when he had offered to have me accompanied to the mine. He wouldn't be able to give me a copy of the pamphlet, he said, as I had expected (I touched the two copies I had in my pocket); he had been hard pressed to find his only copy, and that copy he would need so that he could sue the author. But I could glance through it now if I liked. 'Just think,' he said, 'they call me 'Nero'! And they call my wife 'Donna Rachele'. And read this, such nonsense, can you believe it? To claim that Donna Rachele said: 'I would rather wallpaper the rooms with banknotes than raise your pay!' And that I fired my accountant because his wife wouldn't give up her pew to my wife, in church; and that I fired a miner, Schillati, because he attended his daughter's funeral, and many other enormities. Look, it calls me N the terrible, N the slave-driver, it calls me an insult to Sicily. Ha! Ha!' and he broke into laughter, showing all his teeth. I hurriedly glanced through the pamphlet: it described life in the mines, the starvation wages, the deaths of miners, the feudal conditions of Lercara, a true story. It spoke of the whippings used to force boys between the ages of ten and thirteen to work in the mineshafts, and of the stories that made Signor N roll his eyes and laugh, and of many other stories. I don't know whether those stories are true: but faces speak for themselves, with their appearance and expressions; looking at, and listening to, the faces that surrounded me in that warehouse, I decided that they could all be credible.

Outside, in front of the café, I met a tall, well-dressed man, who greeted me, and said that he had read my books. He was a prominent citizen of the town, a liberal, he said, in favour of Sicilian autonomy. 'You came here at an unfortunate time. There's a strike going on. The sulphur miners are starving. Certainly, Signor N has his faults, but he's not as bad as you may believe. Life is hard for the mine owners, too. The real criminals aren't here, they're in Rome. It's the Sulphur Agency: we are forced to sell sulphur to them at thirty and they resell it at eighty: and those bureaucrats gobble up the difference. Believe me, Rome is eating us alive, us Sicilians.'

In the night, by now pitch dark, young men and old were waiting for me, at the street corners, to show me the way to the Michele Felice Sulphur Miners League. First one, then two, then three, then ten of them escorted me and B, in silence, along the dark narrow lanes, and in that complete darkness I could not see their faces. The League headquarters was a large hall in a little alleyway, filled with benches upon which sat nursing mothers, boys and old men, and between them and all around men crammed into the room; and they all applauded, clapping their hands in a gesture of friendship and human understanding as we passed through. They told me their story, the hardships they had withstood, hunger, abuse, poverty: the life of poor sulphur miners. But that was not what mattered, to them or to me, at the moment. As they spoke of their misfortunes, their eyes and their faces were cheerful, open, smiling. They were gaunt, and some of them were disfigured by accidents, and many, children and adults, bore on their faces the marks of disease, tuberculosis and prolonged hunger. But it seemed that they had forgotten all that, borne up by a gust of excitement at all that was happening, all that they were achieving, all together, all in unison. They were proud, confident of victory, and happy to have discovered themselves as free human beings, happy with a new happiness, deeply moved and deeply moving, on all the faces. These were new faces, the faces of today, eyes that today could see the things that until yesterday had been hidden, eyes that saw themselves. All things considered, I thought to myself, this is nothing more than an ordinary and normal episode of social struggle, identical to thousands that occurred everywhere a hundred years ago, in England, France, throughout Europe, and even in Italy. The thing is that it is no longer a hundred years ago, this is 1951, and the face of Signor N, whom they are struggling against, does not date from a hundred, but a thousand years ago; it is not the face of an English industrialist in 1848, but perhaps that of a master of servants of the glebe from the eighth or ninth century, before the year 1000, and maybe not even that; and even these faces that now shine with rediscovered life were until just yesterday slaves from a remote era. And the pleasure that they experience in sensing that they are alive, and the certainty that they will win, is the ineffable, unconscious sense of having stepped, as actors, into an actual story, into the flowing river of history. Not one of them would have said to me: 'We don't even know where the Madonie are. All we know is the Dog Mountain and Bolognetta (or Lercara and the sulphur mines).' They spoke now as if the entire world had opened up, and secrets and boundaries had vanished. And they even spoke about N without anger, in civil tones. They no longer felt they were alone.

On the far wall hung a portrait of the dead boy, Michele Felice. There were no party insignias or portraits of politicians: he, the dead *caruso*, was the only image. Beneath it was a small crucifix, and another larger crucifix beside it. They were looking at the portrait of their dead comrade with eyes filled with enthusiasm and almost gratitude. It was with him that, for them, life had begun, and the sense of being alive. I could not help but think that those men, who had spent all their days underground, like the dead, in the sulphureous physical hell of the dead, were now living their own Resurrection. They were all satisfied with themselves: the old women, the nursing mothers, the young men, the tall and very handsome Drago, secretary of the League, who led them: as if they had been born yesterday. They all wanted to have their pictures taken: they had found the courage to live, they were no longer enemies of their own image. B complied with their wishes. When he wanted to take a picture of the wall with the portrait of Michele Felice, a miner, with the naive zeal of the neophyte, moved to take the crucifixes down. I asked him to leave them up.

It was late and we had to leave. Many of them escorted us, through the dark alleyways, to the car; and we cheerfully shook hands.

We were driving through the night, with the weak headlights half extinguished, across the vast black expanses of the large landholdings. A marten scurried across the road. Gianni, who didn't know what to think about what he had seen in Lercara, broke the silence at a certain point to say, in his childish way: 'That Signor N really has the face of Ganimence.' (He meant Ganelon of Mayence). And then he went on to tell the stories of the Paladins, cross-eyed Roland, Rinaldo, chief of the forty thieves, Lady Roversa, the enchanted Saracen woman, who could only be killed by Roland's sword, and then only if stabbed in a single place, the most intimate and concealed and feminine place; and how Rinaldo killed her, after stealing, in his usual way, Roland's sword, and lying down amid the dead, running her through in just the right spot, from beneath, as the woman warrior passed by. But already the lights of Palermo were glittering, and we had reached the welcome coast, redolent with seaweed.

Translated by Anthony Shuggar

The 1940s were the time of the celebrated Sicilian bandit Salvatore Giuliano. Strikingly handsome and charismatic, the very incarnation of the romantic outlaw, Giuliano's exploits, photogenic face and flirtatious relationship with the press – not to mention certain politicians and members of the police who were supposed to be hunting him – made the bandit something of an international celebrity. From stealing a diamond ring from a flustered Palermitan noblewoman (he eased it off her finger with a kiss) to gunning down ranks of ambushed *carabineri*, everything Giuliano did sent conflicting waves of horror, fascination and admiration through Sicilian society. He robbed trains, killed *carabineri*, killed leftist activists, killed Mafiosi and anyone he suspected might betray him: it is estimated that as many as four hundred and thirty people became his victims. In 1947, with the left making large and unexpected gains at the polls, Giuliano sent a letter to Harry Truman, informing the American president that henceforth the man known as the King of Montelpre (the mountain village from which he came, and which he made his headquarters) would dedicate himself to fighting 'Communist hounds'. For all his fame and daring, though, Giuliano was a mere child in crime compared to the men who held real power on the island, and in 1947 they made a lethal gull of him.

Portella della Ginestra is a pass between two mountain peaks, at least three thousand feet up, south-west of Palermo, near the remarkable and beautiful mountain town of Piana Degli Albanesi, a community founded by Albanian immigrants in the fifteenth century, where an antique Albanian is still spoken, and the signs are in that language, as well as Italian. On May 1st, 1947, the people of the town went up to the pass at Portella della Ginestra to meet the villagers of St Guiseppe Jato, who lived on the other side of the pass, in order to celebrate international workers day and the return of freedom after Fascism with dancing and feasting. The site commands a fabulous view of the ring of mountains surrounding Piana degli Alabanesi, and is overlooked by a savage and rocky peak: here, with their machine-guns, Giuliano's band waited.

Today the scene is marked with tall stones, standing in the places where each victim fell. The handsome bandit and his gang fired indiscriminately at the men, women and children below them, killing eleven and wounding thirty three. The truth of Giuliano's motives died with him and his murderer, his cousin Gaspare Pisciotta, who was poisoned, probably by the mafia, in the Ucciardone prison. It seems likely that rightist elements in Sicily's political structure, in collusion with the mafia, convinced Giuliano that he would be striking some sort of definitve blow against the left: 'Boys, the hour of our liberation is at hand,' he is said to have told his men, on receiving his orders in a letter, sent by persons unknown. Perhaps he thought that the outrage might somehow count towards his own rehabilitiation.

At least forty biographies of the bandit have been published, as well as Francesco Rosi's film *Salvatore Giuliano* (1961). Here, though, is a piece by the poet Marius Kociejowski, who visited the island in the 1960s, which says as much and more, in its own way, as any of them.

Marius Kociejowski
From *Music's Bride*

Salvatore Giuliano

> *Quid facies odio, sic ubi amore noces?*
> What will you do in your hatred, when you are so cruel in your love?

OVID, *Heroides*

1

We can almost smell the spent cartridges.
These gaunt figures with their wide moustaches are ambassadors come,
As from beyond the grave, counselling reticence,
Saying, *Speak only those words which do not hide what things are,*
And keep thought constantly on the move.
Who are these guns for hire, mouthing parables?
We ask them whom they serve, and, rubbing their stubble,
They hiss, *The ghost of a razor blade.*

The hills deepen with mauve,
And the bloated sun slides, bleeds over the distant pines.
The hour is all nerve.
As though piloted by some ghostly flame,
Suddenly we flare with one whom the devil in ourselves
Gave rise to, a tough who shook this isle.
What does death do with such handsome features?
A phantom of the kind engendered by dialogue
Slips between the colour of what is and the colour of what was,
As smoothly as a hawk on the thermal.
We debate how certain matters came to be,
And so, with a solemn measure that redeems time, we put bare wires to
A myth dipped in formaldehyde.

All geared up to mock sleeping justice,
Our brigands prowl through the village.
They observe, while pretending not to, every move we make,
While somewhere, deep within ourselves,
We can hear their dark, tracking voices:
Psst, the gun slackly held shoots wide.

2

You wished always to be of the people,
And even though you brought them trouble
Who among them would not provide solace?
And who among them would not break the law to preserve the code?
O Turiddu, very flesh of their silence,
You began as some Galahad on a shiny bicycle, upholding justice.
What loser did not bask in your presence?
So who was that other who came, blasting a hole through the haze?
Who gave shape to the darkness behind the hedge?
You were barely out of the cradle, malevolence came,
And men in their dismals began to slide.
A farmer whom misfortune drove over the edge sharpened his knife,
Watched the sun flash upon it, then heard the metal talk,
As talk it must have, for you saw the man smile
While he cupped his ear to the speaking blade.
A butchered snake dangled from the sacred olive tree;
Smelling the strange blood of that creature,
You thrilled to the knowledge of what makes things cease to be.
Pain and death absented themselves,
As though the pity of those words would make you hesitate.
Speed was to become a kind of virtue.
Your whole body drained with the pleasure the mule kick
Of the gun as you watched the sparrow plunge,
Although what you saw was only the slow image of something just gone,
An apostrophe hanging in space.
A scream flew up out of the bramble.
What it really was came from deep inside your throat,
A cry so primitive you blushed for shame.
Here, where the blood of many flows as one,
You would listen to the singing in the nerves,
And, spotting at once a false note, you'd strike as the adder strikes,
Without sorrow, without malice.
This, you darkly swore, the moment requires,
As to parley for but a second more would have been to see the hawk as dove.
The results you dumped in moonlit squares,
A note attached to each bundle, saying this one spoke, or that one took a bribe.
Weep, mothers and daughters and wives.
When finally the moment towered above all else, all time stood false.
The love you fought for, you wrapped in ice.

Your vanity was the vanity of the people,
And the photographer your only muse.

3

All day we grapple with slow commerce,
And now, with tiredness hanging upon us like shackles,
We face the dangers of the interlude.
There's everywhere the stench of failure.
Pah, spit our mild killers, cocked with pride,
Why not complain about the price of oranges?
Signori, you have not come all this distance just to lose
What by the stars above is your mandate.
You might better petition the moon than seek to communicate with one who rumbles
*   in the grave.*
We suggest an aspirin for your many troubles;
What remains of the night is ours to dissolve.

What stronger perfume than a just cause?
We hunger for change, and, where nothing moves, the milk in the dish coagulates;
A sleeping dog whimpers for the missing bone.
Such times these are, men who would aim true foul the line,
Say honour is not what is, but what we prescribe.

4

You made crazy promises for crazy times.
A wily magician, could he have conjured hope, would have ridden
Upon the shoulders of the populace.
A shabby god could be had at any price.
With the mood so ripe, you never slipped once.
So when did you begin to notice a drop in the temperature?
When the mammas stopped sending cakes?
The festive air of May shook with your fire.
The dead lay sprawled all over the place, their wounds bright
As the flags which the living brought here.
Later, you would put the slaughter down to a mistake,
As though a mistake could never be a crime.
Who, then, did you suppose the people were?
Despair had begun to gnaw at your vigilance,
And, as if on purpose, you would stray into the open spaces where
Any punk could draw a bead on fame.

You were destroyed as you deserved to be, by love.
Yes, you who would not allow the heart to meddle with your schemes
Put faith in a man who wore white shoes.
You lay as brothers side by side, the smoke of your cigarettes
Yellowing the white, while outside, the law would fake the circumstances
Of your demise, as though in this place
There can be no such thing as a straight line.
You slept beneath the Judas gaze, only to awake into death's embrace.
The news some hack had prepared well in advance sang through the wires.
The *signora*, your mother, sank to her knees;
With the cameras clicking around her in a circle,
She pressed her lips to where you'd bled over the cobble-stones,
Crying, O *sangue mio.*
You were already on the mortician's stone,
Bits of plaster from the death mask sticking to your face,
A player right down to the grand finale.
The *carabiniere* puzzled over your corpse,
Wondering how so much comes of so little.

Salvatore Giuliano, you may go as you please.
There is nobody here who'll divulge your crimes,
And besides, when the law frolics beneath the blanket with the knave
What's easier than to bribe a judge?
There has been a change in the climate, too,
Which will make recognition barely possible.
The features of all we know rapidly dissolve.
What can the gelding world say of brigandage,
When young women carry guns close to themselves, snugly as babes,
And when, instead of prayer, we place charms among the machines?
All things high and low slide towards the middle.
There is nothing solid we can put a face to.

5

We shed by slow degrees our disquietude.
The sun edges the hills with burning magnesium white,
And the hawk shadows the creeping snake.
All things wriggle into their familiar modes.
A stallholder handles with care the dark glow of aubergines.
A grocer scoops a pound of olives, so precise the reckoning of hand and eye.
We find in this a deeper resonance,

A play ghosting the whole of many lives.
Any worthy thing comes, shall come, of balance.
We called him who would become resolute in hate honourable,
And in doing so filled our house with shame.
The shutters open wide, we must go to our chores.
Our sullen desperadoes fade into the blankness of the page,
Sighing, *We shall be brought down by love.*

Another writer who was fascinated by Giuliano, Gavin Maxwell, lived in Sicily in the 1950s. As well as his book about the bandit, *God Protect Me From My Friends*, Maxwell published *The Ten Pains of Death*, which he dedicated to the people of Sicily, 'who know the ten pains of death.' It contains many remarkable and telling passages: as well as being fluent in Italian (with an ear for the Sicilian dialect), Maxwell seems to have had the gift of persuading all kinds of people to talk freely to him. He lived for a while in Scopello, a fishing village by the Tyrrehian sea. When he arrived at the little cluster of buildings on the northwest coast the writer of *Ring of Bright Water* thought it the most beautiful place he had ever seen. The following piece is more or less a verbatim oral history, that of a fisherman and 'criminal', Enzo.

Gavin Maxwell
From *The Ten Pains of Death*

'Marriage à la mode'

The days went by and the sun grew hotter and I saw the flowers begin to crumple and fade and the summer come back as I had known it. When there was no-one to talk to I would go to the edge of the sea and watch the moving surface; in the height of a Sicilian summer to be at the edge of the waves is as if one experienced for the first time in all one's life the coolness and glitter and the purity of water. All the magic of the element is fixed by contrast; behind is the pale soil, cracked and crumbling now, the vegetation dusty and rasping, then a tumble of white boulders and a strip of fine shingle. The shingle and the rocks are too hot for bare feet to touch. To be in the sea itself would be to lose the contrast.

Because as the season advanced we were forced into the shade and thus into greater privacy, I found my companions ever more ready to speak freely. It was like the Arabian nights; there were not a thousand and one, but if there had been they would not have become wearying, for I was learning more and more about human beings.

Buonaventura had his fingers broken by a tunny's tail, and retired to Castellammare, but Carlo had decided that I was to be trusted, and used to introduce me to his friends with that recommendation. The first time I met one of these, Enzo, he was warm with a litre of the dark sour Scopello wine, and told me much not only of himself but of several of his luckless fellow crewmen.

'Of course we are all criminals, Gavin,' he said cheerfully, 'how can you be a man and not be a criminal? It doesn't make you less good to be a criminal. Take Salvatore who you were talking to this afternoon – you wouldn't think he was a criminal, would you?'

Salvatore was a giant, a great hulk of flesh and muscle who, like half of the other members of the crew, could neither read nor write; his round unshaven face held a babyish innocence and friendliness.

'Well,' Enzo went on, 'it's not his fault that he's not a murderer – he just happens to be a bad shot. He couldn't kill his own son-in-law at five yards with five rounds.'

'Why did he want to?' I asked lazily. I had found that apparent uninterest was the best stimulus to loquacity.

'Well, it's long story, and it's really about things an Englishman wouldn't understand. Do you know all about engagement and marriage in Sicily?'

'A bit, but tell me more.'

'You must be patient – it'll take time to explain, and you have to understand what made Salvatore angry before his story would make sense to you. This is the way we do it in Sicily.

'In each town marriage is part of a tradition – it's one of the most important events in human life, and it's a subject of most careful attention. But while the traditional function of the wedding remains almost the same from town to town, the details are different even between one village and another and not only different but often contradictory. There's a common root from which the different traditions of particular districts branch.

'In Sicily there's no fixed age at which you can marry, but there's the most usual age, which is almost always from twenty years upwards. In fact the majority of marriages are after the age of twenty-one, because in Sicily a youth is absolutely under the thumb of his family up till that age. He achieves a certain independence after he's finished his military service, and not until then can he tell his parents he wants to get married. But by that time he's chosen his girl – a pretty girl and a good housewife, religious, and above all who has never been in love with another man. Usually he's loved this girl for several years, without letting his parents know anything about it. These hidden engagements are called *ammucciuni*.

'We needn't go into details as to how a youth falls in love in Sicily and how tradition affects him – it's an interesting story but too long.

'The famous old Sicilian proverb says "Man is a hunter", and he's got to find his prey. In a Sicilian town the circumstances in which a youth falls in love are always the same; almost, you'd say, traditional. The most truly traditional of the ordinary circumstances is when the girls go to church. A girl very rarely appears alone on the street, not even when she goes to church; she's always accompanied by her mother or a younger sister, or by some older woman. The boys talk among themselves only of the physical attractions of the girls, but sooner or later a youth feels something more than this – he feels the need to see one of them again, to be able to look at her better; the need, really, to be in love with her.

'So the long story of the engagement begins – an engagement which in Sicily traditionally lasts between five and ten years. The youth will pass down the girl's street every evening as soon as he's finished his day's work, usually accompanied by some trusted friend, and hopes that his eyes will meet those of the girl he loves. When that happens he feels certain that the prey is almost his. Then he must make his own intentions known to the girl – there is still much work ahead.

'Every evening at the same time the girl will show herself, apparently indifferent, in front of her door or on her balcony; and he will pass by in his best clothes, and pass and repass until the girl's eyes can no longer make him out in the dark.

'Jealousy is deep rooted in Sicilian character, more especially in matters of love, and in fact the youth won't have many friends with him, for they too might look at his girl, and then you never know. He will go either alone or with one trusted friend, and he keeps an eye on him too, no matter how much he trusts him.

'Now he must make his love known to the girl. It's not an easy matter, and it's not possible without the help of neighbours, or a woman friend of the girl's, or, very often, of the parish priest. The youth in love is up against a hard struggle, and not without risk. He must cultivate the girl's neighbours and find out from them if there are other claimants, and if the girl has ever been touched by another man – and if she has the matter can go no further. He must propose to the girl – but how? Through whom? It's a story that goes on month after month, often for a year, until at last he's found a safe hand to carry a letter – probably not written by him – which always finishes with the words *ti vogghiu beniri* "I love you", and the great step has been taken.

'The reply comes after perhaps a month, after she's consulted with her friends and with the parish priest, and if the advice is favourable she too will end her letter *ti vogghiu beniri*.

'The two now love each other – in the evenings they look at one another and smile; every now and again they exchange letters, but always from a distance, for there are

209

long years to be passed before he may approach his girl. They are secretly engaged; neither dares to say anything even to their own families, even though all the family knows all about it already – as a matter of fact the whole town often knows all about it, but the family's always got to make its weight felt, and quarrels and rebukes would begin.

'The years pass; the youth must do his military service, and when that time comes the boy can say to his father that he's in love and that before he goes away he must give the "word" to the girl's family. The "word" is a kind of permission that the youth's father asks of the girl's family – that they won't pledge her to anyone else while he's serving, and in return the youth's father promises that as soon as his son has finished his service he and his family will come and "ask the marriage". "Asking the marriage" means that the youth's parents ask from the girl's parents permission to marry their son to his daughter.

'Well, he finishes his military service and comes back to the town already of age; he takes up his work again, and first of all he fixes the "appointment" with the family of his fiancée – he fixes, that is, the day on which his family will go to the fiancée's family to "declare" the marriage.

'This declaring is a real traditional function. The youth's family invite their nearest relations to be present at the important happening that is taking place, and the girl's parents do the same. So on the appointed evening all the youth's intimate friends and his relations go together to the home of his fiancée; they walk in double file, the mother in front with her betrothed son. The fiancée is waiting before her door with her father. Greetings are exchanged, and the guests seat themselves in the positions assigned to them by custom. The two young people sit at the middle; at the youth's side is the girl's mother and at the girl's side the youth's mother, all outside the house, and all the other guests sit inside the house. The benedictions begin, thanking Heaven and the Saints, then good wishes to the betrothed couple, and so on. At last the long-awaited moment comes – the youth's mother gives a ring and many other presents to her son, and he, usually very embarrassed, places the ring on his fiancée's finger, and then gives her the other gifts. Then the girl does the same, and all the guests applaud by clapping their hands. The engagement is now official, and everyone celebrates it with wine.

'Now begins the period of official engagement, which will last from three to five years. The youth may go to his fiancée's house every evening, but he must sit at a distance from her – between him and her will be her mother and her grandmother and the rest of the family. They make small talk and joke, but always at a distance. Every Sunday and on days of *festa* the two families will go out together, the youth's mother with her future daughter-in-law, and the youth with his future mother-in-law, and behind them all the rest of the family, brothers, cousins and so on.

'During the time of the engagement the youth's working to get enough money for the wedding, and the girl works at home preparing her trousseau, all of which she customarily sews herself.

'After three or four years of official engagement it's sometimes, but not always, permitted to the couple to sit side by side, but never to kiss each other, or so much as to touch each other.

'Now they can begin to talk about marriage – the girl has almost finished her trousseau, and her fiancé has earned a fair sum working, and there's nothing left to do but to get the documents through and get married. When this decision has been taken another six months will go by before the wedding.

'And so here we are at the week before the wedding day. The two families fix between themselves the day on which the dowries of the engaged couple are to be shown to the public. Usually the girl's dowry is shown first. The families send invitations to all their friends and neighbours, and to their more distant acquaintances too, saying that on such and such days the dowries will be on show. Everyone comes to see the dowry, and everyone leaves some present at this show.

'The dowries are on show for three or four days, and on the last day they send for the priest to bless everything; the linen is put into the appropriate chests, and everything is carried to the house where the couple are going to live.

'The wedding day comes at last. The wedding's almost always in the morning. All the guests assemble at the house of the bride or the bridegroom, according to who's invited them, and wait for the couple to be ready. Then the bridegroom's mother, with her son at her side, and all her guests behind her, repair to the house of the bride. Here a change takes place – the bridegroom stands with his mother-in-law and the bride in front with her own father, and behind them in pairs follow the bridegroom's parents and relations and friends.

'A group of children dressed in white go in front of the bride, then a little girl carrying a bouquet of artificial orange blossoms which will afterwards be given to an altar; and behind the bride there are sometimes unmarried girls, but that doesn't always happen.

'The long procession moves down the street until it reaches the church, all the townspeople ranged along the street watching the wonderful procession, and the girls look at the bride and dream.

'After the religious ceremony there are kisses in the church. Only the women may kiss the bride and the men the bridegroom – there are tears in the eyes of the young couple and of their parents.

'They leave the church again in double file, the bride and bridegroom arm in arm in front. All the guests go to the house of the bridegroom, where there is a real feast. According to the family's means they give the guests beer and sweets and so on. Sometimes there's dancing too, but the unmarried girls can't dance or they would have been "touched" by a man. The youths look at the women and the girls, dreaming of a wedding like this one, and often they fall in love because of it.

'After the feast there's a photograph taken, which will be jealously preserved in their new home.

'To wait so many years for something that only takes place on one day!

'Well, that's what ought to have happened with Salvatore's daughter and son-in-law, but it didn't. I've told you all the stages of what ought to happen so you can see what a shocking thing it is if someone takes the law into his own hands and how angry the parents would get if all this tradition was flouted – and of course it would mean flouting the family itself, which you can't expect them to like.

'Salvatore only had one daughter, but she was very pretty. Such eyes, such breasts, such a behind – she was really *bona*. That's a word we use to mean very very attractive in a sexual sense. There'd been two other daughters, but they'd died during a typhus epidemic years ago, and there were two brothers who'd been in Giuliano's band – both of them are in prison now. So the one daughter, Pietrina, was all Salvatore had left, and he wanted her to make a good marriage.

'You know his son-in-law – he's the young chap in the crew who's got a twisted hand, it doesn't bend properly. That's where his father-in-law shot him; it was meant for the heart, but he's no good with a gun, as I said.

'Three years ago this young man Andrea fell in love with Salvatore's daughter. He went through the first stages in accordance with tradition; he got his letter ending *ti vogghiu beniri* – she didn't write it herself because none of that family can read or write; she got it written by a *spicciafacende* – but the marriage was never 'declared'. Salvatore just put his foot down and said no, and he wouldn't give way an inch. No-one really knew why, and it must have been because he wanted a richer son-in-law, for there was nothing much against Andrea. He could read and write and he had a job as a garage mechanic and he'd never been in trouble with the police, which is saying a lot here.

'But Salvatore made up all sorts of reasons, that he wasn't earning enough money, and that he went regularly to the brothel even while he was secretly engaged – and that was silly, because everyone goes to the *casino*, and more particularly while they're engaged, because then a man wouldn't be human if he could keep his mind off it. At last Salvatore found a real reason, and one that nobody could say was silly. He found out that forty years ago Andrea's great uncle had killed a member of Salvatore's family, and after that he had quite a lot of people on his side.

'Andrea had got to know a maiden aunt of the girl's while he was courting, and through her he begged and pleaded, but it was no use. Salvatore said if he saw Andrea looking at his daughter again he'd kill him. It was about then he got hold of a pistol.

'When Andrea understood that he was really up against it he decided to see how much the girl really loved him. He went to the aunt secretly and told her his plan, and he found her on his side, for old spinsters often have a soft spot for lovers. She was to carry a message asking whether the girl would run away with him. She did this, and when she came back she not only told him that the girl had agreed but she had even arranged the time. Andrea was to be in a *viccolo* (a narrow alley) near to the aunt's house at midnight three days later, and the girl would meet him with what possessions she could carry in a bundle.

'Andrea was overjoyed, and just at that moment it didn't seem to matter that he would have to leave his job and go into hiding. He approached a man we call Uncle Gaspare, who lives in Castellammare – he was once a rich man when Mussolini was in power, but now he's poor like everyone else, and he likes to help people; perhaps it makes him forget that he's not powerful any more. Uncle Gaspare had a little bit of land about six kilometres from the town, with a little two-roomed house on it, and he said Andrea and his new wife could go and live there out of sight until things quietened down, and he also got hold of an old priest to marry them, and he lent them a mule to get from the town to his property.

'Everything went exactly as planned, and four days later the two were set up as man and wife in that little house. Andrea had been saving money for a long time, and now he had enough to last them a few weeks. After that he hoped he'd be able to come back, because when a thing has actually happened the parents are sometimes prepared to forget it so as to avoid public scandal.

'But things didn't look like settling down at all. Salvatore went on raging and shouting and swearing vengeance, and his family and Andrea's family insulted each other with very bad words and there was war between them.

'Andrea heard of all this, and he didn't know what to do. The money was running short, and what was worse the girl began to fret and to say she hadn't known she was going to be shut up there forever. At last Andrea thought that if he could give her some present, something that women like, it might make all the difference.

'So he decided to go to Castellammare and buy her a bottle of scent. He couldn't go openly in the day-time, but as you know, the shops open in the small hours of the morning, so that the women can do their shopping when there's no men about. He thought he could go in then and buy the bottle and get out quick, and if anyone did happen to see him in the town they wouldn't know where he'd gone afterwards.

'He left on foot about two in the morning, and he was at the top of the hill above Castellammare when the sun came up over the Montelepre hills. You know the way the road comes down that hill in a series of hairpin bends, and whenever the bend's to the right you can't see round it. Well, he came down to just before the last bend without seeing anyone. After that there's only a hundred yards of straight and you're in the town.

'He came round that last corner, and there right in front of him was Salvatore's brother, leaning on the wall and looking out over the harbour. He turned his head at the sound of footsteps and he saw Andrea and he took to his heels and away down the road like a frightened rabbit.

'Andrea knew that he had gone to fetch Salvatore, and he was in two minds. One half of him wanted to go on and the other half wanted to run away. He started back and then he felt ashamed of himself and turned round, but by that time he had the corner to go round all over again, and he could hear voices and footsteps beyond it.

'But he went round it, and there fifty paces below him were Salvatore and his brother, and Salvatore had a pistol in his hand and he was coming up the hill as fast as his fat would let him.

'Andrea's heart was thumping like a steam engine and the sweat was running down his legs, but he decided to walk right on just as if those two didn't exist. He went on down and they came up to meet him puffing like pregnant donkeys.

'There were only five paces between them when Salvatore upped with his pistol and started blazing away. The first four shots went God knows where, but the fifth hit Andrea in his left wrist. He screamed, and clutched it with the other hand, and the blood started spurting all over the place and spattered his white shirt, and he was waiting for the last bullet to finish him off, because now he could have touched Salvatore from where he stood.

'But do you know what Salvatore did? He dropped the pistol on the ground, yelling "Oh, my son, my son, what have I done to you?" and he threw his arms round Andrea and started kissing him on the cheeks and begging forgiveness. "Forgive me, forgive me," he blubbered, "you come of a fisherman's family like mine, and all we fishermen have big hearts, big hearts for forgiveness! Forgive me as I forgive you – and marry my daughter with my blessing! Oh, my poor son, my poor son!" And the brother started kissing him too, and all three of them were covered with blood and tears like three babies.

'And it's true, Salvatore *has* a big heart, and he's a good man even if he can't read or write, but you see it wasn't his fault that he didn't kill his son-in-law, and then he'd have been a murderer and spent all his life in jug.

'And now, Gavin, I think I deserve a cigarette.'

The sun was beginning to go down behind Cap St. Vito, and the jackdaws were chattering to themselves as they settled down to roost among the prickly pears on the *faraglioni*. An Egyptian vulture came sailing by, his evil yellow head glancing rapidly from side to side. Enzo threw a stone at it and missed only by inches, though it was thirty yards away. 'Vulture,' he said. 'In the mountains, when there's trouble, the *sbirri* police, watch them and the ravens. They see them gathered together in the air, and they know there's an unburied body.'

I took advantage of Enzo's loquacity. 'Enzo,' I said, 'Rosario walks with a limp. Once I asked him why, and he said he had corns, but today he wasn't wearing shoes, and he's got a big scar like a bullet wound right in the top of his foot. How did he get it?'

'You are very inquisitive, Gavin, but all the same I think you are our friend, so I will tell you. He wouldn't tell you himself, so you must not betray me. He is a fool, is Rosario, or he would never have got that wound. He's not so bad – he's always making jokes or pulling someone's leg, but he's not intelligent. So he gets himself shot in the foot and he's got corns for the rest of his life.

'He's poor, very poor. It's true he's not married, although he's thirty-four, but he likes to smoke, and he never has work except in the spring when he's here at the *tonnara*. So last year when he had no money at all he and a cousin of his got together and they thought how they might make a bit. There's an old couple who live about four kilometres from here; they're both more than seventy years old and they live all alone – they've got a little house and a vineyard that's bigger than most hereabouts. They hadn't got much money, but they'd got some old family silver that they kept in a chest in their bedroom. Rosario had heard about it because his uncle had worked in the vineyard the year before and had seen it himself. Well, you'd think that was a sitting target if ever there was one. And he had to get a bullet through the foot!

'It was like this. Rosario and his cousin had it all worked out how they would get into the house and into the bedroom, very quietly when the two old people were sleeping, and Rosario would open the chest while his cousin stood guard covering the bed with a sub-machine-gun. The chest, you understand, was near the door of the room, at the opposite end from the bed.

'Well, when they got into the room they could hear the old man snoring away quite peacefully and his wife breathing deeply beside him. The chest was standing just inside the door, under the window, and Rosario started to work on it at once, while his cousin stood between him and the bed, covering it with a sub-machine-gun. That cretin Rosario had hardly got started before he dropped something on the floor with a clatter. The old man woke up, and in less time than it takes to tell he'd struck a match and had the candle lit beside the bed. He sat up in bed in his nightgown and nightcap, peering across the room to see what was going on.

'"Don't move!" said Rosario's cousin "keep your hands in front of you and don't move, or you're a dead man!" – but he was trembling all over, because it was the first time he'd ever done anything like this.

'The old boy was a tough one, right enough. He sat staring from behind a moustache like a *disa* broom for a moment or two, while Rosario went on fiddling with the chest, and then cool as you please he bent out of the bed and picked up a

215

slipper and threw it as hard as he could at Rosario's cousin, who had just half turned his head to speak to Rosario.

'The shoe caught him fair in the face and spun him half round towards Rosario, and as he staggered he tightened his finger on the trigger and the gun started going like a motorbike. There was a yell from Rosario and there he was hopping about on one foot and clutching the other in his hands and bawling like a stuck pig. His cousin took to his heels, and Rosario flopped down on the floor and nursed his foot and started crying like a baby.

'The old man was laughing fit to bust. He and his wife bound up Rosario's foot and gave him a lot of wine to make the pain less, and then their labourer, who'd waited long enough after the shooting to feel safe in coming to the house, set off to get the *carabinieri*.

'That's how Rosario got his corns. The old couple pleaded for him in court and because of that he only got four months, although he had been inside twice before. Corns!'

The following week, by a curious coincidence, Rosario's cousin was in the news again. He was found shot through the stomach on the road near to Scopello di Sopra. He was conscious but in great pain; he said he'd been shot by an unknown man whom he'd never seen before. But he broke down under questioning by the *carabinieri*, and told quite a different story. He'd been carrying a pistol to impress his girl-friend in Castellammare, and he had been on his way to meet her there. Caution, however, had over-ruled his instinct for *panache*, and, frightened of being searched by the police, he had decided to unload the pistol and to hide it before reaching the town. While trying to unload it he had shot himself through the stomach. After the first minutes of shock he'd realised that he might escape the penalty for carrying unlicensed firearms if he claimed an unknown assailant, so he had thrown the pistol into the heart of a prickly-pear bush near where he lay.

'Mad,' summed up Enzo, 'absolutely mad. First he shoots poor Rosario through the foot and then he shoots himself in the stomach – it's not prison he needs, it's the madhouse.'

Along with all her many villains – tyrants, bandits, killers, and officially mandated thieves – Sicily has also had her share of heroes, from Timoleon, the Greek Tyrant-toppler, to the judges Giovani Falcone and Paulo Borsellino, who were murdered by the Mafia in 1992. Before them stands another figure, an architect and academic who came from Trieste, was appalled by the conditions of the Sicilian poor, and dedicated his life to improving them: Danilo Dolci. Dolci's non-violent campaign against the mafia and the backwardness of Sicily's administration earned him the title 'the Sicilian Ghandi' in the 1960s, and there are parallels between the two men's methods. Dolci worked for and among the poor, living as one of them. Small fishing communities like Nomadelfia, Trappeto and the town of Partinico were his bases. Partinico is an agricultural settlement in what was once the heart of bandit country in western Sicily. Dolci organised people into works projects, the success of which depended on labour and idealism, rather than the state or regional government. From irrigation, school-building and social services to roadworks, Dolci showed that things could be done without the permission or assistance of indifferent politicians, and in defiance of the Mafia, which had its hands thrust deep into the coffers of private enterprise and public works contracts. Hunger, illiteracy and unemployment were the causes of banditry, he believed. In a simple, almost mathematical process, he sought to expose and understand problems, and then to solve them. He was clearly an extraordinary man, who lived as a very humble one. Carlo Levi met and described him:

> 'We entered Danilo's house, and he greeted us in a friendly and open manner: he was tall, strong, with a large complex northern head, eyes that were lively behind his glasses, cheerful with an inner energy, always present, always disposed, even in his smallest gestures, to action. His tone was not that of the pure missionary or the philanthropist, but rather that of a man of faith, who has faith in others (a general faith in human beings), and who causes faith to blossom around himself, and with this weapon alone feels that he can cause life to spring up where it would have seemed impossible, little by little, by spontaneous force...'

Dolci wrote a great deal. He is carefully absent in much of his writing – forever steering the reader towards his subjects. In *The Man Who Plays Alone*, he lets a hugely diverse collection of Sicilians speak for themselves.

Danilo Dolci
From *The Man Who Plays Alone*

A Street Cleaner

Beautiful, yes, very beautiful – but filthy. Filthy on the outskirts – but also in the centre, in certain places. In Via Maqueda, it's kept clean; in Via Roma and Via Liberta, it's kept clean. But Via Carini, now – that's filthy, and just about all the rest of the city is filthy.

Except for the workers, this is a city that wakes up late. At four o'clock, five o'clock, there's still nothing stirring. About six you begin to get one or two itinerant tradesmen going round the outlying districts, selling brooms, say, or vegetables, and here and there a basket is let down on string from a balcony. The cowmen go round with their cows selling milk, gradually the buses fill up; by about seven o'clock the building workers are on their way to work, some walking, some on bicycles, some on scooters. The bulk of us start work at half past six.

If my beat is here, but I have to go a long way off to tip the rubbish, it'll be an hour before I'm back. And by the time I get back, there's already as much rubbish again as what there was before I started. I mean to say, I sweep all this bit – this is my stretch – but by the time I've finished my stretch they've chucked out a whole lot more rubbish behind me. I can go back again and pick up a second lot in Via Maqueda, and the central bits where the gentry are, but in the less important places like Piazza Capo and Piazza Garraffello, where the filth would make your skin crawl, I'm not allowed to go back, I just have to push straight on.

Sometimes when the lorry doesn't come round we have to leave all the rubbish in the street to be collected next day, piled up in a little back alley – we're supposed to always dump it in the poorest bit, always at the feet and under the noses of the poorest people.

That alley between Piazza Bandiera and Via Napoli, in the centre – that's often completely blocked: the posh shops in the streets round there chuck all their rubbish into the alley, and then people come and pick through it for cardboard and other bits and pieces that might come in handy. Quite a few of the poor streets in the centre are used as rubbish dumps like that.

It's the firm of Vaselli who have the contract from the Council; but because they want to save money and make as much profit as possible, they don't have the proper equipment, so they don't do the job properly. You can take it from me – I know that's why. When the lorry comes round to pick up the refuse at the various collection points – we start work at half past six in the morning, so by quarter past or half past seven our bins are already full, but we have to wait till the lorry comes round before we can unload, and the lorry doesn't come till about quarter past or half past eight. Well, when the lorry does come, we tip in our first load, and then while it stands and waits we go back and fill our bins again. If there's room on the lorry then, you tip in your second load, but if there isn't room you have to hang about there waiting for an hour or an hour and a half, because the lorry has to go a long way off to tip the rubbish. It may be two hours, even, before it's back, but we just have to sit there waiting. And it's not as if our bins were just brim full and hermetically sealed – we pile baskets and stuff on top of the rubbish, too, we pile it up just out of love, every one of us, for the sake of keeping our own particular bit clean.

218

There's another thing, now: it's my day off today, and they're supposed to send another man along to take my place. However, rather than employ someone else, the superintendent will come along to you and say: 'Here, dustman, you'll have to do a bit extra today to cover the next stretch too.' And he'll say the same to the other fellow on the other side; and so the money stays in the pockets of Vaselli and Co, while the dustmen have to toil away even harder.

Lots of people loathe us. The streets are always dirty, no matter how hard we try. There are lots of beautiful houses here, palaces, old ones and new, and all this filth spoils the look of the place. But it's all so difficult. Sometimes you're sent to do a place in the early morning but the rubbish isn't thrown out till later on, after the people have got up, about eight or nine, and so it has to lie there in the street all day.

The Palermo the street cleaners know isn't the same Palermo you'd see by driving round in a posh car – we see it always through dust. One swish of the broom, and up comes the dust, all over the legs of passers-by too – I ask you! But our own noses are so full of it we hardly notice it any more. When you first start, you feel it all going up your nose, and it stinks, and you get it in your eyes; when there's a wind it blows in your eyes and stings, and when you sweep the dust gets in your mouth, and in your ears, and everywhere. One sweep of the broom in an unpaved street will send dust right up to the first floor. People are annoyed, they get cross with us: 'Get along!' they say, 'Is this the time of day to be doing that?'

But it all depends whereabouts you're working. Some people understand all right, but there are others who don't understand at all: 'What are you doing here?' they say. 'Why don't you be off!' – or worse. Of course it's always the best-dressed people who object most when they get dust on them.

Some people do understand what a sacrifice our work is, but others – they really make my blood boil. What I say to them is this: 'All right,' I say; 'if you think I'm not doing anything, or if you think it would be better if I wasn't here at all, just you take the broom and have a go at sweeping yourself!' But on the other hand there are people who pity us – 'Poor devils!' they say, when they see us toiling away in the dust. People come past sometimes while we're sitting waiting at one of the collection points – we're not sitting there just because we fancy it: we have to wait for the lorry – and they say, 'those lazy beggars won't do a hand's turn!' Where I work there's a fellow who's so poor I could buy him for a slave, and he comes by and he says to me: 'You just don't want to do this work!'

The dust gets in our socks, in our shoes, in our trousers; our clothes go quite stiff with all the dust and sweat, they turn into cardboard. You sweep and sweep, and thoughts keep coming into your head; you sweep away and think about home, each one of us as he sweeps is thinking about his own private affairs, thinking his own particular thoughts.

At half past eight or nine, the shops open. Office workers are supposed to start work then too, but... say I'm the head of the office: I go in, ring the bell, and the porter appears: 'Listen, if anyone comes, say I'm in the bar, or tell them I've gone out for a moment.' Some of them just sign the register and go home again. But at the end of the month, they get their pay all right. There are lots of them like that – not all, of course, but there are lots like that in the Regional Government offices, in the Provincial Administration, the Town Hall, the Labour Exchange – all the various Council offices. The Health Insurance place is almost like a brothel at certain moments! Even at eleven o'clock in some offices there's still no one to be seen; and then by one o'clock or half past, they've all disappeared again. We're rotten with that sort of thing. Rotten. That's how Sicily was born, and that's how she's dying.

Giuliano had the whole of Sicily intimidated: he could have put everything right. He should have been King of Sicily and put everything in order. But they killed him: here anyone who wants to do something for the poor gets killed.

Our brooms stir up the dust, dust is stirred up by the lorries, dust is stirred up by the wind. Most passers-by just go about their own business, they carry on walking and keep themselves to themselves, they don't want anything to do with us. Every now and again there may be one who'll talk to us, but usually they don't. I might get one who'd talk to me today, say, and then maybe another the day after tomorrow: you go whole days alone among the dust.

Everybody goes about their own affairs, you don't often get a person sticking his nose into other people's business. But that's another thing I like about Palermo: it's beautiful, even though it is dirty – and it's a city where people mind their own business. Not everybody, but most people mind their own business. The rich man is rich, the poor man is poor, and they all mind their own business. Of course I'd like to be well-off too. But what am I supposed to do about it? Go out stealing? '*Lavoro e Chiesa*,' the saying is: work and Church, which means *Lavoro e Casa*, work and home. I'm just a humble working man.

This eye can't see the other eye. I work as a street cleaner, now, and let's suppose another fellow comes along to work as a street cleaner too: well, I've got my bit of bread, and it's only natural I should be jealous and not want somebody else to take it from me – there are plenty who would. But on the whole people keep themselves to themselves.

We're in two groups, us cleaners: Group A, employed by the Council – there's about two hundred and thirty of them; and Group B, we're about one thousand two hundred or one thousand three hundred, I'm not sure exactly how many, and we're employed by the firm of Vaselli. It's always Vaselli who get the contract. About fifty to fifty-three cleaners work at the Palace of Justice. Then there are the watchmen: in my stretch alone there are eight of them, and about forty or fifty altogether – and I tell you, they do nothing. That's the watchman's job – to do nothing. Then there are about forty supervisors, and they do practically nothing. That's Palermo for you: if you have friends to pull strings, you can make your living doing nothing at all. If not, you stay down in the dust.

In some families the women go out shopping, but often it's the men who go. Men here are strict about keeping their wives and daughters indoors. From one o'clock till two is the busiest time of day, for people and cars. That's when most office workers go for lunch. But building workers mostly eat on the spot, sitting on the pavements. In the poorer quarters they just have bread or chickpea cakes with a bit of cheese or something.

Then the office workers go home for a sleep – and that's the end of their working day: the offices are closed till ten next morning, even if it's a matter of life and death. In the evening, people from upper-class Palermo stroll down towards the centre, and in summer they go down to the sea at Mondello. The poor folk stand in their doorways in the evening, or sit on their balconies; or those who can afford it go down to the harbour and eat oysters and squids. In the poorer suburbs it gets quiet very early because they have to go to work early in the morning. But in the centre, at the Politeama, in Piazza Massimo, in all the posh places, there are crowds of office workers strolling about till one o'clock or even two in the morning.

We knock off at four-thirty, us street cleaners. You feel all chewed up, you're full of dust, filthy, you still stink of all the stuff you've been handling. You can get poisoning sometimes; your eyes sting, and often your skin prickles and itches. If it's cold weather and you get wet, that'll probably bring on the rheumatism. *We* can't go strolling about amusing ourselves till midnight or two o'clock in the morning: by eight o'clock I'm already in bed.

When we go on strike the city becomes a real cess-pit. In two days you can't even walk – paper, rubbish, flies, babies and children all among the filth: but we really have to strike sometimes for our rights, even though we hate to see the city in that state. If I live in this quarter, I like it to be clean; I even have a flower garden at home, I grow jasmine and passion flowers. They say, 'Don't do to others what you wouldn't like them to do to you': I'd like to see the whole city clean – it's my native city, and I'm fond of it.

There are thousands of other people after our job, thousands of applications, thousands of people who'd like to take our place. To get taken on, though... every saint has his own band of faithful. You go and recommend yourself to your own particular little benefactor, and the next man goes to his, and so on. There are thousands who envy us our job! To be sure of getting in, you have to be able to procure a certain number of votes for some friend on the Council when elections come round. Because of the lack of industry here, one of the dreams of the people of the poor quarters of Palermo is to be a street cleaner, so as to have a steady job all the year round, and to get the family allowances.

Sonia Alliata, Duchess of Salaparuta

In my view, the aristocracy live an isolated life, cut off from one another, each within his own narrow family circle.

No one of the aristocracy still lives in the country today: only one or two, perhaps, such as myself and the Princess Paternò here at Bagheria, twelve kilometres from Palermo.

Even in the old days, though, each family lived its own independent life, except that then the families were very rich and could give large parties, and so they kept more in touch with one another.

They had money, but I do not think there was any collaboration at all among the nobility, except within the narrow family circle, children and grandchildren: it didn't even extend to cousins. Each thought only of the glory of his own house, and that cannot but be founded on the poverty of others. That is how it always was, I am quite sure of it.

One goes to the few parties (there are only a few nowadays because it costs so much to give a party), and to the Massimo Theatre; people enjoy showing off their jewels, seeing others envy them: they enjoy trying to outshine everyone else. I enjoy it too, to tell you the truth: as long as I am alive, I hope it may always be said that the house of Villafranca Salaparuta conducted itself worthily, and that I made my contribution to its lustre and to its dignity in modern times.

The nobility is dying: it is the twilight of the gods. Once upon a time we were indeed gods, and all the great geniuses, from Michelangelo to Leonardo, were our subjects, for we are a chosen people. Now we are like museums, good for little more than for people to go and stare at. There is not much life left in us. Even our children are no longer princes and princesses, neither financially nor morally. But I am attached to the old ways: I am old, and I cannot change.

There is one link which, though invisible, binds us all, and that is our pride in belonging to the nobility. A race-horse is not the same as a cart-horse. Some scientist – or perhaps he was a philosopher – once said that it takes many generations for a cart-horse to lose its long hair. Centuries and centuries of refinement.

Nowadays it is all materialism – the spirit no longer has any expression today.

Although it doesn't take any organized form, there is a feeling – a feeling for the defence of certain values, but... it is the twilight of the gods. We no longer have the will to fight back, since ours is a debased coinage. What holds us together still is our resistance to vulgarization.

There is naturally a difference between the great families and the lesser ones, counts and barons. But there are some barons who are worth as much as princes: it is all a question of money. Even within our aristocratic circle, whoever has more money is considered more important, and whoever has none left is considered a nobody. Once upon a time all the peasants used to vote for their master: every nobleman had his own province, so to speak. The house of Villafranca had forty estates. So of course they had their own Senators, whose living depended on them. Everyone votes according to where his daily bread comes from.

Nowadays the lower orders are better off than we are. There is no poverty: if a man is poor it is because he chooses to do nothing. I know Generals' wives, Duchesses – even Princesses, who can no longer afford to keep women-servants because they cost too much, their pretensions are too high. These families only have one or two servants left, it is the end of the relationship between aristocracy and common people: they no longer have their peasants, they no longer have their valets. In the old days, there was a beautiful relationship: our dependents served us willingly for generations (our gardener had been with us for five generations, father to son, father to son). And even today disengaged servants choose rather to go into service with the nobility, even for lower wages, than with the middle classes, because they are humiliated less: 'If I am to serve, I will serve a gentlemen' – not an ordinary person like themselves: they recognize the superiority. The middle classes treat them badly, whereas we treat them in a gentlemanly way, and take them into our confidence.

I find it distressing to see the lower orders getting ahead, because naturally others' gain is my loss. But of course I do recognize, with my head at least, that it has to be that way: I only wish they could do it rather more slowly. *Natura aborret saltum* – sudden changes are painful.

There used to be a paternal relationship, paternalism: '*Voscieza mi benedica*' – 'Your Excellency's blessing on us!' they used to say (and many still do); and the expression shows how they felt themselves to be in this position, in the position of being protected, like a child by its father. Once upon a time it was very very common, but now it is becoming a thing of the past, it is disappearing. The nobility (not the middle classes) were kind to them, though of course always keeping them in their place, you understand – I don't want to make myself out to be better than I am! – always keeping them at a certain distance. I adore dogs, I take them to the vet, feed them, cry when they die – but a dog is a dog. No, it never occurred to them that people's position could change: the peasants were to be peasants for ever – which I personally think is wrong, but I believe there are very few of us who think so. The world is changing, and change brings sorrow to whoever has to pass away: you must be understanding, and try to forgive us.

They ought to be ruthless with breakers of the law. And they ought to abolish the secrecy of the vote. Every man, or woman, ought to have the courage of his convictions and show his loyalty to the person he has chosen to represent him, since there is so much talk of ideals. And voters ought to have the necessary qualifications to vote: that is, they ought to undergo some small examination to prove their mental education, to show they have at least a minimal understanding of social problems, and common sense.

The grandees of the old days used to bring geniuses to their courts and feed them gratis. This is what makes me weep: today, whichever way one turns, one sees idiocies: beatniks – and think of what has happened to music, and painting. Look at these flowers now, these roses: why shouldn't they be a delight? People should think of spiritual joys, of the love of beauty.

We still have one thing to bring us together every day: canasta. There are twenty-four of us who meet to play daily – not for the money, but because it is an intelligent game and there is a spirit of competition amongst us. One day at the Marchioness of X's, another day at Countess Y's: an innocent occupation, very superficial, and of very little value. I play every day – what else would you have me do? I lead a useless life.

IV: The Curse

A S I BEGAN TO LEARN about them, the large-scale map of Palermo on my kitchen wall seemed to develop a horrible sort of mould, spots of blood on this street, and that, and in that block, on this motorway, on the road to Mondello, on those flats, in this suburb and that, in the grove there, around that village, by that railway line... Everywhere are roads named after their victims. They have given an entire, grimly telling vocabulary to Sicily. *Lupara* is literally wolf-shot, a cartridge of large steel balls, which has become shorthand for the sawn-off shotgun from which it is fired. *Omerta*, which meant a sort of manliness, has come to mean silence. *Cosca*, which is a cluster of leaves on an artichoke, has come to mean a nest of 'men of honour', a local branch of 'the honoured society', the most misleading terms of all: there is nothing resembling honour in the doings of these men. *Lupara Bianca*, white shotgun, means a disappearance, when the victim's body is never found. *Piccioti* – young thugs; aspirant, disposable, street-level foot-soldiers. *Pizzo*, means beak, from beak-wetting, meaning extortion, a fixed 'tax' payed by businesses great and small, legal and illegal, to those who thus 'wet their beaks' in every transaction. *Cadaveri Eccellenti* are the eminent corpses: senior businessmen, politicians, policemen, judges and journalists, the upper social crust of the thousands whom they have killed.

On your way into Palermo from the airport you pass two red obelisks on the motorway, marking the spot where in 1992 the entire carriageway was blown up in order to kill Judge Giovanni Falcone. His wife and three members of his escort died with him. Most people in Italy remember where they were when they heard the news; it is the Italian equivalent of America's JFK moment, the bend in the road near Capaci is Sicily's Grassy Knoll, and this in a nation where the former head of state, Aldo Moro, was kidnapped and killed by the Red Brigades.

225

The day after Falcone's death, the newspaper *Repubblica* carried a cartoon on its front page, showing Sicily as a crocodile's head, split open in a fanged grin, its teeth crunching down on a hawk, an eagle of justice, and a pun on Falcone's name. The inference is that the mafia and Sicily are indivisible, that in this terrible moment Sicily opened its mouth and ate civilisation, as if somehow the entire island was responsible for the slaughter. The moment and the response to it brim with the dark ripples of crisis. As the cartoon recognises, it was the moment when the anti-state within seemed to have overtaken the host, as if the cancer had burst out of its victim's body. At the same time the cartoon reveals a fiercely bigoted and disingenuous side of the Italian psyche, which suggests that all the seeds of all the ills of this complex nation reside, thinly hidden, in this strange, off-shore, other land.

This was not just the murder of a man. With Judge Paolo Borsellino (murdered two months later, with five of his escort) and a pool of magistrates, researchers and prosecutors, Falcone had come closer than any man since Mussolini to breaking the curse. Mussolini used whole-sale imprisonment. Falcone and Borsellino used persuasion to win the trust of certain *mafiosi* – disillusioned and terrified by the maniac Toto Riina, then the boss of bosses – who broke their *omerta* and gave evidence. The judges' research and what they learned from these *pentiti* unravelled some of the webs of the mafia's power, and, for the first time, proved it to be a vast and united organisation. Thanks to the judges, membership and association became crimes, three hundred and forty-two men were convicted, and it became possible for the police and judiciary to begin to fight the mafia in a way they should have been fighting them since the beginning. The killing of the judges was a ferocious and ferociously arrogant dismissal of the hope of the people of Sicily and the state of Italy, that the forces of good and order, personified by these superlatively brave and intelligent men, might finally be taking the fight to the mafia, after over a hundred years of defeats.

The word mafia is a worldwide term now, applied to Russian, Balkan, American and Mexican organised criminals, among others. Certain commentators point to other Italian groups, the *n'dranghetta* of Calabria, and the *Camora* of Naples, and say that these are just as vicious, and just as malign. But in the history of crime, there has been nothing to compare with the Sicilian mafia, *Cosa Nostra*: it penetrated its host society more thoroughly, damaged more terribly, and killed more prolifically than any other group. Perhaps only Al Quaeda or the IRA might be measured against it, in terms of organisation, pervasiveness, reach and riches, but the three are so different in aims and character as to render the comparison

226

meaningless. *Cosa Nostra* was never so interested in any kind of social, political or religious change, except when its interests were threatened: stasis served it well, until recently. *Cosa Nostra* wanted only power, and money, through which to obtain more power.

It is necessary for any non-Italian to abandon fundamental misconceptions before considering the question of the mafia. Put aside the dark-eyed Hollywood heros who have done so much to glamorise the term: photographs of the real players reveal a seemingly endless succession of spivs, brutes, thugs and low-life, clustered around the occasional psychopath.

Forget misty notions of a venerable society looking after their own, cocking a snook at inept authorities in the name of a proud and oppressed people, governed by their own code of honour. Torture, kidnapping, drug-dealing, intimidation and extortion on an unprecedented scale are the mafia's tributes to Sicily. To face the mafia is to face the unholy trinity of human life: violence, fear and malign power. To follow its rise and prospering is to study the genesis and processes of evil. As we know, as we have always known, the most frightening thing about evil is the way it insinuates itself into normal life.

One of the standard works in English on the subject is John Dickie's *Cosa Nostra: A history of the Sicilian Mafia*, published by Coronet.

John Dickie
From *Cosa Nostra: A History of the Sicilian Mafia*

The Violence Industry

There was something rather English about the investigation mounted by Leopoldo Franchetti and Sidney Sonnino. Both men were great admirers of British liberalism and Sonnino owed his first name to his English mother. When they travelled to Sicily they were entering a land where the vast majority of the population spoke a dialect they could not understand. In the university and salon milieu that Sonnino and Franchetti left behind, the island was still a mysterious place known primarily from ancient Greek myths and sinister newspaper reports. So they planned for the considerable stresses and dangers of their journey with the resolve of explorers setting off for uncharted territory. Among the equipment they took on their journey in the spring of 1876 were repeating rifles, large-calibre pistols, and four copper basins each. The plan was to fill the basins with water and stand the legs of their camp-beds in them to keep insects away. Because roads were poor or non-existent in the interior of the island, the two researchers often travelled on horseback, choosing their routes and guides at the last possible moment to avoid brigand attacks.

Franchetti in particular was far from entirely naive when he went to Sicily; two years earlier he had hacked across large areas of the mainland of southern Italy on a similar expedition. Yet what he found on the island caused him to feel overcome by 'a profound tenderness' towards the rifle he carried across his saddle. 'The nightmare of a mysterious, evil force is weighing down on this naked, monotonous land,' he later wrote. The notes that Franchetti actually took during the journey have only recently been published; two of the many stories that emerge from those notes can serve to explain the shock of his encounter with Sicily.

Franchetti recorded that, on March 24th, 1876, he and Sonnino rode into the central Sicilian city of Caltanissetta. Two days earlier, a priest had been shot dead in the nearby village of Barrafranca, a mafia stronghold, according to the authorities who informed them of what had happened. Sixty metres from where the priest lay dying stood a witness, a new arrival in Sicily, a government inspector from the northern city of Turin whose job was to supervise the collection of taxes on milled flour. This honest functionary ran to the priest's side in time to hear his dying words of accusation: his own cousin was the murderer.

Profoundly disturbed, the tax inspector jumped on his horse and rode off to tell the *carabinieri*. He then went to inform the victim's family. Not wanting to upset them by blurting out what he knew, he told them to follow him to where the priest needed help. Along the way, he gently broke the news. Grateful for his sensitivity, they told him that the murder was the culmination of a twelve-year feud between the priest and his cousin. The priest himself was a wealthy man with a fearsome reputation for violence and corruption.

Twenty-four hours later local police arrested the tax inspector, threw him in jail, and charged him with the murder. The witnesses against him included the priest's cousin. But the people of Barrafranca, including the murdered man's family, kept quiet. Mercifully for the tax inspector, the government authorities in Caltanissetta got wind of the case; when he was released the real murderer went into hiding.

A week after hearing of this episode, Franchetti and Sonnino arrived in Agrigento, a town on Sicily's southern coast famous for its ancient Greek temples. Franchetti's notebooks tell another story he learned there, of a woman who had taken five hundred lire from the police in exchange for information on two criminals; they were in league with a local boss, a man with a hefty share of government road-building contracts. Soon after she accepted the money, the woman's son returned to this village after a decade in jail. He was carrying a letter from the local mafia detailing what his mother had done. When he confronted her and asked for money to buy some new clothes, her evasive response triggered a furious row after which the man stormed out. He returned shortly afterwards with his cousin and together they stabbed his mother ten times – the son six times and his cousin four. They then threw her body out of the window into the street before giving themselves up.

As they journeyed round Sicily, Franchetti and Sonnino also encountered the seemingly hopeless confusion that had set in around the word 'mafia' during the ten years since it had first been heard. Everyone the travellers interviewed during the two months they were in Sicily seemed to have a different understanding of the new buzzword; everyone seemed to accuse everyone else of being a *mafioso*. The authorities in some places were confused. As one lieutenant in the *carabinieri* lamely told them: 'mafia is an extremely difficult thing to define; you would need to live in Sambuca to get an idea.'

When he subsequently published his findings, Franchetti explained how perplexed he had been to find that the situation was most worrying not in the treeless, yellow interior of the island, where most people would have expected there to be backwardness and crime, but in the citrus groves around Palermo. On the surface, this was the centre of a thriving industry in which the locals took great pride: 'Every tree is looked after as if it were a rare plant specimen.' These initial perceptions, Franchetti wrote, were soon changed by the hair-raising tales of murder and intimidation in the area: 'After a certain number of these stories, the scent of orange and lemon blossom starts to smell of corpses.' The presence of endemic violence in such a modern setting ran counter to one of the beliefs most cherished by Italy's rulers: that economic, political, and social progress all marched in step. Franchetti began to wonder whether the principles of justice and freedom he so cherished 'might just amount to nothing more than well-planned speeches to disguise ailments that Italy cannot cure; they are a layer of gloss to make the dead bodies gleam.'

It was a bleak and perplexing spectacle. But Leopoldo Franchetti was intellectually tenacious as well as brave; he passionately believed in a hands-on engagement with the nation's problems. A patriotic shame burned within him at the thought that foreigners seemed to know Sicily much better than did the Italians. By patiently covering the territory and by studying its history, Franchetti overcame his doubts and confusion. He produced an account of the mafia business that is starkly systematic. Sicily was not chaotic; on the contrary, its law and order problems had an underlying and very modern rationality to them. The island, Franchetti argued, had become home to 'the violence industry'.

Franchetti's account of the genesis of the mafia opens in 1812 when the British, who occupied Sicily during the Napoleonic wars, began the process of abolishing feudalism on the island. The feudal system had been based on a form of joint landownership: the king granted land in trust to a nobleman and his descendants; in return, the noble put his private army at the service of the king when the need arose. Within the nobleman's territory, termed a 'fief' or 'feud', his word was law.

Until the abolition of feudalism, Sicilian history was shaped by tussles between a long series of foreign monarchs and the feudal barons. The monarchs tried to draw more power towards the centre; the feudal barons resisted the monarchy's interference in the running of their estates. In this tug-of-war, it was the nobles who usually had the advantage, not least because Sicily's mountainous geography and atrocious transport infrastructure made it impossible for central government to rule without letting the barons have their way.

Baronial privileges were wide-ranging and long-lasting. A custom dictating that vassals should greet their feudal lord with a kiss on the hand was only formally abolished by Garibaldi in 1860. The title of 'don', which was originally given to the Spanish noblemen who had ruled Sicily, was applied to any man of status for many years after that. (These practices were widespread in Sicily, and were not just mafia habits.)

The abolition of feudalism did not immediately do more than change the rules of the tug-of-war between the centre and the provinces. (The power of the landowners was slow to fade; the last of the great estates was only broken up in the 1950s.) However, forces for long-term change were set loose when feudalism ended; the legal preconditions were put in place for a property market. Quite simply, bits of the estates could now be bought and sold. And land that is acquired rather than inherited needs to be paid for; it is an investment that has to be put to profitable use. Capitalism had arrived in Sicily.

Capitalism runs on investment, and lawlessness puts investment at risk. No one wants to buy new machinery or more land to plant with commercial crops when there is a strong risk that those machines or crops will be stolen or vandalized by competitors. When it supplanted feudalism, the modern state was supposed to establish a monopoly on violence, on the power to wage war and punish criminals. When the modern state monopolizes violence in this way, it helps create the conditions in which commerce can flourish. The barons' ramshackle, unruly private militias were scheduled to disappear.

Franchetti argued that the key to the development of the mafia in Sicily was that the state had fallen catastrophically short of this ideal. It was untrustworthy because, after 1812, it failed to establish its monopoly on the use of violence. The barons' power on the ground was such that the central state's courts and policemen could be pressurized into doing what the local lord wanted. Worse still, it was now no longer only the barons who felt they had the right to use force. Violence became 'democratized', as Franchetti put it. As feudalism declined, a whole range of men seized the opportunity to shoot and stab their way into the developing economy. Some of the feudal lords' private heavies were now acting in their own interests, roaming the countryside as brigand bands that were sheltered by the landlords either out of fear or complicity. The formidable managers called *gabelloti*, who often rented bits of the landowners' estates from them, were also adept at using violence to defend their interests. In the city of Palermo, societies of artisans demanded the right to carry arms so that they could police the streets (and force up prices or run extortion operations).

When modern local government institutions were set up in the towns of the Sicilian provinces, groups that were part armed criminal gang, part commercial enterprise, and part political clique, quickly organized themselves to get their hands on the spoils. Officials complained that what they called these 'sects' or 'parties' – sometimes they were merely extended families with guns – were making many areas of Sicily ungovernable.

The state also set up its courts, but soon found that they were subject to control by anyone who was tough and well organized enough to impose his will. Even the police became corrupted. Instead of reporting crime to the authorities, they would often broker or impose deals between the victims and perpetrators of theft. For example, rather than send stolen cattle along the long chain of intermediaries to the butchers, rustlers could simply ask the captain of the local police to mediate. He would arrange for the stolen animals to be handed back to the original owner in return for money passed on to the rustlers. Naturally the captain would get a percentage of the deal.

In a hellish parody of the capitalist economy, the law was parcelled up and privatized just like the land. Franchetti saw Sicily as being in the grip of a bastard form of capitalist competition. It was a violent market in which there were only notional boundaries between economics, politics, and crime. In this situation, people hoping to run a business could not rely on the law to protect them, their families, and their economic interests. Violence was an essential asset in any enterprise; the ability to use force was as important as having capital to invest. Indeed, Franchetti thought that in Sicily violence itself had become a form of capital.

Mafiosi, for Franchetti, were entrepreneurs in violence, specialists who had developed what today would be called the most sophisticated business model in the marketplace. Under the leadership of their bosses, mafia bands 'invested' violence in various commercial spheres in order to extort protection money and guarantee monopolies. This was what he called the violence industry. As Franchetti wrote,

> [in the violence industry] the mafia boss ... acts as capitalist, impresario and manager. He unifies the management of the crimes committed ... he

231

regulates the way labour and duties are divided out, and controls discipline amongst the workers. (Discipline is indispensable in this as in any other industry if abundant and constant profits are to be obtained.) It is the mafia boss's job to judge from circumstances whether the acts of violence should be suspended for a while, or multiplied and made fiercer. He has to adapt to market conditions to choose which operations to carry out, which people to exploit, which form of violence to use.

Men with commercial or political ambitions in Sicily were faced with two alternatives: either to arm themselves; or, more likely, to buy in protection from a specialist in violence, a *mafioso*. If Franchetti were around today, he might say that threats and murder belonged to the service sector of the Sicilian economy.

Franchetti seems to have seen himself as a kind of Charles Darwin for a delinquent ecosystem, and as such he gives us a powerful insight into the laws of Sicily's rich criminal habitat. Yet in doing so he makes Sicily sound like a complete anomaly. In fact all capitalism has a bit of the bastard in it, particularly in the early stages. Even the English society that Franchetti so admired had had its violent entrepreneurs. In Sussex in the 1740s, for example, semi-militarized gangs made huge profits for themselves and their contacts by smuggling tea. They caused a breakdown in law and order by corrupting customs officials, directly confronting troops, and performing armed robberies as a sideline. One historian has described England in the 1720s as resembling a banana republic, its politicians masters in the arts of patronage, nepotism, and the systematic pillaging of the public revenue. Franchetti's analysis is also limited by the fact that he did not believe that the mafia was a sworn secret association.

Political and Administrative Conditions in Sicily met with a mixture of hostility and indifference on its release. Many Sicilian reviewers berated its author for ignorant prejudice. In part this poor reception was Franchetti's own fault. For one thing, his proposals for solving the mafia problem were outlandish and authoritarian: Sicilians were not to be allowed any say at all in how their island was policed. Franchetti even thought that their whole outlook was so perverted that they gave violence a 'moral value' and considered it ethically wrong to be honest. He seemed not to realize that people very often went along with the *mafiosi* simply because they were intimidated and did not know whom to trust.

Thus a pioneering account of the 'violence industry' failed to make an impact during Franchetti's lifetime. After publishing his research in Sicily, he went on to serve as a backbench MP, but his political career did not take off. In the end, it was the very same grim patriotism that had impelled him to investigate the mafia in 1876 that eventually killed him. (Even friends thought there was something dark and excessive about Franchetti's love of his country.) During the First World War he was tormented by the thought that he had not been called to an important office in the nation's hour of need. In October 1917, when news came through of Italy's catastrophic defeat at the battle of Caporetto, he became so depressed that he shot himself.

The question remains: where did it come from? As good an answer as any is given by Norman Lewis, whose first wife was the daughter of a *mafioso*. Lewis prided himself on being the only man he knew who could walk into any room, anywhere in the world, and cause no stir, comment or even, often, interest. Travel writing has changed much since Lewis. The publisher of this series, Barnaby Rogerson, directs novices like myself to Lewis' *Naples '44: An Intelligence Officer in the Italian Labyrinth*. The depth and sophistication of Lewis' contact with his subject is matched only by the vivid impression he gives his reader of the profound obscurity and mystery of its hinterland, that which he cannot reach, which no outsider could reach. This, Rogerson implies, is as far as Lewis could get: do you really think you can match him?

In his book *The Honoured Society* Norman Lewis begins his account of Sicily with the remarkable story of the allied invasion in 1943, and a portrait of the *mafioso* Don Calogero Vizzini, who played such an extraordinary part in it.

Norman Lewis
From *The Honoured Society*

I

On July 10th, 1943, the allied armies landed on the south coast of Sicily and, thrusting northwards, began their conquest of the island. The task of occupation was divided between the American and combined British and Canadian forces, the former including in their command a small contingent of Free French. The Anglo-Canadian army advancing up the east coast found an enemy poorly equipped to offer resistance. A great deal of ingenuity had gone into the construction of painted wooden cannon, artfully contrived to discharge firecrackers and thus draw fire, which deceived nobody. Key positions were defended by captured Russian guns which could not be fired because no one had been able to translate the operational manuals. Some battery commanders had no idea that they were about to be attacked as the telephone lines connecting them to their headquarters had not yet been laid. In one case, infantry rushed into battle had received an emergency issue of mouth organs but no ammunition. Yet all things considered, despite the fact that they were out-gunned, outnumbered by five to one, and faced by battle-toughened veterans of the Africa campaign, the Italians fought back well and sometimes desperately. It cost the British and Canadian army five slogging weeks, some stiff engagements, and several thousand casualties to reach their objective: the town of Messina on the northeast tip of the island.

The Americans, to whom had been allotted the seemingly stiffer proposition of subduing the mountainous centre and western half of the island, carried out their share of the operation with great speed. After a short initial period when the American Seventh Army seemed almost to be awaiting the signal to move, it suddenly began a brisk advance up two main roads towards Palermo, reaching the north coast of Sicily in only seven days and with hardly a shot fired. General Patton was to describe this campaign as 'the fastest *blitzkrieg* in history'. It was certainly the least costly: casualties, once the Seventh Army had broken out of its beachheads, being negligible.

The key-point in the Italo-German defence system was the area of Mount Cammarata near the towns of Villalba and Mussomeli, and here, in positions dominating both main roads along which the Americans were certain to advance, a mixed brigade of motorised artillery, anti-aircraft guns and 88mm anti-tank guns, plus a squadron of German tanks, including several Tigers, waited to give battle. The Cammarata redoubt had been most carefully chosen. This craggy solitude, with its concealed ravines and its caves reached by secret paths, had been the home of armed resistance since Roman antiquity and had sheltered slave rebellions that had taken decades to quell. Only a few miles away, and in similar terrain, the bandit Giuliano was shortly to hold two fully equipped divisions in check with a force of only a hundred men. In command of the defenders was a Colonel Salemi, a veteran described as possessing an inflexible sense of duty. The Colonel was pessimistic about the final outcome of the battle in view of the lack of air-cover, but he had no doubt of his ability to halt the American advance for a valuable period of days, or even weeks. Cammarata might, in fact, have supplied a foretaste of the unhappy experience of Cassino.

On the morning of July 14th, four days after the landing, an American fighter plane flew low over the town of Villalba, circled and returned to drop a packet which fell near the church. A yellow flag with the letter L in black had been stretched over the side of the plane's cockpit, and when the packet was picked up its contents were found to include a small replica of this flag. Packet and contents were handed over to *Carabinieri* Lance-Corporal Angelo Riccioli, now a sergeant-major in the service at Palermo, who has no objection to discussing the occurrence with an interested visitor.

Next day the plane returned and a second packet was dropped, this time a short distance from the house of Villalba's leading citizen – Calogero Vizzini – for whom it was intended. The packet was recovered by a servant of the Vizzini family, Carmelo Bartolomeo, who must have been looking over his employer's shoulder when it was opened, as he later told a newspaperman that he had seen a yellow silk handkerchief bearing the initial L. Bartolomeo's employer, Calogero Vizzini – generally known as Don Calò – was the head of the mafia of all Sicily, and as such considered by most Sicilians to be the most powerful man in the island.

Next morning, July 15th, a messenger left Villalba on horseback for the neighbouring town of Mussomeli. He was carrying a letter on behalf of Don Calò to Giuseppe Genco Russo, regarded at that time as second to Don Calò in the mafia hierarchy. This letter, which the messenger had been told to swallow if intercepted, was couched in mafia jargon, and its substance was that a certain mafia chieftain known as Turi would be leaving on July 20th to accompany the American motorised division as far as Cerda (within five miles of the north coast), while he, Don Calò, would be going on the same day with the main body of the army. Genco Russo was asked to do all he could in Don Calò's absence for the security and the comfort of the Americans.

On July 20th, in fact, while the advance guard of the Seventh Army was still thirty miles away, a solitary jeep made a dash to reach Villalba and carry off the indispensable Don Calò. The jeep, however, took a wrong turning, came under fire from an Italian patrol, and one of its crew was killed. Later that day three American tanks repeated the attempt and were successful. One of these was flying the by now familiar yellow flag with the black L, and when in the main square an officer climbed out of its turret, he spoke in the authentic Sicilian dialect of the region.

Citizens of Villalba who were present at the encounter between this officer and the formidable Don Calò say that the American seemed surprised by the presence in the flesh of the legendary mafia chief. Characteristically, Don Calò appeared on the scene in his shirtsleeves and braces, waddling unemotionally towards the group of nervous and excited American soldiers standing under the guns of their tanks. At this time he was sixty-six years of age, a man of bulky features and inert expression, but with eyes that moved like lizards. Don Calò's slovenly dress and laconic speech were typical mafia affectations. It was not done for a mafia chieftain to show off in the matter of his clothing or any other way, and sometimes, as in Don Calò's case, this lack of concern for appearances was carried to extremes. From the Prince of Lampedusa's description, Don Calò might well have been the twin brother of Don Calogero Sedara, the unshaven and unscrupulous mafioso mayor of *The Leopard*.

Reaching the shadow of the guns, Don Calò pulled out of his pocket the yellow handkerchief that had been dropped by the plane, and showed it to the officers. He and a nephew, Domiano Lumia, who had returned from the United States a short time before the outbreak of war, were invited to get into one of the tanks, which then moved off, followed by the others. During the whole confrontation Don Calò – true to his reputation for preferring action to speech – is reported not to have opened his mouth.

Next morning, July 21st, on the heights of Cammarata, visible from the town, two-thirds of Colonel Salemi's men were found to have deserted. Some of them have since said that during the night they were approached by mafia agents, who convinced them of the hopelessness of their position and supplied them with civilian clothes and whatever else was needed to get home to their families. The same day, the Italian Commander himself was arrested by a trick while passing through Mussomeli, and confined by the mafia in the Town Hall. At four o'clock on the afternoon of the 21st, Moroccan troops under General Juin, who had been waiting since dawn at the village of Riffi for an order to advance, received the expected signal from a Sicilian agent coming from Mussomeli and began to move forward. The battle of Cammarata was over without a shell having been fired.

Don Calò was away from his capital for six days. During this time the Seventh Army divided itself in two columns, one of which, striking directly north along the Agrigento-Palermo road, reached Cerda, where it was joined by the other column which had carried out a wide encircling movement through Gela, Piazza Armerina, Nicosia, Mistretta and Santo Stefano – all of them notorious as mafia towns. As indicated in the letter to Genco Russo, Don Calò considered his mission to end at Cerda. Here other mafia potentates were ready to shoulder his responsibility.

In reality, although at this time Don Calò was the accepted head of the mafia, there were certain weak links in his chain of command. Mussolini's vigorous attack on the 'Honoured Society', as it was called by its members, had shaken its structure and left it weaker, probably, than it had ever been. Many of the best mafia brains had been hastily converted to Fascism. Others, in 1943, were still in *confino* and only just about to be released. In the heart of western Sicily, the stronghold of great feudal estates, Don Calò – who had been too wily even for Mussolini – remained absolute master; but in the coastal plain between Cerda and Palermo the mafia satraps had become used to their independence and had to be handled with diplomacy. It would be Don Calò's first task to repair this weakness in the organisation.

By the time Calogero Vizzini returned to Villalba the war in western Sicily was at an end. He had dedicated the whole of his life to what the mafia calls 'winning respect', and his prestige was now enormous. He had been nicknamed by the Allies 'General mafia'. Whether or not he was responsible for American strategy in western Sicily, his followers certainly gave him the credit for it, and no one could deny that the mafia had most efficiently cleared all obstacles in the path of the American advance, while in the east the British and Canadians were still fighting their way round the slopes of Etna and it was to be three more weeks before they reached their goal at Messina.

But the war in western Sicily had been terminated bloodlessly, rapidly, and to the satisfaction of all but a few diehard senior Axis officers like the unfortunate Salemi. The Sicilians, always anti-Fascist, to all intents and purposes were now anti-Italian too. In so far as the loyalties of kinship were felt they were towards America, where by 1943 two million Sicilians, or first- or second-generation Americans of Sicilian origin, were living in a prosperity that was almost incredible by island standards. Many islanders were totally dependent on money sent back by relations in the States. Moreover, American Intelligence had seen to it that the Sicilian component of the invading force was as high as fifteen per cent. Hatred of the war had become so intense that, shortly after the invasion began, there were cases of Sicilian civilians attacking and destroying Italian military camps left unguarded by the rushing of troops to the beach-heads. To the Sicilians, resistance of any kind only signified a painful delay in an occupation wholeheartedly desired by all.

There was a precedent for the display of yellow flags and handkerchiefs which heralded this happy conclusion of hostilities on the western Sicilian front. The exchange of silk handkerchiefs was commonly practised among the mafia and had become the equivalent of a password when an identity had to be established. In 1922 a certain Lottò, an associate-member of the mafia of Villalba, committed a murder so outrageously ill-planned and with such an arrogant disregard for any attempt at concealment, that his arrest and conviction were inevitable. This kind of overconfidence was in breach of mafia rules, which called for consultation and approval at high level before a liquidation could be carried out. But, to have left a 'man of honour' to his fate would have damaged the authority and prestige of the mafia and have caused Don Calò himself serious 'loss of respect'. He therefore arranged to have Lottò declared insane and transferred to a criminal lunatic asylum at Barcellona, where mafia infiltration had been particularly successful. Soon after Lottò's arrival, he officially died. The 'corpse' was removed for burial in a specially prepared and ventilated coffin, after which Lottò was supplied with false identity documents and smuggled away to the United States. On arrival in New York, he was met by a group of friends who had been warned to expect him, and to these he identified himself by the production of a yellow silk handkerchief given to him by Don Calò, which in this instance carried the initial C.

The bold black L on the flags flown at Villalba on these fateful days in July stood for Luciano. Lucky Luciano, originally Salvatore Lucania, had been born in Lercara Friddi, the next town of any size along the main road from Villalba to Palermo, and as head of the mafia in the United States – which he had almost certainly become – Luciano would undoubtedly have been in regular contact with his opposite number in Sicily. In 1943, Luciano, who had been found guilty on sixty-two counts of compulsory prostitution, was serving a thirty to fifty year prison sentence. He had recently been transferred at the US Navy's request from the State Penitentiary at Dannemara, a maximum security prison known to the criminal fraternity as 'Siberia', to the Great Meadows Penitentiary, where he was more conveniently accessible to parties of naval officers in plain clothes who went there to confer with him.

In February of that year – five months before the invasion of Sicily took place – he appealed through his lawyer, George Wolf, for a reduction of his sentence in consideration of 'services rendered to the nation'. Following this, he appeared in 1945 before the State Parole Board, where some squeamishness seems to have been displayed by naval intelligence officers called upon to testify on his behalf. Whatever had been promised Luciano in return for his co-operation – and Luciano protested that it was his freedom – the naval authorities refused to be drawn in, and the fact that Luciano was eventually freed and deported to Italy was due to the action as a private individual of Commander Haffenden, a naval officer prominent in these negotiations, and his confidential letters to members of the Parole Board.

The late Senator Estes Kefauver, Chairman of the Senate Crime Investigating Committee 1950-51, has referred in his book *Crime in America* to the background of these circumstances.

During World War II there was a lot of hocus-pocus about allegedly valuable services that Luciano, then a convict, was supposed to have furnished the military authorities in connection with plans for the invasion of his native Sicily. We dug into this and obtained a number of conflicting stories. This is one of the points about which the committee would have questioned Governor Dewey, who commuted Luciano's sentence, if the Governor had not declined our invitation to come to New York City to testify before the committee.

One story which we heard from Moses Polakoff, attorney for Meyer Lansky, was that Naval Intelligence had sought out Luciano's aid and had asked Polakoff to be the intermediary. Polakoff, who had represented Luciano when he was sent up, said he in turn enlisted the help of Lansky, an old associate of Lucky's, and that some fifteen or twenty visits were arranged at which Luciano gave certain information...

On the other hand, Federal Narcotics Agent George White, who served our committee as an investigator for several months, testified to having been approached on Luciano's behalf by a narcotics smuggler named August Del Grazio. Del Grazio claimed he 'was acting on behalf of two attorneys ... and ... Frank Costello who was spearheading the movement to get Luciano out of the penitentiary,' White said.

'He [Del Grazio] said Luciano had many potent connections in the Italian underworld and Luciano was one of the principal members of the mafia,' White testified. The proffered deal, he went on, was that Luciano would use his mafia position to arrange contacts for undercover American agents 'and that therefore Sicily would be a much softer target than it might otherwise be.'

There have been many apocryphal versions of what followed these transactions, some of them wildly improbable. It has, for example, been reported that Luciano was secretly released from prison in 1943 to accompany the invasion force, that he was freely to be seen in the town of Gela where the Seventh Army's first headquarters were established, and even that he was a member of the crew of the tank that picked up Don Calò at Villalba. There is no evidence of Don Calò and Luciano getting together, however, until 1946, when they occupied adjoining suites in a Palermo hotel during the formation of the Sicilian Separatist Party.

The day after Don Calò's return to his capital, an intimate little ceremony took place in the barracks of the *carabinieri* at which he was appointed Mayor by the American Officer of Civil Affairs. A sketch made from a photograph taken at the time captures the spirit of the historic moment. It shows Don Calò, who has agreed to put on an untidy jacket for the occasion, listening while the Civil Affairs Officer, who has been told that the new Mayor is illiterate, reads out the document conferring the honour upon him. The artist shows Don Calò's attention as incompletely held by the ceremony, an eye swivelled sideways as if distracted by something that is happening behind his back. In fact, in the square below a cheering crowd had gathered, and among the cheers Don Calò was slightly embarrassed to hear cries of 'Long live the Allies. Long live the mafia.'

That evening the new Mayor gave a party for the Allied officers – 'the sheep' as Don Calò called them – and a number of his selected friends. The friends were the members of the mafia of Villalba and such mafia notabilities from the surrounding districts as could attend at short notice. Some of them wore their hair closely cropped, and their faces still bore the pallor of Mussolini's prisons. Don Calò introduced them to the officers as victims of Fascism, as indeed they were. His enthusiastic recommendations easily persuaded the military authorities to issue firearms permits all round – 'to guard against the possibility of any attempted Fascist coup'. Thus Don Calò had restored to him the armed bodyguard that had been taken away by Mussolini in 1924. The first of many victims of this resurgence of democracy was Pietro Purpi, the very *carabinieri* non-commissioned officer whose rueful task it had been to countersign the firearms permits.

Don Calò's next step was a more important one – so important indeed that Sicily has not yet recovered from its far-reaching effects. He compiled a list of suitable candidates for the office of mayor throughout the whole of western Sicily, and this too was found acceptable. Many of these partisans of democracy, as Don Calò pointed out, had spent long years in confinement. No one seems to have had time to investigate his claim that his nominees had suffered for their political ideals, rather than for crimes ranging from armed train-robbery to multiple homicide. In a matter of days, half the towns in Sicily had mayors who were either members of the mafia or were at least closely associated with it. One or two had been bandits into the bargain. A noteworthy appointment was that of Serafino Di Peri to be Mayor of Bolognetta near Palermo. Di Peri's first task as head of the municipality was to form a band of 109 desperadoes, who thereafter terrorised the outskirts of Palermo for the next five years. Thus for the first time, due to the military authorities' complete incomprehension of the situation in which they found themselves, the mafia ruled directly, instead of, as in the past, exerting its influence indirectly through the control of corrupt public officials. Within days the maleficent genius of Don Calò had been able to repair much of the damage done to the 'Honoured Society' in the twenty years of Fascism. Now, in the absence of a constituted government, the mafia chieftains had become the real rulers of Sicily.

A ceremony with a strangely archaic flavour brought this period to a close. A whispered suggestion to the Allies set the ball rolling with a gift to the municipality of Villalba of two Fiat trucks and a tractor taken from an abandoned Italian depot. The trucks were usefully employed in the black market, and the tractor was sold for scrap iron. Following this lead, presents for Don Calò began to pour in from all over Sicily. Every notability contributed to this avalanche of flour, cheeses, pasta, and stolen military equipment. Under the innocent gaze of the Allied Military Government a spontaneous revival took place of an ancient custom dating back to the days of Roger the Norman. Don Calò had become, for the second time in his life, a feudal ruler, and these gifts were the tributes of vassals who accepted him as their overlord.

Strangely, not all those who came to press Don Calò's hand or to present their ceremonial offering were sycophants. Aside from the natural awe they felt for him, many people genuinely admired the head of the mafia, and even those he had victimised sometimes seemed unable to repress their grudging esteem. Don Calò was a natural artist in the control of men, through their affections as well as through their fears. His immense dignity, the Johnsonian pithiness of his rare but massive utterances, the majestic finality of his opinions, appealed to the human search for leadership. Even men of education and intellectuals admitted their susceptibility to a strange power of attraction not uncommonly possessed by a capo-mafia, and certainly highly evident in Don Calò. The Mayor of Villalba would have shaken his head at the puerility of anyone who could really have believed he was a criminal. He almost certainly saw himself as the head of a self-created aristocracy of the intellect, to which had been committed, as if by some divine right, the arcana of government. He believed in himself as only a *mafioso* could and with the stolid unwavering faith of religious fanaticism – and almost as though by telepathic contact, he forced those around him to become believers too. Don Calò knew that only he, the inspired realist in command of the mafia, could rule Sicily as it should be ruled, and had anyone dared to oppose this assumption – which he would never have bothered to claim in so many words – he would have pointed to the total ruin Mussolini had left behind after a mere twenty years of Fascist rather than mafia rule. Such *mafiosi* of the old school were only criminals in the eyes of the law and of abstract justice – and in a more confused and unfocused way in those of the peasantry they exploited. To the rest of the community they were 'men of respect', and of sincere if inscrutable purpose.

A conversation fifteen years later between a newspaperman and Don Calò's chauffeur, after the old capo-mafia's death, illuminated a curious facet of his remarkable character.

'Did Don Calò pay you well?'

'He never gave me a lira.'

'You mean you never had any wages? In that case, how did you live?'

'I suppose you might say I robbed him. I used to tell him we needed a new set of tyres for the car. Or maybe it was petrol or oil. Once I told him we had to have a new engine. I just put the money in my pocket. He never said a word.'

'But didn't he realise what was happening all the time?'

'Of course he did. Nothing ever got past him. Don Calò knew everything that was going on. He just wanted it that way. He never gave me any wages, so I cheated him and he pretended not to notice it. That was the way he wanted it.'

2

The word mafia probably derives from the identical word in Arabic and means 'place of refuge'. As such, it no doubt recalls the predicament of the relatively civilised Saracens after the conquest of Sicily by the Normans in the eleventh century. The Arabs had introduced smallholdings and scientific irrigation. Their rule by comparison with anything the island had known before (or since) was mild and beneficent. Had they remained, there is no reason why the prosperity and civilisation of Sicily should not have equalled that of Spain, but the Normans dislodged them and plunged the country back into the polar night of feudalism. Most of the Arab smallholders became serfs on the reconstituted estates. Some escaped to 'the mafia'.

241

These are the dry bones of probability as unearthed by the historians. But scratch below the surface and the evidence of an even earlier origin comes to light. One discovers archaic – even Bronze Age – ingredients in the seemingly down-to-earth, devil-take-the-hindmost materialism of the men of the 'Honoured Society'. In times of crisis, men like Don Calogero Vizzini tend sometimes to behave not so much like big-scale black-market operators of the twentieth century as like the *personae* of a Greek tragedy, whose motives are often so remote from our own as to be incomprehensible. This – from our viewpoint – irrational element in mafia behaviour comes out strongly in the great feud between the Barbaccia and Lorello families of Godrano, near Palermo.

The two families quarrelled back in 1918 over the possession of a wood. This in itself is perhaps significant, because the wood, standing unaccountably intact in a country denuded of trees since Roman times, may have survived through its supposed possession of sacred or magic attributes. The dispute over this ragged patch of stunted oaks and thorny underbrush cost these two families dozens of lives, until, it is supposed, Don Calò Vizzini – that great advocate of mafia unity – intervened in 1942 to help repair the quarrel. Following age-old custom, the thing now would have been to arrange a marriage between two suitable members of the opposing families. This could not be done through lack of mutually acceptable candidates, and in 1944 the war flared up again with the commission by the Lorellos of what to the men of honour is considered the most odious of all crimes: Francisco Barbaccia, head of his family, was kidnapped and never seen again. It is at this point that the archaic component of the mafia mentality – its utter separation from the outlook of the ordinary criminal of modern times – is apparent. The killing of Barbaccia was bad enough, but the final offence – held to be ten times more execrable than the killing itself – was the concealment of the body so that vengeance could not be ritually sworn 'in the presence of the corpse'. By 1960, nearly one-tenth of the population of Godrano had become casualties as the feud developed and spread, the latest victim – in the absence of eligible adults – being a boy of twelve.

The mafia stands outside Christian morality, but the uncorrupted form of the mafia found in feudal Sicily has an iron morality of its own. No *mafioso* sees himself as a criminal, and the mafia has always been the enemy of petty crime – and therefore, to a limited extent, the ally of the police, both in Sicily and the United States. The organisation demands blind obedience from its members, but will defend them in return through thick and thin – and in an alien land even extends its powerful protection to all immigrants of Sicilian birth. It can be regarded as a form of primitive human society that has somehow survived in the modern Western world; its cruel laws are those of tribesmen exposed to continual danger who can only hope to survive by submitting to the discipline of terrible chieftains. The capo-mafia considers himself a law-giver, concerned with the welfare of his people, and prides himself on watching over the advancement of deserving juniors in the organisation with the assiduousness of the master of novices of a religious order. In his own eyes, he never steals from the community, but he can see no objection to exploiting his power over men to enrich himself. To delinquents he awards only one punishment, usually after a warning: death. He is self-righteous and full of justifications. Listen to Nick Gentile, an American capo-mafia, discussing the ethics of eliminating an uncontrollable young criminal: 'There was nothing we could do with him, so he had to be rubbed out. We embalmed the body and sent it back to his people in Sicily. His folks were poor – they didn't have anything – so we put a diamond ring on his finger, the way they'd see it as soon as they opened the casket. I guess we did the right thing. We figured otherwise he'd have finished up in the chair or the gas-chamber. That way they wouldn't even have had his body back.'

A primeval law transcends the bonds of blood-relationship, and mafia honour demands precedence over ordinary human loyalties. Between 1872 and 1878 there took place in the neighbourhood of the towns of Bagheria and Monreale the most calamitous vendetta known to history. The two clans involved, the Fratuzzi and the Stoppaglieri, were both active in the same area, frequently treading on each other's toes but on the whole successful in keeping on terms of limited hostility. In 1872 Giuseppe Lipari, a member of the Fratuzzi clan, committed what the mafia calls *infamità* by denouncing a Stoppaglieri to the police. The Stoppaglieri sent an emissary to their opponents describing what had happened, and calling upon the Fratuzzi to observe mafia law and execute Lipari. This the Fratuzzi failed to do, and the feud was on. Within a short time all the close relations of the original disputants had been killed, and as more remote degrees of kinship were forced into the vendetta, the whole population began a terror-stricken rummaging back into its ancestry in search of dangerous ties of blood. By 1878 a man might be approached by some enshrouded, tragic crone he had never seen before – the female head of one of the clans – who would inform him that he was now the surviving head of the Fratuzzi, or the Stoppaglieri, and that he must consider himself in a state of ritual vendetta with some cousin he had never seen or heard of and who might even have had the foresight to take refuge in Tunisia or the USA. A case occurred of a young boy being assisted to fulfil his ritual duty by an outsider, who charitably loaded his blunderbuss for him and carried it to the place where it had been decided to stage an ambush. By the time the feud ended, fear of involvement had brought about the depopulation of the countryside. The survivors of the two clans were reconciled in characteristic fashion. A survivor of the Fratuzzi, Salvatore D'Amico, who had lost all his family, went to the police and told all he knew of the malfeasances of the Stoppaglieri. It was an act tantamount to suicide, of a man tired of life, as D'Amico made quite clear in his statement. This time the Fratuzzi did the right thing. They killed their clan member, and to make sure of his recognition, his body was displayed prominently, with an amulet of the kind worn by the Fratuzzi, made from a vestment stolen from an image of the Madonna, placed over each eye.

There are mild and rustic men, goatherds and ploughmen, drawn without hope of escape into these ancient, tragic games whose rules were established perhaps before their ancestors reached the shores of the Mediterranean. In 1944 I was engaged in army duties in Naples which committed me to a number of lugubrious visits to the prison of Poggio Reale. There I was introduced by the head warder to a Sicilian, D'Agostino, who had committed five vendetta murders. The maximum sentence for an 'honour' killing in Italy is ten years, so that D'Agostino was serving a total of fifty years. He was put on display for the benefit of privileged visitors with what can only be described as a sort of modest pride. D'Agostino was treated with immense respect. He was the only prisoner, not excluding a general occupying a cell in Poggio Reale at that time, who was addressed in the third person singular, being given a courteous *lei* instead of the familiar and slightly contemptuous *tu*. D'Agostino was small, puzzled, and yet resigned. He was slightly under five feet in height, with tiny hands and feet and hardly more than the frame of a child. His crime had been committed with an axe – the tomahawk-like weapon that Prefect Mori, Mussolini's destroyer of the mafia, had permitted shepherds to keep – and he had wiped out a whole family. This was the end of a period of close confinement, and on the assumption that after three years the prisoner had come to a working arrangement with despair, the forty-seven years that remained would pass under a slightly relaxed prison régime. D'Agostino always expected to be asked whether he would commit his crime again could the clock be put back, and his reply was always the same: 'Surely you don't imagine I had any choice, one way or the other? Honour's honour and a vendetta's a vendetta. You might say that destiny put its big fat thumb in my neck and squashed me like a beetle.' The warders nodded their sympathy and their agreement. That was the way it was.

What would Don Vito Cascio Ferro, who established his image as a forward-looking man by making a pioneer trip in a balloon and was head of all the mafia until his final arrest by Prefect Mori, have said to anyone who pointed out to him that the organisation he commanded was psychologically still entangled in the prehistory of humanity? The sophisticated Don Vito can hardly have realised, either, that mafia symbolism – the system of graded warnings from the cutting down of a vine and the maiming of an ass or mule, to the depositing at a man's door of his beheaded dog or a sheep with its throat cut – is shared with certain African tribes of the Republic of Mali. How strange, too, that the custom of vendetta of Corsica, Sardinia and Sicily – whose peoples have presumably been separated for thousands of years – should be so similar in all its curious detail: the ritual denunciation of the slayer by the professional mourners at the funeral (ignorance of his identity will be feigned, if necessary, up till this point); the entrusting of the vendetta to the male nearest-of-kin by the senior female member of the household; the kissing, even the pretended sucking of the wounds, by close relations such as mother, wife or brother, followed by the spoken formula: 'In this way may I drink the blood of the man who killed you'; the final consummation of the act of vengeance, which ideally should take place, after a period of ritual preparation, in full sunshine – an archaic blueprint for the *mise-en-scène* of *High Noon*.

The vendetta was the weapon ready to hand of the poor and otherwise defenceless in a society where law did not exist and justice meant the baron's court and the baron's torture chamber. Sicily – the America of the ancient world – has been a colony exploited by the use of slave labour, either openly or in a disguised form, for two thousand years. The Roman armies marched to the conquest of Gaul and Britain on bread made from corn grown by Sicilian slaves. When, with the fall of Rome, the Papacy took over the great Sicilian estates, it was the chain gangs of Sicilian peasant labourers that provided three-fourths of its wealth. Sicily was exploited by Norman, German, Frenchman, Aragonese, Spaniard, and finally the Bourbons, but nearly always from a distance. After the Germans there was no central government, no monarch, no court, no resident hierarchy. So long as the corn was shipped out of Sicilian ports each year, nothing else mattered. Defining the seemingly endless ice-age of feudalism in Sicily, Filangieri, the social historian, said that an overbearing despotism had grown up to separate the Crown from the people. As a result, Sicily was a political hermaphrodite, neither monarchy nor republic, 'which suffered from all the dependency of the former, while lacking the advantages of a constitution, and all the turbulence of the latter, although deprived of its liberties'.

And then, just at the time when the first stirring of the modern world were visible elsewhere in Europe, another tragic yoke was laid upon the Sicilian neck by the establishment of the Inquisition. And in Sicily, through the remoteness of the Crown, its effects were even more deadening than in Spain itself. More and more to the modern observer the Holy Office appears as a device concerned primarily with economic situations, and only secondarily with matters of faith. Drawing its revenues from heresy, it saw to it that heresy was abundant. In Spain heresy provided an excuse for the ruin and annihilation of a class of rich Christianised merchants of Jewish or Moorish origin. In Sicily its objectives were all-embracing, although vaguer. Heresy started as religious dissent, but as religious dissenters – understandably enough – were remarkably few, the Inquisition widened its scope to include a miscellany of bigamists, 'philosophers', usurers, sodomites, priests who married their concubines, and finally opponents of any kind, who automatically became classed as heretics. Membership of the Inquisition, like that of an exclusive club, was open only to the aristocracy, and in Sicily the barons enrolled themselves with enthusiasm as familiars. All convictions were accompanied by forfeiture of property, and the Inquisition gave no receipts. In procedural matters the scales were heavily weighted against those whose reputation for original thought or whose conspicuous possessions happened to attract the Holy Office's attention. Arrests were made on suspicion, often as the result of anonymous denunciation. The accused was presumed guilty and the functions of prosecutor and judge were combined. Women, children and slaves could be called as witnesses for the prosecution, but not for the defence. Nor could the victim be allowed a lawyer to plead his case, as this would have been tantamount to opposing the Inquisition, and, as such, an act of heresy.

The familiars of the Inquisition dominated Sicily for three centuries. Until the time of their disbanding in 1787 there were never less than two thousand of these psalm-singing marauders, each in command of his own band of retainers – all of whom enjoyed the same extra-legal privileges. They stripped rich men of their property, and sentenced them to *murus largus* – the most comfortable kind of incarceration the day had to offer. The poor were punished for their lack of seizable goods by torture and *murus strictis*, which meant that they were flung, fettered, into a deep dungeon and endured 'the bread and water of affliction' until they died. Horrified by these excesses, which he was quite powerless to check, the Spanish Viceroy, the Duke of Medinaceli, wrote: 'It would take a year to describe the things they do. Unheard of things – the most hideous and frightful enormities.' The poor man's only shield was the mafia and the vendetta. Justice was not to be come by, but the association of men of honour, silent, persistent and inflexible, could at least exact a bloody retribution for the loss of a wife or daughter, or the burning down of a house. Colafanni, an authority on the period, sums up: 'The mafia in Sicily under the Bourbons provided the only means for the poor and humble to make themselves respected ... To the mafia, then, went all the rebels, all those that had suffered injuries, all the victims.'

It was in the school of the vendetta, too, that the traditional character of the *mafioso* was formed. The common man, a victim of absolute power, had to learn to stomach insult or injury with apparent indifference so that vengeance could be delayed until the opportunity for its consummation presented itself. The *mafioso* therefore developed a kind of self-control closely resembling that quality known as *giri* by the Japanese, and so much admired by them. A true man of honour never weakened his position or armed his enemy in advance by outbursts of passion or of fear. When he sustained some grave injury he made a pact with himself to be revenged, and thereafter would wait patiently and unemotionally, half a lifetime if necessary, until his moment came – often seemingly on excellent terms with the man he proposed to destroy.

But when a man lost his head, threw mafia-inculcated secrecy and caution to the wind and struck back openly, his only chance of salvation was to take to the *maquis*. For this reason there was never a time when Sicily was without its bandits. At the end of the Second World War thirty separate armed bands terrorised western Sicily, while even in the late winter of 1962–3 motorised bandits were still staging highway robberies on the main provincial highway between Castellamare and Ballestrate. A hundred and fifty years ago the Bourbon authorities decided to deal with this situation by creating the first pseudo-police force. The only qualification for enrolment in the 'Armed Companies', as they were called, was ruthlessness. Many of these upholders of the law were ferocious criminals reprieved from the gallows and allowed to rehabilitate themselves in this way. What the familiars of the Inquisition had overlooked, the Armed Companies took. After the depredations carried out in the name of religion, Sicilians were now doomed to suffer voicelessly under the agents of the State. Since then they have quite simply turned their backs on authority of any kind. For this reason the police charged with the investigation of the highway robberies of February 1963 met with nothing but the most intractable hostility from local villagers, while even the victims of the robberies appear not to have been specially helpful. For this reason, when a man is found lying seriously wounded, possibly dying, and the police appeal to him to identify his aggressor, the reply is usually couched in a formula: 'If I die, may God forgive me, as I forgive the one who did this. If I manage to pull through, I know how to settle my own accounts.'

This is the famous Sicilian *omertà* – 'manliness', which rules the public conscience and is sustained so often even in the face of death. It is a word which calls for further examination, and is best understood by the study of an extreme case of *omertà* in action.

Some four or five years ago one of two brothers living together in a Sicilian farmhouse disappeared. The men were known to have been on the worst possible terms for years, and the younger and stronger one frequently knocked his older brother about and even threatened to kill him. Finally the older brother vanished and the police got to hear about it, searched the farmhouse, and found inefficiently cleaned-up bloodstains on the floor. It is a popular misconception that a case for murder cannot be made out if no body can be found. In this case it was decided by the examining magistrate that a *corpus delicti* existed, constituted by the threats of murder known to have been made, the man's disappearance, the bloodstains, and the suspect's immediate assumption of his brother's property. The younger brother was accordingly tried for murder, found guilty, and sentenced to imprisonment for life.

A year or two later a *carabiniere*, who knew the older brother, suddenly found himself face to face with the 'murdered' man. He was working quietly as a labourer on a farm in the mountains, only two miles away. It emerged that as part of his plan to be revenged on his brother, the man had changed his name, although most of his fellow labourers and some of the neighbours knew who he was all the same. This was *omertà* with a vengeance. It simply did not occur to these people to go to the police, despite the terrific injustice that had been done. It was 'manly' to solve one's own problems in one's own way and leave others to do the same, and one 'lost respect' by poking one's nose into other people's affairs.

The Sicilian conscience is further bedevilled by an unfortunate linguistic confusion, arising out of the similarity between the words *omertà* and *umiltà* – humility, the Christian virtue so much extolled in the Church. Many illiterate Siciliane have combined the two words to produce a hybrid of mixed pagan and Christian significance. The virtuous man is in mafia fashion 'manly' and silent, and as a Christian, humble.

Far from protecting the underdog, the mafia today has taken the place of the oppressors of old, but it still benefits from a moral climate formed in past centuries. The Sicilian is a trifle cynical and quite self-sufficient. He fights his own battles, keeps his mouth shut, and has little interest in the doings of humanity outside the circle of his family, extended perhaps to include his second cousins. 'Manliness', once a barricade raised against injustice, now serves to keep justice out.

In the past it was the mafia – the product of weak government that had developed its own vested interest in governmental weakness – that whipped up the frantic *jacqueries* of 1820, 1840 and 1866. The savageries of these outbursts of peasant hatred are quite inexplicable to anyone unaware of the long years of contempt that had preceded them. As in Spain, the targets of popular fury were always the same: the landlord, the Church, the police. There is no better description of the kind of thing that could happen than that given by Giovanni Verga in his story *Liberty*, which is largely factual and based on the rising at Brontë, put down by Nino Bixio, lieutenant of Garibaldi – the man who was to have given the land to the peasants.

Like the sea in storm, the crowd foamed and swayed in front of the club of the gentry, and outside the Town Hall, and on the steps of the church – a sea of white stocking-caps, axes and sickles glittering. Then they burst into the little street.

'Your turn first, baron! You who have had folks cudgelled by your estate guards!' At the head of all the people a witch, with her old hair sticking up, armed with nothing but her nails. 'Your turn, priest of the devil, for you've sucked the soul out of us!' ... 'Your turn, police-sergeant, you who never took the law on anybody except poor folks who'd got nothing!' 'Your turn, estate guards, who sold your own flesh and your neighbour's flesh for ten pence a day!'

Now they were drunk with the killing. Sickles, hands, rags, stones, everything red with blood. The gentry! Kill them all! Kill them all! Down with the gentry!

'Don't kill me,' pleads the priest, 'I'm in mortal sin!' Neighbour Lucia being the mortal sin; neighbour Lucia, whose father sold her to the priest when she was fourteen years old, at the time of the famine winter. But the priest is hacked to pieces on the cobblestones of the street. Then it is the turn of the apothecary, the lawyer, and the lawyer's eleven-year-old son. The estate guards fire on the crowd from the castle, but the castle is stormed and the defenders massacred, the baron's young sons trampled to death, the baroness and her baby thrown from her balcony to the street.

And then suddenly the slaughter is over. They are free of the gentry and rage is dead. Now they have their liberty, but nobody knows what to do with it. And in any case there is no time to learn, for the Army, with its firing squads, is on the way. Quietly and sadly, arms folded, they sit waiting behind closed doors.

In those days the mafia was still with the people; then, gradually, as it gathered its power it began to draw apart. The mafia was paid for its part in Garibaldi's triumph, it organised the plebiscite (at Lampedusa's Donnafugata – Voters, 515; Voting, 512; Yes, 512; No, zero); its chieftains, like his illiterate Sedaras, married their daughters to penniless princes. From that time on the mafia began to elbow the feudal aristocracy aside. By 1945 the process was complete. Don Calogero Vizzini was the feudal overlord of all Sicily as well as head of the mafia. And thereby he had become the worst single thorn in the peasants' side since the bad old days of the Bourbons.

Don Fabrizio, the ruminative and unworldly princeling of Lampedusa's novel, philosophical in his acceptance of Garibaldi and the mafia, felt queasy at the first sight of the infant democracy newly delivered at Donnafugata. 'Something had died, God only knew in what back-alley, in what corner of the popular conscience.' People always had done, and always would do, what they were told, and he found it in some way demeaning that anyone should find it necessary to construct this elaborate edifice of pretence dedicated to the lie that free will and freedom of choice actually existed.

However sickening to Don Fabrizio's stomach the newly imported democracy might have been, for the mafia it was an invention as promising as the new steam-engine. In the old days the Viceroy had given the orders – at most, and as a matter of courtesy, taking the advice of his council of nobles. Now it was to be the turn of anyone who could fight his way to the controls of this wonderful new machine. In 1881 communal elections were held at Villalba – the town that was to become Don Calogero Vizzini's capital – and the Marchese of Villalba, supported by the mafia, took his precautions ten days in advance. The two hundred and fourteen citizens possessing the qualifications entitling them to vote were locked up in a granary, from which they were released, eight at a time, and escorted by the Marchese's armed guards to the polls. The Marchese was elected.

Later the mafia invented and perfected new methods of democratic suasion. By the time the government of Giolitti reached power, the mafia had become the only electoral force that counted in Sicily and the Government was realistic in its acceptance of the fact. Alongi, who published a study of the mafia in 1902, describes the arrangements for voting he had witnessed a year or two previously: 'Some short distance from the polling station the road was barred by a group of sinister figures. Here each voter as he approached was seized, thoroughly bastinadoed, and forced to drink a huge glass of wine. There followed a thorough search of his person, after which the government candidate's voting slip was put into his hand and he was led or dragged to the ballot box, where the president took the slip from him and put it in.'

Later still, this physical suppression of the element of choice gradually came to be considered unnecessary; it was found that the same result could be obtained by making the voter understand what he stood to lose by voting for the wrong side. As it was never explained to the voter what programme the candidates stood for, and he was assumed to be quite ignorant of the function of Parliament, the contending parties might be represented by symbols such as the mule and the ox, and the agricultural voters warned that it was either a case of voting for the mule or looking elsewhere for work in future. The system recalls the last election held under French tutelage in parts of then colonial West Africa, where bloody disputes took place between villages over the relative merits in terms of strength, courage and sagacity of the lion and the elephant, which were the symbols adopted by two of the parties soliciting their votes.

This somewhat special interpretation of the democratic process persisted in Sicily even after the end of the Second World War. In 1945 when the mafia and most of Sicily's aristocracy were hoping that Sicily would secede from Italy to become an American state, or at worst a British colony, a Separatist congress was convened at which Don Calogero Vizzini appeared unexpectedly and without formal invitation. When asked who he represented, he replied with proud simplicity: 'I have only to whistle, and every man in the province of Caltanisetta will vote Separatist.'

When a year or two after that the mafia threw the idea of Separatism overboard, and became, by order of Don Calò, Christian Democrat, there was one serious breach in the honoured society's political unity in the person of the awe-inspiring Don Vanni Sacco, head of the mafia of Camporeale. To the remonstrations of Don Calò, when he refused to accept a badge sent him in the form of a cross on a shield – the Party emblem – Vanni Sacco replied: 'I've been a liberal all my life, and my father before me. After all, politics, as I see it, is a stick, and I've got used to the feel of this one.' It took lunch with the Archbishop of Monreale, Monsignor Filippi, and the Archbishop's consent to Vanni Sacco's request that his daughter, Giovanna, should be granted the honour of christening the cathedral's new bell, before Don Vanni would agree to change his politics.

At the turn of the century, with the political machine finally and firmly under control, and the manicured hands of that distinguished ruffian Don Vito Cascio Ferro on its levers, the mafia could go ahead and trim up the details of the 'state within a state' that existed until the coming of Mussolini, and was to re-emerge in 1945 under the generalship of Don Calogero Vizzini of Villalba.

It was Don Vito who developed with a certain artistry the system of the '*pizzi*', as he called it – an onomatopoeic and picturesque word from the Sicilian dialect which translates rather flatly into English as 'racket'. *Pizzi* means the beak of a small bird, such as a canary or a lark, and when Don Vito with his inborn habit of understatement spoke of levying a mafia toll, he called it in Sicilian *fari vagnari a pizzi* – 'wetting the beak'. By the time Prefect Mori had succeeded in putting Don Vito away on his faked-up charge, beak-wetting was included in almost every conceivable activity in Sicily.

A great gathering of vulturine chieftains had collected to wet their beaks at the expense of the farmers, whose produce they bought dirt cheap on the spot and carried to the market in the mafia's own beautifully decorated carts – or later, trucks. In the market only those whose place had been 'guaranteed' by the mafia were allowed to buy or sell at prices the mafia fixed. The mafia wetted its beak in the meat, fish, beer and fruit businesses. It moved into the sulphur mines, controlled the output of rock salt, took over building contracts, 'organised labour', cornered the plots in Sicily's cemeteries, put tobacco-smuggling on a new and more profitable basis through its domination of the Sicilian fishing fleets, and went in for tomb-robbing in the ruins of the Greek settlement of Selinunte – the results of its archaeological excavations being offered at bargain prices to foreign tourists. Looking round for further sources of revenue, the mafia decided to recommend the owners of country houses and estates, however small, to employ guardians for their property, and after a few stubborn landowners had declined to supply sinecures for ex-convicts and had seen their property burned down, the practice became universal. There were advantages, too, to be gained by stringing along. The mafia gave monopolies to shopkeepers in different trades and then invited them to put up their prices – at the same time, of course, increasing their mafia contribution. Some of the mafia beak-wettings were picturesque in a sort of depraved oriental way. Beggars, for example, would be granted exclusive rights to a certain pitch, thus guaranteeing a display of distorted limbs freedom from competition by simulated idiocy.

The most evident of the mafia's criminal functions – and one that had been noted by the Bourbon attorney-general back in the 'twenties of the last century – now became the normally accepted thing. The mafia virtually replaced the police force, offering a form of arrangement with crime as a substitute for its suppression. When a theft, for instance, took place, whether of a mule, a jewelled pendant, or a motorcar, a mafia intermediary was soon on the scene, offering reasonable terms for the recovery of the stolen object. In this way the matter was usually settled rapidly, and to the satisfaction of all concerned. The victim got his property back without delay. The thief received a relatively small sum, but at least escaped the risk of police interference, since no one would have dared to call in the police once the mafia had interested itself. The mafia intermediary, of course, wetted his beak at the expense of both parties. The situation was and is an everyday one in Sicily. The police charge nothing to restore stolen property but are only successful in one case out of ten. The mafia is expensive, and may impose a commission charge of thirty-three and a third per cent. However, the mafia is successful ninety percent of the time.

But it was not only the farmer and the merchant who felt the weight of the mafia's New Order. The rich man, drawing his income, perhaps, from investments, could not be allowed to escape the net, and he became increasingly the target of letters of extortion. Such letters are commonplace in Sicily, but most of them are composed by novice delinquents who give themselves away by their brusqueness, their semi-literacy, and their habitual decoration with drawings of skulls and crossbones and dripping daggers. Letters of this kind go into the wastepaper basket, or may even be handed over to the police. The genuine mafia letter-writer is unmistakable in his style, which is likely to have a touch of the nineteenth century about it, with outmoded epistolary flourishes and protestations. It may even express regret for the inconvenience caused. As no second requests are sent, it is usual for payment to be made promptly.

Some of the rackets sound a trifle fantastic, such as the tax imposed on lovers in Don Vito's day when they went to carry on their courtship in the Spanish fashion with a girl who sat behind a barred window, and had to pay a mafia concessionaire 'the price of a candle' for his protection.

More fantastic was the racket – or rather the interlacing series of rackets – built up around religious devotion. The mafia – always ready to ally itself with the Church as a matter of expediency, in the manner of Don Calogero Vizzini –

moved cautiously at first. By the middle of the last century it controlled the confraternities devoted to the cults of the various patron saints, and more important, it directed the standing committees of the cults. It was the standing committees that raised the funds required for the saint's annual feast day; for the processions, the illuminations, and the firework displays. Later a mafia trust interested itself in the manufacture of devotional candles, and obtained a virtual monopoly. In nearly all Sicilian churches the seats are private property, and it was the mafia that hired the seats. The mafia took over the manufacture of religious objects of all kinds, and, being on the whole free of sentimental prejudices, attacked the problems of manufacture and distribution in an entirely dispassionate manner. With the advance of the twentieth century and the streamlining of production, its factories produced statues of saints and madonnas and religious medallions by the million. It employed the most persuasive travelling salesmen, appointed the most go-ahead retail firms as exclusive stockists, awarded bonuses and special quantity discounts, and supplied tasteful window displays to the shops in the bigger cities. Many of the faithful liked to have their religious medallions blessed by a bishop, and the mafia had no objection to arranging that – and blessed they were, in basketfuls and by the thousand.

Back in the last century the mafia had turned its attention to the lucrative business of manufacturing relics. The process was a simple one, requiring only the co-operation of the sacred object's custodian – in most cases a village priest. The relic was usually some portion of the body of a saint or a lock of his hair, or occasionally a more fanciful object of devotion such as a miniature urn full of the ashes of Abraham, or a bone from one of the fishes multiplied by Christ in the miracle of the loaves and fishes. All that was necessary to create a second relic having a large portion of the virtue of the original was to bring the new object into contact with it. Although the authorities of the Church frown upon the practice, relics were and are mass-produced by the thousand in this way. The manufacturing process is simplified by the existence of a tremendous number and diversity of saintly remnants upon which local cults are centred. In the course of a recent study of mafia penetration of devotional practices, the Italian publication *Le Ore* carried out, with remarkable results, a brief numerical survey of the most important of such relics. The paper discovered the existence of seventeen arms attributed to St Andrew, thirteen to St Stephen, twelve to St Philip, and ten each to St Vincent and St Tecla. Sixty fingers belonging to St John the Baptist were in circulation, and forty heads were revered as that of St Julian.

The mafia seems to have decided that there were profitable pickings to be made in this direction shortly after 1870, when, as a measure of reform, the Italian Government decided to close down a number of religious institutions and the relics they contained were dispersed. Most of these were bought up by the mafia. A number of extra copies of each were made up from materials furnished by an abandoned cemetery, and duplicates of the original seals of authenticity attached by the Congregation of Rites of the Vatican were assiduously faked. A vigorous overseas market for such spurious articles of devotion – particularly in the Americas – quickly developed. *Le Ore* discovered that in 1962 alone minor sales to the United States made by the organisation they had investigated included twenty suits of armour of Joan of Arc, twenty monastic gowns worn by St Francis of Assisi, fifty rosaries alleged to have belonged to Bernadette, and – as a triumphant culmination of mafia salesmanship – the wand carried by Moses when he led the Children of Israel into the Promised Land.

Where there was no saint, no holy relic, and consequently no flocking of pilgrims to be fleeced, the mafia did its best with artificial substitutes. A well-publicised 'miracle', such as the apparition of the Madonna to a child, filled the specially-chartered buses, the shops, and the hotels, and produced an upswing – however short-lived – in the sales-curve for religious merchandise. Thus it was with Padre Pio, the 'stigmatised' monk of San Giovanni Rotondo, whose cult was thought important enough to justify the transfer of a mafia commando to the Italian mainland itself.

The appearance of a monk whose followers claimed that his hands miraculously reproduced Christ's wounds from the Cross's nails was enough to provoke a delirium of commercial speculation. Within a few years the remote hamlet near Foggia had turned into a sort of embryo Lourdes, with half a dozen prosperous hotels, innumerable boarding-houses, and a hospital with a helicopter landing-stage on its roof, to which rich patients were brought to be exposed to the saintly influence. Books were sold by the hundred thousand, describing Padre Pio's miracles, and records by the million of the father saying mass or at prayer. The photographs of the monk displaying his wounds would not have convinced the hardened sceptic, as the negative had obviously been subjected to crude retouching and the prints daubed all over with a red dye, but they were happily bought by the pilgrims who poured into San Giovanni Rotondo. Such was the clamour to be confessed by Padre Pio (ninety-five percent of the applicants were women), that confessions had to be booked, and the waiting-list grew so long that pilgrims had to spend days and even weeks in the town's expensive hotels awaiting their turn. By arrangement with the mafia, however, and on payment of a substantial sum, the queue could be jumped. mafia agents waited, too, at the bus terminals, ready to carry off new arrivals to be confessed on the spot for sums varying between two and five thousand lire by false Padre Pios who awaited their prey in hastily faked-up backstreet rooms.

Most impudent of all was the sale of revolting relics of the monk's 'stigmata' – hundreds of yards of blood-soaked bandages displayed on market stalls outside the convent. Even when in 1960 the newspapers published analyses showing the blood to be that of chickens, the sales did not slacken.

It is this scene of the mafia presiding over charlatans selling cock's blood and amulets against the evil eye that reminds us how fully the wheel has turned. The mafia that had come into being as the peasants' refuge against the worst abuses of the Middle Ages now gleefully resuscitated all the bagful of medieval tricks to exploit the peasants' ignorance. The mafia that had fought feudalism, that had lain in wait on the moonless night for the baron no officer of the law could touch, now elected and manipulated politicians who would guarantee to fight for the survival of the feudal order. But far worse was to come under the absolute rule of Don Calogero Vizzini, General mafia of Villalba, still known as *Il Buonanima* – the Good Soul – to the many thousands who cherish his memory. It was Don Calò whose hired killers silenced the voices of protest when the postwar democracy turned out to be a crueller fake than Fascism itself. And when the voices crying in the wilderness of the Sicilian feudal estates swelled into a furious chorus, it was Don Calò and his feudal allies who called in Giuliano, the cleverest and bloodiest bandit in Sicilian history, to fight their battles for them.

The Sicilian writer whose work is most closely associated with an understanding of the mafia is Leonardo Sciascia. He came from Racamulto, a town in the south, where he was born in 1921, and where he is commemorated with a large bronze statue and a foundation in his name. His first novel, *The Day of the Owl (Il Giorno della Civetta)*, is an historical document, as well as an engrossing read, representing the first response in Sicilian art to the mafia as we now know it, with its endless, transverse tentacles, its deep and fearful roots in the population, and its long, clinging shoots, reaching up into the politics of Rome and beyond. Sciascia is published in English by Granta, and though one should be wary of seeing only the mafia when one visits Sicily, it is never far away, and Sciascia teaches his readers where and how to see it. There are many complete short-stories which would serve here to illustrate Sciascia's achievement, but the scene with which his novel begins, at dawn in a small mountain town, with a bus standing in a silent square, is essential reading.

Leonardo Sciascia
From *The Day of the Owl*

The bus was just about to leave, amid rumbles and sudden hiccups and rattles. The square was silent in the grey of dawn; wisps of cloud swirled round the belfry of the church. The only sound, apart from the rumbling of the bus, was a voice, wheedling, ironic, of a fritter-seller; fritters, hot fritters. The conductor slammed the door, and with a clank of scrap-metal the bus moved off. His last glance round the square caught sight of a man in a dark suit running towards the bus.

'Hold it a minute,' said the conductor to the driver, opening the door with the bus still in motion. Two earsplitting shots rang out. For a second the man in the dark suit, who was just about to jump on the running-board, hung suspended in mid-air as if some invisible hand were hauling him up by the hair. Then his brief-case dropped from his hand and very slowly he slumped down on top of it.

The conductor swore; his face was the colour of sulphur; he was shaking. The fritter-seller, who was only three yards from the fallen man, sidled off with a crablike motion towards the door of the church. In the bus no one moved; the driver sat, as if turned to stone, his right hand on the brake, his left on the steering-wheel. The conductor looked round the passengers' faces, which were blank as the blinds.

'They've killed him,' he said; he took off his cap, swore again, and began frantically running his fingers through his hair.

'The *carabinieri*,' said the driver, 'we must get the *carabinieri*.'

He got up and opened the other door. 'I'll go,' he said to the conductor.

The conductor looked at the dead man and then at the passengers. These included some women, old women who brought heavy sacks of white cloth and baskets full of eggs every morning; their clothes smelled of forage, manure and wood smoke; usually they grumbled and swore, now they sat mute, their faces as if disinterred from the silence of centuries.

'Who is it?' asked the conductor, pointing at the body.

No one answered. The conductor cursed. Among passengers of that route he was famous for his highly skilled blaspheming. The company had already threatened to fire him, since he never bothered to control himself even when there were nuns or priests on the bus. He was from the province of Syracuse and had had little to do with violent death: a soft province, Syracuse. So now he swore all the more furiously.

The *carabinieri* arrived; the sergeant-major, with a black stubble and in a black temper from being woken, stirred the passengers' apathy like an alarm-clock: in the wake of the conductor they began to get out through the door left open by the driver.

256

With seeming nonchalance, looking around as if they were trying to gauge the proper distance from which to admire the belfry, they drifted off towards the sides of the square and, after a last look around, scuttled into alley-ways.

The sergeant-major and his men did not notice this gradual exodus. Now about fifty people were around the dead man: men from a public works training centre who were only too delighted to have found such an absorbing topic of conversation to while away their eight hours of idleness. The sergeant-major ordered his men to clear the square and get the passengers back on to the bus. The *carabinieri* began pushing sightseers back towards the streets leading off the square, asking passengers to take their seats on the bus again. When the square was empty, so was the bus. Only the driver and the conductor remained.

'What?' said the sergeant-major to the driver. 'No passengers today?'

'Yes, some,' replied the driver with an absent-minded look.

'Some,' said the sergeant-major, 'means four, five or six... I've never seen this bus leave with an empty seat.'

'How should I know?' said the driver, exhausted from straining his memory. 'How should I know? I said 'some' just like that. More than five or six though. Maybe more; maybe the bus was full. I never look to see who's there. I just get into my seat and off we go. The road's the only thing I look at; that's what I'm paid for... to look at the road.'

The sergeant-major rubbed his chin with a hand taut with irritation. 'I get it,' he said, 'you just look at the road.' He rounded savagely on the conductor. 'But you, you tear off the tickets, take money, give change. You count the people and look at their faces... and if you don't want me to make you remember 'em in the guardroom, you're going to tell me now who was on that bus! At least ten names... You've been on this run for the last three years, and for the last three years I've seen you every evening in the Café Italia. You know this town better than I do...'

'Nobody could know the town better than you do,' said the conductor with a smile, as though shrugging off a compliment.

'All right, then,' said the sergeant-major, sneering, 'first me, then you... But I wasn't on the bus or I'd remember every passenger one by one. So it's up to you. Ten names at least.'

'I can't remember,' said the conductor, 'by my mother's soul I can't remember. Just now I can't remember a thing. It all seems a dream.'

'I'll wake you up,' raged the sergeant-major, 'I'll wake you up with a couple of years inside...' He broke off to go and meet the police magistrate who had just arrived. While making his report on the identity of the dead man and the flight of the passengers, the sergeant-major looked at the bus. As he looked, he had an impression that something was not quite right or was missing, as when something in our daily routine is unexpectedly missing, which the senses perceive from force of habit but the mind does not quite apprehend; even so its absence provokes an empty feeling of discomfort, a vague exasperation as from a flickering light-bulb. Then, suddenly, what we are looking for dawns on us.

'There's something missing,' said the sergeant-major to Carabiniere Sposito, who being a qualified accountant was a pillar of the Carabinieri Station of S, 'there's something or someone missing.'

'The fritter-seller,' said Carabiniere Sposito.

'The fritter-seller, by God!' The sergeant-major exulted, thinking: 'An accountant's diploma means something.'

A *carabiniere* was sent off at the double to pick up the fritter-seller. He knew where to find the man, who, after the departure of the first bus, usually went to sell his wares at the entrance of the elementary schools. Ten minutes later the sergeant-major had the vender of fritters in front of him. The man's expression was that of a man roused from innocent slumber.

'Was he there?' the sergeant-major asked the conductor.

'He was,' answered the conductor gazing at his shoe.

'Well now,' said the sergeant-major with paternal kindness, 'this morning, as usual, you came to sell your fritters here... As usual, at the first bus for Palermo...'

'I've my licence,' said the fritter-seller.

'I know,' said the sergeant-major, raising his eyes to heaven, imploring patience. 'I know and I'm not thinking about your licence. I want to know only one thing, and, if you tell me, you can go off at once and sell your fritters to the kids: who fired the shots?'

'Why,' asked the fritter-seller, astonished and inquisitive, 'has there been shooting?'

In Palermo today many of the bus shelters and advertisement hoardings carry large signs with black type on a light blue background *La Mafia Fa Schifo – Defendiamo Nostra Liberta* (*The Mafia Makes us Sick – Defend our Freedom*). On the cash points there are worn stickers protesting against the blanket extortion Cosa Nostra applies to the city's businesses, great and small – *Denounce the Pizzo!* On many streets the death's-head features of the photo-fit of 'boss of bosses' Bernardo Provenzano stare out from the walls, (the 'face' of the man on the run for forty-three years was so familiar to Sicilians that he needed no naming) beside a picture of a youth smoking a joint. The caption reads *Who finances him? You do! Taking drugs supports the Mafia.* When they caught him in 2006, hours after it became apparent that Berlusconi was going to lose the destabilised (by him) and partially fraudulent election by a few votes, *zu Bernu* – '*il trattore*', (uncle Bernie – 'the tractor') looked a little happier than his photo-fit, but otherwise remarkably like it. You would have thought that its assemblers must have known someone who had seen him quite recently. But then, since he was found in his own house just outside his own town of Corleone, you might have thought someone could have knocked him up anytime over the last forty years, had it not been against the interests of powerful people. If it was coincidence that the two men came down together, it was a very Sicilian synchronisation. The mafia, on this occasion, came out quietly; '*il trattore*' grinding his teeth. In Rome, more predictably, '*il Cavaliere*' dived for cover and his gun, shooting up the political landscape.

To someone who had not been to Sicily for a few years, the signs and stickers represent an amazing change of attitude: the unspoken is now spoken; what was once denied is now loudly condemned. The change began with the campaign of Falcone and Borsellino, and was accelerated by their deaths. The battle has come out of the shadows, though it is not necessarily being won. The streets of Palermo no longer echo with gunfire, as they did not so long ago, but every day the *Giornale di Sicilia* carries some new story of the mafia's doings. There are small-scale arrests of Pizzo collectors; a pronouncement by the Chief Prosecutor that the tentacles still reach far into politics; a small paragraph reporting that last night three grocer's shops caught fire in different corners of the city – someone late with their protection money. They call it the Pax Mafiosa, which goes to show what things were like in the '80s and '90s, the times of mafia war. In my time in the city there was excitement and worry at the murder of Maurizio Lo Iaconno – a drug smuggling and extortion specialist, thought to be allied to Provenzano, shot at least ten times on the school run in Partinico, where he was boss of the local *cosca*. It is thought that the killing was a message to Provenzano on behalf of hardliners, in prison and out, that his 'work' and policies were unsatisfactory. The harsh prison regime known as *41 Bis*, and the failure of mafia-friendly politicians to sufficiently undo Falcone's judicial advances is causing severe inconvenience to men accustomed to favourable string-pulling. They have lost patience with Provenzano's strategy of 'submersion', built on the principle of out-of-sight, out-of-mind, which does not involve killing the eminent or bombing the Italian mainland, the tactics of Toto Riina's rule.

You can see Riina's face on the streets too, a bull-necked, blank-eyed thing, on the covers of books sold at various stalls. He and Provenzano were friends, or at least allies, from Corleone, and they masterminded the Corleonesi take-over of *Cosa Nostra*, a blood-bath which unified the organisation and left them standing, kings of a hill of corpses. The mafia's bosses lead from the front – they have killed at least forty men each, personally, and been responsible for the deaths of many, many hundreds. Provenzano had the reputation of being an excellent shot; Riina an adept strangler. They were known as 'the beasts', and they put the fear of God into godless, fearless men – Riina particularly. The idea of a mass-killer like Riina being allied to, even cordially friendly with, the Italian prime minister is fantastical, ludicrous, but it seems that is exactly what happened. In his book *Midnight in Sicily* the Australian writer, Peter Robb, details the affair. A former nightclub bouncer, traveller and English teacher who stopped off in Naples on his way to south America and stayed for years, Robb made a temporary base in an outstanding Palermo restaurant, *Sant Andrea*, and set to work. An inscribed copy of *Midnight...* now stands proudly on a windowsill there.

Robb is a demon researcher, and the book is an elegant crash-course in an extraordinarily bloody period of Sicily's recent history. Though much of what it contains has been covered in Italian, and is familiar to natives, it provides an outsider with a gripping overview of the Corleonesi rise to power, and Cosa Nostra's alliance with, and subsequent war against Italy's ruling Christian Democrat party, and its repulsive, infamous, seven-times prime minister, Giulio Andreotti. In the following extract the DC are the Christian Democrats, Orlando is Leoluca Orlando, a famously brave anti-mafia mayor of Palermo, and Tommaso Buscetta is the one of the first and certainly the most significant of the mafia deserters, the *pentiti*, who revealed to Giovanni Falcone the structure of the organisation, and even the name it gave itself, *Cosa Nostra*, which had previously been thought an Americanism, used exclusively by the mob on the other side of the Atlantic. One of the key connections between the killers in Palermo and the powers in Rome was Salvo Lima, Palermo city councillor, DC politician, member of the European Parliament, and one of the men behind the Sack of Palermo in the '50s and '60s, a decade-long festival of uncontrolled and corrupt construction when the old centre was sacrificed in favour of a vast fungus of concrete which consumed the citrus groves of the Conca d'Oro and sent motorways snaking across the island.

Peter Robb
From *Midnight in Sicily*

All that afternoon I pondered The Kiss. I went back to the rabbit warren hotel and lay on my back in a darkened room, breathing in the smell of roasting coffee and raking over memories of body language in the Mezzogiorno. *It is not a crime to kiss the boss of Cosa Nostra*, Orlando had said that morning. *Very bad taste, yes, but not a crime. Ça manque de bon ton.* Orlando was merely correcting an emphasis. He knew very well it was no ordinary kiss. He knew as well as anyone how much more was involved. Like most of the rest of the story, the kiss was a men's affair. It was exchanged, if at all, in 1987. Eight years later it was occupying the finest and most highly paid legal minds in Italy. A moment of physical intimacy was witnessed, recalled, denied, hypothesized, contextualized, theorized, reconstructed and deconstructed. It had led the legal minds to call on others, anthropologists, psychologists, historians, students of the ways of power and affection. The aim was always the same, to establish in principle, after the manner of Italian intellectuals, that it could or could not ever have taken place. And thus that it did or did not take place in 1987. A lot of history hung on this kiss.

In 1987, in the heat of another Palermo September, the Sicilian DC had held that year's annual Friendship Festival. It was a sort of regional fair of the ruling party that ran for a week from the 19th to the 27th. It'd been well known for months before that the Hon. Andreotti would be coming to Palermo to take part and he was awaited with excitement. For nearly twenty years the alliance with Salvo Lima had made Palermo the heartland of Andreotti's power. On the second day of the festival, in fact, he was scheduled to speak twice. At ten-thirty in the morning he would be speaking on *Europe, Sicily and the Countries of the Mediterranean Basin*. After lunch, at three in the afternoon, he would speak on *Overcoming Ideological Thinking and the Risk of Mere Pragmatism in Political Alignments*. This second speaking engagement was later put off until six in the evening. The dog days of the Sicilian summer were barely over, and someone may have suggested to the organizers that the theme was a little heavy to handle straight after lunch.

Andreotti duly flew to Palermo on September 20th, and duly spoke at the party festival that morning. Then he went to the Villa Igiea, his usual hotel when he came to Palermo, a temple of *art nouveau* built on the water and that day crowded with demochristian politicians. At lunch time Andreotti dismissed his police security escort, and arranged to meet them later in the afternoon. He didn't in fact join his fellow politicians for lunch in the hotel restaurant, and his absence was noted. Nobody saw him again until he reappeared in the late afternoon and met up again with his escort. Andreotti had left the Villa Igiea at half past two in the afternoon. In another part of Palermo at exactly the same time, Salvatore Riina's driver Baldassare Di Maggio was collecting the head of Cosa Nostra as instructed from a prearranged address. Di Maggio arrived smartly dressed, as Riina had told him to. He drove Riina in a white VW Golf turbo to the gracious home of Ignazio Salvo in No 3, piazza Vittorio Veneto.

Ignazio Salvo and his cousin and business partner Nino Salvo, who'd died of a brain tumour in a Swiss clinic a year earlier, had been for decades two of the richest businessmen and most powerful demochristians in Sicily. Ignazio Salvo was at home that day in 1987 because he was under house arrest, awaiting sentence in the maxitrial. Di Maggio couldn't remember, when he spoke about it in 1993, the exact day in September 1987 he drove Riina to Salvo's house, but he remembered everything else. He described with precision the concealed side entrance to the basement garage of No 3, and the private lift that ran from the garage directly to the Salvo apartment. He identified the man of honour called Rabito, Salvo's personal driver and assistant, who'd met them at the garage gate and taken them up to the house. He described walking down a hall and being shown into a room on the right at the end of it. He and Riina had entered a sitting room suite with a parquet floor and a big carpet. On the left had been a large bookcase and a desk in dark wood. There'd been a sofa in front of the desk and another at right angles to it, and an armchair. On the other side he'd seen a table and chairs. The room had led out on to a large terrace and he'd seen a lot of plants growing there. The walls had been hung with paintings, he couldn't remember of what, or their styles, which given his background as a car mechanic and killer wasn't all that surprising, and the windows with long heavy curtains. Sitting on the sofa he'd seen Ignazio Salvo. He'd seen the Hon. Salvo Lima and the Hon. Giulio Andreotti, *whom I recognized without a shadow of doubt*. They'd all stood up when Riina entered.

> I shook hands with the parliamentarians and kissed Ignazio Salvo ... Riina,
> on the other hand, kissed all three persons, Andreotti, Lima and Salvo.

This was The Kiss. Di Maggio had then gone back down the passage to wait with Rabito in another room. After three hours, perhaps three and a half, Ignazio Salvo had called him back to the sitting room, where he'd shaken hands again with Andreotti and Lima and left with Riina. On the way back in the car, Riina had made no mention as they chatted of what had passed between himself and Andreotti, but Di Maggio had had his own strong reasons for believing they'd talked about the maxitrial. He couldn't really imagine the subject having been anything else, and he'd interpreted the kiss between Riina and Andreotti as *a sign of respect ... for as long as things went well*. Back at the Friendship Festival, the Hon. Andreotti arrived with his security escort barely in time to address the faithful at six on *the risk of mere pragmatism* in politics.

I tried to imagine the scene Di Maggio described to the magistrates. The luxurious drawing room on a hot Sicilian summer afternoon. The small, hunched and fragile figure of the minister for foreign affairs rising from the sofa as the stocky and uncouth mass murderer entered the room. What'd passed through that subtle mind as they'd embraced? Andreotti had never been known for physical effusiveness. He was already sixty-eight then, but he'd little changed over the years. The long lipless downward curving mouth, the *moneybox mouth* hardly seemed made for kissing. He'd said once that he never recalled his widowed mother kissing him as a child, and the ways of affection are learnt. There was no trace in Andreotti of affection or carnality, no intimation of closeness. A friend of mine as an exuberant young woman in the early '70s once had the job of tottering across an exhibition hall in swimming costume and high heels and proffering to prime minister Andreotti a satin cushion bearing the ceremonial scissors he'd use to cut a ribbon and open an international trade fair. She's never quite got over the lemonsucking narrow-eyed glare of disapproval the head of government shot her as he reached for the instrument. Andreotti's voice was dry and small. Utterance was concise, formal, throwaway, deprecatory, minimalist. It was deliberately flat, clerical, ordinary, except for the intermittent verbal echoes and elaborations of the little flashes of malice and cynicism that glinted behind the lenses. These had earned him a reputation for irony.

He was a politician grown in the shelter of the Vatican, a government minister since his twenties who'd never had to ingratiate himself with the people he served. He'd never had to press the public flesh with those *diaphanous* hands. By the '70s, after sealing his alliance with Salvo Lima, he'd eliminated all challengers to the power he held, even if the party game and the parliamentary ritual had required a certain rotation of posts. He'd perfected a system that revolved around himself. He'd provoked admiration rather than affection in his followers, but this was never a minus. The famously sentimental Italians had always nursed a deeper feeling for the sly and heartless, for the diabolically clever. His admirers, at the height of his power, called him *the god Giulio*. Others called him Beelzebub, which of course was a more colourful name for Satan. Former men of honour said they'd known him as *Uncle Giulio*.

The person you had to imagine Andreotti embracing was eleven years younger and also short, formerly known indeed to his colleagues as *Shorty*, though stocky and a lot more robust. *He'll be even shorter when we're through with him*, they'd said in Palermo once, but they'd been wrong and very soon they were dead. He was a country person, a peasant from Corleone without formal education, who spoke limited Italian and hardly wrote at all. He'd used figures scribbled in a little notebook to run a multinational business with an annual turnover of many billions of dollars. His wife had studied Machiavelli at school, which might've helped hone the family management skills. A jovial figure and an expert cook, Uncle Totò Riina was said to have shown the strength of a bull when he throttled his guests after banquets. In his ten-year rise to total power in Cosa Nostra, he'd killed or had killed eight hundred men of honour. In Cosa Nostra they'd stopped calling him *Shorty* and started calling him *The Beast*. He'd eliminated all challengers to the power he held and perfected a system that revolved around himself. What'd passed through that subtle mind as the two embraced?

On page 761 of *The True History of Italy* I found a section of seven pages on *the meanings of the rituality of the greeting between Riina and Andreotti*. It turned out to be a tiny sketch of Cosa Nostra and its relations with the Italian state. Unscrewing a plastic lampshade that fell into two pieces in my hand, in the full glare of the light shed by the fifteen watt bulb of the hotel reading lamp, I studied it. *The kiss*, Andreotti's defence had submitted, was *a hypothesis sailing through the rarefied atmosphere of the absurd.* And since the kiss had become the image of the case against Andreotti, symbolic and concrete, *The True History* had to demonstrate that the notion of the vastly powerful man with the fine political mind kissing the illiterate peasant killer, *Italy's most wanted criminal,* wasn't at all absurd. That it was, in the circumstances, inevitable. First you had to acknowledge Cosa Nostra's existence. The hardly trammeled growth of Cosa Nostra from the end of the war until the eighties had been enabled, the prosecutors said, by the state's refusal to believe that the mafia existed as an organization, a refusal reflected in the attitudes and practices of criminal investigators and trial judges in mafia cases.

That a coherent overall picture of Cosa Nostra had never been articulated was no accident. Interested parties in the media, the judiciary, the church and in parliament had always been ready to muddy the waters, to dismiss the mafia as a literary chimera or communist propaganda or an insult against Sicily. Police practice and judicial practice, the very articles of the law, reflected a belief that Cosa Nostra didn't exist. Nobody even knew its name until Tommaso Buscetta revealed it in 1984. And the police and magistrates who'd had open eyes and the wit to make sense of what they found had soon been identified as dangers and soon removed. Cesare Terranova, for instance, had known. When the Sicilian judge Leonardo Sciascia, called *an acute and implacable enemy of the mafia,* had returned from parliament in Rome in 1979 to head the investigative office in Palermo, he was murdered before he could start, shot in his car as he left home for work.

His tough and determined successor as chief prosecutor, Rocco Chinnici, had known too. He'd encouraged Falcone's early investigations of the heroin traffic between the Asian golden triangle and Sicily, when a ship was seized in the Suez canal carrying two hundred and thirty-three kilos of refined heroin to Sicily. Chinnici spoke out against the mafia in schools and piazzas at a time when nobody else mentioned the word, and was blown up by a car bomb with two of his escort and a bystander in 1983. A few months earlier Ciaccio Montalto, another judge who'd known, had been shot in Trapani. The season of *distinguished corpses* was beginning in those first years of the '80s.

These murders were partly a sign of the growing strength of Riina's brutal Corleonesi, though if Cosa Nostra had never killed magistrates before, it really hadn't needed to. Chinnici had left a private diary when he died, that named names, recording his private suspicions and fears and accusing many of his colleagues in the Palermo justice building of complicity with Cosa Nostra. When this became known its contents were assimilated with hints that Chinnici had become paranoid. After the murders of these vigorous and intelligent magistrates, it seemed the final defeat for anti-mafia activism when a frail elderly magistrate on the verge of retirement called Antonino Caponnetto came down from Tuscany to replace his two murdered predecessors in Palermo, remarking that *at sixty-three one should be used to living with the idea of death*. Yet Caponnetto formed the anti-mafia pool with Falcone and Borsellino and the others, and the maxitrial verdict was the pool's work, the final recognition in law that Cosa Nostra was a single body. All those magistrates had been murdered to prevent that.

The prosecutors of Andreotti underlined Cosa Nostra's permanent aim of eliminating the *historic memory* built up by those few who'd understood that Cosa Nostra was *a state within the state*. Cosa Nostra, *The True History* reminded you, was a state organized territorially, divided into clans, governed by a central commission known as the Cupola at the apex of its pyramid and served by thousands of members at its base, who were controlled through rules and sanctions. It wasn't *an indistinct galaxy of criminal gangs, often at war among themselves and without a unified organization and leadership*. Cosa Nostra was a state that maintained relations with professional, political and judicial representatives of that other state, the Italian republic.

> This state within the state murdered the president of the regional government, the leader of the main opposition party, the provincial secretary of the main governing party, the prefect of Palermo, two chief state prosecutors, an advisory judge, two heads of the investigative police, two commanders of the *carabinieri*, the director general of the ministry of justice, a deputy prosecutor. It has also killed dozens of other citizens loyal to the state's institutions, doctors, businessmen, magistrates, law enforcement officers and hundreds of ordinary people.

The anti-state of Cosa Nostra had featured

> ... in the darkest pages of the history of the republic from the end of the war to the present: the massacre of Portella della Ginestra, the BORGHESE coup d'etat attempt, the MORO kidnapping, the P2 affair, the CALVI case, the SINDONA case, etc.

When Totò Riina had entered the Salvo drawing room that summer afternoon, he'd entered as a head of that other state, and it was as such that the past and future leader of the Italian government had greeted him. It was a summit. They were Kennedy and Krushchev, Nixon and Mao, and thus the two leaders greeted each other.

At the time of The Kiss, the maxitrial had been going for a year and a half, and it had only three months more to run. As the trial moved inexorably to its conclusion, the leaders of Cosa Nostra were becoming more and more perturbed. Two legal attempts to derail proceedings had failed. They'd challenged the presiding judge in April 1986, accusing him of partiality and misconduct two months into the trial. This had failed in the appeal court. Six months later defence lawyers had tried a kind of filibuster, requesting that all the documents on the case be read out in full in court. Since the prosecution's case alone ran to nearly nine thousand pages, this would have prolonged the trial beyond the legal limit for preventive custody, and freed the hundreds of the accused *mafiosi* before the verdict was reached. In early 1987 the Italian parliament quickly passed a new law to prevent this happening. The DC, to the great anger of Cosa Nostra, had done nothing to stop this law being passed. At one point Cosa Nostra had decided to express their dissatisfaction with the feeble performance of their defence lawyers by waxing a few of them, *pour encourager les autres*, but the project stalled over which barristers to eliminate. Cosa Nostra was unhappiest of all with the demochristians who seemed to be doing nothing to impede or compromise the maxitrial. They hadn't been given votes to do nothing. It was this that Giulio Andreotti had to answer for to Totò Riina that afternoon of The Kiss. Cosa Nostra wanted reassuring.

To teach the DC a lesson, Cosa Nostra had ordered a switch in votes in the 1987 elections, away from the DC. All the candidates supported by Cosa Nostra had been elected, and while the DC vote had increased in the rest of Italy, it'd fallen sharply in Palermo, in some central Palermo electorates dropping by more than half. It'd been a nasty little taste of a possible future for Andreotti, whose electoral strength in Sicily, assembled and mediated by Salvo Lima, was the source of his power. Lima himself, the man of honour who'd gone on from being mayor of Palermo to be Andreotti's under-secretary of the budget in Rome, was in a delicate position by 1987, now that the Corleonesi had taken over Cosa Nostra. Lima had always dealt with the old guard, civilized *mafiosi* who'd understood the ways of mediation. He wasn't known or trusted by the new bosses. The new Cosa Nostra did business differently and their dissatisfaction over the maxitrial had left Lima dangerously exposed. They'd been less flexible, less gracious than the *mafiosi* they'd eliminated. *Stick to the agreement or we'll kill you and your family*, the new Cosa Nostra had told him. This was an overriding reason for Andreotti to respond to Riina's request for a summit.

Italy's most wanted criminal came without the slightest fear of arrest or entrapment. When he kissed Andreotti, a kiss the prosecutors described Andreotti as having *undergone*, Riina was taking the initiative and sending a complex message. It was a reassurance offered on Cosa Nostra's own territory in a moment of crisis, prelude to a new understanding between the states. It must have been a relief. When he'd come down secretly to Palermo seven years earlier, to get an explanation for Cosa Nostra's murder in 1980 of Piersanti Mattarella, president of the Sicilian regional government, Andreotti had been shouted at by the Palermo boss Stefano Bontate.

In Sicily we give the orders. And if you don't want to wipe out the DC completely you do what we say. Otherwise we'll take away your vote. Not only in Sicily but also in Reggio Calabria and all through southern Italy. You'll only be able to count on the vote up north, and up there they all vote communist anyway. You can make do with that.

Riina was now more quietly reminding Andreotti of his commitments. Politically, Andreotti had less room for manoeuvre than before. Vito Ciancimino, the former mayor of Palermo, and the Salvo cousins, his link with Cosa Nostra, had all been charged as *mafiosi*. A dossier on Salvo Lima had been tabled in the European parliament in Strasbourg. The maxitrial was being followed closely.

Riina suspected that Andreotti now wanted to slither out of his undertakings to the mafia without losing the electoral power base Cosa Nostra guaranteed. It was another instance of the Andreotti *double game*. So Riina had to remind him. He had to remind Andreotti that he couldn't *distance himself*, that Riina and Andreotti, like Lima and Salvo and the others in the room, were *the same thing*. Cosa Nostra is *our thing* and a man of honour identifies another as *la stessa cosa*, the same thing, and the four powerful figures present that afternoon were all the same thing and were in it all together. It made little difference, *The True History* said, whether or not Andreotti had been formally sworn in. Whether Andreotti's finger had been pricked by a senior man of honour in the presence of other men of honour, whether he had dropped blood on to a sacred image and held it burning in his hands as he prayed *that my flesh may burn like this holy image if ever I betray my vow*. This, said the Palermo prosecutors, didn't matter.

> The one thing that mattered, and what [Riina] wanted to remind [Andreotti] once again, is that whoever had made a pact of mutual loyalty and assistance with Cosa Nostra had got to understand that there could be no grounds for withdrawing from that pact for the rest of his life. And to keep that clearly in mind.

At such a meeting, the kiss wasn't *absurd* at all. The kiss and the embrace were inescapable.

Baldassare Di Maggio, the witness of The Kiss in 1987 and the man of honour who'd led the police to Riina in 1993, had started adult life as a mechanic. He was the son of a *mafioso* shepherd in the old mafia town of San Giuseppe Jato, thirty kilometres inland from Palermo, and three years older than Givoanni Brusca, son of the district boss. He'd been approached in his twenties and done his first killing in 1981 with the Brusca son. He'd had no idea who he was killing or why and knew not to ask. Then he was taken to a country property nearby and met Totò Riina and his wife and four children. The house had been made available to the Riinas by a Palermo doctor. After takeaway roast chicken, the boys told Riina they'd been impressed by Di Maggio's grace under pressure. He'd returned the fire of a *carabiniere*. Four months later Di Maggio was initiated by Brusca senior. Over the next five years, Di Maggio had killed, for Riina and Brusca, twenty-three people in a variety of ways. He'd torched a number of houses, including an ex-mayor of Palermo's, and dealt in drugs and public works. He'd become a particular favourite of Riina's, who often said *Baldo's in my heart* and made Di Maggio his driver. Thus, when Brusca senior was in jail and Brusca junior exiled to a remote island, Di Maggio was made boss of their *cosca*, their mafia family. He'd built a million-dollar villa, with swimming pools and pillars and *original art work* on the walls.

It turned bad when he lost interest in his wife and fell for a girl that Brusca junior also wanted. It turned nasty when Brusca came home and wanted to take command as well. In early 1992 a conference was called with Totò Riina, to make the peace. At the end of the discussion Riina confirmed his trust in Di Maggio, and kissed him. *Baldo's not some old orange to chuck away*. Di Maggio, however, knew his boss's ways. He'd seen too many scenes like that not to realize Riina's was a Judas kiss. He realized he was about to be killed. Uncle Totò had *Baldo in his heart* and was going to kill him. He was choosing the Bruscas. It was like that with Riina. Di Maggio fled with his heavily pregnant girlfriend to Canada. Unable to get a visa, they returned to Italy, going north to Novara where Di Maggio had a friend. The police knew this, knew about the quarrel, and arrested him in the first days of 1993, just after the birth of Di Maggio's child. The violence of Riina's Cosa Nostra in 1992 had plunged a lot of men of honour into crisis. *Profoundly shaken by the terrible atrocities committed against judges Falcone and Borsellino*, the leading man of honour and Riina intimate Gaspare Mutolo had decided to talk three months earlier. *Cosa Nostra has undertaken an irreversible strategy of death*, he said. It was the thought of being sent to Palermo, of being surrounded by men at Riina's orders in the Ucciardone that now turned Di Maggio. *I'm a dead man*, he said. *But I'm a man of honour. I can take you to Riina*. And he did. And when Riina was taken, Di Maggio, Mutolo, Buscetta, Mannoia, all the *pentiti* who knew the most overcame their last inhibitions. Unknown to each other, in their secret safe houses in Italy and America, in 1993 the men of honour all started talking for the first time about Giulio Andreotti.

Corleone is a grey-roofed little mountain town, tightly clustered around up-thrusts of rock in the middle of western Sicily. Thanks to Mario Puzo's *Godfather* series the name is world-famous, though the worst doings of some of its citizens post-date the books. Many tourists make a sort of anti-pilgrimage to the town now, not knowing quite what they are looking for, but guaranteed some shade of the eerie, sickly feeling that comes from an encounter, however mediated, with horror. It is such a small and innocuous place. It seems hard to believe anything has ever happened here, until you catch a certain light in someone's eye: in my case she was an elderly woman, who was exchanging a few words with a neighbour across a narrow street. She had white hair, a straight nose, and clever blue eyes. I looked directly at her and said good afternoon. She looked at me with a thin blankness, beneath which was complete contempt. I held her gaze, and she forced a response out of herself, through a constricted throat. We both knew why I was there. And we both knew that however many books I might have read, however many facts assembled, however accurate my knowledge of the numbers of Corleone's dead and disappeared might be, I knew nothing – nothing. 'I was a *mafioso*,' one of them once said, 'the others were merely men.' How much less than a man, how much less than the merest Sicilian, is a tourist in Corleone, I felt, as she looked through me.

There is as yet no conclusion to the story of the curse. Whether the organisation that emerges is led by Salvatore 'The White Fox' Lo Piccolo: a Palermitan in the old-style tradition of Provenzano, or by Matteo Messina 'Diabolik' Denaro: a monster in the Riina mould, the beast lives yet. Only the future will reveal whether it is true that merely cutting off its head does not kill it. The outcome will be a measure of how far we – Italy and Europe – have really come in two hundred years.

At the end of his life Leonardo Sciascia believed the worst: 'When I speak out against the mafia it also makes me suffer because within me, as within every Sicilian, the residue of *mafioso* feeling is still alive. So when I struggle against the mafia I'm also struggling against myself; it is like a split, a laceration.' For what it is worth, I believe, having met and been embraced by many Sicilians, and having come to know some well, that Sciascia, unless he equated 'mafia' simply with human evil, was quite wrong about this, as he was, towards the end, quite wrong about other important things. In 1987, half way through the maxi trial, he accused the crusading judges of ignoring civil liberties in the same way the Fascists had done, and noted: 'There is nothing better for getting ahead in the magistracy than taking part in mafia trials.' It was unworthy of an intelligent man, and a bitter blow to those like Paolo Borsellino, who saw Sciascia as an intellectual figure-head, and who knew there was no surer way of getting killed than to pursue the mafia through the courts. It is the very nub of the issue, though. To know where evil lies, and to witness how it emerges and works, is the lot of many men and women, and many Sicilians. It is not the same thing as being responsible for it, or complicit with it.

269

V: The Life

THERE WERE SIX of us for dinner. Francesca, the hostess, who had made the feast; Paolo, her husband, my friend; the Priest, an old school friend of Paolo's, the Lawyer, and his wife, Angela. We ate like Gods. Francesca laughed a lot and kept pressing more on us, on me particularly, because I was the youngest, and the stranger. 'Courage!' she said, as we reached the chops, two main courses in, and she served me the largest. Angela talked about things she had read in the *Giornale di Sicilia*, the men ate steadily, and at last we reached the pudding, then the fruit, then the coffee, and then the politics. I was talking to the lawyer, who looked at me benevolently, the way one looks at a child. I asked him, in view of Italy's declining economy, and Berlusconi's endlessly broken promises (he specialised in extravagant verbal give-aways, followed some time afterwards, when pressed, with his catchphrase, 'You have misunderstood me!') – was it not best simply to hold one's nose and vote for the left, and Prodi? (Many Italians, on all sides of the spectrum, think him odious.)

The lawyer launched into a long speech. It was eloquent, elegant, subtle, and argued for absolutely nothing. No change, no hope, no point, he said, even thinking about it. They are all as bad as each other, Prodi and the left especially. The priest peeled his fruit, nodding, with an amusedly raised eyebrow, as if to suggest that all this worldly stuff was as consequential as a dog race, though if you made him back one, he was certainly with Berlusconi. Paolo concentrated on his figs, occasionally raising one hooded eye. When the lawyer had quite finished, and you might have thought the last word had been said, Paolo, who had now concluded his dealings with the feast, spoke. In his quiet certainty, his sadness, his anger and barely controlled passion, he was extraordinary. Suddenly the terribly urgent necessity, and simultaneously the apparent impossibility, of meaningful change for the better, of the hopeless

270

prospect yet desperate need for advance beyond decades of stasis, empty rhetoric, and foul and careless corruption – all was suddenly on the table, among the nutshells, cores and fruit-peel. Neither the lawyer nor the priest raised even a syllable of contradiction.

Plain and passionate speaking in front of a stranger was not a common thing in the Sicily of my experience. Things were complicated enough for natives: how could an alien like me be expected to understand them? Besides, allusion, dialect and coded references are fundamental to communication here: there are barriers in the unspoken language as much as in what is said. Ironically, one of the simplest ways into contemporary Sicily is through a man, a fictional character from a fictional south Sicilian town, who loves his food, and will not speak until he has finished eating, who does not believe anyone, even his most trusted lieutenant, especially not his superiors, really understands the subtleties of Sicilian matters as well as he does, and tends, therefore, to keep them in the dark.

Inspector Salvo Montalbano of the Vigata Police department is one of the world's most famous imaginary Sicilians: if he has not yet reached the magnitude of the audience familiar with Lampedusa's Prince or Puzo's Corleone family, he is not far behind. His creator, Andrea Camilleri, a former teacher from Porto Empedocle, near Agrigento, has not been seen in his home town for some years. Camilleri now lives in Rome, but he must spend much of his inner life on the island. The Montalbano books pullulate with Sicilian dialect, history, manners and mindset. They are ingenious, very funny, and rarely fail to have a dig at the 'some people' who do not consider crime writing to be literature. It is true that the food is portrayed with more depth and attention than the female characters, but then the Inspector has to eat at least three times a day and rarely meets his girlfriend, who lives in Rome, more than once per book. The novels follow an Ian Fleming-type pattern, which ensures that should you enjoy one you will be afforded at least as much pleasure by the next. They tend to begin with Montalbano waking up on an unpleasant day in a terrible mood. At some point in what follows there will be a beautiful woman, a ghastly crime, at least one car-crash, various failed attempts to either discipline or promote the inspector, an inconclusive encounter with the mafia, and a lot of eating. There will also be some sort of spiritual crisis. The following taste comes from *The Snack Thief (Il Ladro di Merendine)*. It begins with Montalbano, absent without leave, phoning his office, Vigata Police Station, where the calls are taken by Sergeant Catarella, butt of a thousand jokes, who speaks an all-but incomprehensible (and untranslatable) Sicilian.

Andrea Camilleri
From *The Snack Thief*

'It's Montalbano, Cat.'

'Izzat really 'n' truly you in person, sir?'

'It's really and truly me in person. Let me speak with Inspector Augello.'

'Hello, Salvo. Where are you?'

'At home. Listen, Mimì, I don't think I can come in to work.'

'Are you sick?'

'No. I just don't feel up to it, not today nor tomorrow. I need to rest for four or five days. Can you cover for me?'

'Of course.'

'Thanks.'

'Wait. Don't hang up.'

'What is it?'

'I'm a little concerned, Salvo. You've been acting weird for the last couple of days. What's the matter with you? Don't make me start worrying about you.'

'Mimì, I just need a little rest, that's all.'

'Where will you go?'

'I don't know yet. I'll phone you later.'

Actually, he knew exactly where he would go. He packed his bag in five minutes, then took a little longer to select which books to take along. He left a note in block letters for Adelina, the housekeeper, informing her he'd be back within a week. When he arrived at the trattoria in Mazàra, they greeted him like the prodigal son.

'The other day, I believe I understood that you rent rooms.'

'Yes, we've got five upstairs. But it's the off-season now, so only one of 'em's rented.'

They showed him a room, spacious and bright and looking straight onto the sea.

He lay down on the bed, brain emptied of thoughts, chest swelling with a kind of happy melancholy. He was loosing the moorings, ready to sail out to the country of sleep, when he heard a knock on the door.

'Come in, it's unlocked.'

The cook appeared in the doorway. He was a big man of considerable heft, about forty, with dark eyes and skin.

'What are you doing? Aren't you coming down? I heard you were here and so I made something for you that …'

What the cook had made, Montalbano couldn't hear, because a sweet, soft melody, a heavenly tune, had started playing in his ears.

For the last hour he'd been watching a rowing boat slowly approaching the shore. On it was a man rowing in sharply rhythmic, vigorous strokes. The boat had also been sighted by the owner of the trattoria; Montalbano heard him cry out, 'Luicì! The cavaliere's coming back!'

The inspector then saw Luicino, the restaurateur's sixteen-year-old son, enter the water to push the boat up onto the sand so the passenger wouldn't get his feet wet. The cavaliere, whose name Montalbano did not know, was smartly dressed, tie and all. On his head he wore a white Panama hat, with the requisite black band.

'Cavaliere, did you catch anything?' the restaurateur asked him.

'A pain in the arse, that's what I caught.'

He was a thin, nervy man, about seventy years old. Later, Montalbano heard him bustling about in the room next to his.

'I set a table over here,' said the cook as soon as Montalbano appeared for dinner, and he led him into a tiny room with space for only two tables. The inspector felt grateful for this, since the big dining room was booming with the voices and laughter of a large gathering.

'I've set it for two,' the cook continued. 'Do you have any objection if Cavaliere Pintacuda eats with you?'

He certainly did have an objection: he feared he would have to talk while eating.

A few minutes later, the gaunt septuagenarian introduced himself with a bow.

'Liborio Pintacuda, and I'm not a cavaliere,' he said, sitting down. 'There's something I must tell you, even at the risk of appearing rude,' the non-cavaliere continued. 'I, when I'm talking, do not eat. Conversely, when I'm eating, I don't talk.'

'Welcome to the club,' said Montalbano, sighing with relief.

The pasta with crab was as graceful as a first-rate ballerina, but the stuffed bass in saffron sauce left him breathless, almost frightened.

'Do you think this kind of miracle could ever happen again?' he asked Pintacuda, gesturing towards his now empty plate. They had both finished and therefore recovered the power of speech.

'It'll happen again, don't worry, just like the miracle of the blood of San Gennaro,' said Pintacuda. 'I've been coming here for years, and never, I repeat, never, has Tanino's cooking let me down.'

'At a top-notch restaurant, a chef like Tanino would be worth his weight in gold,' the inspector commented.

'Yes he would. Last year, a Frenchman passed this way, the owner of a famous Parisian restaurant. He practically got down on his knees and begged Tanino to come to Paris with him. But there was no persuading him. Tanino says this is where he's from, and this is where he'll die.'

'Someone must surely have taught him to cook like that. He can't have been born with that gift.'

'You know, up until ten years ago, Tanino was a small-time crook. Petty theft, drug dealing. Always in and out of jail. Then, one night, the Blessed Virgin appeared to him.'

'Are you joking?'

'I try hard not to. As he tells it, the Virgin took his hands in hers, looked him in the eye, and declared that from the next day forward, he would become a great chef.'

'Come on!'

'You, for example, knew nothing of this story of the Virgin, and yet after eating the bass, you specifically used the word 'miracle'. But I can see you don't believe in the supernatural, so I'll change subject. What brings you to these parts, Inspector?'

Montalbano gave a start. He hadn't told anyone there what he did for a living.

'I saw your press conference on television, after you arrested that woman for killing her husband,' Pintacuda explained.

'Please don't tell anybody who I am.'

'But they all know who you are, Inspector. Since they've gathered that you don't like to be recognized, however, they play dumb.'

'And what do you do of interest?'

'I used to be a professor of philosophy. If you can call teaching philosophy interesting.'

'Isn't it?'

'Not at all. The students get bored. They no longer care enough to learn how Hegel or Kant thought about things. Philosophy should probably be replaced with some subject like, I don't know, 'Basic Management'. Then it still might mean something.'

'Basic management of what?'

'Life, my friend. Do you know what Benedetto Croce writes in his *Memoirs*? He says that he learned from experience to consider life a serious matter, as a problem to be solved. Seems obvious, doesn't it? But it's not. One would have to explain to young people, philosophically, what it means, for example, to smash their car into another car one Saturday night. And to tell them how, philosophically, this could be avoided. But we'll have time to discuss all this. I'm told you'll be staying here a few days.'

'Yes. Do you live alone?'

'For the fifteen days I spend here, very much alone. The rest of the time I live in a big old house in Trapani with my wife and four daughters, all married, and eight grandchildren, who, when they're not at school, are with me all day. At least once every three months I escape and come here, leaving no phone number or forwarding address. I cleanse myself, take the waters of solitude. For me this place is like a clinic where I detoxify myself of an excess of sentiment. Do you play chess?'

On the afternoon of the following day, as he was lying in bed reading Sciascia's *Council of Egypt* for the twentieth time, it occurred to him that he'd forgotten to tell Valente about the odd agreement he'd made with the colonel. The matter might prove dangerous for his colleague in Mazàra if he were to continue investigating. He went downstairs where there was a telephone.

'Valente? Montalbano here.'

'Salvo, where the hell are you? I asked for you at the office and they said they had no news of you.'

'Why were you looking for me? Has something come up?'

'Yes. The commissioner called me out of the blue this morning to tell me my request for a transfer had been accepted. They're sending me to Sestri.'

Valente's wife, Giulia, was from Sestri, and her parents also lived there. Until now, every time the vice-commissioner had asked to be transferred to Liguria, his request had been denied.

'Didn't I say that something good would come out of this affair?' Montalbano reminded him.

'Do you think – ?'

'Of course. They're getting you out of their hair, in such a way that you won't object. And they're right. When does the transfer take effect?'

'Immediately.'

'See? I'll come and say goodbye before you leave.'

Lohengrin Pera and his little gang of playmates had moved very fast. It remained to be seen whether this was a good or a bad sign. He needed to do a foolproof test. If they were in such a hurry to put the matter to rest, then surely they had wasted no time in sending him a message as well. The Italian bureaucracy, usually slow as a snail, becomes lightning-quick when it comes to screwing the citizen. With this well-known truth in mind, he called his commissioner.

'Montalbano! For God's sake, where have you run off to?'

'Sorry for not letting you know. I've taken a few days off to rest.'

'I understand. You went to see – '

'No. Were you looking for me? Do you need me?'

'Yes, I was looking for you, but I don't need you for anything. Just rest. Do you remember I was supposed to recommend you for a promotion?'

'How could I forget?'

'Well, this morning Commendator Ragusa called me from the Ministry of Justice. He's a good friend of mine. He told me that, apparently … some obstacles have come up – of what kind, I have no idea. In short, your promotion has been blocked. Ragusa wouldn't, or couldn't, tell me any more than that. He also made it clear that it was useless, and perhaps even unwise, to insist. Believe me, I'm shocked and offended.'

'Not me.'

'Don't I know it! In fact, you're happy, aren't you?'

'Doubly happy, Commissioner.'

'Doubly?'

'I'll explain when I see you in person.'

He set his mind at rest. They were moving in the right direction.

The following morning, Liborio Pintacuda, a steaming cup of coffee in hand, woke the inspector up when it was still dark outside.

'I'll wait for you in the boat.'

He'd invited him to a useless half day of fishing, and the inspector had accepted. Montalbano put on a pair of jeans and a long-sleeved shirt. Sitting in a boat with a gentleman dressed to the nines, he would have felt silly in a bathing suit.

Fishing, for the professor, proved to be exactly like eating. He never opened his mouth, except, every now and then, to curse the fish for not biting.

Around nine in the morning, with the sun already high in the sky, Montalbano couldn't hold back any longer.

'I'm losing my father,' he said.

'My condolences,' the professor said without looking up from his fishing line.

The words seemed flat and inappropriate to the inspector.

'He hasn't died yet. He's dying,' he clarified.

'It makes no difference. For you, your father died the very moment you learned he was going to die. Everything else is, so to speak, a bodily formality. Nothing more. Does he live with you?'

'No, he's in another town.'

'By himself?'

'Yes. And I can't summon the courage to go and see him in this state, before he goes. I just can't. The very idea scares me. I'll never have the strength to set foot in the hospital where he's staying.'

276

The old man said nothing, limiting himself to replacing the bait the fish had eaten with many thanks. Then he decided to talk.

'You know, I happen to have followed an investigation of yours, the one about the 'terracotta dog'. In that instance, you abandoned an investigation into some weapons trafficking to throw yourself heart and soul into tracking a crime from fifty years ago, even though solving it wasn't going to yield any practical results. Do you know why you did it?'

'Out of curiosity?' Montalbano guessed.

'No, my friend. It was a very shrewd, intelligent way for you to keep practising your unpleasant profession, but by escaping from everyday reality. Apparently this everyday reality sometimes becomes too much for you to bear. And so you escape. As I do when I take refuge here. But the moment I go back home, I immediately lose half of the benefit. The fact of your father's dying is real, but you refuse to confirm it by seeing it in person. You're like the child who thinks he can blot out the world by closing his eyes.'

Professor Liborio Pintacuda, at this point, looked the inspector straight in the eye.

'When will you decide to grow up?'

Montalbano's Sicily is a recognisable version of the place it seems now: if not exactly in step with today's Europe, then at least within easy reach of it. Many of Camillieri's protagonists and perpetrators leave, come back, go and come again. None of them can quite escape it. There are old stories of returning emigrants dropping dead with heart attacks, overcome with emotion on the decks of ships, at last within sight of their homeland. More recent returnees have found a happier isle than that which they or their forefathers abandoned. Two American women of Sicilian descent, Mary Taylor Simeti and Theresa Maggio, came back to discover their roots. Both formed relationships with Sicilian men – Simeti married and stayed – and both women penetrated far below the surfaces tourists touch, and wrote books about what they found here. Simeti writes from the perspective of one struck with amazement, horror and wonder, struggling to adjust to a new life on the island – like Montalbano she encounters it all at once – while Maggio crosses and recrosses it, renting temporary homes here and there, and recording her finds thematically, like a student of a new world. Mary Taylor Simeti and her husband Tonino, like many of the more fortunate Palermitans, have a house in the country, in Bosco, in their case.

Mary Taylor Simeti
From *On Persephone's Island: A Sicilian Journey*

Chapter Five

There are no lions or lambs in Sicilian iconography: March is quite simply considered mad. Dark clouds scud back and forth across the sky, caught in a cosmic tennis match played out between the *sirocco*, the hot wind blowing up from the Sahara, and the *tramontana*, whose gusts have been chilled by Alpine glaciers. The temperature changes abruptly at every swing, and the pace is furious, allowing the clouds no pause to unload their precious burden of water. Despite the many grey days this winter, little rain has actually fallen into the reservoirs, already depleted by two years of drought, and the prospects for the summer are very grim. Water in Palermo has been rationed for more than a year now, in theory at least, but the supply system is such a tangled maze of modern tie-ins to Bourbon conduits that the aqueduct office is hard put to know how the water gets from one point to another, much less to insure an equitable distribution. At least a third of the input leaks out through the rotting pipes before it reaches its destination.

The situation is much worse in the towns in the interior, where water often arrives only every five or ten days. Here too it is man who is at fault, not nature, for Sicily is rich in water that flows to the sea unexploited. The government's neglect is part ingrained, part instigated: the mafia controls the major wells and springs that tap the subterranean water layers, and it sells its water at high prices. One must admire, however, the mafia's adaptability; when a popular movement led by Danilo Dolci forced the government to approve the construction of a huge dam on the Belice River, local *mafiosi* bought, for next to nothing, some of the wheat fields that were to be flooded and applied for government subsidies to transform them into first-class vineyards (the government foots sixty percent of the bill for this kind of land improvement). When the land was expropriated for the dam, the government reimbursed these new owners at vineyard prices, which were much much higher than what it would have paid for the original wheat fields.

On the few days that rain does fall, the clouds, exhausted by so much activity, drop everything at once. The water descends in a solid wall, choking Palermo's inadequate sewers and bringing traffic to a standstill. The countryside is overcome, unable to drink in such an exuberant serving, the water drains off to the sea, carving deep furrows in the plowed fields and carrying away the seeds and seedlings of the farmers who had hoped to get an early start on their *novara*.

Beneath the grey skies the fava beans are in bloom. These flowers alarmed the Greeks, who read in the black markings on the petals a *theta*, the first letter of *thanatòs*, of death. In fact, the Greeks used fava beans for funerary rites rather than as food; the Pythagoreans even considered eating a fava bean to be cannibalism, since the stalk, one of the few in nature to be absolutely hollow, was the passageway for the exchange of souls between the living and the dead. Fortunately for us, the Romans recuperated the fava bean to the table of the living: picked while they are still small, very green and tender, and cooked with bacon, or in *fritedda*, sautéed in olive oil and a little broth together with new peas and finely sliced artichokes, fava beans deserve their place in spring's cornucopia.

Another Lenten flower stands sentinel along the roadsides: the asphodel, grey-green stalks supporting a spear of pallid flowers, white barely tinged with pink, pale flesh, the flowers that covered the meadows of Hades. I remember – and am touched by how telling a memory it is – that my mother was bitterly disappointed by her first sight of the asphodel, for the poets had led her to expect something far more magnificent.

Except in Arcadia, where acorns were plentiful, the roots and seeds of the asphodel were probably the basis of the Greek diet before the introduction of grain, and Pythagoras thought this, the spontaneous production of nature, to be the perfect food. Chased to the Netherworld by the introduction of agriculture, the asphodel has now returned, together with the poppy, to invade the fields abandoned in the exodus from the countryside, a white flag marking capitulation to poor soil and inadequate cultivation.

But Lent is also a time of preparation, to which nature contributes by adding new colours to her palette. The hedgerows, still yellow and orange from February's flowering, are now awash with the watery blue of the borage flowers and streaked bright pink by the campion. In the garden the daffodils herald the change in season, the big gold trumpets that multiply each year towering over the miniatures I put in last December, while round them the grape hyacinths run a ribbon of purple-blue. Each day brings some new flower, some new sign that spring is coming, though not in the sense of a New England spring, as tenuous promise, veiled allusions of green over grey, pastel colours and faint perfumes. The Sicilian spring is building up to a vivid and violent explosion of bloom and heat and colour and smell, of pagan rite and Christian procession, in which nature, agriculture, and cultural tradition meet in perfect synchronization.

In the city March begins with another sort of explosion, literal and tragic. On the afternoon of the first, a bomb goes off in the courtyard of the new police commissariat in Brancaccio, the 'South Bronx' neighbourhood where the Favara Palace lies. Nine people are injured; one of them, a young policeman, is on the critical list.

This storm has been brewing for some time, ever since the Minister of the Interior and the prefect of Palermo announced their intention to introduce a commissariat into this neighbourhood as a response to the mafia violence that has been steadily increasing there over the past two years. The only available site was a pair of adjoining apartments, the property of the municipal government, in a new building in the heart of Brancaccio, just down the road from the Favara. The building's residents rebelled, protesting that the commissariat would constitute a danger for them and their families and that the coming and going of patrol cars would prevent the children of the building from using the courtyard as a playground. But after several meetings with police representatives they seemed to have accepted the government's decision.

And then this afternoon a car drove into the courtyard, and a young man leapt out and threw a bomb under the patrol car parked there. Attracted by the cries of a man who was sitting at a window, one of the policemen doing guard duty at the still-unopened office ran out to see what was happening. As he neared the car the bomb went off, tearing the patrol car in two and smashing the car next to it against the wall. The policeman lost both legs, and flying glass slightly injured other people. Fortunately the weather was not good; otherwise the courtyard would have been filled with children.

After a moment of shocked silence a crowd formed rapidly in the courtyard, on one side the building's residents, some wounded, some in shock, all terrified and angry; on the other, the police, distressed by the fate of their colleague, dismayed and embittered to find themselves under attack from the people they believe themselves to be defending.

In Alcamo, our friend has made a formal complaint to the police, and as of yesterday morning his phone has been tapped. In the afternoon a phone call comes, but to his father's house:

'Tell your son we are waiting for an answer.'

Apparently it is not uncommon in Alcamo for professionals to pay protection; one of Tonino's friends says that several people have come to the bank where he works, desperate to raise the money.

It is too easy for me to consider Bosco the repository of all that I love in Sicily, and Palermo the incarnation of all that is worst. I stand rebuked by this morning's newspaper, which bears a reminder that pastoral settings are not reserved for idylls. Two sons of our local shepherd have been arrested, together with some twenty-five other people of the area, on charges of belonging to a criminal organization and of attempted extortion. During the night the *carabinieri* cordoned off the area between Partinico, Balestrate, and Alcamo and arrested the whole gang, mostly shepherds, who they claim have been exerting pressure on local landowners to rent or even sell land for pasturage at very low prices.

Tonino had heard no rumors of anything like this, and we speculate as to whether it is generational turnover or indicative of the power void at the top. All the local *pezzi di novanta*, the big shots, are in hiding because of the drug war, and a lot of petty criminals are making amateurish attempts to carve out a space for themselves in the absence of the bosses.

I have long been a champion of shepherds, albeit for ridiculous reasons: just about the best thing one can eat in Sicily is a bowl of hot curds and whey ladled from the cauldron in which the shepherds are making *ricotta*, and I bitterly resent the fact that we are seldom on visiting terms with the shepherds who live nearby. Perhaps it was basically greed that prompted me to consider Tonino's profound distrust of shepherds as an inherited and unreasonable prejudice, something out of *Oklahoma*. 'Oh, the cowboys and the farmers should be friends' would run through my head whenever he embarked on the subject.

When we first began to spend time at Bosco, the shepherd whose house and sheep pens are just up the road sent his son to ask permission to pasture the sheep in the stubble after our wheat had been harvested. It seemed that this might mark the onset of a thaw in our relations with shepherds, and the following Easter I took Natalia and her cousin Martina to get some *ricotta*, as we had been invited to do. Following Tonino's instructions we walked up the road, forked left and left again onto a track that led up over a little rise and into a muddy yard blackened with sheep droppings and pockmarked by the passage of tiny hooves. In front of us was the traditional whitewashed one-room farmhouse with a sloping tile roof, to the left a shed and a modern, flat-roofed house stuccoed in a pattern of brown and green, to the right the railings of the sheep pens and a small vegetable garden.

Smoke was coming out of the shed, and it was there that we found the shepherd's wife, a grey-haired woman perhaps in her early fifties, and her teenaged daughters, hard at work on the *ricotta* from the morning's milking. In the summer they have to make the cheese twice a day, but in April the nights were still cold enough to keep the evening's milk from spoiling so that the two batches could be processed together. The first lot of milk had already been boiled and separated, and the curds, destined to become *pecorino*, had been packed into rush baskets and were draining on wooden trays in one room of the shed. In the other room the women were taking turns at stirring the whey that was heating together with more milk in an enormous copper cauldron, big enough to take a bath in, propped up on stones in one corner of the shed over a blazing fire fed by four- or five-foot-long logs that were shoved farther and farther into the flames rapidly consuming them. The smoke circled the rafters and went out the door; the women seemed accustomed to it, but the little girls and I couldn't manage to stay in the room for more than a few minutes at a time.

As she pushed the long-handled twig brush round and round to keep the milk from scorching and sticking to the bottom of the cauldron, the wife talked to me about her life: the hard work involved in making cheese twice a day (as welcome as the open fire was in the damp chill of an April morning, it wasn't difficult to imagine what it would mean in the Sicilian summer), the difficulties and the loneliness of bringing up seven children out in the Sicilian countryside, without electric light or running water until eight years ago, her worry that her sons would be unable to find wives willing to put up with the hardships of a shepherd's life. They managed to get a good price for their cheese, she said, because instead of selling it to a middleman she herself took it in the car to Partinico every day and delivered it direct to her customers. I remarked on how unusual it was to find people living full time on the land. Her husband had always needed her help, and although they had had a house in Alcamo 'with all the proper furniture,' somehow she had never managed to live there, and finally they had saved up enough money to build a house with all the modern comforts here in the country.

'Come, let me show you.' Turning the brush over to one of her daughters, she led us to the brown and green house we had seen as we came in. 'There wasn't any point in letting my furniture just rot there in Alcamo where nobody could see it.'

With great pride she showed us through a shiny, tiled and marble-floored house full of brand-new furniture that looked as if it had never been sat on. It was all what the Italians call '*in stile*,' modern replicas approximating styles from the past, as opposed to *moderna*. (But then there is also what an architect I know calls '*stile moderna*' – built by someone who has heard of modern furniture but never seen any.) A sofa and armchairs upholstered in velvet and fringed in silk sat about a dining room suite that was vaguely French in inspiration, heavy with gilt and pink marble. The kitchen had the matching cabinets known as '*all'americana*'; the master bedroom was, she proudly announced, '*stile veneziana*' and was very handy when her married daughters came to spend the night. Of the other two bedrooms, only the one where her son slept showed any sign of human passage, and I couldn't figure out if the gleaming ceramic tiles of the bathroom got polished up every morning after the men had washed or whether that too was off limits for daily use.

When I asked her if she had learned the art of cheese making from her mother, she seemed almost offended. 'Oh, no, signora, I wasn't born to this. I grew up in Balestrate, my father was a *bottaio*, a cooper.' The craft of making and maintaining wine casks is many rungs above shepherding, so she saw her life as one of disappointment and decline.

When we returned to the cheese shed, the milk had boiled and curdled and she pronounced it ready. Her daughter lifted up the brush, shook off the drops of whey clinging to the twigs, and passed it over the cauldron in the sign of the cross before carrying what was left of the logs outside to plunge in a bucket of water.

The shepherd's wife filled up my plastic container with *ricotta* from the cauldron and then insisted that we eat some while it was still hot. Natalia and Martina could not manage the soup plates full of steaming whey while standing up, so one of the daughters ushered us into the old farmhouse and sat us down at a table. One look showed me that this was where the real business of living was conducted. The room that occupied the front half of the house was at once kitchen and living and dining room; to the back were two alcoves, closed off by curtains, where presumably the parents and the two daughters still living at home slept. The flaking whitewashed walls were dotted with pots, coat hooks, and pictures of saints, and the furniture was old and lopsided, whatever *stile* it once had had blurred by many coats of paint.

As we sat at the table mopping up the *ricotta* with fat slices of fresh bread, a voice, high and wavering with age, suddenly spoke up from behind one of the curtains. I couldn't make out anything it was saying, until I realized to my astonishment that it was declining a Latin noun.

'*Buon giorno*,' I answered, at a loss for any more adequate response.

The answer came in Italian, quite correct and without a trace of dialect: 'You aren't Sicilian, are you, signora? By your accent I would say you were either English or American.'

'You're quite right, I'm an American,' I replied, still having no idea to whom I was talking, or even if it was a he or a she.

'English is a *very* beautiful language.' This time the voice was speaking in English. The daughter who was attending to us must have noticed my growing perplexity, for she intervened.

'My father has very bad legs, and ever since his gallstone operation last fall he hasn't been able to get out of bed.' She drew back the curtain just enough so we could see an elderly man in a woollen nightcap propped up in a large double bed under many layers of blankets. I bowed, he nodded, and we continued our conversation, this time in Italian.

The old shepherd was greatly saddened that age, sickness, and the harsh adversities of the pastoral life to which fate had so unjustly delivered him were such that they prevented him from rising from his bed of pain to greet me properly, honoured as he was to welcome to his humble dwelling someone who not only belonged to a family with which he had long had the honour to be acquainted and of which he held particularly sacred the memory of the *buon'anima* ('the good soul,' the Sicilian way of saying 'the late') of Don Turiddu, in whose footsteps his grandson (Tonino) was following, a man of honour the Cavaliere Simeti, respected throughout the neighbourhood for his honesty and beloved for his generosity, of which he, the shepherd, was not the only beneficiary, for Don Turiddu had ever been ready to lend money to some poor unfortunate without ever asking as much as a *soldo* of interest, but also he was honoured to welcome someone who spoke English, which was music to his ears, bringing back to him as it did the time when he had been in the service of the British crown, for he had studied English in school, since he had not been intended for the miserable life of a shepherd but would have been an accountant had not the war intervened, sending him to fight in Africa, where he was taken prisoner by the British and sent to Ceylon, where he was interned in a prison camp in which he was able, by virtue of his knowledge of the English language, to serve as an interpreter, but this was the last stroke of fortune in a long and luckless life, for upon his return to Alcamo at the end of the war he was to discover that his widowed father had first remarried and then expired, and that all that was to have been his had finished in the pockets of a son by a previous marriage of his wily stepmother, save for the small piece of land on which this house where we were was built and some few sheep, and if it hadn't been for the *buon'anima* of Don Turiddu, who had lent him the money to enlarge his flock, he didn't know where he would be, but as it was, thanks be to God and ever struggling against the bestiality and the suffering of a shepherd's life, which is certainly the most desperate and *disgraziata* occupation that God ever created for man, he and his family had managed well enough, although after all he had endured he was now still further tried by the pains in his legs, but he and his family did their best to maintain their dignity and furthermore he was in frequent correspondence with Queen Elizabeth II!

That visit marked the high point in our relations with this family. The warm weather allowed the old shepherd to hobble about with the help of canes, and he and his wife returned the visit, but it soon became clear that we would have to look sharp. Things borrowed took a very long time to come back, the sheep wandered too often out of the stubble to nibble on the grapevines, the flock took shortcuts over freshly plowed fields (even though their hooves are tiny, when a flock of sheep passes through a vineyard, it packs the earth down solidly, suffocating the vine roots), and then the youngest son took a fancy to Christmas trees.

One day some *carabinieri* in a patrol car jolted down the road and stopped to ask me directions to the shepherd's house. With my usual naïveté I thought they probably wanted to buy some ricotta. That evening we heard that the elder son was being held for questioning in connection with a murder. (The case was never solved, and the boy was released after a few months.) When he came over once with his father to protest the fact that another shepherd (quite uninvited) had brought his flock to graze in our stubble, which they considered to be their own monopoly, he said, by way of recommending himself to me: 'We treat your things as if they were our own!' ...

History has made the Sicilian dialect almost a language apart, so great is the legacy of the Greeks, the Arabs, the French, and the Spanish. The dialect is full of marvellous metaphors, strong and vivid and with a rude vitality that has long since been ironed out of Italian, for centuries a literary, official language more often than a spoken one. My mother-in-law, for example, an insomniac of many years' standing, would complain enviously about how easily her husband slept: '*Ha il sonno attaccato col laccio* – He has sleep tied on with a string,' and in my mind would appear a soft, quilted cloud, like a balloon tied on by string to the bedpost, which at a gentle tug from my father-in-law would slowly descend to envelop him in sleep.

The dialect has a rich range of epithets as well, covering the spectrum from sworn enmity to momentary hostility in a traffic jam. My husband tends to disparage Palermo drivers as *scricchiapanelli*, '*panelli*-chompers,' reserving the true Sicilian offense, *cornutu*, for graver occasions. *Cornutu* means having horns, cuckold and therefore dishonored, and when said without a smile is about as much of an offense as one might need, but Tonino prefers to embroider, as in *cornutu abbiveratu*, an 'irrigated cuckold,' who thanks to watering has grown particularly long and flourishing horns, or *chiù cornutu di un panere di babaluci*, 'having more horns than a basket full of snails.'

Sicilians will usually laugh at my attempts to use their dialect: they proudly claim that no one who was born off the island can properly pronounce the double *d* that has taken the place of the Italian double *l*, as in *bedda matre e beramente*, 'by the beautiful Mother and verily,' a phrase with which a Sicilian protests his sincerity, or in '*adduzzu*, 'little rooster,' the word Tonino makes me say to prove, to his perpetual amusement, that I am still unable to locate the particular spot between palate and throat from which the tongue must launch the double *d*.

Sicilian has a different grammar as well; it tends, like Latin, to put the verb at the end of the sentence, and it uses its tenses differently from the Italian. The future tense is lacking altogether, so contemplated actions are perforce tinged with an element of constriction – 'I have to go' for 'I shall go' – as if to underline how rarely the Sicilians have been masters of their own fate ...

Making the year's supply of tomato sauce is *the* most important domestic ritual in the Sicilian summer, and each housewife believes in the efficacy of her favourite method with fervour equal to that with which she believes in the efficacy of her favourite saint. There are basically two rival schools of thought: the one favours passing the scalded tomatoes through the tomato mill, then sterilizing the filled and capped bottles in boiling water; the other prefers to heat up the empty bottles, fill them with boiling hot tomato sauce, and then lay them in a nest of woollen blankets, so well wrapped that they will take several days to cool off. Then of course there are many minor variations: some prefer to add a few onions to the cooking tomatoes, some don't cook the tomatoes at all but pass them raw, still others disdain the widespread habit of putting a sprig of sweet basil in each bottle.

Preparations begin early, in the spring actually, when cracked pots and old five-kilo salted sardine tins are seeded with the tiny-leafed basil that is preferred for sauce making; these are assiduously watered into big and brilliant balls of green. Then crate after crate of empty beer and soda bottles are lifted down from the lofts, rinsed out, and left upside down to drain in the July sun for at least two weeks, so as to eliminate the least bead of moisture. At the same time the Wednesday morning street market at Alcamo is crowded with outsize gas burners, huge aluminum and copper cauldrons, gigantic ladles and mammoth colanders.

Sauce making is no small undertaking for the average peasant family, which in one day will put up anywhere from fifty to one hundred and fifty bottles, or even more if there are married daughters to be supplied, or the *padrone* to be served. In fact, when I was first in Sicily, the little sauce that sufficed for my in-laws' needs came from bottles prepared by the Pirrellos or by Peppino. (One year the bottles Peppino left in homage in the stairway behind the front door at Alcamo exploded, painting the entire staircase red, and I have often wondered whether it was chance or, like the green fruit, one more act of guerrilla warfare.)

It was therefore not my mother-in-law who initiated me into the rites of sauce making, but Teresa Vivona, Turiddu's wife. When we were first at Bosco, Turiddu had not yet inherited the piece of irrigated land where he now grows their family vegetables, and each summer he would plant tomatoes and other vegetables at Bosco, for their use and ours. As soon as Turiddu announced that a sufficient number of tomatoes had properly ripened, the whole family would arrive at dawn to do the picking and then, when ten or fifteen crates were filled, we would set up our assembly line in the shade of the almond trees. Teresa, Franca and I hosed down the tomatoes in large plastic buckets and plucked out the star-shaped green stems, which have a bitter taste, while Turiddu ignited the fire under our big copper cauldron, its bottom black from years of smoke, and spread out on old iron bed trestles the enormous sieve he had made by wiring thin young canes together. Gino, Felice, and Francesco carried out tables and strung an extension cord from the kitchen for the electric tomato mill that a thoughtful friend had once given me.

And there we worked, across the morning and on into the early afternoon, stirring and ladling and passing and capping. Teresa was in charge of the cauldron, filling it with tomatoes while she stirred until it was time to ladle them out onto the canes, so as to drain off the incredible amounts of watery juice that these plants had managed to suck up from the dry soil. Felice, still young enough then to be fascinated by *any* form of machine, operated the mill and sent the thick red sauce cascading into a plastic bucket, while I spooned it into the bottles into which

Franca had first poked a sprig of basil. Turiddu and Gino capped the bottles and lowered them gently into the big oil drum, each layer covered with straw to keep them from cracking against each other in the boiling water. Francesco and Natalia ran errands for as long as their interest held out, then disappeared, not to show themselves again until all the bottles, filled with sauce and covered with heating water, lay in the oil drum and the last remaining sauce was being ladled out onto big plates of pasta. Our meal was interrupted by frequent trips out to shove the flame-consumed logs farther under the drum and to see if the boiling point had been reached and we could begin to keep an eye on our watches.

After forty-five minutes of boiling the fire was scraped away and the Vivonas went home, leaving the drum and its contents to cool off in the night air. The next day Turiddu came back to lift out the bottles and wipe away the bits of wet straw that clung to them, separating the green glass of mine, formerly filled with my mother-in-law's mineral water, from the sturdier brown of the beer and *gassosa* bottles that Teresa preferred, and I would carry mine into the house and set them in rows on the shelves of the *palmento*, where I could give them a proud glance each time I passed.

I must confess that sauce making lost much of its appeal when the Vivonas no longer came to share it with me, and after two years of solitary efforts that left me flattened for three days afterward, I proceeded to put aside my cornucopia complex and make a hard-hearted estimate of our real consumption. It is thus without too much grief that Natalia and I pick, cook, and pass three crates of tomatoes this morning, and when Tonino and Francesco return from commitments elsewhere to do their part, they find some twenty-five bottles of sauce, an adequate yet unostentatious supply, waiting to be loaded into the drum and boiled.

Such self-control is fleeting, however, and the energy saved in cutting down on sauce is consumed in the days that follow in relishes and chutneys and jams and pickles. Figs must be opened like clams and put out to dry in the sun, or pickled in sugar and vinegar; the green tomatoes, whose skins, unaccustomed to all the water that the rain has brought, would split if left to ripen on the vine, must be chopped up in relish and chutney; the purple plums that are bending down the branches of the two young trees in the valley must be boiled into jam; and then there is the pickled watermelon rind, and the bread-and-butter pickles, and the India relish, and all the other American delights to which I rashly have introduced my family and which they now claim they cannot live without. And while one hand stirs the pot, the other must wield a paintbrush, since the winter rains and summer sun that have forged all this bounty have also wreaked havoc on the varnish of the shutters, the doors, and the windows. Tradition decrees that wood is my province, while Tonino must keep the rust at bay on anything – like the outer doors and the latticed grills on the downstairs windows – that is made of iron.

One of the classic sights of Sicily, and the Italian south, is the lines of bright washing, hanging from balconies and on lines strung across streets and courtyards. My flat had no washing machine, and Palermo has, as far as I can tell, no laundrettes, though there are a few very expensive dry cleaners. Washing your own clothes by hand is wretchedly hard work, but thanks to the wind and sun they take virtually no time to dry. In this first, delightful extract from her book, Theresa Maggio reads the lines of washing as if they were signal flags.

Theresa Maggio
From *The Stone Boudoir*

Washing on the Line

'Well hung, half ironed.' That's what the women say about hanging wet laundry. It's a folk art – the draping without wrinkles, the juxtapositions of shapes and colours, the shock of white sheets. The wash line tells a story in a semaphore code anyone can read. Without speaking or even being seen, a woman can say: 'Ha! I have my wash hung before you're even up.' Or she can hang boys' briefs, men's work clothes, and black shawls to say: 'I have three sons, two are out of diapers, my husband's got a job, and my widowed mother lives with us.' You can tell from her wet laundry if a woman is lonely or overworked, or how many times she will patch her husband's pants before letting him wear the new ones. And a woman can signal her lover it is safe to come up by leaving only her nightgown on the line.

I have only seen a dryer once in Sicily, and that was in my American girlfriend's house. Appliances and the fuel to run them are expensive. And in Sicily the sun shines most of the time anyway. Pinning laundry to a line is an excuse for a woman to be outside, or at least to linger on her balcony without being deemed wanton.

I have seen, in Giuliana, laundry flutter like prayer flags from a line strung between a balcony and a church steeple. I have seen sheets strung across a cobblestone street in Locati where they would have blocked traffic had there been any. The woman who hung them had washed them in a tin tub, sloshed the rinse water onto the stones, and swept the stones while they were wet. The whites were wrung into tight gourds ready to be snapped flat and pinned up. The white-haired woman hid behind a sheet when she saw me, a stranger with a camera. When I asked to take her picture, she stepped in front of the sheets taken from the bed she still shares with her husband and smiled sweetly.

288

I had heard that in Geraci Siculo there lived an American woman who had married a man from Palermo. They had met in London, where they both had jobs. Neither she nor her husband had family in this town in the Madonie Mountains but had moved there with their two young daughters, from England and out of the blue, because the town was beautiful – a very un-Sicilian thing to do. One day I found her. Melissa Gay Rose was a former dancer and contortionist from Mississippi. Her clothes line was closely watched.

She had made concessions to the culture when she moved here. 'I don't iron underwear, towels, or sheets, but I do iron everything else,' she said. One day she hung five identical black socks on her line. A week passed, another washday, and she hung another five socks. That afternoon a neighbour lady she rarely spoke to hailed her in the street and said, 'Oh, Rosa, I am so glad you found your husband's other sock. I said a prayer that you would find it.'

An explorer like Theresa Maggio has an incomparable advantage over one like me. While it is generally the case that men enjoy a greater freedom and peace of mind in solitary travel, for those women who are prepared to brave the stares, who can handle the isolation and are confident of taking care of their own security, Sicily offers hundreds of doors which are closed to a single man. Which is not to say it is a particularly easy place for lone women.

Theresa Maggio
From *The Stone Boudoir*

Without a Man

One day in Polizzi I sat on a blue stool in Enza Dolce's nameless store next to an empty ice cream freezer. She was thirty-eight, single, thin as a rail, with black hair and almond-shaped eyes. She had just returned from her winter job in Tuscany, where she glued abrasive pads onto sponges at her brother-in-law's factory. We'd met the year before. She lived with her mother and owned this store where she sold soda, chewing gum, potato chips, juice, cocktails, and espresso. In the summer she was famous for her homemade gelato. But this was late March; Piazza Trinità was deserted, and Enza was depressed.

I was to learn that Polizzi's tolerance does not necessarily extend to Sicilian women. 'Some people here don't like the fact that I've made it this far without a man,' she said.

She had just had another run-in with a neighbour who claimed the parking space that she used beside her store was his private territory, and he demanded she move her car. He said he needed it empty for easy access to his garage. Enza knew the laws and claimed the space was public property. The appropriate town stamp did not appear on her neighbour's store-bought 'No Parking' sign, and furthermore she never blocked access to his garage. That evening he'd entered the store, nodded at me, turned to Enza where she sat on her stool behind the counter, and yelled insanely in dialect for twenty seconds, then left.

'At least he was brief,' I said when he was gone.

'Brief and very concise,' Enza said. 'Did you hear what he said? He'd have my hide. That means kill me.' The threat seemed excessive for a dispute about a parking spot; this battle of wills had been escalating for years. With no man to champion her, Enza was easy prey. Someone had slashed three tires and had scratched the paint on her car.

Enza took the threats and verbal abuse. She could leave Polizzi and stay in the north, where she had sisters, 'but I love the stones here,' she said. She could just give in and park elsewhere, but parking wasn't the point. 'The point is that the man must win over the woman,' she said, and this one wanted her store closed. Enza drew a line and wouldn't budge.

I admired her. I was a little like her. We had both tasted the pleasures of autonomy – making plans and carrying them out. She was ambitious, quick-witted, independent, tenacious, hardworking, and thrifty, a wonderful mix for a man but a volatile combination for a woman in a small Sicilian town. Her gifts marginalized her.

My friends the Riccobene sisters, unmarried twins who run a pharmacy in Locati, twenty minutes from Polizzi, ran into similar problems. Independent, unmarried, childless women like Enza, Rosaria, and Antonietta are rare birds in Sicily. They all say it irks some Sicilian men to see them succeed. Maybe their discomfort is the reaction of insecure men to proof that they are not indispensable.

Most Sicilian country women don't have to contend with such problems because they'd never find themselves in Enza's situation. I know plenty who seem to live happily with clipped wings. For fleeting moments I've envied their safe, ordered, socially approved lives. Most Sicilian country girls grow up in patriarchal families, learn to clean, go to grammar school and high school, fill their hope chests with cutwork linens, marry suitably, have children, attend Sunday Mass, keep house, and stay at home. Those who work outside the home have the permission and protection of a father, husband, or son. But this was not Enza's fate.

Her father had died when she was a toddler, leaving seven children fatherless. From age two to eleven she was raised by Franciscan nuns in a Polizzi *collegio* similar to the one in nearby Geraci Siculo. For Enza, Polizzi's Collegio di Maria was a poor child's nightmare. At the time of her father's death, the roof was off their house in preparation for an expansion, and her mother, Peppina, had no money to pay the workers. She sent the two oldest girls, who were thirteen and fourteen, to Germany, to work and send back money to finish the house. She sent three of the younger girls, including Enza, to the Collegio di Maria in the center of Polizzi, where the Region of Sicily paid the Franciscan nuns to feed and educate her children. Some of the students were paying boarders; others, like Enza and her sisters, were state-subsidized orphans. After five years, Enza's older sisters went to work in Germany too and left the seven-year-old to fend for herself in the convent.

Her mother was not allowed to visit the orphanage; it would have been too disruptive. If on Sunday Enza turned around in church to search out her mother's eyes, the nuns punished her for disobedience. Students who paid tuition were allowed to have long hair, but the nuns gave the orphan girls a military buzz cut. They said they did it in the name of hygiene, but the paying girls did not have to submit; for Enza, a shaved head was mortification. 'Maybe they did it to cut down on the electric bill.' She had to bathe with other girls and keep her underwear on. They made her eat food she hated. Once the nuns locked her in the dining room for ten hours in front of a plate of polenta because she had refused to eat it.

The nuns taught her to read, do sums, and keep house and to sew, embroider, crochet, knit, do cutwork, and make lace. 'When I made a mistake, instead of showing me the right way, the nun would poke my hand with a needle,' Enza said. Enza had none of her childhood works in her hope chest because the nuns bought them for pennies, then sold them at a profit. The mother superior put Enza's meager earnings in the child's piggy bank, but once a year she collected all the girls' banks to pay for their dues in a Catholic youth league, for which they received a paper certificate of membership in return.

One of Enza's friends wet the bed at night, but instead of sending her to a doctor, the nuns made her wear her underwear on her head as a punishment, Enza said. 'The nuns were bitter women who took out their own frustrations on those weaker than them,' she said. While they were teaching her that the weak must submit, Enza was making other plans.

When she was eleven her mother was finally able to bring her home. The first thing she did was to grow her hair long. At eleven she sold Avon products door to door. At twelve she went to work for a tailor who paid her five thousand lire a week. Polizzi once had many tailors, one of whom was the father of the designer Domenico Dolce, of *Dolce e Gabbana*. Enza said the designer was ostracized because he was gay, and when he left he vowed never to return. When the mayor later gave him the key to the city, Dolce sent a representative to collect it. (Polizzi is a fountainhead of talent; Martin Scorsese's father, Charles, was born here, too.) Enza saved for five years and was the first girl in Polizzi to own a motor scooter, which she paid for in cash. She had eclectic tastes in music and became the Madonie region's first woman deejay, broadcasting from a Polizzi disco inside what was once the writer Giovan Battista Caruso's house and drawing partiers from Palermo and Catania. Her mother screamed at her nightly for coming home late. Enza scandalized Polizzi by taking a job as a home health assistant, then considered too lowly a job for a woman of decent family. But she was saving for a dream: to own a business and be her own boss.

When she was twenty-seven Enza went deep into debt, flew to Parma to buy pasta machines, and opened her own fresh-pasta business in a rented storefront in Polizzi. The *chiesa e casa* – church and home – women's brigade insinuated that she must have sold her body to buy the machines. 'People made bets about when my business would fold,' she said. This hurt her. Enza had created her own job, harmed no one, paid for her permits, and offered a service to the public, but her neighbours reviled her. She couldn't sell enough pasta to stay in business. When she sold her equipment a truck came to pick it up. She told no one about the good deal she had struck with the buyer. 'People stopped the driver on his way out of town and asked him how much I'd sold the machines for,' Enza said. Before she left the store that day, she got down on her knees and prayed for something that would let her save face. For a while, the wags thought they'd won. But Enza took a night course to earn a business license and in a few weeks she opened her ice cream store in the same locale.

Most of her friends now are from out of town. She tries to ignore jealous criticism and live her honest life; she has a kind heart and will not let them change her. She remembers to put drops in her old widower landlord's eyes twice a day. She cleans the house of her best friend's widowed father, because her best friend married and moved to Germany. He gives her bunches of chicory in return.

Enza lives in town with her mother; they take care of each other. But Enza's dream is to retire at the small orchard house she has bought, three miles out of town and a world away from troublesome men.

Catania, the island's most modern-feeling and forward-looking town ought to be, for those reasons, the easiest place to be a woman alone. It takes about a minute to understand the enmity between Sicily's first and second cities. Palermo is an antique town, wry and reserved; several different times exist there: thousands have been, thousands will come – what is all this twenty-first century fuss?

Catania, on the other hand…

Palermo is classy, ancient and fragile. It is relatively clean and deeply provincial. Secure in its ring of mountains and its golden shell it has never had to try: the world has come to Palermo, stayed or blown through, wondering, and Palermo has barely raised a heavy eyelid.

Catania, however…

Palermo is golden, fair and beautiful.

Catania, meanwhile…

'In Palermo we go to bed early, because we are aristocrats,' my landlord informed me, laughing. 'In Catania they go out…'

They certainly do. Catania is filthy. Catania is black. It wears its extraordinary monochrome architecture like a goth on a big night out, and like the same goth the next morning, Catania is bedraggled, smeared, madly cool. The gorgeous black and white lava baroque buildings seem like a fabulous coat, inherited from a great grandmother, which young Catania now intends to wear for a hard weekend. The charred colours make the city feel as though it has been scorched naked by wild fire, and now the vivid hues of its citizens flood the gullies and cuts of the streets like new life returning, redoubled. I have seen Palermo, at one am, extraordinarily, eerily dead, and wondered that a modern city could be so silent. At one am on the same weekday night, Catania is just beginning to jump.

You can go book shopping at two am. The lovely piazzas seem to inhale all the smoke and noise of the city and blast it down the narrow streets. At *The Stag's Head* English Pub they were having a wild west night, which meant bar staff dressed up as impossibly handsome cowboys and sexy indians; about two hundred Catanians, French and Americans drinking stout and a stage loaded with rather comely line dancers, touching their hats and kicking their heels to country and western classics, blared out in a thick Italian accent. It was loud, laughing and deeply surreal. The next morning I could have bought six live octopi in a bucket of water at the hectic market. They looked very melancholy and down in the mouth. Obviously intelligent, they seemed to have given up hope. I have never come across a market to beat Catania's. You feel the squid would escape if only everyone would look the other way. The prawns and shrimps kick, rattle and expire. Butchers toss knives from hand to hand and eye you like mechanics appraising a car. You look lively: they could unscrew you and lay out your constituent parts in an instant, as they have with dozens of lambs, pigs and cows, whose neatly sorted bits bedeck every centimetre of their stalls. It cannot have been so different when it was Katane, and the townspeople spoke Greek. At the same time, Catania is with the right now: modern, online and hi-tech. Nokia and various software companies have hubs in Catania. The university and the students are a constant presence, unlike in Palermo, where they keep relatively quiet.

Palermo has the Tyrrenhian sea, and more than a sniff of Tunisia and Morocco, thanks to the Arab history and recent immigrants. Catania has the Ionian sea: it looks towards Greece, Egypt, Libya, Australia and everywhere else. It is definitely part of the Global Village (Palermo would not contemplate such a crude abstraction). You would not catch a group of Palermitans betting handfuls of ten euro notes on heads or tails, as I saw in Catania.

A Londoner feels almost at home here, especially one who has lived south of the river. It is entirely apt that the city's symbol should be a mad black elephant, which looks as if it has fallen out of a Christmas cracker (actually solid lava, hewn in the seventeenth century) carrying a wacky and disproportionate Egyptian obelisk on its back, with, for good measure, a cross on top of that. It is tempting to ascribe the louche and haphazard air of the city to the presence of the great volcano which fills its northern sky. It looks too far away to be threatening, but as you gaze up at its majesty, like a squat white-haired giant with an immensely fat stomach, you can imagine that one day, in the wrong frame of mind, it might just burst its guts all over the streets and try to kill everyone. Not that the Catanians are worried. They will just run screaming out of the way, stopping only to light their cigarettes, yell into their phones, embrace their mates, beep their horns, and, perhaps, haul the odd bucket of resigned octopi to temporary safety.

It is appropriate that Catania should be the home and setting of the writer who has done the most to expose the unspoken, reveal the denied, and blow the lid off the ancient know-your-place gallantry and sexism of Sicilian attitudes towards women. Her real name is a mystery, her first book has sold millions, and she was not yet twenty when she wrote it: the diary of a Catania teenager, Melissa P, called *One Hundred Strokes of the Brush Before Bed*.

The graphic sex and the heroine's plunge into and through degradation accounts, no doubt, for a good cut of Melissa's sales. But it earns its place in any story of Sicilian literature: an angry, bloody banner of protest and truth-telling, in the face of centuries of restriction and misogynist repression. Having read even a bit of it you will not look at a Sicilian girl on a moped in quite the same way you did before, and nor should you.

Melissa P
From *One Hundred Strokes of the Brush Before Bed*

September 28th, 2001, 9:10 am

School started a little while ago, and already the air is thick with strikes, demonstrations, and meetings over the usual issues. Already I'm imagining the reddened faces of the politicians when they clash with the protesters. The first assembly of the year will begin in a few hours, and the issue is globalization. Right now I'm sitting in a classroom during a period with a substitute teacher; behind me sit some of my schoolmates gabbing about the speaker who will lead this morning's meeting. They say he's not only very smart but good-looking, with an angelic face. When one girl says she's much less interested in the intellect than in the face, they burst into giggles. They're the same girls who went around talking trash about me a few months ago, saying I'd given it up to some guy who wasn't my boyfriend. I'd confided in one of them, told her everything about Daniele, and she'd hugged me, uttering an 'I'm sorry' that was obviously hypocritical.

'What's so funny? Wouldn't you let a guy like that bang you?' asks the girl who expressed more interest in the face.

'No, I'd rather rape him,' answers another with a laugh.

'What about you, Melissa?' she asks. 'What would you do?'

I turned around and told them I don't know him, and therefore I don't feel like doing anything. Now I hear them laughing, and their laughter blends with the shrill, metallic sound of the bell that signals the end of the hour.

4:35 pm

Perched on the platform built for the assembly, I didn't care about the demolished Customs building or the torched McDonald's, even though I'd been chosen to write a report on the event. I was seated in the centre of the long table; on either side of me were the representatives of the opposing sides. The guy with the angelic face sat next to me, gnawing on a pen in the most obscene way. And while the confirmed rightist engaged with the tenacious leftist, my eyes studied the blue pen wedged between his teeth.

'Write down my name among the participants,' he said at a certain point, his face bent over a slip of paper filled with notes.

'What is your name?' I asked tactfully.

'Roberto,' he said, although this time he looked at me, surprised that I didn't already know it.

He stood up to speak. His speech was strong and compelling. I watched him as he moved with self-confidence, holding the microphone and the pen. The extremely attentive audience smiled at his ironic quips, which he made at just the

295

right moments. He's a law student, I thought, which explains his rhetorical skills. Every so often he would turn to look at me. Somewhat mischievously, although in the most unaffected manner, I started unbuttoning my blouse from the neck down, revealing the white swell of my breasts. Perhaps he noticed my gesture. At any rate, he began to turn more frequently, and with a mixture of curiosity and slight embarrassment he started making eyes at me, or at least so I thought. After finishing his speech, he sat down again and stuck the pen back in his mouth, ignoring the applause that was directed at him. Then he turned toward me – I had meanwhile gone back to writing my report – and said, 'I don't recall your name.'

I felt like playing. 'I still haven't told you,' I replied.

He lifted his head a bit and said, 'Right...'

I smiled and watched him resume taking notes, pleased that he might be waiting for me to tell him my name.

'Aren't you going to tell me?' he asked, scrutinizing my face.

I beamed. 'Melissa,' I said.

'Mmmm... Your name is the Greek for 'bee'. Do you like honey?'

'Too sweet,' I replied. 'I prefer stronger tastes.'

He shook his head, smiled, and each of us continued writing on our own. After a while he stood up to smoke a cigarette, and I saw him laugh and gesture excitedly to another guy (who was also quite handsome). At times he would glance at me and smile, letting the cigarette dangle from his mouth. From a distance he appeared thinner, and his hair seemed soft and scented, bronze-coloured ringlets that fell gently on his face. He stood leaning against the streetlight, shifting all his weight to one hip, which he seemed to be holding up with the hand in his trouser pocket. A green-checked shirt flounced out, disarranged, and round glasses completed his intellectual look. I'd seen his friend a few times outside of school, handing out leaflets. He invariably had a small cigar in his mouth, lit or not.

When the meeting ended, I was gathering the sheets of paper scattered on the table – I had to submit them with my report – and Roberto returned. He squeezed my hand and said goodbye with a broad smile.

'*Arrivederci*, comrade!'

I started laughing and confessed that I liked being called comrade, it's amusing.

'Come, come!' said the assistant principal, clapping his hands. 'What are you doing there chattering away? Do you not see that the assembly has ended?'

Today I'm happy. I had this lovely encounter and hope it doesn't end here. You know, Diary, I truly persevere if I want to achieve something. Now I want his phone number, and I'm sure I'll manage to get it. After his number I'll want what you already know – namely, to inhabit his thoughts. But before that happens you know what I must do.

It's a wet, melancholy day. The sky is grey, the sun a faded smear. This morning there was some light rain, but now a few flashes of lightning would be enough to unleash a downpour. Still, the weather doesn't make a difference to me: I'm very happy.

Stationed at the school entrance were the usual vultures wanting to sell you books or to persuade you with leaflets, undeterred even by the rain. Roberto's friend was there, a cigar in his mouth, wearing a green raincoat and handing out red flyers, a smile stamped on his face. When he approached to give me one as well, I stared at him, flabbergasted, since I didn't know what to do, how to act. I mumbled a timid thanks and dragged my heels, thinking that a golden opportunity like this wouldn't happen again. I wrote my number on the flyer, turned around, and handed it back to him.

'Why are you returning it? Why don't you just throw it away like everybody else?' he asked me, smiling.

'No, I want you to give it to Roberto,' I said.

Bewildered, he protested, 'But Roberto has hundreds of these.'

I bit my lip. 'Roberto will be interested in what's written on the back.'

'Ah, I understand.' He seemed even more bewildered. 'Don't worry, I'll see him later, and he'll get it.'

'*Grazie!*' I'd have preferred to give him a loud kiss on the cheek.

As I was leaving, I heard someone call me. I turned, and it was him, breaking into a run.

'I forgot,' he panted, 'my name's Pino, pleased to meet you. You're Melissa, right?'

'Yes, Melissa. I see you couldn't wait to read the back of the flyer.'

'Well... What of it?' he said, smiling. 'Curiosity is a sign of intelligence. Are you curious?'

I closed my eyes and said, 'Immensely.'

'You see, then you're intelligent.'

My ego appeased, sated with happiness, I said goodbye and headed toward the piazza in front of the school, a hangout that was now half-empty because of the nasty weather. I didn't start the scooter right away. The traffic at that hour is terrible, even on a motorino. A few minutes later my phone rang.

'Yes?'

'Ummm... Ciao, it's Roberto.'

'Whoa!... Ciao.'

'You surprised me, you know?'

'I like to take chances. You could have not called me. I ran the risk of getting a door slammed in my face.'

'You did the right thing. I would've come to ask after you one of these days. Except that... you know... my girlfriend goes to the same school.'

'So you're taken.'

'Yes, but that doesn't matter.'

'It doesn't matter to me either.'

'Tell me, what made you look for me?'

'What would make you come looking for me?'

'I asked you first.'

'I want to get to know you better, spend some time with you.'

Silence.

'Now it's your turn.'

'Same here. As long as you know the premise: I'm already committed.'

'I don't really believe in commitments. They end when you stop believing in them.'

'Feel like meeting up tomorrow morning?'

'No, not tomorrow, I have school. Let's meet Friday – the day of the strike. Where?'

'In front of the university cafeteria at 10:30.'

'I'll be there.'

'Ciao, then, till Friday.'

'Till Friday. *Un bacio.*'

October 14th, 2001, 5:30 pm

As usual I arrived incredibly early. The weather has been the same for four days, an incredible monotony.

From the cafeteria came the smell of garlic, and from where I stood I could hear the cooks making a racket with the pots and bad-mouthing some co-workers. A few students passed by and winked at me; I pretended not to see them. I was more attentive to the cooks' conversation than my thoughts. I was calm, not in the least nervous; I let myself be swept away by the external world, and I didn't pay much attention to me.

He arrived in his yellow car, wrapped up in the most exaggerated way, with an enormous scarf covering half his face, leaving only his glasses uncovered.

'So I won't be recognized, you know how it is... my girlfriend. We'll use the back roads,' he said once I'd got into the car. 'It'll take a bit longer, but at least there won't be any risk.'

The rain beat harder on the windscreen; I thought it might shatter. We were headed for his summer home on the slopes of Etna, outside the city. The brown, withered branches of the trees tore tiny cracks in the cloudy sky; flocks of birds flew laboriously through the dense rainfall, yearning to reach some warmer place. I too wanted to soar in order to reach a warmer spot. Yet I felt no yearning: it seemed as if I were leaving home to start a new job that was far from exciting – a dutiful, laborious job.

'Open the glove compartment. There should be some CDs.'

I found a couple and chose Carlos Santana.

We talked about my school and his university, then about us.

'I don't want you to think badly of me,' I said.

'Are you joking? That would be like thinking badly of myself. We're both doing the same thing, in the same way. For me it might be even more dishonourable, since I'm spoken for. But you see, she –'

'Doesn't give you any,' I interrupted with a smile.

'Exactly,' he said with the same smile.

He entered a narrow, badly paved road and stopped before a huge green gate. He climbed out of the car and opened the gate. When he got back inside, I noticed the face of Che Guevara printed on his drenched T-shirt.

'Fuck!' he complained. 'It's still autumn, but the weather is already so lousy.' Then he turned to me and asked, 'Aren't you a little excited?'

I closed my lips so tightly that I wrinkled my chin. I shook my head and after a brief pause said, 'No, not at all.'

To reach the door I covered my head with my bag. Running in the rain, we laughed non-stop, like two idiots.

The house was completely dark. When I entered, I felt an icy cold. I groped my way in the pitch darkness; he was evidently used to it. He was familiar with every corner and therefore walked with a certain confidence. I planted myself in a spot where there seemed to be more light and made out a couch, where I placed my bag.

Roberto came up from behind, turned me around, and kissed me, thrusting his entire tongue into my mouth. I found this kiss a bit repulsive; it wasn't at all like Daniele's. He was swapping spit with me, letting it trickle from our lips. I backed off tactfully, without revealing my disgust, and wiped my mouth with the palm of my hand. He took me by the same hand and led me into the bedroom, which was just as dark and just as cold.

'Can't you switch on the light?' I asked while he was kissing my neck.

'No, I like it better like this.'

He left me on the huge bed, knelt down, and removed his shoes. I was neither excited nor impassive. I felt I was doing everything just to please him.

He undressed me as if I were a mannequin in a window display, the way a fast, detached shop assistant strips the dummy and leaves it bare.

He was shocked to see my stockings. 'You're wearing thigh-highs?' he asked.

'Yes, always,' I replied.

'You filthy pig!' he roared.

I was embarrassed by his comment, so out of place, but I was even more struck by his transformation from a polite, well-bred young man to a coarse, vulgar beast. His eyes were flaming, ravenous, his hands rummaged around beneath my blouse, inside my panties.

'Do you want me to keep them on?' I asked to comply with his wishes.

'Definitely, leave them, you're dirtier like this.'

My cheeks flushed again, but now I felt my fireplace start to blaze, and reality gradually receded. Passion was getting the upper hand.

I got down from the bed, and my feet touched the smooth, incredibly cold floor. I waited for him to take me and do what he wanted.

'Suck my dick, slut,' he whispered.

I ignored my shame, immediately banished it, and did what he asked me to do. I felt his member turn hard and swollen. He grabbed me by the armpits and lifted me to the bed.

He positioned me on top of him like a defenceless doll and aimed his long lance toward my sex, still so little opened, so little wet.

'I want to make you feel pain. Come on, scream, let me hear how I'm hurting you.'

There was in fact pain, I felt the walls burning, and the dilation occurred against my will.

I screamed as the dark room spun around me. My embarrassment had vanished and in its place was only the desire to make him mine.

'If I scream,' I thought, 'he'll be happy, he asked me to do it. I'll do anything he tells me.'

I screamed and felt pain, no trace of pleasure passed through me. He, however, exploded, his voice was transformed, and his words turned obscene and vulgar.

He hurled them at me, and they pierced me with a violence that exceeded even his penetration.

Then everything returned to the way it was before. He picked up his glasses from the bedside table, took off the condom with a tissue and threw it away, calmly dressed, caressed my head, and when we got into the car, we talked about bin Laden and Bush as if nothing had happened.

October 25th, 2001

Roberto calls me often. He says hearing me fills him with joy and the desire to make love. He says the latter in a low voice, partly because he doesn't want to be heard, partly because he's embarrassed to admit it. I tell him that I feel the same way, that I often think about him when I touch myself. It isn't true, Diary. I say it only to stroke his ego; he's full of himself. He's forever saying, 'I know I'm a good lover. Women really like me.'

He's an arrogant angel, he's irresistible. His image hounds me during the day, but I think of him more as the polite young man than as the passionate lover. And when he is transformed, he makes me smile: I think he knows quite well how to maintain his equilibrium, how to be different people at different times. Unlike me, always the same, always identical. My passion is everywhere, so is my cunning.

December 1st, 2001

I told him my birthday is the day after tomorrow, and he exclaimed, 'Great. Then we'll have to celebrate in an appropriate fashion.'

I smiled and said, 'Robi, we just celebrated yesterday. Aren't you satisfied?'

'Uh, no. I meant your birthday should be special. You know Pino, don't you?'

'Yes, of course,' I replied.

'Do you like him?'

Worried about saying something that would distance him from me, I hesitated a little, then decided to tell the truth: 'Yes, quite a lot.'

'Perfect. I'll come to pick you up the day after tomorrow.'

'OK.' I shut my phone, curious about this strange excitement of his. I trust him.

December 3rd, 2001, 4:30 am

My sixteenth birthday. I want to stop right here and not go any further. At sixteen I'm mistress of my actions, but also the victim of chance and unpredictability.

Epilogue: Departure

THE FIRST TIME I LEFT Sicily was by boat from the port of Palermo. The ship towered above the quay, and as the moment of departure approached a large crowd gathered there, in the dusk, to see it off. A party of Palermitan school children was going on a trip to the mainland; their families had come to wave goodbye. As well as parents there were grandparents, older siblings, younger children, babes in arms, and friends. They held cameras, phones and handkerchiefs, they called out advice, cautions and loving farewells: it was a large and very noisy assembly. The school children lined the decks, leaning over the rails, waving and shouting back. The engines rumbled and the ropes were let go, raising fresh cries from both groups. There was a great feeling of turmoil, the thrill of adventure coupled with longing, love and the sorrow of parting; some of the mothers left behind were in tears and the noise between us all was quite deafening: shrieks and yells from the children, shouts from the quay, a real uproar. As the water boiled under the sides of the ship and a gap began to open between the hull and the land the noise still grew, across the widening divide, and suddenly I felt as though we had all fallen through time, and I was witnessing the departure of another boatload of Sicilian emigrants, another generation of the island's young pulled away to the world and a future in which nothing was certain but that it would not be Sicily. Everyone, those watching and those leaving, seemed to fall quiet at once, as we all wondered what would happen and how long it would be before we saw one another again.

W H Auden
Good-Bye to the Mezzogiorno

Out of a gothic North, the pallid children
    Of a potato, beer-or-whisky
Guilt culture, we behave like our fathers and come
    Southward into a sunburnt otherwhere

Of vineyards, baroque, *la bella figura*,
    To these feminine townships where men
Are males, and siblings untrained in a ruthless
    Verbal in-fighting as it is taught

In Protestant rectories upon drizzling
    Sunday afternoons—no more as unwashed
Barbarians out for gold, nor as profiteers
    Hot for Old Masters, but for plunder

Nevertheless—some believing *amore*
    Is better down South and much cheaper
(Which is doubtful), some persuaded exposure
    To strong sunlight is lethal to germs

(Which is patently false) and others, like me,
    In middle-age hoping to twig from
What we are not what we might be next, a question
    The South seems never to raise. Perhaps

A tongue in which Nestor and Apemantus,
    Don Ottavio and Don Giovanni make
Equally beautiful sounds is unequipped
    To frame it, or perhaps in this heat

It is nonsense: the Myth of an Open Road
    Which runs past the orchard gate and beckons
Three brothers in turn to set out over the hills
    And far away, is an invention

Of a climate where it is a pleasure to walk
    And a landscape less populated
Than this one. Even so, to us it looks very odd
    Never to see an only child engrossed

In a game it has made up, a pair of friends
    Making fun in a private lingo,
Or a body sauntering by himself who is not
    Wanting, even as it perplexes

Our ears when cats are called Cat and dogs either
    Lupo, *Nero* or *Bobby*. Their dining
Puts us to shame: we can only envy a people
    So frugal by nature it costs them

No effort not to guzzle and swill. Yet (if I
    Read their faces rightly after ten years)
They are without hope. The Greeks used to call the Sun
    He-who-smites-from-afar, and from here, where

Shadows are dagger-edged, the daily ocean blue,
    I can see what they meant: his unwinking
Outrageous eye laughs to scorn any notion
    Of change or escape, and a silent

Ex-volcano, without a stream or a bird,
    Echoes that laugh. This could be a reason
Why they take the silencers off their Vespas,
    Turn their radios up to full volume,

And a minim saint can expect rockets—noise
    As a counter-magic, a way of saying
Boo to the Three Sisters: 'Mortal we may be,
    But we are still here!'—might cause them to hanker

After proximities—in streets packed solid
    With human flesh, their souls feel immune
To all metaphysical threats. We are rather shocked,
    But we need shocking: to accept space, to own

That surfaces need not be superficial
    Nor gestures vulgar, cannot really
Be taught within earshot of running water
    Or in sight of a cloud. As pupils

We are not bad, but hopeless as tutors: Goethe,
    Tapping homeric hexameters
On the shoulder-blade of a Roman girl, is
    (I wish it were someone else) the figure

Of all our stamp: no doubt he treated her well,
    But one would draw the line at calling
The Helena begotten on that occasion,
    Queen of his Second *Walpurgisnacht,*

Her baby: between those who mean by a life a
    Bildungsroman and those to whom living
Means to-be-visible-now, there yawns a gulf
    Embraces cannot bridge. If we try

To 'go southern', we spoil in no time, we grow
    Flabby, dingily lecherous, and
Forget to pay bills: that no one has heard of them
    Taking the Pledge or turning to Yoga

Is a comforting thought—in that case, for all
    The spiritual loot we tuck away,
We do them no harm—and entitles us, I think
    To one little scream at A *piacere,*

Not two. Go I must, but I go grateful (even
    To a certain Monte) and invoking
My sacred meridian names, *Vico, Verga,*
    Pirandello, Bernini, Bellini,

To bless this region, its vendanges, and those
    Who call it home: though one cannot always
Remember exactly why one has been happy,
    There is no forgetting that one was.

Bibliography

Auden, W H. *Collected Poems* (Faber)

Brydone, Patrick. *A Tour through Sicily and Malta in a Series of Letters to William Beckford* (Strahan and Cadell, London 1773)

Buffalino, Gesualdo. *The Plague-Spreader's Tale*. Trans Patrich Creagh (Harvill, London 1999)

Camilleri, Andrea. *The Snack Thief*. Trans Stephen Sartelli. (Picador, London 2004)

Cary, Henry. *Herotodus: The Histories* (H G Bohn 1852)

Cicero, Marcus Tillius. *The Verrine Orations* (H G Greenwood, Heinemann 1928)

Cronin, Vincent. *The Golden Honeycomb* (Harvill, London 1992)

Dickie, John. *Cosa Nostra: A History of the Sicilian Mafia* (Hodder and Stoughton, London 2004)

Diodorus Book IV: The Loeb Classical Library Diodorus of Sicily III. Trans C H Oldfather (William Heinemann 1939)

Dolci, Danilo. *The Man Who Plays Alone*. Trans Antonia Cowan (MacGibbon and Kee 1968)

Goethe, Johann Wolfgang von. *Goethe's Travels in Italy: Letters from Italy* (George Bell and Sons, London 1885)

Gower Chapman, Charlotte. *Milocca: A Sicilian Village* (Allen and Unwin, London 1973)

Homer. *The Odysseys of Homer*. Trans George Chapman (John Russell Smith, London, Soho Square 1857)

Jubayr, Ibn. *The Travels of Ibn Jubayr*. Trans R J C Broadhurst (Jonathan Cape, London 1952)

Kociejowski, Marius. *Music's Bride* (Anvil Press Poetry 1999)

Lampedusa, Giuseppe Tomasi di. *The Leopard*. Trans Archibald Colquhoun (Vintage, London 2005)

Lawrence, D H. *Poems* (Martin Secker 1929)

Levi, Carlo. *Words are Stones: Impressions of Sicily*. Trans Anthony Shuggar (Hesperus Press 2005)

Lewis, Norman. *The Honoured Society: The Sicilian Mafia Observed* (Eland, London 2003)

Maggio, Theresa. *The Stone Boudoir: In Search of the Hidden Villages of Sicily* (Review 2002)

Maxwell, Gavin. *The Ten Pains of Death* (Longman's, London 1959)

P, Melissa. *One Hundred Strokes of the Brush Before Bed.* Trans Lawrence Venuti (Serpent's Tail 2004)

Pindar. *Pindar's Victory Songs.* Trans Frank J Nisetich (John Hopkins University Press, Baltimore and London 1980)

Pirandello, Luigi. *Horse in the Moon: Twelve Short Stories.* Trans Samuel Putnam (E P Duton and Co Inc, New York 1932)

Pirandello, Luigi. *Six Characters in Search of an Author and Other Plays.* Trans Wilfred David (Lindsay Drummond and Wilfred David, London 1948)

Plutarch. *Plutarch's Lives.* Revised Arthur Hugh Clough (J M Dent, London and Toronto 1927)

Quasimodo, Salvatore. *Complete Poems.* Trans Jack Beavan (Anvil Press Poetry, London 1983)

Robb, Peter. *Midnight in Sicily* (Harvill, London 1998)

Rossetti, D G. *Italian Poetry chiefly before Dante* (A H Bullen, Stratford upon Avon) [Enzo and Jacopo da Lentini poems]

Runciman, Steven. *A History of the Mediterranean World in the Later 13th Century* (Cambridge University Press, Cambridge 1992)

Sciascia, Leonardo. *The Day of the Owl.* Trans Archibald Colquhon and Arthur Oliver (Granta 2001)

Servadio, Gaia. *Motya: Unearthing a Lost civilisation* (Victor Gollancz 2000)

Taylor Simeti, Mary. *On Persephone's Island: A Sicilian Journal* (Viking 1996)

Theocritus. *The Idylls of Theocritus.* Trans R C Trevelyan (Cambridge University Press, Cambridge 1947)

Thucydides: The History of the Peloponnesian War. Trans The Rev Henry Dale (George Bell and Son, London 1899)

Verga, Giovanni. *Cavalleria Rusticana and Other Stories.* Trans G H McWilliam (Penguin 1999)

Vittorini, Elio. *Conversations in Sicily.* Trans Wilfrid David (Canongate 2004)

Further Reading

Classics:

Aeschylus: *Seven Against Thebes* (A favourite for performance at the Greek theatre at Segesta)

Livy: *The Punic Wars?*

Virgil: *The Aeneid*

Landscape and Place:

David, Elizabeth: *Italian Food*

Lewis, Norman: *In Sicily*

Maupassant, Guy de: *La Vie Errante*

Phelps, Daphne: *A House in Sicily*

Tasca Lanza, Anna: *The Heart of Sicily*

Verdura, Fulco de: *The Happy Days of Summer: A Sicilian Childhood*

People:

Battaglia, Letizia: *Passion, Justice, Freedom: Photographs of Sicily*

Crowley, Aleister: *Diary of a Drug Fiend*

Durrell, Lawrence: *Sicilian Carousel*

Fallowell, Duncan: *To Noto: London to Sicily in a Ford*

Gilmour, David: *The Last Leopard: The Life of Giuseppe di Lampedusa*

O'Faolain, Sean: *South to Sicily*

Poetry:

Bonaffini, Luigi: *Dialect Poetry of Southern Italy*

Buttitti, Ignazio: *Lo Faccio Il Poeta?*

History:

Ahmad, Aziz: *A History of Islamic Sicily*

Astarita, Tommaso: *Between Salt Water and Holy Water: A History of Southern Italy*

De Tocqueville, Alexis: *Voyage en Sicilie?*

Lewis, Norman: *Naples '44*

Mack Smith, Denis: *A History of Sicily*

Norwich, John Julius: *The Normans in the South 1016-1130, The Kingdom in the Sun 1130-190*

Tregaskis, Richard: *Invasion Diary*

Mafia:

Falcone, Giovanni: *Men of Honour: The Truth about the Mafia*

Orlando, Leoluca: *Fighting the Mafia and Renewing Sicilian Culture*

Sterling, Claire: *Octopus: The Long Reach of the International Sicilian Mafia*

Stille, Alexander: *Eminent Corpses?*

Fiction:

Agnello Hornby, Simonetta: *The Almond Picker*

Consolo, Vincenzo: *The Smile of the Unknown Mariner*

Maraini, Dacia: *The Silent Duchess*

Puzo, Mario: *The Godfather, The Sicilian*

Radcliffe, Anne: *A Sicilian Romance*

Roberto, Federico de: *The Viceroys*

ELAND

61 Exmouth Market, London EC1R 4QL
Tel: 020 7833 0762   Fax: 020 7833 4434
Email: info@travelbooks.co.uk

Eland was started in 1982 to revive great travel books that had fallen out of print. Although the list has diversified into biography and fiction, it is united by a quest to define the spirit of place. These are books for travellers, and for readers who aspire to explore the world but who are also content to travel in their own minds. Eland books open out our understanding of other cultures, interpret the unknown and reveal different environments as well as celebrating the humour and occasional horrors of travel.

All our books are printed on fine, pliable, cream-coloured paper. Most are still gathered in sections by our printer and sewn as well as glued, almost unheard of for a paperback book these days. This gives larger margins in the gutter, as well as making the books stronger.

We take immense trouble to select only the most readable books and therefore many readers collect the entire series. If you haven't liked an Eland title, please send it back to us saying why you disliked it and we will refund the purchase price.

Extracts from each of our books can be read on our website, www.travelbooks.co.uk. If you would like a free copy of our detailed catalogue, please contact us at the above address.